NEW
ENGLISH
KEY NOTES

Leaving Certificate 2017 – Higher Level

Series Editor: Pat O'Shea
Tony Lake

MENTOR BOOKS

Published in 2015 by

Mentor Books
43 Furze Road
Sandyford Industrial Estate
Dublin 18
Tel: 01–295 2112 / 3
Fax: 01–295 2114

Website: www.mentorbooks.ie
e-mail: admin@mentorbooks.ie

Edited by: Daniel McCarthy
Design and Layout by: Kathryn O'Sullivan

ISBN: 978-1-909417-37-3

Contents

Contents: Poetry Notes

Contents: Poetry Notes

Note to Students

The purpose of *New English Key Notes* is to offer some practical assistance and advice to students preparing for Leaving Certificate Higher Level English – Paper 2. The notes presented here explain and analyse the three elements of the literature syllabus:

• Single Text (*Hamlet*)   • Comparative Study   • Poetry.

New English Key Notes aims to promote a clear-minded, analytical approach to the exam. The range of aspects considered in these notes is not intended to be either exhaustive or prescriptive. Essential phrases are in **bold type**.

Single Text: This sections includes a Scene-by-Scene Summary and Commentary on *Hamlet*. Key Points are listed at the end of each scene, stressing the most important aspects in relation to plot development, characterisation, themes, style, etc. Following Exam Guidelines, a variety of Exam Topics are addressed. Finally, the Characters of the play are also examined in terms of their traits and dramatic function. Key Adjectives are listed at the end of each section to highlight each character's most striking qualities.

Comparative Study: This section examines three popular, accessible texts: *The Plough and the Stars, The King's Speech* and *Foster* in terms of the three prescribed comparative modes:

     A. Theme or Issue: Complex Relationships

     B. General Vision and Viewpoint

     C. Literary Genre.

Key Points of Comparison / Contrast are listed at the end of each section. With such a wide range of texts from which to choose, the aim here is to encourage a coherent comparative approach to the three texts chosen. Sample Answers are provided at the end of each mode. Finally there are Guidelines for Answering Exam Questions.

Poetry: This section discusses the poems of eight poets individually. Key Points are listed at the end of each poem. The Sample Answers given here are considerably longer than the responses expected of students in the exam itself (most responses are three to four A4 pages). The lengthy answers given here are designed to suggest a wide range of areas of possible discussion and to discourage rote learning of such answers. The emphasis throughout this section is on the central importance of personal engagement grounded in the text. Finally there are extensive Guidelines on Answering Exam Questions.

The last section explains **Key Literary Terms**.

Hamlet

Exam Topics & Themes

The Characters

Introduction

Hamlet is a tragedy believed to have been written by William Shakespeare between 1599 and 1601. This play is located in Denmark after a new king – Hamlet's uncle, Claudius – has begun his reign following his killing of his own brother and Hamlet's father, King Hamlet. Claudius' twin goals in this unnatural act were to usurp his brother's crown and claim his wife for himself. In essence, this play is based on Hamlet's obligation to avenge the death of his father, killed in an act of regicide.

This play engages and holds the interest of the audience from the outset through to the conclusion, offering us a combination of such enduringly relevant themes as treachery, revenge, madness (real and feigned), the role of women, corruption, the struggle between good and evil and the contrast between appearance and reality. The complexity of Hamlet's character adds to the play's appeal. All of Shakespeare's tragic protagonists are flawed by one major weakness in particular and this generalisation clearly applies to Hamlet who, flawed by indecision, tends towards procrastination. It is very difficult to predict how Hamlet will act in certain contexts in Acts 1-4, but he ultimately develops into a composed, calm and decisive character following his return from England towards the close of the play.

The struggle between Hamlet and Claudius proves to be one of the most interesting aspects of the play, with them proving to be closely matched adversaries possessed of contrasting personalities.

Another fascinating feature of *Hamlet* is its portrayal of women. Women's inequality is patently clear from the outset of the play set in the patriarchal Danish court that is Elsinore. Hamlet's profoundly sceptical view of his mother's relationship with Claudius colours his attitude towards Ophelia in a very significant manner ('Frailty, thy name is woman.').

The struggle between good and evil and the contrast between appearance and reality lie at the heart of this, and indeed every Shakespearian tragedy, with such themes being timeless and universal. The supernatural aspect of the play (represented by the ghost of Hamlet's father) further enhances its appeal, as does its richness in dramatic incident. It is difficult to imagine the closing scene of any play being more compelling or dramatic with its many twists and turns, or imagine a protagonist more complex than Hamlet who delivers some of the most philosophical soliloquys in any Shakespearian tragedy.

Scene-by-Scene Summary and Commentary

Act 1 Scene 1

The opening scene is full of dramatic tension. Two sentries, Marcellus and Barnardo, are on duty at the royal castle of Elsinore. It is midnight and bitterly cold. The sentries are nervous and filled with foreboding (apprehension / misgiving / dread) because they have twice seen a ghost, to whom they refer to as 'this dreaded sight' and 'this apparition'. They have asked Horatio, a respected scholar, to join their watch in the hope that he may be able to explain this strange happening. The fact that the ghost resembles the dead king is especially intriguing.

When the ghost appears again, the initially sceptical Horatio admits to being filled 'with fear and wonder'. The sentries encourage Horatio to speak with the apparition, but the ghost quickly disappears. It is apparent that the dead king was highly respected by his subjects as the three friends remember his reign with obvious nostalgia. King Hamlet is remembered as a strong and brave leader: 'our valiant Hamlet'.

The dramatic appearance of the ghost is regarded as an event of some significance. Horatio sees the apparition as a sign of some national disaster to come: 'But in the gross and scope of my opinion, this bodes some strange eruption to our state'. He also refers to the ghost as a 'harbinger' and 'omen' (a sign pointing to the future). Barnardo also sees the ghost as a sign pointing to the future, referring to the ghost as 'this portentous figure'. Both men wrongly conclude that the appearance of the ghost is connected with the threat to Denmark posed by young Fortinbras of Norway.

The opening scene provides the audience with important background information necessary for the development of the plot. Horatio speaks of the strained relations between Denmark and Norway. We learn that King Hamlet killed King Fortinbras of Norway, and that, as a consequence, Norway lost territory to Denmark. Horatio describes young Fortinbras as a fiery young man ('of unimproved mettle hot and full'), bent on reversing this defeat and on regaining these lost lands. Treaties and international agreements seem to mean little to the impulsive Fortinbras, who now seems poised to attack Denmark. With this attack seemingly imminent, the dramatic tension increases. The theme of revenge that is so central to the play is, in this way, introduced in the opening scene.

At the close of this scene Horatio decides to tell Hamlet what they have seen: 'Let us impart what we have seen tonight unto young Hamlet'.

KEY POINTS

- Opening scene conveys a sense of dramatic tension.
- Horatio is portrayed as a respected scholar.
- The appearance of the ghost is seen as a very significant happening and as an omen (a warning in relation to the future).
- The theme of revenge is introduced, with Fortinbras, Prince of Norway whose father was killed by King Hamlet, young Hamlet's father, poised to attack Denmark.

Act 1 Scene 2

This scene is set in the Danish court and there is a great sense of pomp and ceremony. **Claudius, King Hamlet's brother and successor on the throne, addresses the court. He tactfully balances expressions of grief at his brother's death with expressions of joy at his own recent marriage to King Hamlet's widow, Gertrude:** 'With mirth in funeral and with dirge in marriage, in equal scale weighing delight and dole'. At this point the audience is unaware of the extent of Claudius' hypocrisy, but we are struck by the unseemly, improper haste with which the new king married his widowed sister-in-law.

Claudius initially makes quite a positive impression. He appears to be statesmanlike in his measured response to the threat posed by Fortinbras, sending ambassadors to the old King of Norway with a request that he restrain his fiery young nephew. While appearing to be in control of affairs of state, he also comes across as overly accommodating and eager to please. Laertes, the son of his chief courtier Polonius, is granted permission to return to France: 'What wouldst thou beg Laertes . . . What wouldst thou have Laertes?' Claudius is particularly anxious to placate Hamlet, addressing him as 'my cousin . . . and my son'. **However, it is immediately apparent that all is not well between Claudius and Hamlet, who has no desire for a closer relationship with his uncle: 'A little more than kin and less than kind'.**

Hamlet's black clothing and equally black mood set him apart from everyone else in the Danish court. The mood of the court is one of joyful celebration, but Hamlet is in a state of melancholy. He is an isolated figure and a deeply disillusioned young man. The king's attempts to win Hamlet's favour meet with a sharp, abrupt response from his sullen nephew. Hamlet's contempt for his uncle is expressed through bitter puns. When Claudius asks him why 'the clouds still hang' on him, Hamlet replies: 'Not so, my lord, I am too much in the sun". Claudius goes to great lengths in his efforts to win Hamlet's loyalty and affection, pointing out that he is the heir to the throne ('the most immediate to our throne'). However, none of this lessens Hamlet's deep hatred of his uncle.

While Claudius at first appears to be an admirable, even likeable, character, there are early signs of his true self. Claudius' excessive desire to please virtually all in court hints at his own sense of insecurity. Claudius puts on a display of grace and exaggerated good humour because he is aware of the falsity of his position. His insensitivity and hypocrisy are apparent when he describes Hamlet's grief as 'unmanly' and as 'a fault to heaven'. Claudius' refusal to allow Hamlet to return to Wittenberg points to his cunning nature – he will keep his most dangerous enemy under his sharply watchful eye.

From the beginning of the play we see Gertrude as a weak, dependent character. In her desire to see her son get along with her new husband, she too seems to be insensitive to Hamlet's deep grief: 'Why seems it so particular with thee?' Hamlet's bitter response ('Seems', madam! Nay, it is; I know not 'seems') suggests that the Danish court is a world of false appearances, a world where people are not always what they seem to be. Here Hamlet may be hinting at his mother's artificiality. Ultimately, neither Gertrude nor Claudius succeeds in their attempts to appease (placate / pacify) Hamlet.

Hamlet's opening soliloquy offers us a range of insights into his deeply troubled state of mind. Hamlet's disillusionment with life is total: 'How weary, stale, flat and unprofitable seem to me all the uses of this world!' The image of the world as an unweeded garden reflects Hamlet's belief that he is living in a world of 'rank and gross' corruption. This soliloquy presents us with the reasons for Hamlet's intense anguish. **His beloved father is not even dead two months and his mother has already remarried. Hamlet is outraged by his mother's decision to marry a man such as Claudius. In sharp contrast to what Hamlet sees as his perfect, godlike father, Claudius is seen as a repulsive beast. In Hamlet's eyes, his father was Hyperion (the beautiful god of**

the sun) while Claudius is a disgusting satyr (a mythical creature that was half man, half goat).

Hamlet is outraged by his mother's disloyalty to his father's memory. Gertrude seemed to be utterly devoted to King Hamlet ('Why, she would hang on him as if increase of appetite had grown by what it fed on'), yet she married again within a month of his funeral. **Disgust at Gertrude's weakness dominates Hamlet's mind and soul and is the primary cause of his depression. Her weakness and disloyalty cause Hamlet to lose faith in all women: '. . . frailty, thy name is woman'.** Hamlet angrily declares that 'a beast that wants discourse of reason would have mourned longer'. He is disgusted by what he regards as the 'incestuous' relationship between Gertrude and Claudius, predicting that this relationship 'cannot come to good'.

When Hamlet meets Horatio, he sarcastically remarks that 'the funeral baked meats did coldly furnish forth the marriage table', underlying his feelings of disillusionment and anger. Horatio is Hamlet's trusted friend and the one person in whom he confides. Hamlet idealises his dead father, believing him to have been an excellent king, a perfect husband and a complete man: 'He was a man, take him for all in all, I shall not look upon his like again'. When Horatio tells him about the appearance of the ghost, Hamlet is determined to speak with the apparition. He immediately suspects 'some foul play', but believes that evil deeds will eventually come to light: 'Foul deeds will rise, though all the earth overwhelm them, to men's eyes'.

KEY POINTS

- While Claudius at first seems to be an admirable character and an able king, his exaggerated politeness and excessive desire to please suggest his insincerity and sense of insecurity.
- Hamlet is a deeply disillusioned young man whose black clothing and dark disposition set him apart from a Danish court celebrating Claudius' accession to the throne.
- Hamlet's opening soliloquy helps us to see why he feels so angry and bitter – he thoroughly resents Claudius and is disgusted by Gertrude's betrayal of his father.
- Gertrude's decision to re-marry so soon after King Hamlet's death suggests that she is a fundamentally weak, dependent character.
- Horatio is the one person in whom Hamlet can confide.
- Hamlet is determined to speak with the ghost, sensing that something is fundamentally wrong in Denmark.

Act 1 Scene 3

This scene is concerned with the family affairs of Polonius, his son Laertes and his daughter Ophelia. As the play unfolds, we see that the lives of all three members of this family become closely intertwined with that of Hamlet. All three ultimately die, with Hamlet incontrovertibly (unarguably / undeniably / indisputably) bearing some responsibility for all three deaths. Polonius becomes Hamlet's enemy because he epitomises (personifies / embodies) the falseness of the Danish court. Ophelia is driven to insanity and suicide by Hamlet's rejection of her and by her father's death at the hands of the man she loves. Laertes becomes Hamlet's implacable enemy when he dedicates himself to avenging the deaths of his father and sister.

Before Laertes returns to France, he speaks to

Ophelia about her relationship with Hamlet. He sounds rather pompous as he delivers a moral lecture to do with the importance of virtue and honour. Laertes advises his sister to be very cautious in her dealings with Hamlet because, as heir to the throne, Hamlet will not be free to choose his own wife: '. . . his will is not his own, for he himself is subject to his birth'. Laertes suggests that Hamlet's apparent affection for her will not last. He urges Ophelia not to be too trusting ('too credent') and to guard her virtue: 'Be wary then, best safety lies in fear'. Ophelia listens respectfully to Laertes' lecture but shows a degree of independence and spirit when she expresses the hope that her brother will follow his own advice.

No sooner has Laertes finished sermonising Ophelia than he himself is forced to listen to a typically lengthy lecture from Polonius. Of course, Polonius never tires of listening to the sound of his own voice. Polonius offers Laertes shrewd and practical advice rather than moral instruction. Essentially, he urges his son to be very cautious in his dealings with others: 'Give every man thine ear, but few thy voice . . . Neither a borrower nor a lender be'. Polonius sounds rather idealistic when he tells Laertes that the most important thing is to be true to himself ('This above all, to thine own self be true'), but he is basically telling him to put his own self-interest before everything else. **We soon see that, far from being idealistic, Polonius is in fact a deeply cynical character.**

We see the unattractive side to Polonius in the advice that he gives to Ophelia. Like Laertes, Polonius disapproves of the relationship between Ophelia and Hamlet. He dismisses any possibility that Hamlet's feelings for Ophelia might be genuine, telling his daughter that she is naïve to believe Hamlet's declarations of love: 'You speak like a green girl!' Using the cold language of commerce, he tells her: '. . . you have taken his tenders for true love which are not sterling'. Polonius' cynical view of love is reflected in the animal imagery that he uses to suggest the greater freedom that Hamlet enjoys: '. . . with a larger tether may he walk than may be given you'. **Polonius sees young people as farm animals that need to be controlled. He does not believe in Hamlet's sincerity or decency: 'Do not believe his vows'. Ophelia agrees to be guided by her father: 'I shall obey, my Lord'.**

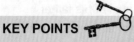

KEY POINTS

- Laertes advises Ophelia not to be too trusting of Hamlet because, in his view, their relationship will not last.
- Polonius offers Laertes shrewd and practical advice, in essence telling his son that his actions should at all times be guided by the principle of self-interest.
- Polonius' advice to Ophelia reveals his deeply cynical view of life and of human relationships – he never considers the possibility that Hamlet may genuinely love Ophelia.
- Ophelia is young and easily manipulated – she unhesitatingly agrees to be guided by her father.

Act 1 Scene 4

We are now brought back to the dark, cold battlements as Hamlet and his companions wait for the ghost to appear again. As they watch, they hear the sounds of a late-night party within the castle. Hamlet, a man of high moral standards, is disgusted by the heavy drinking that, in his view, has tarnished the Danes' reputation among other nations: 'This heavy-headed revel east and west makes us traduced and taxed of other nations. They clepe us drunkards . . .' The king's fondness for this drunken revelry is an indication of his moral weakness in Hamlet's eyes.

When the ghost finally appears, Hamlet immediately wants to know why this spirit is walking the earth: '. . . tell why thy canonized bones, hearsed in death, have burst their cerements?' The ghost beckons Hamlet to follow it and, ignoring the advice of Horatio and Marcellus, Hamlet does not hesitate to follow the ghost's instructions.

Marcellus is convinced that the appearance of the ghost is a sign that 'something is rotten in the state of Denmark'. Horatio believes that Heaven will control the outcome of events: 'Heaven will direct it'.

KEY POINTS

- Hamlet has high moral standards and is disgusted by the king's late night partying and heavy drinking.
- Hamlet is fiercely determined to speak with the ghost, following the beckoning spirit – against the advice of Horatio.
- Marcellus restates the idea that the appearance of the ghost is a sign that something is fundamentally wrong in the Danish state.

Act 1 Scene 5

The climax of Act 1 occurs when Hamlet comes face to face with his father's ghost. In this scene Claudius' crime is revealed and the duty of avenging his father's death is laid squarely on Hamlet's shoulders.

The ghost's reference to 'sulphurous and tormenting flames' suggests that he is now paying for his sins in life. King Hamlet was obviously not as perfect as his son imagines him to have been and must remain in Purgatory until, in his own words, 'the foul crimes done in my days of nature are burnt and purged away.' The vivid account of the ghost's sufferings evokes feelings of pity in the audience. Claudius had poured poison into one of King Hamlet's ears as he slept. The ghost's dramatic command that Hamlet 'revenge his foul and most unnatural murder' meets with a passionate response:

'Haste me to know it, that I with wings as swift as meditation or the thoughts of love, may sweep to my revenge'. The ghost reveals that King Hamlet was not killed by a serpent, but by his own brother: 'The serpent that did sting thy father's life now wears his crown'. The serpent image suggests that Claudius is devious (sly) and evil. Hamlet's response to this dramatic revelation indicates that he had always suspected Claudius of involvement in his father's death: 'O my prophetic soul!' His natural instincts are now shown to have been correct.

In describing Claudius as 'that incestuous, that adulterate beast', the ghost echoes the feelings of disgust so powerfully expressed by Hamlet in his opening soliloquy. While the reference to adultery points to additional wrongdoing on the part of Gertrude and Claudius, there is no conclusive proof that they were involved in an illicit relationship before King Hamlet died (although, in the Closet Scene, Gertrude refers to 'black and grained spots' on her soul). Their relationship was 'incestuous' in that the Church regarded it as incest for a man to marry his brother's widow. **By repeatedly describing the relationship between Gertrude and Claudius as 'incestuous', both Hamlet and the ghost give powerful expression to their shared sense of revulsion.**

The ghost feels betrayed by Gertrude and is bitterly disappointed by her weakness of character: 'O Hamlet! What a falling off was there'. When he speaks of 'my most seeming-virtuous queen', the ghost touches on one of the central themes of the play: the contrast between appearance and reality. He believes that Gertrude's relationship with Claudius is based on lust rather than love. Once again, the imagery underscores the ghost's sense of deep disgust: 'So lust, though to a radiant angel linked, will sate itself in a celestial bed and prey on garbage'.

The ghost underlines the enormity of Claudius' crime when he points out that, in killing him, Claudius took his life, his crown and his queen. Furthermore, by killing him when he was in a state of sin, Claudius condemned him to the torment of Purgatory: 'Thus was I sleeping by a brother's hand of life, of crown, of queen at once dispatched, cut off even in the blossoms of my sin . . .' Claudius' crime was utterly 'unnatural' and the ghost expects Hamlet to set things right if he has 'nature' in him: 'If thou hast nature in thee, bear it not'. While Hamlet is expected to avenge his father's death, the ghost does not want him to take any action against his mother – Gertrude is to be left to heaven and to her own conscience ('those thorns that in her bosom lodge to prick and sting her').

Hamlet immediately dedicates himself to the business of gaining revenge, telling the ghost: 'And thy commandment all alone shall live within the book and volume of my brain . . .' He now sees his mother as 'most pernicious woman' and Claudius as a 'smiling, damned villain'. Hamlet is forcibly struck by the king's

falseness and by the contrast between appearance and reality: 'That one may smile and smile and be a villain'.

Hamlet is profoundly shocked by what he has learned; indeed in the immediate aftermath of his dramatic encounter with the ghost he struggles to retain his mental and emotional stability. Horatio can make little sense of Hamlet's 'wild and whirling words'. Of course when we consider the series of traumatic events that Hamlet has experienced, we should not be surprised that he struggles to maintain the balance of his mind. He has lost his beloved father to murder, his mother has married his uncle with unseemly haste, he has just learned that his father was murdered by his own brother (who is now Hamlet's step-father) and, finally, he has been told that he must avenge his father's death and set everything right.

At the close of this dramatic scene, Hamlet tells Horatio of his intention of wearing a mask of madness: 'As I perchance hereafter shall think meet to put an antic disposition on'. Hamlet's act of madness is a tactic designed to confuse Claudius and so give him an advantage over his arch-enemy. The battle of wits between Hamlet and his uncle is now underway. **Of course, in the light of his earlier incoherence, the audience may well question whether Hamlet's madness is pretended or real.** Hamlet's adoption of a mask of madness must also be viewed in the context of the falseness of the Danish court. Hamlet knows that he is living in a world of false appearances where people are rarely what they seem to be. By pretending to be mad, Hamlet is equipping himself to survive in a world of deception.

Hamlet's remarks at the close of this scene suggest that he is a reluctant avenger: 'The time is out of joint. O cursed spite that ever I was born to set it right'. Hamlet had earlier promised the ghost that he would 'sweep' to his revenge but, once his passion subsides and he has time to reflect, he draws back from the idea of revenge. **The audience is now aware of the complexity of Hamlet's character. While Hamlet has a passionate side, he is a thinker**

rather than a man of action and the more he thinks, the less likely he is to act. In this sense Hamlet seems to be temperamentally unsuited to the role of avenger.

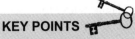

KEY POINTS

- This is one of the most dramatic scenes in the play – Hamlet speaks with his father's ghost and learns the horrifying truth about his death.
- The ghost's dramatic revelations confirm Hamlet's suspicions regarding Claudius and reinforce the disgust he feels towards his mother.
- By ordering Hamlet to 'revenge his foul and most unnatural murder', the ghost sets the main action of the play in motion.
- The theme of false appearances is to the fore in this scene. Gertrude seemed to be devoted to King Hamlet, yet she betrayed his memory by marrying so soon after his death, and is also accused of betraying him in life by committing adultery. Claudius, apparently the lawful king, is a usurper (an illegal king) and a 'smiling damned villain'.
- Hamlet is profoundly affected by his encounter with the ghost and is quite incoherent when he meets Horatio immediately afterwards.
- Hamlet will pretend to be mad in order to gain an advantage on Claudius.
- We become aware of the complexity of Hamlet's character when he initially declares that he will 'sweep' to his revenge before cursing the heavy duty with which he has been burdened.
- Hamlet is more a thinker than a man of action, and consequently is temperamentally unsuited to gaining revenge.

Act 2 Scene 1

This scene throws some light on the character of Polonius. While he had earlier lectured Laertes about his behaviour, it is apparent that his own moral standards are not very high. While his final piece of advice to his son ('This above all, to thine own self be true') is high-sounding, we quickly realise that, far from being noble, Polonius is in fact an utterly cynical and unscrupulous character who does not even trust his own children. Laertes is in Paris and Polonius sends his servant Reynaldo to spy on him. He even tells Reynaldo to make false accusations about Laertes so that others might be encouraged to speak openly about any vices or weaknesses that Laertes may have. Polonius is a Machiavellian character who believes that the

end justifies the means: 'And I believe it is a fetch of warrant you laying these slight sullies on my son . . . Your bait of falsehood take this carp of truth'. The idea of a father instructing someone to tell lies about his own son is reprehensible, but Polonius sees nothing wrong with tarnishing his son's reputation. He is a devious and thoroughly unpleasant character whose falseness renders him perfectly suited to the role of adviser to the equally false king.

Ophelia is very upset by her encounter with Hamlet. She is troubled by Hamlet's disordered appearance ('his doublet all unbraced, no hat upon his head, his stockings fouled . . .'), **and is particularly disturbed by the strange look on his face** ('And with a look so piteous in purport as if he had been loosed out of hell to speak of horrors . . .'). While this may be an early example of Hamlet's 'antic disposition' (acting madness), it is more likely that he is genuinely disturbed by recent experiences, notably his encounter with the ghost. Hamlet has to deal with his feelings of grief and betrayal and come to terms with the weighty responsibility that has been laid on his shoulders. It may also be the case that Hamlet is upset by Ophelia's rejection of him. **Her refusal to meet with him heightens Hamlet's sense of isolation in the Danish court. Ophelia is completely obedient to Polonius: '. . . as you did command, I did repel his letters, and denied his access to me'.**

Polonius believes that Hamlet's love for Ophelia is the cause of his strange behaviour: 'This is the very ecstasy of love . . .' Ever anxious to ingratiate himself with the king, Polonius hurries off to report to Claudius: '. . . come, go we to the king, this must be known'.

KEY POINTS

- Polonius' willingness to spy on his own son reveals him to be a cynical, unscrupulous, devious character.
- Ophelia is greatly disturbed by Hamlet's strange appearance.
- Ophelia's rejection of him heightens Hamlet's sense of isolation within the Danish court.
- Polonius is a servile character who is always anxious to please the king.

Act 2 Scene 2

Suspicious of Hamlet's strange behaviour, Claudius sends for Rosencrantz and Guildenstern, schoolmates of his nephew. Basically, they are in Elsinore to act as spies for the king. Claudius hopes that their friendship with Hamlet will enable them to 'glean' (gather) information which may explain the prince's odd behaviour. The king is anxious to get to the root of 'Hamlet's transformation'. Once again we see Claudius' innate ability to flatter when he addresses 'dear Rosencrantz' and 'gentle Guildenstern'. Smiling and welcoming, he appears to be a kindly monarch. However, once again his exaggerated politeness suggests his falseness and insincerity.

Claudius appears to be a capable king. His successful management of affairs of state is seen when his two ambassadors return from Norway, having successfully completed their diplomatic mission. The Fortinbras affair has been resolved peacefully. The ambassadors report that the elderly king of Norway has rebuked the fiery Fortinbras, making his nephew vow not to attack Denmark. In return, Fortinbras has requested permission to march through Denmark on his way to Poland on another adventure.

Like Claudius, the queen is also troubled by the change in Hamlet, but unlike him, she is concerned for her 'too much changed son'. She understands Hamlet better than anyone else and believes that the reasons for his apparent madness: 'I doubt it is no other but the main, his father's death and our o'er hasty marriage'. She too hopes that Rosencrantz and Guildenstern can solve the riddle of Hamlet's strange behaviour.

Polonius believes that he has discovered the cause of Hamlet's madness – his unrequited love for Ophelia. It is comically ironic that this most longwinded of characters should proclaim that 'brevity is the soul of wit'. Exasperated by his verbosity, the queen demands that he get to the point: 'More matter, with less art'. Polonius proposes spying on Hamlet in order to 'find where truth is hid' and suggests using his own daughter as a pawn in his spying game. Ophelia will act as the 'bait' to trap Hamlet: 'I'll loose my daughter to him . . .' He speaks of his daughter as he might a farm animal. Once again, Polonius' use of animal imagery highlights his cynical view of human love. **Polonius and the king will secretly watch the encounter between Hamlet and Ophelia – spying is second nature to both of these double-dealing characters.**

When Hamlet meets Polonius, he uses his 'antic disposition' to poke fun at him. **It is ironic that Polonius should regard Hamlet as a harmless lunatic, all the while failing to see that Hamlet is ridiculing his foolishness and self-importance.** Hamlet sees Polonius as one of 'these tedious old fools' that populate the Danish court. He describes Polonius as 'a fishmonger', possibly suggesting that he is always fishing for information for the king or that he is a man of low moral standards. **Hamlet questions Polonius' honesty, again revealing his deep disillusionment with the falseness of court life** when he declares that 'to be honest as this world goes, is to be one man picked out of ten thousand'. **There is always a point to Hamlet's seemingly meaningless ramblings.** When he speaks of the sun breeding maggots 'in a dead dog', we see his disgust at the idea of procreation. His disillusionment with love and with life itself is conveyed by means of a clever pun: 'Let her (Ophelia) not walk i' the sun. Conception is a blessing, but as your daughter may conceive, friend look to 't'. Even Polonius recognises that there is a logic to Hamlet's remarks: 'Though this be madness, yet there is method in it'.

When Polonius leaves, Hamlet is approached by Rosencrantz and Guildenstern. When Hamlet wearily describes Denmark as 'a prison', Rosencrantz and Guildenstern believe that they have discovered the reason for the dramatic change in Hamlet. They suggest that Hamlet feels imprisoned in Denmark because his ambition to be king has been frustrated. In reality, Hamlet feels imprisoned by the inescapable duty to avenge his father's death.

While Hamlet is initially friendly towards his friends, he becomes angry when he realises that they are spies in the pay of the king – they are enemies posing as friends. **Hamlet's disillusionment with the falseness of court life again comes to the fore when he asks Rosencrantz and Guildenstern to 'deal justly' with him,** before telling them: 'I know the good king and queen have sent for you'. Here we see that Claudius will not easily gain an advantage on the shrewd Hamlet. It is already becoming apparent that the two are well-matched adversaries.

Hamlet expresses his world-weariness when he describes the earth as 'a sterile promontory'. He is utterly disenchanted with the world and with mankind. He cannot find joy in anything: 'Man delights not me, no, nor woman neither'. Hamlet goes on to reflect on the fickle nature of popular opinion – those people who once regarded Claudius with contempt now pay a lot of money for his portrait. Interestingly, Hamlet seems to admit that he is not genuinely mad when he tells Rosencrantz and Guildenstern: 'I am but mad north-north-west: when the wind is southerly, I know a hawk from a handsaw'. Hamlet ridicules Polonius in front of his school friends when he addresses him as 'old Jephthah'. Again, it is apparent that there is real meaning behind Hamlet's seemingly nonsensical remarks. Jephthah was an Old Testament figure who thought he was pleasing God by sacrificing his daughter – in a sense, Polonius sacrifices Ophelia to please Claudius.

The arrival of the players sees a dramatic change in Hamlet's mood, affording him an opportunity to briefly rise above the depressing realities of court life. **Hamlet loves everything associated with the theatre** and is very much at ease in the company of these travelling actors. This is the first time that the audience sees a chatty, sociable Hamlet. Hamlet recites a speech from one of his favourite plays and reveals his expert knowledge of drama. However, a speech from one of the players has the effect of bringing Hamlet sharply back to reality. This speech, telling the story of Pyrrhus, Priam and Hecuba is concerned with the theme of revenge, reminding Hamlet of his own duty to avenge his father's death. In this speech revenge is portrayed as something brutal and bloody – after a moment's hesitation, Pyrrhus brings his sword on King Priam, 'mincing' his limbs. Later in the play Hamlet will raise his sword over the head of the kneeling Claudius but, unlike Pyrrhus, he will spare his victim. Unlike Pyrrhus, the reflective Hamlet is not suited to the business of gaining revenge.

Hamlet is deeply affected by the passionate manner in which the actor delivers his speech. He observes the tears in the actor's eyes when he describes Hecuba's grief at her husband's death. The actor's passion causes Hamlet to feel guilty about his own lack of passion. Unlike the actor, Hamlet has real reasons to be passionate, yet he does nothing: 'What's Hecuba to him or he to Hecuba that he should weep for her? What would he do had he the motive and the cue for passion that I have?' Hamlet wonders if his inaction is caused by cowardice: '. . . it cannot be but I am pigeon-livered and lack gall'. The passionate outburst that follows suggests that Hamlet is finally about to act: 'Remorseless, treacherous, lecherous, kindless villain! O vengeance!' However, moments later,

Hamlet's more reflective side is apparent in his determination to have concrete proof of the king's guilt. He considers the possibility that the spirit he saw may have been an evil one: 'I'll have grounds more relative than this: the play's the thing wherein I'll catch the conscience of the king". Hamlet will ask the actors to put on a play which will basically portray the murder at Elsinore and will observe the king's reaction to it. This scene vividly highlights both the passionate and reflective aspects of Hamlet's character.

It is interesting to note that it is a chance event (the arrival of the travelling players at Elsinore) that re-awakens Hamlet's sense of purpose. He had promised the ghost that he would think only of his command to gain revenge. However, there followed a lengthy period of inaction as Hamlet seemed to lose his sense of purpose. Prior to the arrival of the actors, Hamlet seemed to have no plan of action. Now he seems to be more clear-minded and purposeful as he sets out to establish beyond doubt the king's guilt.

KEY POINTS

- Rosencrantz and Guildenstern arrive at Elsinore to act as spies for the king.
- Polonius is a deeply cynical character who is even prepared to use his own daughter as 'bait' to 'trap' Hamlet.
- Hamlet uses his 'antic disposition' to ridicule Polonius.
- Hamlet's world-weariness and cynicism are very evident in his conversations with Polonius and with Rosencrantz and Guildenstern.
- The actor's speech describing Pyrrhus' revenge on Priam reminds Hamlet of his obligation to the ghost, while the actor's passion makes him aware of his own lack of passion.
- By the end of Act 2 Hamlet has finally formulated a plan – he will test the king's guilt by observing his reaction to a play depicting the murder at Elsinore.

Act 3 Scene 1

Feeling threatened by Hamlet's 'turbulent and dangerous lunacy' Claudius asks Rosencrantz and Guildenstern if there is any way that they can discover the cause of his nephew's strange behaviour. However, Hamlet's so-called friends admit that they have failed in their attempts to probe his mind. Rosencrantz tells the king that Hamlet is not anxious to be 'sounded' (questioned) about the reasons for his distracted state. **Guildenstern speaks of Hamlet's 'crafty**

madness', explaining how he cleverly avoids answering questions to do with his state of mind.

At this point the king prepares to test the validity of Polonius' theory that Hamlet is behaving in a peculiar manner because Ophelia has rejected him. Using Ophelia as 'bait', Polonius slyly sets up an encounter between his daughter and Hamlet. Neither the king nor his chief adviser hesitates to spy on what should be a private meeting between Ophelia and Hamlet. Polonius directs his daughter as he would an actor on a stage: 'Ophelia, walk you here . . . Read on this book'. Ophelia is directed to read a book and to appear to be praying. Polonius observes that appearances can often be misleading, pointing out that a seemingly holy appearance can often hide or disguise evil: ''Tis too much proved, that with devotion's visage and pious action we do sugar o'er the devil himself'. This observation on human hypocrisy provokes a guilty response in Claudius: 'How smart a lash that speech doth give my conscience!' Claudius goes on to speak about a 'heavy burden' of guilt. This aside reveals the king's troubled conscience, making him a more credible villain. Claudius and Polonius hide as Hamlet approaches.

It is at this point that Hamlet delivers his most famous speech. **In his 'To be, or not to be' soliloquy Hamlet reflects on philosophical issues relating to life and death.** We see his indecision as he wonders whether he should 'suffer the slings and arrows of outrageous fortune' or 'take arms against a sea of troubles' – in other words, he wonders if he should simply endure or confront life's problems. One part of Hamlet is drawn to the idea of death as eternal sleep. However, he fears that the sleep of death may not bring peace: 'For in that sleep of death what dreams may come?' Perhaps Hamlet is suggesting that he cannot escape the duty to avenge his father's death, and that his father's ghost will haunt him even beyond the grave. **Ultimately, death does not appeal to Hamlet because the next world is an unknown quantity.** Towards the close of this soliloquy, Hamlet makes an observation that largely explains his own indecisive nature, pointing out that the more we think the less likely we are to act: 'Thus conscience does make cowards of us all, and thus the native hue of resolution is sicklied o'er with the pale cast of thought'. Where Hamlet is concerned, excessive reflection or moral awareness certainly undermines his will to act. **This philosophical soliloquy reminds us that Hamlet is essentially a scholar and a thinker rather than a man of action.**

Hamlet's treatment of Ophelia in what is known as the 'Nunnery Scene' is shockingly cruel. When Ophelia attempts to return his letters, Hamlet denies ever having given them. He questions Ophelia's honesty: 'Are you honest?' He taunts her, telling her 'I did love you once', before declaring, 'I loved you not'. Hamlet dismisses Ophelia in an extremely harsh manner: 'Get thee to a nunnery. Why wouldst thou be a breeder of sinners?'

Hamlet's cruel treatment of Ophelia is caused by his loss of faith in women in general. Disillusioned and embittered by his mother's weakness, Hamlet denounces all women: 'God hath given you one face and you make yourselves another, you jig, you amble, and you lisp, you nickname God's creatures and you make your wantonness your ignorance'. Hamlet now regards all relationships between men and women with total disgust, no longer believing in the idea of love and marriage: 'I say we will have no more marriage'. In addition to Hamlet's loss of faith in women, there may be a more specific reason for the vicious outburst directed against Ophelia. Hamlet's remarks suggest that he knows that Polonius is spying on them and that Ophelia is conspiring with her father and the king against him: 'Let the doors be shut upon him that he may play the fool nowhere but in his own house'.

Ophelia is greatly distressed by Hamlet's strange behaviour and concludes that he has lost his mind: 'O what a noble mind is here o'erthrown!' Ophelia describes Hamlet as having had the qualities of the complete man. In her eyes, Hamlet was the finest example of Danish manhood ('The expectancy and rose of the fair state') and she struggles to come to terms with the dramatic change in the man she loves.

The eavesdropping Claudius shrewdly concludes that Hamlet's strange behaviour is not caused by his love for Ophelia: 'Love? His affections do not that way tend'. He also wonders about the nature of Hamlet's 'madness': 'Nor what he spake, though it lacked form a little was not like madness'. **Hamlet and Claudius are well-matched adversaries in that they are both very astute. The king understands the dangerous nature of Hamlet's melancholy, sensing that his nephew is hatching a plan:** 'There's something in his soul o'er which his melancholy sits on brood'. He fears that such a plan will prove dangerous to him: 'And I do doubt the hatch and the disclose will be some danger'. Claudius decides to move quickly to counter the threat posed by Hamlet by sending his nephew to England without delay to collect revenue owed to Denmark.

Polonius still clings to his theory that Hamlet's strange behaviour was originally caused by 'neglected love'. The plan he now proposes involves Gertrude meeting privately with Hamlet and asking him the cause of his unhappiness, while he himself listens in on their conversation – he will be 'in the ear of all their conference'. Once again we see that Polonius has no respect for the privacy of others. **For his part, Claudius knows that he must keep a close eye on Hamlet:** 'Madness in great ones must not unwatched go'.

KEY POINTS

- Polonius uses Ophelia as 'bait' to 'trap' Hamlet.
- Neither Claudius nor Polonius has any qualms about spying on Hamlet – the king and his chief adviser are similarly devious and unscrupulous.
- In a revealing aside, Claudius admits to bearing a 'heavy burden' of guilt.
- In his most famous soliloquy ('To be, or not to be . . .'), Hamlet wonders whether or not he should 'take action against a sea of troubles'. He is clearly a thinker rather than a man of action.
- Hamlet knows that he is inhibited by his conscience, concluding that the more he thinks, the less likely he is to act.
- Hamlet treats Ophelia in a harsh and cruel manner before going on to launch a bitter attack on women in general.
- Ophelia is greatly distressed by Hamlet's apparent loss of sanity.
- Claudius feels threatened by Hamlet's peculiar behaviour, and decides to send him to England.
- The ever-devious Polonius proposes even more spying – this time he will listen in on what should be a private conversation between Hamlet and his mother.

Act 3 Scene 2

Hamlet gives one of the players advice on how to speak his lines. **Hamlet is very knowledgeable about drama and acting.** He tells the player that he must at all times remain in control of his emotions: '. . . for in the very torrent, tempest, and whirlwind of your passion, you must acquire and beget a temperance that may give it smoothness'. **It is rather ironic that Hamlet fails to heed his own advice about remaining in control of one's passion.**

The purpose of the play that Hamlet is about to stage ('The Murder of Gonzago' or, as Hamlet entitles it, 'The Mousetrap') is to reflect real life: 'to hold, as 'twere the mirror up to nature, to show virtue her own feature'.

In conversation with Horatio, **Hamlet reflects on the falseness of court life where flattery is used for the purpose of self-advancement:** '. . . let the candied tongue lick absurd pomp, and crook the pregnant hinges of the knee where thrift may follow fawning'. Hamlet admires Horatio because of his balanced personality: '. . . blest are those whose blood and judgement are so well commeddled'. Horatio possesses the correct temperamental balance between 'blood' and 'judgement' or between passion and reflection. Hamlet himself does not possess this perfect temperamental balance. While Horatio is to be admired because he is not 'passion's slave', Hamlet is on occasions ruled by his emotions. Horatio is a stoical character who takes life's ups and downs in his stride. Noble and trustworthy, he is the only person in whom Hamlet confides. **Hamlet tells Horatio of his plan to stage a play to test the king's guilt.** Craving certainty, he asks his one true friend to also observe the king's reaction to the play.

Hamlet speaks with Ophelia before the play begins, sarcastically remarking on how happy his mother looks 'and my father died within two hours'. Hamlet exaggerates the speed with which Gertrude re-married in order to highlight her fickleness and disloyalty. When Ophelia observes that it is 'twice two months' since King Hamlet died, we realise how much time has passed since the appearance of the ghost. **We are reminded of Hamlet's failure to deliver on the promise he made to the ghost.**

Before the play begins there is a Dumb-Show which is an exact imitation of what happened in the orchard when King Hamlet was murdered. The Dumb-Show heightens the tension before the play itself is performed. The play itself starts at a leisurely pace, before the Player Queen delivers lines designed to cut to Gertrude's heart: 'In second husband let me be accursed; none wed the second but who killed the first'. The Player Queen goes on to express Hamlet's sentiments when she declares: 'The instances that second marriage move are base respects of thrift and none of love'. **Hamlet believes that Claudius' marriage to Gertrude has more to do with self-advancement and lust than love.**

Hamlet asks his mother for her opinion of the play. Naturally, Gertrude cannot accept the Player Queen's view of second marriages: 'The lady doth protest too much methinks'. When Hamlet explains that the poisoner is 'nephew to the king', Claudius feels threatened as well as exposed. The king's guilt is confirmed when he abruptly leaves. Hamlet tells Horatio: 'O good Horatio, I'll take the ghost's word for a thousand pound'. Guildenstern reports that Claudius 'is in his retirement marvellous distempered'.

Rosencrantz continues with his efforts to probe Hamlet's mind, asking him about the reason for his disturbed state. **Hamlet deliberately misleads him when he replies that he is frustrated by his lack of promotion:** 'Sir, I lack advancement'. Shortly afterwards, Hamlet vents his anger at his so-called friends' attempts to discover what lies behind his strange behaviour: '. . . you would pluck out the heart of my mystery . . .'s blood, do you think I am easier to be played on than a pipe?'

When Polonius enters the scene, Hamlet highlights and ridicules his falseness when he has a conversation with him about the shape of a cloud. The foolish, sycophantic courtier agrees with Hamlet every time he changes his mind about the shape of the cloud, by turn agreeing that it resembles a camel, a weasel and a whale. **Hamlet is intensely frustrated by the falseness of court life:** 'They fool me to the top of my bent'. At the close of this scene Hamlet finally seems poised to act when he passionately proclaims: '. . . now could I drink hot blood and do such bitter business as the day would quake to look on'.

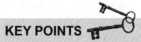

KEY POINTS

- Hamlet is disillusioned and frustrated by the falseness of court life.
- He expresses his admiration for Horatio's balanced temperament.
- He stages 'The Mousetrap' to test the king's guilt.
- Claudius leaves the play abruptly, confirming his guilt.

Act 3 Scene 3

Claudius takes immediate action to have Hamlet removed from the Danish court. He decides to send him to England, escorted by Rosencrantz and Guildenstern. **He sees his nephew as a very real threat to his kingship:** 'The terms of our estate may not endure hazards so near as doth hourly grow out of his brows'.

In addition to causing Claudius to feel threatened, 'The Mousetrap' also pricks the king's conscience. Claudius' soliloquy offers us important insights into his state of mind. **He is painfully aware of the enormity of his crime:** 'O my offence is rank, it smells to heaven'. Claudius feels that there is 'not rain enough in the sweet heavens' to wash the blood from his hands. While he longs to repent, he is incapable of praying because he will not give up all that he has gained through his crime: 'My crown, mine own ambition and my queen'. Claudius knows that he can avoid justice in the corrupt world in which he lives ('In the corrupted currents of this world offence's gilded hand may shove by justice'), but acknowledges that there can be no escaping divine justice: 'But 'tis not so above,

there is no shuffling, there the action lies in his true nature'.

As Claudius struggles with his guilt and tries in vain to pray, Hamlet enters and has his first opportunity of killing the king: 'Now might I do it pat, now he is praying'. However, he hesitates, claiming that he does not want to kill his father's murderer when he is at prayer: 'A villain kills my father, and for that I his sole son do this same villain send to heaven'. If we take Hamlet's sentiments at face value, he does not take this opportunity to finally kill Claudius because he wants a complete revenge that also involves the king's damnation. Hamlet declares that he would sooner kill him 'when he is drunk asleep, or in his rage, or in the incestuous pleasure of his bed'. While Hamlet may indeed crave a complete revenge, it is very likely that he is simply trying to justify his inability to act. **He again postpones revenge because he cannot bring himself to kill Claudius in cold blood.**

It is of course ironic that Hamlet draws back from killing Claudius because he believes him to be in a state of prayer when in reality the king is unable to pray. **Here again we see an interesting contrast between appearance and reality.**

KEY POINTS

- Claudius sees Hamlet's madness as a serious threat to his kingship and decides to send him to England.
- Claudius' soliloquy reveals a man tormented by his conscience, but incapable of praying for forgiveness.
- Hamlet's indecision is brought into clear focus when he has an opportunity to kill Claudius, but draws back from killing the king when he is praying.

Act 3 Scene 4

This is the most dramatic scene in the play. In it Hamlet rashly slays Polonius (an event that will have a number of very significant consequences) and angrily confronts his mother. To add to the drama, the ghost appears to remind Hamlet of his duty to gain revenge.

Polonius hides behind a curtain in order to eavesdrop on Hamlet's conversation with his mother. He plans to go and report to the king on the reasons for Hamlet's strange behaviour. On Polonius' advice, Gertrude rebukes Hamlet, accusing him of offending his father. However, Hamlet turns this accusation back on her: 'Mother, you have my father much offended'. It is Gertrude who is severely chastised in this scene. Hamlet is determined to make his mother more self-aware: 'You go not till I set you up a glass where you may see the inmost part of you'. However, the queen is alarmed by Hamlet's aggressive, threatening behaviour and cries out for help. When Polonius foolishly echoes the queen's cry for assistance, Hamlet unthinkingly runs his sword through the arras, killing the servile courtier.

Gertrude rightly describes the killing of Polonius as 'a rash and bloody deed'. This dramatic event will impact in a profound way on the lives of the central characters of the play. Ophelia will lose her sanity and ultimately take her own life, while Laertes will become Hamlet's mortal enemy as he also assumes the role of avenging son. Hamlet later recognises that both of them come to share a common cause. The impetuous killing of the king's unscrupulous adviser marks a critical turning point in the play because all of the other deaths in the play follow on from it.

Hamlet shows little feeling for the dead Polonius, coldly dismissing him as a 'wretched, rash, intruding fool'. He expresses no regret for his impulsive act; indeed he seems to be completely unaffected by what he has done. The contrast between this dramatic scene and the Prayer Scene brings Hamlet's complex and unpredictable nature into sharp focus:

the man who could not bring his sword down on the guilty king does not hesitate to run his sword through a curtain, killing Polonius. The fact that Hamlet thought that it was Claudius hiding behind the curtain ('I took thee for thy better') indicates that he is capable of killing his uncle, but only in the heat of the moment. **When Hamlet has time to think, he draws back from the idea of revenge.**

Hamlet now vents his anger at his mother, bitterly describing her marriage to Claudius as 'an act that blurs the grace and blush of modesty'. He believes that Gertrude's disloyalty has stained the original beauty of her love for her first husband: '. . . takes off the rose from the fair forehead of an innocent love and sets a blister there'. **Hamlet believes that his father was the perfect man:** 'A combination and a form indeed where every god did seem to set his seal'. In contrast, Claudius is depicted as 'a mildewed ear' of corn, infecting others with the disease of corruption. Hamlet angrily demands that Gertrude open her eyes to the reality of Claudius' character: 'Have you eyes?'

Hamlet certainly succeeds in forcing his mother to examine her conscience. We see a sign of Gertrude's humanity when she admits to her sinful state: 'Thou turn'st mine eyes into my very soul and there I see such black and grained spots as will not leave their tinct'.

Hamlet's loud, angry attack on his mother is very dramatic. While Hamlet's anger is understandable, his self-righteous tone and the delight he seems to take in tormenting Gertrude are unattractive aspects of his character. He uses repulsive animal imagery to describe her relationship with Claudius, comparing them to pigs 'honeying and making love over the nasty sty'. Hamlet is utterly disgusted by his mother's 'incestuous' marriage to a man he despises. Gertrude is deeply pained by Hamlet's ferocious outburst, comparing his words to daggers and begging him to say no more.

This scene is full of dramatic happenings. At this point the Ghost briefly appears to remind Hamlet of his duty to gain revenge: 'This visitation is but to whet thy almost blunted

23

purpose'. The Ghost displays some concern for Gertrude when he asks Hamlet to help her in her inner struggle. The queen cannot see the Ghost and concludes that Hamlet is hallucinating: 'This is the very coinage of your brain'. Hamlet urges his mother to dramatically change her ways: 'Confess yourself to heaven. Repent what's past . . .'. He wants Gertrude to end her relationship with Claudius and not to add to the corruption that is the key feature of his reign: 'And do not spread the compost on the weeds to make them ranker'. Hamlet's preoccupation with the physical aspect of the Gertrude-Claudius relationship is an unappealing aspect of his mentality: '. . . by no means that I bid you do, let the bloat king tempt you again to bed'.

Hamlet admits to his mother that his madness is an act: 'I essentially am not in madness, but mad in craft'. Gertrude promises not to reveal Hamlet's secret to anyone: 'I have no life to breathe what thou hast said to me'. While she does not subsequently detach herself from Claudius, she proves to be true to her word, never sharing her son's secret with the king.

Hamlet and Claudius are engaged in a battle of wits throughout the play. As adversaries they are evenly matched, both being sharp-witted, shrewd and ruthless to varying degrees. Hamlet reminds Gertrude that he will shortly be going to England in the company of Rosencrantz and Guildenstern. Of course there is more to this trip than meets the eye. While Hamlet is unaware of the king's devious plan to have him killed, he knows that he cannot trust his so-called friends, whom he compares to 'adders fanged'. Furthermore, he is confident that he can out-wit them: 'But I will delve one yard below their mines and blow them at the moon'.

At the close of this very dramatic scene **Hamlet again expresses his contempt for the dead Polonius,** dismissing him as 'a foolish prating knave'. He had no respect for the servile courtier when he was alive and he has scant respect for him now that he is dead: 'I'll lug the guts into the neighbour room'.

KEY POINTS

- Hamlet's killing of Polonius profoundly influences the course of events in the play.
- Hamlet expresses no remorse for 'this rash and bloody deed'.
- Hamlet forces his mother to examine her conscience and admit to her sinful state.
- The Ghost appears to remind Hamlet of his duty to gain revenge.
- Hamlet tells Gertrude that his madness is only an act.
- Hamlet is confident of out-witting Rosencrantz and Guildenstern.

Act 4 Scene 1

Gertrude informs Claudius of the death of Polonius, but does her best to protect Hamlet by attributing the killing of Polonius to his madness: 'In his lawless fit . . . kills the unseen good old man'. Claudius' response to the death of Polonius underlines the extent to which he is self-absorbed. He realises that Hamlet meant to kill him rather than Polonius: ('It had been so with us, had we been there') and sheds no tears for his loyal courtier, instead worrying that he may be blamed for failing to control his 'mad' nephew. While Claudius and Hamlet are well-matched enemies, this scene illustrates one advantage that the king enjoys over his nephew. **In contrast to the indecisive, procrastinating Hamlet, Claudius is clear-minded and decisive.** He decides to send his dangerous nephew to England without delay: 'The sun no sooner shall the mountains touch but we shall ship him hence'.

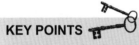

KEY POINTS

- Gertrude does her best to shield Hamlet from blame. She remains loyal to Hamlet and does not tell Claudius that her son's madness is an act.
- Claudius remains utterly self-absorbed – he is largely unmoved by the death of Polonius.
- Claudius moves swiftly to deal with the threat that Hamlet now poses, deciding to send him to England without delay.

Act 4 Scene 2

Hamlet refuses to tell Rosencrantz and Guildenstern where the body of Polonius is. Adopting his 'antic disposition', he challenges his 'friends' to a game of 'hide and seek'. **Hamlet knows that Rosencrantz and Guildenstern have no genuine interest in him and are** **motivated only by self-interest.** He describes Rosencrantz as 'a sponge' that 'soaks up the king's countenance, his rewards, his authorities'. Hamlet uses his mask of madness to suggest that Claudius is not the rightful king: 'The body is with the king, but the king is not with the body. The king is a thing . . . '

KEY POINTS

- Hamlet tells Rosencrantz and Guildenstern that he knows they are only interested in what they can gain from the king.

Act 4 Scene 3

Claudius' shrewdness is very apparent in this scene. He will not have Hamlet arrested and put on trial because of his popularity with the Danish people: 'He's loved of the distracted multitude'. Claudius is a clever political animal who will not do anything that might jeopardise his kingship. He uses disease imagery to describe Hamlet, suggesting that he will need to take extreme measures to cure this disease: 'Diseases desperate grown by desperate appliance are relieved or not at all'. **Hamlet uses his 'antic disposition' to make little of Claudius' kingship,** telling his uncle that king and beggar end up as food for maggots. We see Hamlet's black humour when he tells the king that the dead Polonius is unlikely to go anywhere: 'He will stay till you come'. Claudius tells Hamlet that he must go to England for his own safety. Interestingly, Hamlet never questions this decision – he is prepared to go to England even though he has still not gained revenge. At the close of this scene Claudius looks forward to England curing him of the disease that is Hamlet: 'Do it England, for like the hectic in my blood he rages, and thou must cure me'. Claudius' plan to have Hamlet killed in England highlights his devious, ruthless nature. **While Hamlet procrastinates, Claudius does not hesitate to kill his enemy.**

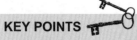

> **KEY POINTS**
> - Claudius is an astute politician – he will not subject Hamlet to the rigours of the law because he fears he might provoke a popular uprising against his kingship.
> - Hamlet uses his 'antic disposition' to make little of Claudius' kingship.
> - Claudius' plan to have Hamlet executed in England underlines his ruthlessness.

Act 4 Scene 4

While on his way to the harbour, Hamlet sees unfamiliar troops. He learns that these are Fortinbras' troops on their way to Poland to fight for a small area of territory ('A little patch of ground'). This bold action by Fortinbras sharpens Hamlet's desire for revenge: 'How all occasions do inform against me and spur my dull revenge'. **Hamlet is filled with guilt at his own inaction.** He realises that his failure to act is the result of 'thinking too precisely on the event'. Hamlet reflects on the contrast between Fortinbras and himself. It seems to him that Fortinbras is brave and daring, while he seems incapable of acting. He considers how Fortinbras is prepared to risk his own life and the lives of twenty thousand men 'for a fantasy and trick of fame', while he himself does nothing despite having far more compelling reasons to act ('a father killed, a mother stained'). **At the close of this scene, Hamlet passionately re-dedicates himself to gaining revenge:** 'O from this time forth, my thought be bloody or be nothing worth!'

> **KEY POINTS**
> - The sight of Fortinbras boldly marching through Denmark on his way to Poland to fight for 'a little patch of ground' causes Hamlet to feel guilty at his failure to act on the ghost's command.

Act 4 Scene 5

We learn that Ophelia has lost her sanity following the death of her father. A gentleman tells the queen: 'She is importunate, indeed distract. Her mood will needs be pitied'. Ophelia herself enters the scene at this point, singing sad love songs to the king and queen. Her insanity is the result of her father being killed by the man she loved as well as Hamlet's rejection of her. Her mind is too sensitive to cope with the horror of what has happened. **Ophelia is a pathetic figure, an innocent victim of the corruption and treachery that lies at the heart of the Danish court.** Gertrude is filled with foreboding, fearing that this tragedy is a sign of some great disaster to come: 'To my sick soul, as sin's true nature is, each toy seems prologue to some great amiss'. It is significant that Gertrude again acknowledges her sinful state. However, she remains loyal to Claudius in spite of all that Hamlet has told her.

Laertes has secretly returned from France and now makes a dramatic entrance, bursting into the throne room at the head of an angry mob. The king is told: 'Young Laertes in a riotous head o'erbears your officers'. **The angry and impetuous Laertes holds the king accountable for his father's death** and demands answers. Gertrude tries to protect Claudius, even holding onto Laertes. While the queen may not have been involved in King Hamlet's murder, she is guilty of supporting Claudius even after she has been made aware of the extent of his crimes. **Gertrude is a weak woman who is seemingly incapable of an independent existence.**

We see Claudius at his manipulative best in his handling of Laertes. He insists that Gertrude let Laertes go, wisely allowing him to vent his anger before gradually winning him around to his way of thinking. **Claudius' hypocrisy is very apparent when he tells Gertrude that she need not be concerned for his safety** because 'there's such divinity doth hedge a king'. While a king was seen as God's representative on earth, Claudius hardly fits this description since he is a usurper who killed the lawful king so that he could have both his crown and his queen for himself.

While both Laertes and Hamlet seek to avenge a father's death, there are two striking differences between them. Firstly, while Hamlet procrastinates Laertes acts on impulse. Secondly, while Hamlet is paralysed by his conscience, Laertes will not allow his conscience to prevent him from gaining revenge: 'Conscience and grace to the profoundest pit!' His desire for revenge is heightened by the pitiable sight of the insane Ophelia: 'Hadst thou thy wits and didst persuade revenge, it could not move thus'. Claudius handles Laertes with consummate skill, gradually turning a potentially dangerous enemy into a useful ally and instrument of his will. He combines the usual flattery ('Good Laertes') with blatant lies ('I am guiltless of your father's death'), before going on to 'commune' with Laertes' grief. Claudius comes across as a very plausible character, particularly when he tells Laertes that he will give him all that he owns if he finds him to have been in any way involved in his father's murder. By the end of this scene, Laertes has calmed down and no longer poses a threat to the king. From this point on, Claudius sets about using Laertes' passionate desire for revenge as a means of destroying Hamlet.

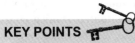

KEY POINTS

- Ophelia loses her sanity following Hamlet's killing of Polonius.
- Laertes is intent on avenging his father's death.
- Claudius skilfully manipulates Laertes for his own devious ends – he plans to use him as the instrument of Hamlet's destruction.

Act 4 Scene 6

Horatio receives a letter from Hamlet describing his eventful voyage to England, and revealing that he is now on his way back to Denmark. **One of Horatio's important dramatic functions is to update the audience on important developments offstage.** This scene is brief, but dramatically important. Hamlet's letter explains how he fell into the hands of pirates who have in fact treated him well. The chance encounter with the pirates would seem to suggest that fate or providence is now finally working in Hamlet's favour. Hamlet asks Horatio to deliver letters to the king and then to come to him.

KEY POINTS

- Hamlet's return to Denmark heightens the dramatic tension, filling the audience with a sense of expectation.

Act 4 Scene 7

Claudius convinces Laertes that Hamlet was responsible for Polonius' death. He cleverly seems to take Laertes into his confidence when he suggests that he could not arrest Hamlet for fear of upsetting his relationship with the queen ('The Queen his mother lives almost by his looks, and for myself . . . she is so conjunctive to my life and soul . . .') and of turning public opinion against him. **Claudius is a shrewd politician with a strong instinct for political survival** and is wary of 'the great love the general gender bear him' (Hamlet). **He continues to manipulate Laertes** with remarkable ease, telling him: 'I loved your father, and we love ourself'. The naïve Laertes agrees to be 'ruled' by Claudius who has now devised a plan for ridding himself of Hamlet in such a way that no blame will attach to him: 'And for his death no wind of blame shall breathe'. As is apparent throughout the play, Claudius is both cunning and unscrupulous.

Laertes is pleased to learn of Hamlet's imminent return because he cannot wait to confront him: 'It warms the very sickness in my heart'. His desire for revenge is so intense that he has no scruples about how he kills Hamlet – he would even be prepared to 'cut his throat in the church'.

While Hamlet and Laertes are driven by the same desire to avenge a father's death, the latter never allows his conscience to stand in the way of gaining revenge. Claudius continues to incite Laertes, telling him that 'revenge should have no bounds'.

Claudius unintentionally pays tribute to Hamlet's nobility when he remarks that his nephew is too trusting to wish to examine the foils before the fencing contest: '. . . he being remiss, most generous and free from all contriving will not peruse the foils'. However, **there is no sign of Laertes' nobility** – in fact he appears to be an utterly unscrupulous character who will stoop to any moral depths to gain revenge. Both Claudius and Laertes are prepared to use poison to kill Hamlet – if Laertes' poisoned sword does not kill Hamlet, then Claudius' poisoned wine will be used to eliminate him. It is impossible to imagine Hamlet ever using such underhanded, treacherous methods.

Ophelia's suicide is a particularly tragic event. She is simply too innocent to survive in the harsh, male-dominated Danish court. At the close of the scene, we are again reminded of Claudius' hypocrisy when he tells Gertrude of 'how much' he had to do to calm Laertes.

KEY POINTS

- Claudius continues to manipulate Laertes, the latter foolishly agreeing to be 'ruled' by the king.
- In contrast to Hamlet, Laertes is not in any way restrained by his conscience when it comes to planning his revenge.
- Claudius devises a cunning plan to kill Hamlet.
- Ophelia's death highlights the play's tragic dimension.

Act 5 Scene 1

The Graveyard Scene provides some light relief, but there is always **a dark side to the humour** here. The gravediggers' banter is entertaining, but Hamlet is reminded of the grim reality of death. The Second Gravedigger asks: 'Who builds stronger than a mason, a shipwright or a carpenter?' The response underlines the finality of death: 'A grave-maker. The houses he makes last till doomsday'. Yorick's skull reminds Hamlet of human mortality. He is disgusted by the sight and smell of death: 'My gorge rises at it'. **Hamlet makes little of Claudius' kingship** when he tells Horatio that the greatest of leaders such as Alexander and Caesar ended up as dust.

As Hamlet sees Laertes approaching in a funeral procession, he describes him as 'a very noble youth'. This is very ironic given the devious methods Laertes employs in order to gain revenge. Hamlet is shocked to discover that it is Ophelia who is being buried: 'What, the fair Ophelia?' Flower imagery once again underlines Ophelia's innocence: 'Lay her in the earth and from her fair and unpolluted flesh may violets spring'. Gertrude is genuinely upset by Ophelia's tragic death: 'I thought thy bride bed to have decked, sweet maid, and not have strewed thy grave'.

An emotional Laertes leaps into the grave to hold Ophelia in his arms. This exaggerated display of grief angers Hamlet. The confrontation that follows culminates in the two men grappling with each other in Ophelia's grave. While this is unseemly behaviour, Hamlet is in control of himself in this dramatic scene. The warning that he issues to Laertes is **an indication of the fundamental change in his character since his return from the sea voyage:** 'For though I am not splenetive and rash, yet have I in me something dangerous which let thy wisdom fear'. Here Hamlet is pointing out that he is capable of acting decisively. He insists that he loved Ophelia and that the love of 'forty thousand brothers' could not match his love for her. **Gertrude again shows her loyalty to Hamlet by blaming his unseemly behaviour on his madness:** 'This is mere madness and thus a while the fit will work on him'.

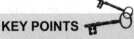

KEY POINTS
- Hamlet is angered by Laertes' exaggerated display of grief.
- His warning to Laertes is an indication of a fundamental change in his character – he is finally capable of decisive action.

Act 5 Scene 2

The Hamlet who returns from the voyage to England is very much a new man. He is calm, composed and decisive. One of the key factors underlying this fundamental change in Hamlet's character is **his new belief in the power of providence.** He now sees no point in endless planning because the best laid plans may come to nothing: 'There's a divinity that shapes our ends, rough-hew them how we will'. He sees the guiding hand of providence behind everything that happened to him during the voyage. He discovered the letter from the king sending him to his death in England. He was able to seal the altered letter with his father's signet ring: 'Why, even in that was heaven ordinant'. Even the encounter with the pirates works in Hamlet's favour because they brought him back to Denmark. The 'new' Hamlet is no longer paralysed by his conscience. Rosencrantz and Guildenstern are sent to their deaths without hesitation because they are believed to be responsible for their own demise: 'They are not near my conscience, their defeat does by their own insinuation grow'. Hamlet logically lists four reasons why he can finally kill Claudius with 'perfect conscience'. He explains to Horatio that Claudius killed his father, tarnished his mother, took the crown that was rightfully Hamlet's and even tried to have Hamlet killed.

We also see a nobler Hamlet in the closing scene. He tells Horatio that he regrets his earlier confrontation with Laertes because he now sees that **both of them are driven by the desire to avenge a father's death:** 'For by the image of my cause I see the portraiture of his'.

The courtier who brings the details of the fencing contest is Osric. Hamlet ridicules Osric's falseness in the course of a conversation about the weather. Every time that Hamlet changes his mind about the weather, the servile Osric agrees with him. Osric is as false and as untrustworthy as Polonius, whom Hamlet had earlier ridiculed in the course of a similar conversation about the shape of a cloud.

Hamlet is filled with foreboding before the duel, telling Horatio: 'Thou wouldst not think how ill all's here about my heart'. However, firmly believing in the power of providence, he presses on: '. . . there's a special providence in the fall of a sparrow'. Hamlet will be ready to respond to unfolding circumstances: 'The readiness is all'. We again see the noble Hamlet when he apologises to Laertes before the contest begins. Laertes accepts the apology, but subsequently goes ahead with the king's treacherous plan. Events move very quickly as the Queen drinks the poisoned wine meant for Hamlet. Claudius makes only a half-hearted effort to save the woman he claimed to love, sacrificing her in order to save himself: 'Gertrude, do not drink'. Laertes and Hamlet end up wounding each other with the poisoned sword. **Laertes accepts the justice of his own death** ('I am justly killed with mine own treachery'), making an attempt to redeem himself by pointing to the king's guilt. It is at this point that Hamlet finally gains his revenge, stabbing Claudius with the poisoned

sword and forcing him to drink the poisoned wine. There is an obvious poetic justice to the manner of the king's death. Right to the end of the play, Hamlet's mind is primarily dominated by feelings of disgust: 'Thou incestuous, murderous, damned Dane'. **Before he dies, Laertes exchanges forgiveness with 'noble Hamlet', absolving him of all blame for both his own and his father's deaths.**

Horatio's final dramatic function will be to tell Hamlet's story to the world: 'Horatio, I am dead, thou livest, report me and my cause aright to the unsatisfied'. **Horatio's loyalty to Hamlet** is such that, in the manner of an ancient Roman, he is prepared to take his own life when he sees that his best friend is close to death: 'I am more an antique Roman than a Dane'. However, Hamlet insists that Horatio live on, before going on to give his blessing to Fortinbras as the next king of Denmark. Horatio's moving tribute to Hamlet's nobility reminds us of the prince's finer qualities 'Now cracks a noble heart. Goodnight sweet prince, and flights of angels sing thee to thy rest'.

As the person who will restore order to Denmark, Fortinbras has the final word. He praises **Hamlet's royal nature, suggesting that he would have been a good king:** 'For he was likely, had he been put on, to have proved most royal'.

KEY POINTS

- Hamlet returns from the sea voyage a new man – calm, composed and decisive.
- Hamlet now believes in the power of providence and is finally able to act with a clear conscience.
- Hamlet finally gains revenge, responding decisively to rapidly unfolding circumstances.
- The closing scene emphasises Hamlet's finer qualities – he exchanges forgiveness with Laertes and prevents Horatio from taking his own life. Our admiration for him is reinforced by the way in which different characters testify to his nobility.

Guidelines for Answering Exam Questions

Structure your Answer

1 A brief plan – this should be no more than key words or phrases.

2 An introduction – this should outline your general response to the question.

3 Aim for a points-based answer, avoiding excessive narrative.

4 Make one main point per paragraph.

5 Points should be discussed in a logical order.

6 The opening sentence in each paragraph (the paragraph sentence) should state the main point of the paragraph.

7 Maintain focus on, and refer back to, the terms of the question.

8 Support your points by close reference to, and quotation from, the text.

9 A brief conclusion.

Main Areas for Exam

1 The manner in which characters are portrayed.

2 The importance / role / dramatic function of particular characters.

3 Themes.

4 Key scenes.

5 Soliloquys.

6 Language, imagery and symbolism.

7 Your personal response to the play.

Hamlet
Exam Topics & Themes

Exam Topics & Themes

The Characters

Exam Topics & Themes

1. 'Is Hamlet a noble hero?'

There are many reasons why a modern audience might feel unsympathetic towards Hamlet. Hamlet himself seems to be keenly aware of his personal faults when he speaks of having 'more offences at my beck than I have thoughts to put them in'. Certainly his **bitterness, cruelty and cynicism** do not endear him to the audience, and there are times when we have to remind ourselves that Hamlet is in fact the hero of the play. However, **Hamlet's worst excesses can be explained, if not excused**, by reference to the stress and strain of the state of affairs in which he finds himself. It is also the case that we see a nobler Hamlet towards the close of the play, ensuring that our final impression of him is a positive one. Finally, it is significant that, at different points in the play, all of the central characters testify to Hamlet's nobility. **While acknowledging his complexity and flaws, we ultimately see Hamlet as an essentially noble character.**

Hamlet's opening soliloquy leaves the audience very unimpressed with the depth of his disillusionment and self-pity. He describes the world as 'weary, stale, flat, and unprofitable', and expresses his disappointment at God's laws forbidding 'self-slaughter'. While Hamlet's utterly negative outlook and lack of interest in life can be explained, they are seriously unpleasant aspects of his character.

Hamlet's treatment of Gertrude is cruel and callous. He is not content with simply making his mother aware of her sins ('. . . set you up a glass where you may see the inmost part of you'), instead setting out to 'speak daggers' to her. He uses repulsive (disgusting) imagery to describe Gertrude's relationship with Claudius: '. . . to live in the rank sweat of an unseamed bed, honeying and making love over the nasty sty'. Gertrude begs her son to be patient with her: 'No more, sweet Hamlet'. **Hamlet's obsession with what he perceives to be the 'incestuous'** relationship between Gertrude and Claudius is a strange, disturbing aspect of his mentality. We can understand why it is so important to him that the queen grows in self-awareness, but Hamlet's treatment of her amounts to a form of mental torture. The Hamlet who takes such a heartless delight in tormenting his own mother is a very unattractive character.

Hamlet's treatment of Ophelia is similarly inhuman. His mother's weakness has caused Hamlet to lose faith in all women: 'Frailty, thy name is woman'. Hamlet questions Ophelia's integrity: 'Are you honest?' He teases her by declaring 'I did love you once', before remarking 'I loved you not'. The audience is shocked by the extent of Hamlet's cruelty towards Ophelia: 'Get thee to a nunnery. Why, wouldst thou be a breeder of sinners?' Hamlet bitterly denounces all women ('. . . you jig, you amble and you lisp, you nickname God's creatures and make your wantonness your ignorance'), leaving Ophelia feeling dejected and bewildered.

Hamlet's killing of Polonius is rightly described by Gertrude as 'a rash and bloody deed'. There can be no justification for this impulsive, irrational act. While the false and servile Polonius is an utterly distasteful (unpleasant) character, he does not deserve to meet his end in this manner. Hamlet expresses no real regret or remorse for this rash act, dismissing the dead courtier as 'a foolish prating knave'. His blatant disrespect for the dead Polonius ('I'll lug the guts into the neighbour room') tends to further alienate the audience.

Hamlet coldly sends Rosencrantz and Guildenstern to their deaths, without giving them a chance to have their sins forgiven. They are to be killed as soon as they deliver the altered letter, 'not shriving time allowed'. This may be seen as further evidence of his cruel and ruthless nature.

Hamlet's unseemly behaviour during Ophelia's burial scene also reflects badly on him. He seems to envy Laertes his grief, ultimately grappling with him in Ophelia's grave. This is not the type of behaviour that we expect from a supposedly noble hero. Gertrude tries to make excuses for her son's utterly inappropriate action by attributing it to his madness: 'This is mere madness, and thus a while the fit will work on him'.

However, Hamlet's worst excesses can be explained by reference to the extraordinary circumstances in which he finds himself. Hamlet's innate (natural) nobility and idealism are undermined by a series of dramatic events: the death of his beloved father, his mother's hasty remarriage, the ghost's dramatic revelations, and the fact that he is burdened with the duty of gaining revenge. Avenging his father's death is a task for which Hamlet, as a thinker and a man of conscience, is unsuited. The melancholy, bitter and cynical Hamlet that we meet at the start of the play seems to be unrecognisable from his earlier self. Gertrude speaks of her 'too much changed son', while Claudius refers to 'Hamlet's transformation'.

There is much evidence of Hamlet's nobility, especially towards the close of the play. We admire Hamlet because he is a man of conscience, anxious to do what is right. His noble nature is evident in his idealistic view of his father and in his devotion to his memory ('A combination and a form indeed where every God did seem to set his seal'). We see Hamlet's finer qualities in his knowledge and enjoyment of drama. He is at his happiest chatting with the actors who visit Elsinore. The noble Hamlet is particularly evident in the final scene when he apologises to Laertes ('Give me your pardon, sir. I have done you wrong') and prevents Horatio from committing suicide. The fact that Hamlet inspires such remarkable loyalty in a character such as Horatio is in itself compelling evidence of his noble nature.

All of the major characters in the play refer to Hamlet's nobility at various points in the play. The ghost addresses him as 'thou noble youth'. Ophelia describes Hamlet as 'the expectancy and rose of the fair state'. Even Claudius acknowledges that his troublesome nephew is 'most generous and free from all contriving', while also pointing out that he 'is loved of the distracted multitude'.

At the close of the play Laertes exchanges forgiveness with 'noble Hamlet'. Horatio pays his dying friend a moving tribute: 'Good night sweet Prince, and flights of angels sing thee to thy rest'. For his part, Fortinbras suggests that Hamlet possessed the qualities of a king: 'For he was likely, had he been put on, to have proved most royal'.

The audience comes to admire Hamlet for ultimately avenging his father's death and for ridding the Danish court of Claudius, its primary source of corruption. Hamlet's actions in the dramatic closing scene enable his father's ghost to finally rest in peace, while also helping to restore Denmark to a state of health. **We also respect Hamlet for the open, public manner in which he finally gains revenge – while Claudius tries to kill his nephew by deceitful and underhanded means, Hamlet's sense of honour prevents him from resorting to such immoral methods.** Finally, we admire Hamlet for giving his blessing to Fortinbras as the next king of Denmark – even as he draws his final breath, he displays a patriotic concern for the good of his country.

Hamlet is clearly an imperfect hero who at times comes close to alienating the audience. However, we can explain, if not condone (excuse) his worst excesses. **Ultimately we come to view him in a positive light, impressed in particular by his honourable and decisive actions at the close of the play.**

2. *Hamlet's Personal Development*

Hamlet's character undergoes a dramatic transformation in the course of the play. **In Acts 1-4 Hamlet is very unpredictable, generally thinking too much and procrastinating, yet on occasions failing to think and acting rashly.** Given to extremes of both reflection and passion, Hamlet lacks the balanced personality that he so admires in his best friend, Horatio. **However, the Hamlet who returns to Denmark from the voyage to England is a new man, displaying remarkable composure and decisiveness.** He is a more balanced character and no longer given either to the inaction or rashness that characterises his behaviour earlier in the play.

We are aware of the complexity of Hamlet's character from the early stages of the play. In Act 1 Scene 5 Hamlet passionately promises the ghost that he will 'sweep' to his revenge. However, by the close of this scene he is cursing the fact that it is up to him to set everything right: 'The time is out of joint. O cursed spite that ever I was born to set it right'. It is already apparent that while there is a passionate side to Hamlet's character, he is essentially a thinker rather than a man of action. As the play unfolds, we see Hamlet procrastinating – the more he thinks, the less likely he is to act.

As time passes, the indecisive Hamlet fails to act on the ghost's command to avenge his 'foul and most unnatural murder'. It is a chance happening – the arrival of a group of travelling actors in Elsinore – which rekindles Hamlet's passion for revenge. One of the actors delivers a speech (describing how Pyrrhus killed old Priam in an act of vengeance) with such passion that Hamlet feels guilty about his own lack of passion and inaction: 'What would he do had he the motive and the cue for passion that I have?' At the close of this scene we again see how Hamlet is, by turns, passionate and reflective. Speaking of Claudius, he passionately declares: 'Remorseless, treacherous, lecherous villain. O vengeance!' **However, when he has time to reflect, his passion diminishes and he** concludes that he needs concrete proof of the king's guilt since the ghost may have been an evil spirit: 'I'll have grounds more relative than this. The play's the thing wherein I'll catch the conscience of the king'. *The Mousetrap* is staged to give Hamlet the certainty he craves.

Hamlet's reflective, scholarly nature is evident in his most famous soliloquy ('To be or not to be ...') in which he ponders some fundamental philosophical questions – questions that relate directly to his own situation. He wonders whether it is better to 'suffer the slings and arrows of outrageous fortune' or 'take arms against a sea of troubles'. Basically, Hamlet is an indecisive character who wonders whether or not he should take action. One part of him is attracted to the idea of death as eternal sleep, yet he knows that even in death he may not be able to escape the obligation to gain revenge: 'For in that sleep of death what dreams may come?' Hamlet knows that he is paralysed by his tendency towards excessive reflection: 'Thus conscience does make cowards of us all, and thus the native hue of resolution is sicklied o'er with the pale cast of thought'.

Taken together, the Prayer Scene and the Closet Scene dramatically highlight Hamlet's complexity and unpredictability. The Prayer Scene brings Hamlet's indecision and procrastination into clear focus. *The Mousetrap* has provided Hamlet with concrete proof of the king's guilt and in the Prayer Scene he is presented with the perfect opportunity to gain revenge. However, instead of acting decisively, Hamlet starts to reflect, concluding that killing Claudius when he is praying would result in his father's killer going to heaven. This appears to be more an excuse than a genuine reason for inaction. As a thinker and a man of conscience, Hamlet seems to draw back from the idea of cold-blooded revenge.

Shortly afterwards, we are presented with the most dramatic example of Hamlet's uncontrolled passion when, in the Closet

Scene, he impulsively runs his sword through the curtain, killing Polonius. Hamlet believed that it was Claudius hiding behind the arras: 'I took thee for thy better'. However, the killing of Polonius is truly 'a rash and bloody deed'. While Hamlet cannot bring his sword down on the guilty Claudius in the Prayer Scene because he thinks too much, he unthinkingly kills his adviser Polonius in a moment of uncontrolled passion. Where Hamlet is concerned, there is either excessive reflection leading to inaction, or an absence of reflection resulting in rashness. **Hamlet greatly admires Horatio for finding a balance between 'blood' (passion) and 'judgement' (reflection):** 'Blessed are those whose blood and judgement are so well comingled that they are not a pipe for fortune to sound what stop she pleases'. **However, Hamlet himself seems to be incapable of achieving a similar temperamental balance.**

Hamlet's inaction results in a visitation from the ghost who reminds him of his failure to gain revenge. The ghost wants to sharpen Hamlet's sense of purpose: 'This visitation is but to whet thy almost blunted purpose'. Once again, Hamlet feels guilty over his failure to act on the ghost's command.

Hamlet's sense of guilt at his own inaction is heightened by the sight of Fortinbras boldly leading his army through Denmark on his way to fight for 'a little patch of ground' in Poland. He again acknowledges that his failure to gain revenge is the result of 'thinking too precisely on the event'. He feels guilty and ashamed that twenty thousand men are willing to die for a seemingly worthless prize, while he, with powerful reasons to act, does nothing: 'How stand I then, that have a father killed, a mother stained, excitements of my reason and my blood, and let all sleep?' **There follows another passionate outburst in which Hamlet re-dedicates himself to the business of avenging his father's death:** 'O from this time forth, my thoughts be bloody, or be nothing worth!' **However, as before, Hamlet seems to lose his sense of purpose as soon as his passion wanes.** Hamlet still has not gained revenge by the time

Claudius arranges for him to sail to England.

Hamlet's experiences during the voyage to England have a profound impact (effect) on his personal development and he returns to Denmark as 'a new man'. He is no longer a slave either to his passion or his conscience. **He is composed and purposeful, viewing the world and his place in it with a new clarity. Hamlet finally seems to possess the type of balanced personality that he so admires in Horatio.** He tells Laertes that he is 'not splenitive and rash' and warns him that he is capable of decisive action: 'Yet have I in me something dangerous which let thy wisdom fear'.

The key factor underlying the fundamental change in Hamlet's character is his new belief in the power of providence. Experience has taught him that the best-laid plans can come to nothing ('our deep plots do pall') and that there is nothing to be gained from endless thinking. He realises that what is most important is the ability to respond decisively to events: 'Our indiscretion sometimes serves us well'. He now believes that heaven exercises a decisive influence on the course of human life: 'There's a divinity that shapes our ends . . . '. He attributes his discovery of the letter ordering his death, as well as the fact that he had his father's signet ring in his purse (to reseal the altered letter) to the power of providence: 'Why even in that was heaven ordinant'.

The 'new' Hamlet is first to be seen in the course of the voyage to England. He responds decisively to the discovery of the letter sending him to his death. For once there is neither procrastination nor rashness on Hamlet's part. He does not hesitate to send Rosencrantz and Guildenstern to their deaths: 'They are not near my conscience: their defeat does by their own insinuation grow'. Their deaths are entirely their own fault in Hamlet's eyes. **Finally, we see a Hamlet capable of thinking clearly and acting decisively.**

Hamlet now believes that he can kill Claudius with a clear conscience. His clarity of thought is very evident in the manner in which he logically lists the reasons why his killing of Claudius is entirely justified: 'He that hath killed my king and whored my mother, popped in between the election and my hopes, thrown out his angle for my proper life . . . is it not perfect conscience to quit him with this arm?' Indeed Hamlet believes that he himself will be deserving of damnation if he fails to eliminate the disease that is his corrupt uncle: 'And is it not to be damned to let this canker of our nature come in further evil?'

Hamlet does not plan the killing of Claudius, believing that providence will provide him with an opportunity to kill the king. He tells

Horatio that everything is divinely ordained: 'There's a special providence in the fall of a sparrow'. Hamlet appears to be confident of his new-found ability to respond decisively to whatever opportunity providence provides for him: 'The readiness is all'. In the dramatic concluding scene Hamlet responds decisively to unfolding events. When Laertes points to Claudius' villainy ('The king, the king's to blame'), Hamlet does not hesitate to kill the 'incestuous, murderous, damned Dane'. In killing Claudius, Hamlet finally avenges his father's death and brings to an end the corruption poisoning the Danish court.

3. 'Hamlet's Madness'

Hamlet's madness is a contentious issue. Is Hamlet's madness mere pretence or is the Prince of Denmark genuinely mad? While Hamlet states his intention of adopting an 'antic disposition' and his 'madness' may simply be seen as a clever ploy intended to give him an advantage over his enemies, he does on occasions seem to be genuinely mentally disturbed.

Hamlet's decision to wear a mask of madness is a clever tactic. Following his encounter with his father's ghost, Hamlet confides in Horatio: 'As I perchance hereafter shall think meet to put an antic disposition on'. **By pretending to be mad, Hamlet confuses and troubles his arch-enemy, Claudius.** The king is unsettled by Hamlet's 'turbulent and dangerous lunacy', regarding his nephew's strange, unpredictable behaviour as a threat to his kingship: 'I like him not, nor stands it safe with us to let his madness range . . . The terms of our estate may not endure hazards so dangerous as doth hourly grow out of his brows'. Hamlet is too important and influential a figure for his apparent lunacy to be ignored: 'Madness in great ones must not unwatched go'.

Hamlet's 'antic disposition' also allows him to ridicule the falseness and hypocrisy of such characters as Polonius, Rosencrantz and Guildenstern. Hamlet tells Polonius that he is 'a fishmonger' and later addresses him as 'Old Jephthah' (an Old Testament figure who was

willing to sacrifice his daughter to please God). Rosencrantz is dismissed as a 'sponge' that 'soaks up the king's countenance, his rewards, his authorities'.

By pretending to be mad, Hamlet can freely express his feelings of anger and bitterness at his mother's betrayal of his father. He tells Ophelia: '. . . look you how cheerfully my mother looks and my father died within two hours'. Under the guise of madness, Hamlet launches a bitter attack on women: 'God hath given you one face and you make yourselves another, you jig, you amble and you lisp, you nickname God's creatures and make your wantonness your ignorance'.

Hamlet's adoption of an 'antic disposition' must be seen in the context of his belief that he is living in a world of false appearances. Hamlet knows that he is living in a world of widespread deception, where few people are what they appear to be: 'To be honest as this world goes is to be one man picked out of ten thousand'. In their different ways, Claudius (a 'smiling damned villain'), Gertrude (King Hamlet's 'seeming virtuous queen'), Polonius (the sycophantic courtier), Rosencrantz and Guildenstern (spies masquerading as friends) are two-faced and insincere. **By pretending to be mad, Hamlet is equipping himself to survive in a world of false appearances.**

Not everyone is taken in by Hamlet's 'antic disposition'. Polonius speaks of 'a method' in Hamlet's madness, observing that his replies are often full of meaning: 'How pregnant sometimes his replies are'. Guildenstern refers to Hamlet's 'crafty madness' which enables him to avoid answering any difficult questions that they put to him – Hamlet remains 'aloof' when his former school friends 'would bring him on to some confession'. Having eavesdropped on his nephew's conversation with Ophelia, Claudius concludes that Hamlet is not as mad as he appears to be: '. . . what he spake, though it lacked form a little, was not like madness'.

Claudius regards Hamlet's madness as a threat to his kingship. The king is a shrewd character who realises that he cannot afford to ignore his nephew's strange, unpredictable behaviour. He speaks of Hamlet's 'turbulent and dangerous lunacy'. Hamlet is a very important figure in Denmark because he is heir to the throne and is hugely popular among the Danish people. Claudius knows that he must keep a close eye on his chief adversary: 'Madness in great ones must not unwatched go'. He believes that Hamlet's peculiar behaviour may threaten his kingship: 'The terms of our estate may not endure hazards so dangerous as doth hourly grow out of his lunacies'. Rosencrantz and Guildenstern are invited to Elsinore because Claudius wants to get to the root of 'Hamlet's transformation'. They, like Polonius, are used by the king to spy on Hamlet.

Hamlet's 'madness' is explained in different ways by different characters – a clear indication that he succeeds in confusing his enemies. Polonius believes that Hamlet's strange behaviour is caused by his unrequited (unreturned) love for Ophelia. Rosencrantz believes that Hamlet is frustrated in his ambition to be king. Gertrude understands her son better than anyone else, telling Claudius: 'I doubt it is no other but the main, his father's death and our o'er hasty marriage'.

There has been considerable debate about the precise nature of Hamlet's madness. Is it pretended or real? There is little doubt but that Hamlet's madness is essentially an act. He tells Horatio of his plan to adopt 'an antic disposition'. Before watching *The Mousetrap*, Hamlet deliberately wears the mask of the mad prince in order to deceive the court: 'I must be idle'. He seems to admit to Rosencrantz and Guildenstern that he is not always mad: 'I am but mad north-north-west: when the wind is southerly, I know a hawk from a handsaw'. Hamlet confides the true nature of his 'madness' in his mother: '. . . I essentially am not in madness, but mad in craft'.

However, not all of Hamlet's strange behaviour can be explained by reference to his deliberate adoption of 'an antic disposition'. There are times in the play when Hamlet is clearly under considerable mental and emotional pressure. This pressure inevitably has some impact on the balance of his mind. Hamlet is so disturbed by his encounter with his father's ghost that he is almost incoherent when he meets Horatio immediately afterwards. Horatio can make little sense of what Hamlet is saying to him: 'These are but wild and whirling words, my lord'. Ophelia's description of Hamlet's disordered appearance ('No hat upon his head; his stockings fouled, ungartered and down-gyved to his ankle') and the look of horror on his face ('with a look so piteous in purport as if he had been loosed out of hell to speak of horrors . . .') give us an insight into Hamlet's personal hell. Overwhelmed by a series of traumatic events (the death of his beloved father, his mother's hasty marriage and his dramatic encounter with the ghost), Hamlet battles to retain his mental and emotional stability.

While Hamlet never completely loses the balance of his mind, there are occasions when he loses his self-control. After being at the receiving end of one of Hamlet's passionate outbursts, Ophelia sadly concludes that Hamlet's 'noble mind' has been 'o'erthrown'. Hamlet's harsh and bitter treatment of his mother also reflects his utter lack of self-restraint on occasions. Indeed his strange obsession with his mother's relationship with Claudius also has the audience questioning his state of mind.

Hamlet's killing of Polonius is another impulsive act of passion, with Claudius later declaring that 'Hamlet in madness hath Polonius slain'. **However, Hamlet's occasionally irrational and unreasonable behaviour is not evidence of genuine insanity. Rather is it the case that Hamlet is sometimes a slave to his passion.**

In conclusion, Hamlet's 'madness' is essentially an act – a clever tactic in his deadly conflict with Claudius. Hamlet uses his 'antic disposition' to disguise his real intentions, to gain an advantage over Claudius and to speak his mind. While there is some evidence to suggest that Hamlet sometimes genuinely struggles to retain the balance of his mind, the final act leaves us in no doubt but that he is perfectly sane. **The Hamlet who returns to Denmark from the voyage to England is so composed, clear-minded and rational that any lingering doubts about the nature of his 'madness' are banished.**

4. 'The Conflict between Hamlet and Claudius'

The conflict between Hamlet and Claudius is a particularly fascinating one because they appear to be such evenly matched adversaries. We learn a great deal about both characters through their interaction with each other. **The battle of wits underlying their deadly power struggle shows them both to be very astute (shrewd) and, to different degrees, unscrupulous.** While Claudius never hesitates to undertake any course of action, Hamlet procrastinates because he is a man of conscience – however, Hamlet ultimately acquires a ruthless streak.

Claudius is a clever and perceptive villain. His cleverness is to be seen in a variety of ways. **Early in the play he wins public approval by diplomatically balancing expressions of grief and joy:** 'With mirth in funeral and with dirge in marriage, in equal scale weighing delight and dole'. **He cleverly tries to appease Hamlet** by publicly declaring that he is heir to the throne: 'You are the most immediate to our throne'. **When he fails to placate the angry young prince, he shrewdly decides to keep Hamlet close to him,** asking him not to return to Wittenberg: 'And we beseech you, bend you to remain here in the cheer and comfort of our eye, our chiefest courtier, cousin and our son'.

Claudius makes regular and effective use of flattery to manipulate people into doing his bidding. Hamlet's former school friends are addressed as 'dear Rosencrantz' and 'gentle Guildenstern'. He tells Polonius that he is 'a man faithful and honourable', while clearly fawning over the angry Laertes: 'I loved your father, and we love yourself'.

He cunningly devises the swordfight in such a manner as to ensure that no blame for Hamlet's death will attach to him. He tells his co-conspirator, Laertes: 'And for his death no wind of blame shall breathe'. He is particularly anxious that Gertrude should suspect nothing.

Claudius' cleverness is evident in his ability to present a cool, unflappable exterior regardless of the strained nature of the circumstances. For example, when Hamlet clearly snubs him in the early stages of the play, Claudius retains his composure. While Hamlet pointedly ignores the king's request that he remain in Elsinore rather than return to Wittenberg, he replies to a similar request from his mother by saying: 'I shall in all my best obey you, madam'. Claudius tries to avoid further embarrassing exchanges by declaring: 'Why 'tis a loving and a fair reply'. We also see Claudius retaining his composure when the angry Laertes breaks into the throne room. He tells Gertrude: 'Let him demand his fill'.

Claudius is unquestionably an unscrupulous character. He ultimately comes into conflict with Hamlet following his utterly unscrupulous murder of his own brother in order to usurp (unlawfully take) the Danish throne.

His lack of ethics (scruples) is readily apparent in his willingness to spy on people. Claudius uses Polonius as a spy and, along with his chief adviser, personally spies on Hamlet's encounter with Ophelia. He is also quick to agree to Polonius' suggestion that he (Polonius) eavesdrop on Hamlet's meeting with Gertrude, his mother. The king deviously employs Rosencrantz and Guildenstern to spy on Hamlet, instructing them to 'glean' whatever information they can from their former school friend.

Claudius does not hesitate to order Hamlet's death when he feels seriously threatened by his nephew. Under the pretence of collecting monies owed to Denmark, he sends Hamlet to England in the hope of ridding himself of the troublesome prince: 'Do it England, for like the hectic in my blood he rages . . .' He incites and manipulates Laertes' grief and anger in an attempt to eliminate Hamlet: 'What would you undertake to show yourself your father's son in deed more than in words?' His unprincipled nature is strikingly evident in the manner in which he plans the swordfight – he even prepares a chalice of poisoned wine to ensure Hamlet's death. Claudius' willingness to let Gertrude drink the poisoned wine rather than risk pointing to his own guilt is yet another striking example of his lack of morality. His attempt to save the woman whom he claims to love is selfishly half-hearted: 'Gertrude, do not drink'.

Like Claudius, Hamlet is sharp-witted, with his cleverness similarly apparent throughout the play. Hamlet expresses his deep resentment of Claudius through a series of **clever puns**. He adopts an **'antic disposition'** to mask his true intent. This mask of madness is a clever tactic which confuses Claudius, giving Hamlet an advantage in his battle of wits with the king. **Hamlet sees through Rosencrantz and Guildenstern's false façade of friendship.** He sees his former friends for the spies that they are: 'I know the good king and queen have sent for you'. He realises that they are attempting to discover the cause of his 'madness': 'You

would play upon me, you would seem to know my stops, you would pluck out the heart of my mystery…' He aptly describes them as 'sponges' that soak up the king's favour and rewards. **Hamlet imaginatively devises *The Mousetrap* to test the King's guilt:** 'The play's the thing wherein I'll catch the conscience of the king'.

While Hamlet is often restrained by his conscience, he shows himself to be unscrupulous on a number of occasions. His treatment of Ophelia is extremely harsh. In the Nunnery Scene he taunts her and questions her honesty, ordering her to 'get to a nunnery'. **He treats his mother in a similarly cruel manner in the Closet Scene.** Hamlet sets out to make Gertrude more self-aware, but his treatment of her amounts to a form of mental torture. His mother begs him to be patient with her: 'These words like daggers enter my ears. No more, sweet Hamlet'. **Hamlet impulsively kills Polonius and expresses no regret afterwards:** 'Thou wretched, rash intruding fool, farewell! I took thee for thy better'. He treats the dead Polonius with utter contempt: 'I'll lug the guts into the neighbour room'. **He sends Rosencrantz and Guildenstern to their deaths without a moment's hesitation, believing that they are responsible for their own demise:** 'They are not near my conscience, their defeat does by their own insinuation grow'.

Ultimately, Hamlet and Claudius prove to be well-matched adversaries and their conflict holds the attention of the audience through to the end of the play. While both men are clever and shrewd, Claudius proves to be the more unscrupulous of the two. Hamlet's conscience restrains him for much of the play and, while he can be unscrupulous, it is impossible to imagine him ever stooping to use the devious methods employed by Claudius. This deadly conflict can only have one winner, and it is Hamlet who eventually triumphs. Upon his return from the voyage to England he puts his trust in providence and, in the closing scene, takes the opportunity presented to him to finally avenge his father's death and restore order to the Danish state.

5. *Claudius: A Credible Villain*

Claudius is clearly the villain of the play. He is **a murderer and a usurper**. He **ruthlessly** kills his own brother because he wants both his crown and wife for himself. He **cleverly hides his true self** behind a kindly exterior. He skilfully and **unscrupulously manipulates others for his own ends.** Claudius is **a shrewd villain** and clearly perceives that Hamlet (even when appearing to be mad) poses a serious threat to his kingship. He is **utterly self-centred**, putting himself before all others, including Gertrude, the woman he claims to love. What is most interesting about Claudius is his **troubled conscience**. He is no one-dimensional evil-doer, being deeply troubled by his crime but unwilling to give up all that he has acquired through his evil deed. While he is a thoroughly unappealing character, he is not without humanity. **Claudius' complexity makes him an entirely credible villain.**

Claudius initially appears to be a capable monarch, comfortable in the execution of his kingly responsibilities. He responds to the threat posed by young Fortinbras of Norway in a measured and decisive manner. By sending ambassadors to the King of Norway, he puts the onus on him to restrain his fiery young nephew.

Claudius plays the part of the kindly monarch very convincingly. He tactfully expresses both grief at his brother's recent death and joy at his own marriage: 'With mirth in funeral and with dirge in marriage, in equal scale weighing delight and dole'. He seems anxious to please: 'What wouldst thou beg, Laertes? What wouldst thou have Laertes?' He makes a great effort to placate (pacify) and win round his sullen nephew. He publicly declares that Hamlet is the heir to the throne ('You are the most immediate to our throne'), going on to describe him as 'our chiefest courtier, cousin and our son'. The contrast between what Claudius appears to be and what he actually is enrages Hamlet: 'That one may smile and smile and be a villain!'

Claudius is utterly ruthless, poisoning his own brother because he wants both his crown and his wife for himself. His ruthlessness is again apparent in his decision to send Hamlet to England to be executed: 'Do it England, for like the hectic in my blood he rages . . .' **Claudius is clever and unscrupulous** in the way he manipulates others into doing his bidding. He is very adept (skilful) at using false kindness and flattery to win people round. There are signs of the king's falseness in his exaggerated politeness and desire to please. He welcomes 'dear Rosencrantz' and 'gentle Guildenstern' to Elsinore, unscrupulously using Hamlet's friends to spy on him. Claudius reinforces Polonius' loyalty by telling him that he regards him as 'a man faithful and honourable'. The sycophantic (flattering) Polonius is ever anxious to do the king's bidding, not hesitating to eavesdrop on private conversations. Claudius' powers of manipulation are highlighted by the skilful manner in which he turns Laertes from a potential enemy into a useful ally. He tells 'good Laertes': 'I loved your father, and we love ourself". Of course, he deliberately incites (provokes) Laertes by asking him what he would do to show himself his father's son 'in deed more than in words'. Claudius plans to use Laertes to get rid of his greatest enemy, Hamlet: 'You must put me in your heart for friend'. His cleverness is also apparent in his devising of a plan which will ensure that he is not in any way connected with the death of his troublesome nephew: 'And for his death no wind of blame shall breathe'.

Claudius is shrewd and cunning. After spying on Hamlet's meeting with Ophelia, he concludes that his nephew's strange behaviour has nothing to do with unrequited love. He feels that Hamlet is not genuinely mad: '. . . what he spake, though it lacked form a little, was not like madness'. He speaks of Hamlet's 'turbulent and dangerous lunacy'. He perceives that Hamlet is deeply troubled and senses that he is plotting against him. 'There's something in his soul o'er which his melancholy sits on brood, and I do doubt the hatch and the disclose will be some danger'. Claudius has sharp political instincts. He knows that he must be vigilant where his nephew is concerned: 'Madness in great ones must not unwatched go'. Claudius realises that Hamlet poses a threat, both to his kingship and his life: 'I like him not, nor stands it safe to let his madness range . . . The terms of our estate may not endure hazard so near as doth hourly grow out of his lunacies'. He understands the significance of Polonius' death: 'It had been so with us had we been there'. He shrewdly decides against arresting Hamlet for Polonius' murder because Hamlet's popularity is such that his arrest might provoke a popular uprising against him: 'Yet must not we put the strong law on him. He's loved of the distracted multitude who love not in their judgement, but in their eyes'. **He is a good judge of character, recognising that Hamlet is too noble and too trusting to examine the foils before his duel with Laertes:** 'He being remiss, most generous and free from all contriving will not peruse the foils'. **This tribute to Hamlet reflects a surprising generosity of spirit in Claudius, adding to his credibility.**

Claudius is completely unscrupulous, never letting his conscience prevent him from doing what he deems to be necessary. He ruthlessly murders his own brother, King Hamlet, because he wants both his crown and his queen for himself. He uses poison ('a leprous distilment') to kill his brother and later uses it in an attempt to murder his nephew, Hamlet. He does not hesitate to send Hamlet to his death in England: 'Do it England, for like the hectic in my blood he rages'. He has no scruples about spying, using Polonius, Rosencrantz and Guildenstern to spy on Hamlet. He is even prepared to use Ophelia as 'bait' to 'trap' Hamlet so that he and Polonius can assess his nephew's strange behaviour.

Claudius is utterly self-centred. He expresses no grief at Polonius' death, merely observing he himself might well have been Hamlet's victim: 'It had been so with us had we been there'. He is concerned that he himself will be held accountable for failing to keep Hamlet under control: 'It will be laid to us, whose providence should have kept short, restrained and out of haunt this mad young man'. He seems to be unmoved by the death of Ophelia. He claims to love Gertrude, but callously allows her to die when he makes only a half-hearted effort to prevent her from drinking the poisoned wine: 'Gertrude, do not drink'. To order Gertrude not to drink the wine intended for Hamlet would be to point to his own guilt and Claudius is primarily interested in preserving his own life and advancing his own interests.

Claudius is a hypocrite. When he addresses the Danish court, he speaks of 'our dear brother's death'. He tells Hamlet that his grief at his father's death is 'a fault to heaven, a fault against the dead'. Bearing in mind that Claudius had murdered his own brother, his hypocrisy here is truly breathtaking. After inciting Laertes, he hypocritically tells Gertrude of his efforts to calm him: 'How much I had to do to calm his rage'. Hamlet is keenly aware of the king's falseness and hypocrisy: 'That one may smile and smile and be a villain'.

Our attitude towards Claudius is strongly coloured by Hamlet's hatred of him. Hamlet compares his uncle to a disgusting, lustful 'satyr' (a mythical creature that was half-man, half-goat). He describes him as a 'treacherous, lecherous, kindless villain". He compares him to a 'mildewed' ear of corn that spreads the disease of corruption. He warns his mother not to have anything more to do with 'the bloat king'.

What makes Claudius an interesting and credible villain is the fact that he has a troubled conscience. *The Mousetrap* visibly pricks his conscience, causing him to retire to his room 'marvellous distempered". The Prayer Scene presents us with the image of the guilt-ridden Claudius who is painfully aware of the enormity and gravity of his crime: 'O my offence is rank, it smells to heaven'. He imagines that there is not enough rain in the heavens to wash his brother's blood from his hands. However, while he wrestles with his conscience, he is unable to pray for forgiveness because he is unwilling to give up all that he has gained through his crime: 'My crown, mine own ambition and my queen'. Claudius knows that while he can avoid justice in the corrupt world in which he lives, he will ultimately face divine retribution: 'In the corrupted currents of this world, offence's gilded hand may shove by justice . . . but 'tis not so above. There is no shuffling, there the offence lies in his true nature'. In Claudius we see the struggle between ambition and conscience.

However, Claudius is ultimately unwilling to let his conscience get in the way of his ambition. The fact that Claudius is guilt-ridden does not detract from the enormity of his crime, but it does make him a more believable villain.

---

6. The Characterisation of the Women in the Play

Shakespeare portrays the women in the play in an essentially negative light. While Gertrude and Ophelia are very different characters, both are intrinsically (fundamentally) weak and dependent, playing passive roles in the male-dominated Danish court. Gertrude lives in Claudius' shadow, while Ophelia is dominated by the men in her life: her father, her brother and her lover. The fundamental weakness of these women is summed up in Hamlet's bitter generalisation: 'Frailty, thy name is woman'.

Gertrude is weak and dependent. She lives in the shadow of two kings and is seemingly incapable of an independent existence. According to Hamlet, she was totally dependent on King Hamlet: 'She would hang on him as if increase of appetite had grown by what it fed on'. She is similarly dependent on Claudius whom she marries with unseemly haste following the death of King Hamlet. While Claudius refers to her as 'the imperial jointress' of the state, she has little in the way of real power or influence. Her dependent nature is underlined by the fact that she remains loyal to Claudius even after Hamlet's dramatic revelations about his crime.

Gertrude is shallow and fickle (changeable). Not only does Gertrude betray the memory of King Hamlet by re-marrying within weeks of his death (Hamlet cynically observes that 'the funeral baked meats did coldly furnish forth the marriage tables'), but it seems that she also betrayed him in life by involving herself in an adulterous relationship with Claudius. The ghost tells Hamlet that Claudius 'won to his shameful lust the will of my most seeming-virtuous queen'.

She is insensitive to Hamlet's grief. Gertrude's 'o'er hasty marriage' is the cause of her son's deepest anguish (distress). She displays her insensitivity towards Hamlet's grief by asking him to set aside his mourning clothes: 'Good Hamlet, cast thy nighted colour off'. Her only concern is that Hamlet should get along with his new step-father, Claudius. She is extremely naïve in her hope that her son will readily accept all that has happened. She infuriates Hamlet by asking him why his father's death 'seems' to be so 'particular' with him.

Gertrude is morally blind, being unable or unwilling to see Claudius for the villain that he is. She even tries to defend him from the angry Laertes when he storms into the throne room following the killing of his father, Polonius, despite Hamlet having informed her that Claudius had murdered King Hamlet. Hamlet refers to her as 'most pernicious (wicked, malicious) woman'.

However, despite her many failings, Gertrude possesses a number of redeeming features. She knows and understands her son better than anyone else, clearly perceiving the true reasons for Hamlet's strange behaviour: 'I doubt it is no other but the main, his father's death and our o'er hasty marriage'. **She remains loyal to Hamlet,** never revealing the secret of his 'antic disposition' to Claudius: 'I have no life to breathe what thou hast said to me'. She tries to protect him from blame after he kills Polonius by attributing the killing to Hamlet's madness: 'Hamlet in madness hath Polonius slain'. Gertrude again does her best to protect him from blame after his inappropriate behaviour at Ophelia's graveside: 'This is mere madness, and thus a while the fit will work on him'. She delights in Hamlet's performance in the fencing contest and dies drinking to his success.

Gertrude has a conscience. When Hamlet forces Gertrude to look deep into her soul, she admits to seeing 'such black and grained spots as will not leave their tinct'. Her realisation of her wrongdoing causes her great distress: 'These words like daggers enter in mine ears; no more, sweet Hamlet!' Later in the play she acknowledges her spiritual sickness when she speaks of her 'sick soul'. **Ophelia's tragic death affects her deeply.** Gertrude's humanity is clearly evident at Ophelia's graveside: 'I thought thy bride-bed to have decked, sweet maid, and not have strewed thy grave'.

In conclusion, Gertrude is weak and shallow (superficial) rather than evil. She retains her maternal instinct, her conscience and her humanity. She pays the ultimate price for her weakness and moral blindness, dying a victim of Claudius' treachery. **Ophelia is a passive, docile character and, like Gertrude, is clearly dominated by the men in her life.** Ophelia is used by the king and by her father and abused by the man she loves.

Ophelia is obedient to her father: In Elizabethan times, fathers had absolute control over their daughters. As the daughter of a royal courtier, Ophelia has a strong sense of duty to her father and to her family. She is conditioned to be subordinate to her father and consequently never defies him or challenges his authority. She is lectured by Polonius who dismisses her as a 'green girl' and orders her not to believe Hamlet's vows. She obediently agrees to be guided by her father: 'I shall obey, my lord'. She subsequently returns Hamlet's letters and refuses to see him: '. . . as you did command I did repel his letters and denied his access to me'.

Ophelia appears to defer (yield) to her brother as she listens politely to Laertes talking down to her, telling her that Hamlet's love is 'sweet, not lasting' and warning her to be wary since 'best safety lies in fear'. Ophelia would have been accustomed to such patronising attitudes in the male-dominated Danish court. However, she shows **some spirit** when she reminds Laertes that he should not preach virtue to her while following 'the path of dalliance' himself.

Ophelia is manipulated and exploited by Polonius and Claudius, allowing herself to be used as bait to trap Hamlet: 'Ophelia, walk you here . . . Read on this book'. In this way she inadvertently becomes enmeshed in the deception and double-dealing that characterises life in the Danish court.

She is cruelly abused by Hamlet. In Act 3 Scene 1 Ophelia becomes the focus of all Hamlet's negative feelings towards women: 'Get thee to a nunnery. Why wouldst thou be a breeder of sinners?' Ophelia does not understand this tirade (an angry speech) and it takes its toll on her. She is deeply affected by Hamlet's apparent insanity: 'O, what a noble mind is here o'erthrown! The courtier's, scholar's, soldier's eye, tongue, sword . . . '

Ophelia is innocent and naive: She is the epitome of innocence and sweetness. The flowers that surround her during her madness symbolise her beauty and innocence. At her graveside Laertes hopes that violets will spring from her 'fair and unpolluted flesh', and calls her the 'Rose of May'.

She is unable to cope with the harshness of the world which she inhabits. Through no fault of her own Ophelia finds herself drawn into the world of corruption and violence that is the Danish court. Her father's death at the hands of the man she loves proves too much for her sensitive mind, and she loses her sanity. Her songs deal with unrequited love, suggesting that Hamlet's harsh treatment of her is partly responsible for her breakdown. She is a pitiable figure at this point: 'She is importunate, indeed distract. Her mood will needs be pitied.'

Both Gertrude and Ophelia have to live in a world dominated by men. Both are clearly subordinate to the men in their lives and both die as a consequence of male power struggles.

7. *The Female Characters in* Hamlet: *Their Importance / Role / Dramatic Function*

(a) Gertrude

Gertrude is the catalyst (a person or thing that accelerates change) for much that happens in the play. Claudius killed his brother, old King Hamlet, because he wanted his crown and, seemingly, his wife (speaking to Hamlet, the Ghost claims that Claudius and Gertrude had an adulterous affair). Claudius is unable to repent because he is unwilling to give up all that he has gained through his crime, including his new wife: 'My crown, mine own ambition and my queen. May one be pardoned and retain the offence?'

Gertrude is a symbol of the weakness of women in the Danish court. Dependent and submissive, she is content to live in the shadow of two kings. Her weakness is such that she remains loyal to Claudius even after Hamlet's dramatic revelations about how he murdered King Hamlet.

The brevity of Gertrude's grieving of King Hamlet's death is the primary cause of Hamlet's profound disillusionment with life – 'O God, a beast that wants discourse of reason would have mourned longer'. Hamlet regards Gertrude's marriage to Claudius with absolute revulsion: 'Such an act that blurs the grace and blush of modesty, calls virtue hypocrite, takes off the fair rose from an innocent love and sets a blister there', 'O most pernicious (wicked, malicious) woman'. Horror and disgust at his mother's behaviour dominate the soul of Hamlet, colouring his view of all women, including Ophelia: 'Frailty thy name is woman'.

(b) Ophelia

Ophelia is also a symbol of the weakness of women in the Danish court. She is abused by Hamlet, lectured by Laertes, manipulated by Polonius and exploited by Claudius. The cynicism and disgust with which Hamlet comes to regard marriage is patently clear in his instruction to Ophelia to get 'to a nunnery' and in the horrified question he asks her: 'Why, would'st thou be a breeder of sinners?' Hamlet tells Ophelia that if she wishes to marry, she should 'marry a fool, for wise men know well enough what monsters you make of them . . .'

Ophelia's behaviour heightens Hamlet's sense of isolation in the Danish court. She facilitates Polonius' spying by acting as 'bait' for Hamlet, who seems to know that he is being spied upon and may feel that Ophelia has betrayed him: 'Where's your father? . . . Let the doors be shut upon him that he may play the fool nowhere but in's own house.'

She is a symbol of innocence and beauty – The flower imagery with which Ophelia is associated sharply contrasts with the weed imagery representative of the corruption of the Danish court. While the garland of flowers she wears towards the close of her life is suggestive of her insanity, it is also a symbol of her innocence. Gertrude had planned to strew Ophelia with flowers had she married Hamlet, the man she loved: 'I thought thy bride bed to have decked sweet maid, and not have strewed thy grave.' At her graveside, Laertes expresses the hope that violets will spring 'from her fair and unpolluted flesh.'

Ophelia's insanity and death highlight the play's tragic dimension. Her innocence, sweetness and beauty cannot survive in the 'rank and gross' Danish court. More than any other character in the play, Ophelia evokes feelings of profound pity. It is impossible not to be moved by her suffering: 'She is importunate, indeed distract, her mood will needs be pitied'. She is too sensitive and too innocent to survive in a male-dominated world characterised by deception, double-dealing and violence. She is the play's most tragic victim because she is so innocent. While Gertrude's demise can in part be attributed to her own weakness of character, Ophelia's tragic death is not caused by any personal flaw.

8. *Horatio: His Importance / Role / Dramatic Function*

Horatio features in the play before Hamlet. He is, along with three others, a guard on the battlements and consequently is among the first to see the Ghost of the dead king, Hamlet's father. **As we don't see him do or hear him say a great deal in the course of the play, some may be dismissive of his overall importance. In reality, Horatio proves to be a character of considerable substance and fulfils a number of important dramatic functions.**

Horatio acts as a spokesman / commentator on Danish affairs. In the opening scene Horatio displays an expert knowledge of Danish history as he provides the audience with important background information on the conflict between Denmark and Norway. He explains why Fortinbras is intent on attacking Denmark. He offers us an insight into the character of Fortinbras: 'young Fortinbras, of unimproved mettle hot and full'. Later in the play Horatio informs us about Hamlet's experiences during his voyage to England. From Hamlet's letter to Horatio we learn that the former has fallen into the hands of pirates who have in fact treated him well. This scene is dramatically important because it informs us that Hamlet will return to Denmark.

Horatio is a key witness in identifying the ghost. Marcellus, a fellow guard, encourages Horatio to speak with the ghost in the opening scene because he is a respected 'scholar'. Horatio recognises the ghost's armour as that worn by King Hamlet when he defeated the King of Norway. **He underlines the significance of the ghost's appearance.** He believes that the appearance of the ghost is a sign pointing to the future, suggesting that it may foretell some disaster to come for the Danish state: 'But, in the gross and scope of my opinion, this bodes some strange eruption to our state'. Filled with foreboding, Horatio helps to create the dramatic tension that draws the audience into the play.

It is Horatio who informs Hamlet about the appearance of the ghost. He regards it as his duty to report all that he has seen to his good friend: 'Let us impart what we have seen tonight unto young Hamlet'.

Horatio acts as Hamlet's confidant. He is the only person in the Danish court in whom Hamlet can confide. **We see the real Hamlet in his soliloquys and in his conversations with Horatio.** He tells Horatio of his anger at his mother's hasty marriage: '. . . the funeral baked meats did coldly furnish forth the marriage tables.' Hamlet speaks to Horatio about the falseness of court life 'where thrift may follow fawning'. He tells him of his plan to test the king's guilt, requesting him to also observe Claudius' reaction to the play: 'And after we will both our judgements join in censure of his seeming'. After observing the king's reaction to *The Mousetrap*, Hamlet tells Horatio that he is now convinced of his uncle's guilt: 'O good Horatio, I'll take the ghost's word for a thousand pound'. Hamlet confides in Horatio regarding the fate of Rosencrantz and Guildenstern, declaring that they are responsible for their own deaths and that his own conscience is untroubled: 'They are not near my conscience, their defeat does by their own insinuation grow.' Indeed it is in his account to Horatio of the dramatic happenings during the voyage to England that we see a new, decisive Hamlet. In the closing scene Hamlet explains to Horatio why he can finally kill Claudius 'with perfect conscience'.

Horatio acts as a foil (contrast) to Hamlet. Unlike Hamlet, Horatio is neither a slave to his passion or to his conscience. **He personifies the balanced personality that Hamlet so admires:** '. . . blest are those whose blood and judgement are so well comeddled . . . Give me that man that is not passion's slave, and I will wear him in my heart's core, ay in my heart of hearts'. In this sense **Hamlet regards Horatio as a role model.** When Hamlet speaks with Horatio after his encounter with the ghost, the latter's calmness and self-possession contrast with Hamlet's incoherence: 'These are but wild and whirling words, my lord'.

Horatio is a symbol of loyalty and integrity

in the corrupt Danish court. His fundamental honesty and decency stand in stark contrast to the falseness of such characters as Claudius, Polonius, Rosencrantz, Guildenstern and Laertes. **He is a true patriot with a genuine love of his country and an expert knowledge of its history. His devotion to Hamlet is beyond question.** He tries to prevent Hamlet from taking part in the fencing contest with Laertes after Hamlet tells him of his sense of foreboding. Horatio's loyalty to Hamlet is such that, in the noble, indeed self-sacrificing, manner of an ancient Roman who has lost his best friend, he is even prepared to take his own life when he sees that his good friend is about to die: 'I am more an antique Roman than a Dane'.

It falls to Horatio to tell Hamlet's story to the world. At the close of the play the stage is littered with bodies, but Horatio survives the carnage. Hamlet charges Horatio with the responsibility of telling the world all that has happened in Elsinore: 'Horatio, I am dead, thou livest, report me and my cause aright to the unsatisfied'. As a confidant of Hamlet and as a respected figure in the Danish court, Horatio is ideally qualified to fulfil Hamlet's final request. His willingness to deliver a comprehensive account of all that he knows is reflected in his determination to speak 'of carnal, bloody and unnatural acts . . . '

Horatio testifies to Hamlet's nobility. At the close of the play Horatio reminds us of Hamlet's finer qualities when he pays a moving tribute to his dead friend: 'Now cracks a noble heart. Good night sweet prince. And flights of angels sing thee to thy rest'.

9. *The Dramatic Importance of the Ghost*

The appearance of the Ghost creates a great sense of dramatic tension in the opening scene and arouses the immediate interest of the audience. The guards, Marcellus and Barnardo, are very much on edge. Horatio asks if 'this thing' has appeared again. Marcellus describes the Ghost as 'this dreaded sight' and 'this apparition', while Horatio declares that the appearance of the ghost fills him 'with fear and wonder'.

The appearance of the Ghost is seen as a sign of some deep disturbance in the Danish kingdom. This supernatural happening is invested with great significance – the spirit is variously described as a 'harbinger', an 'omen' and a 'portentous figure'. Horatio, whose judgement is much respected, declares that the appearance of the ghost 'bodes some strange eruption to our state'. When Hamlet learns about the Ghost, he is convinced that something fundamental is wrong in the state of Denmark: 'My father's spirit in arms? All is not well, I doubt some foul play.' Shakespeare intensifies the suspense by making the audience wait another scene before he brings the two together.

Hamlet's meeting with the Ghost is the basis of another very dramatic scene. Hamlet is so startled by the ghost's appearance that he declares: 'Angels and ministers of grace defend us!' The tension mounts as the ghost beckons to Hamlet to follow him. Horatio and Marcellus urge Hamlet not to follow the ghost, fearing that it may be an evil spirit that will lead him on to his destruction. Ignoring these words of warning, Hamlet follows the Ghost, fearing that he will 'burst in ignorance' if he does not speak with him.

Without the appearance of the Ghost there would be no play. It is the Ghost's dramatic revelations to Hamlet that get the action of the play underway: 'The serpent that did sting thy father's life now wears his crown'. His father's spirit confirms Hamlet's worst suspicions: 'O my prophetic soul!' **The Ghost points to Gertrude's disloyalty:** '. . . won to his shameful lust the will of my most seeming-virtuous queen. O Hamlet what a falling off was there!' **He also underlines the enormity of Claudius' crime:** 'Thus was I by a brother's hand of life, of queen, of crown at once dispatched, cut off even in the blossoms of my sin.' The spirit's dramatic account of Claudius' villainy has profound repercussions for every other major character in the play, ultimately leading to the deaths of Polonius, Laertes, Gertrude, Ophelia and Hamlet himself.

The task of vengeance that the Ghost imposes on his son causes Hamlet intense suffering. He imposes on Hamlet a duty to which he is temperamentally unsuited – the duty to avenge 'his foul and most unnatural murder.' Hamlet struggles with this weighty burden throughout Acts 1-4. Because he is essentially a thinker rather than a man of action, Hamlet cannot deal with the weighty burden laid upon him, and his inner conflict is intense. Having initially promised the Ghost that he would 'fly' to his revenge, he soon curses the fact that he 'was born to set it right'. We see that the more Hamlet thinks, the less likely he is to act: 'Thus conscience does make cowards of us all'. Hamlet's inner conflict is the most fascinating aspect of the play – it is a deep-rooted dispute between his sense of duty to the ghost and his troubled conscience. He only finally reconciles himself to the duty of gaining revenge after he returns from the voyage to England. By this point Hamlet believes in the power of providence to bring about a just resolution of events, and finally feels able to kill the king 'with perfect conscience'.

Hamlet's uncertainty regarding the true nature of the Ghost adds to the play's dramatic tension. He considers the possibility of the ghost being a devil, and decides to stage *The Mousetrap* to confirm the king's guilt: 'The spirit that I have seen may be a devil . . . The play's the thing wherein I'll catch the conscience of the king.' After Claudius' abrupt departure from the play effectively confirms his guilt, Hamlet no longer doubts the ghost: 'O Horatio, I'll take the ghost's word for a thousand pound'.

The appearance of the Ghost in the Closet Scene reminds Hamlet of his failure to gain revenge: 'Do not forget. This visitation is but to whet thy almost blunted purpose'. Hamlet feels guilty about his failure to act on the Ghost's 'dread command', and his sense of purpose is renewed. The ghost also pleads with Hamlet to help Gertrude in her inner struggle, speaking of her 'fighting soul'. Hamlet urges his mother to end her relationship with Claudius: 'Good night, but go not to my uncle's bed'. This is the Ghost's last appearance in the play. Having pricked his son's conscience, he has no other dramatic function to perform.

10. *Polonius: Comic creation or sinister character?*

We can view Polonius in very different ways. On one hand we may share Hamlet's view of him as **'a foolish prating knave'**. However, he may be regarded as **a deeply cynical, unscrupulous and deceitful character** who does not display even a hint of moral difficulty with the business of spying. A contrastingly positive perception of Polonius is put forward by Claudius who sees his courtier as **'a man faithful and honourable'**.

Hamlet regards Polonius as one of the 'tedious old fools' that populate the Danish court. This observation follows his conversation with Polonius about the shape of a cloud. Hamlet highlights Polonius' falseness and foolishness as the king's adviser by turn agrees that the cloud looks 'like a camel . . . like a weasel . . . like a whale'. His contempt for Polonius is very apparent in his lack of remorse after he has killed him. He describes the dead courtier as 'a foolish prating knave' and as 'a wretched, rash, intruding fool'. **Polonius is pretentious and self-important.** He pretends to be knowledgeable about the theatre, telling Hamlet of his acting experience as a university student. However, the only observation he can make about a speech from one of the travelling players' is that it is 'too long'. **Polonius' longwinded speeches are largely without substance,** his verbosity prompting the queen to demand that he get to the point: 'more matter with less art'.

In contrast to Hamlet, Claudius has a high regard for Polonius, describing him as 'a man faithful and honourable.' This positive view of Polonius is easily explained. A dutiful courtier who is unwaveringly loyal to the throne, Polonius is prepared to do anything to ingratiate himself with the king: 'I hold my duty as I hold my soul, both to my god and my gracious king'. Gertrude describes the dead Polonius as 'the unseen good old man'.

Polonius is a shallow and cynical character. The advice he offers Laertes is based on the principle of always looking after his own interests: 'Give every man thine ear, but few thy voice . . . ' While his final piece of advice to his son ('This above all, to thine own self be true.') sounds idealistic, we quickly realise that there is nothing remotely high-minded or noble about Polonius. The advice that he offers Ophelia in relation to her relationship with Hamlet further reflects his utterly sceptical (distrustful) view of male-female relationships. He dismisses any possibility that Hamlet's love for Ophelia might be genuine, describing his daughter as naïve for believing Hamlet's declarations of love: ' . . . you speak like a green girl . . . you have ta'en these tenders for true love which are not sterling'. Polonius contemptuously dismisses Hamlet's promises: 'Do not believe his vows'. He lack of belief in the concept of romantic love is reflected in the animal imagery that he uses to debase love to the level of lust and young people to the level of farmyard animals. Polonius believes that Hamlet 'walks with a larger tether'

than Ophelia, later telling Claudius that he will 'loose' his daughter to Hamlet. His willingness to use Ophelia as a pawn in his spying games underlines his lack of concern for her feelings: 'Ophelia, walk you here . . . Read on this book'. He indifferently instructs his daughter as a director might order an actor around a stage. Hamlet addresses Polonius as 'old Jephthah', an Old Testament figure who thought that he was pleasing God by being prepared to sacrifice his own daughter. In a sense Polonius is willing to sacrifice Ophelia in order to please Claudius.

Polonius is a Machiavellian character who believes that the end justifies the means. He sends his servant Reynaldo to Paris to spy on Laertes, even encouraging him to tarnish his son's reputation if it helps him to get to the truth of his behaviour:

'I believe it is a fetch of warrant, you laying these slight sullies on my son . . . ' His lack of scruples are again apparent in his willingness to spy on what should be a private meeting between Hamlet and his mother. Ever anxious to curry favour with the king, he tells Claudius that he will 'be placed . . . in the ear of all their conference.'

In conclusion, Polonius' primary concern is ingratiating himself with the king and he will do anything to achieve that end. Entirely unscrupulous, there is a sense of poetic justice in the manner in which Polonius meets his end, dying a victim of his own treacherous scheming.

11. *The Theme of Revenge – (Hamlet, Laertes, Fortinbras)*

The theme of revenge is central to the play. The desire for revenge is the driving force behind the plot. Three young men – Hamlet, Laertes and Fortinbras – are driven by a desire to avenge a father's death. However, while they share a common goal, their differing personalities mean that they pursue this goal in very different ways. Both Laertes and Fortinbras act as foils to Hamlet.

Hamlet
Hamlet is given the duty of avenging his father's 'foul and most unnatural murder.' He promises that he will 'sweep' to his revenge, but in reality is not temperamentally suited to gaining vengeance because he is essentially a thinker and a man of conscience: 'O cursed spite that ever I was born to set it right.' Hamlet's soliloquys bear testimony to his reflective

nature. His soliloquys highlight his reflective, philosophical disposition. In his famous 'To be or not to be' soliloquy Hamlet is attracted to the idea of death as eternal sleep (. . . ''tis a consummation devoutly to be wished'). He acknowledges that 'conscience doth make cowards of us all.'

As a thinker and a man of conscience, **Hamlet looks for concrete proof of Claudius' guilt before he acts.** He considers the possibility that the ghost may have been a devil: 'The play's the thing wherein I'll catch the conscience of the king.' **The First Player's passionate delivery of a famous speech causes Hamlet to feel guilty about his own lack of passion:** 'What's Hecuba to him or he to Hecuba that he should weep for her? What would he do had he the motive and the cue for passion that I have?' **Even after *The Mousetrap*** (the play within the play) **seems to confirm the king's guilt** ('O good Horatio, I'll take the ghost's word for a thousand pound'), **Hamlet still hesitates.** The Prayer Scene is the classic example of his procrastination. Hamlet's claim that he does not want to send his father's killer to heaven by killing him while he is praying seems like an excuse for inaction. In reality, Hamlet, the thinking man, draws back from the idea of cold-blooded revenge.

As Fortinbras boldly marches through Denmark on his way to Poland where he will fight for 'a little patch of ground', Hamlet is filled with guilt at his own inaction. Fortinbras is willing to risk his own life and the lives of twenty thousand men for 'a little patch of ground'. In contrast, Hamlet does nothing even though he has far more compelling reasons to act: 'a father killed, a mother stained'. He acknowledges that his failure to act is the result of 'thinking too precisely on the event.'

In Acts 1-4 Hamlet lacks a balanced personality, and is given to extremes both of passion and reflection. He either acts without thinking (e.g. killing Polonius) or else thinks so much that he is incapable of acting (e.g. the Prayer Scene). All of his passionate declarations ('Now could I drink hot blood . . .', 'O from this time forth my thoughts be bloody or be nothing

worth!') come to nothing – when his passion subsides Hamlet loses the impetus to gain revenge. By the time he is sent to England, he still has not gained revenge.

In Act 5 we see a new Hamlet, a man with a balanced personality, capable of thinking clearly and acting decisively. After he returns from the voyage to England, Hamlet believes in the power of providence: 'There's a divinity that shapes our ends.' He understands the best-laid plans can come to nothing ('our deep plots do pall') and believes that providence will provide him with an opportunity to avenge his father's death. He declares that he must be ready to take advantage of such an opportunity: 'The readiness is all'. The second important development in Hamlet is his ability to act without being continually hindered by his conscience. Evidence of a new, decisive Hamlet is to be found in the manner in which he dispatches Rosencrantz and Guildenstern: 'They are not near my conscience, their defeat does by their own insinuation grow.' When he returns to Denmark Hamlet finally believes that he can kill Claudius 'with perfect conscience'. He logically lists four reasons why he can now gain revenge without hesitation: Claudius killed Hamlet's father, 'whored' his mother, took the crown that was rightfully Hamlet's, and even tried to have him killed.

Laertes
Like Hamlet, Laertes has compelling reasons for seeking revenge: 'a father killed, a sister driven into desperate terms'. **However, where the pursuit of revenge is concerned, he differs fundamentally from Hamlet in his personality.** While Hamlet's conscience means that he is reflective and slow to act, Laertes deliberately sets his conscience aside and is impulsive.

Laertes acts on impulse. When he learns of his father's death, he storms into the throne room at the head of a riotous mob: 'Young Laertes in a riotous head o'erbears your officers'. **The intensity of Laertes' desire to be 'revenged most thoroughly' for his father is such that it destroys his finer instincts.** He wants revenge at all costs, and will not allow himself to be troubled by considerations of conscience: 'To hell allegiance, vows to the blackest devil, conscience and grace to the profoundest pit'. He tells Claudius that he is even prepared to cut Hamlet's throat 'i' the church'. This remark highlights the sharp contrast between Laertes and Hamlet – the latter cannot bring himself to kill Claudius when he is praying.

Laertes foolishly allows himself to be manipulated by Claudius, who cynically uses him for his own ends: 'My lord, I will be ruled'. Here he **displays a naivete that is never apparent in Hamlet.**

Unlike Hamlet, **Laertes is prepared to use underhanded means in his unthinking quest for revenge** – he has no qualms about using a sharpened foil with a poisoned tip in what is supposed to be a test of skill. It is impossible to imagine Hamlet plumbing such moral depths – when Hamlet finally avenges his father's death, he does so in full view of the Danish court.

Laertes' finer qualities are apparent at the close of the play when he ultimately realises that he was misguided in seeking revenge against Hamlet. In the closing scene he acknowledges his own wrongdoing: 'I am justly killed with mine own treachery'. **Laertes attempts to redeem himself** by identifying Claudius as the chief villain: 'The king, the king's to blame'. **In his final words he exchanges forgiveness with Hamlet and recognises his honourable character:** 'Exchange forgiveness with me noble Hamlet'.

Fortinbras

Similar to both Hamlet and Laertes, Fortinbras wants to avenge a father's death. He also wants to regain lands lost by Norway to Denmark. Like Laertes, Fortinbras acts as a foil to Hamlet. **While Hamlet is a thinker, Fortinbras is very much a man of action. However, Fortinbras can be reckless in his actions.** The first reference to Fortinbras clearly indicates that he is a man of action. Horatio suggests that Fortinbras can be impetuous: 'Young Fortinbras, of unimproved mettle hot

and full'. He has gathered together a troop of desperate adventurers ('a list of lawless resolutes') to regain by force those lands lost by Norway to Denmark.

Fortinbras is prepared to attack Denmark to achieve his ends. He is restrained from doing so by his elderly uncle, the King of Norway, following diplomatic manoeuvring by Claudius. The fact that Fortinbras is prepared to attack Denmark in breach of a legally-binding treaty suggests that he can be reckless in the pursuit of his goals.

Fortinbras' decisiveness contrasts with and highlights Hamlet's indecision and procrastination. Fortinbras' willingness to risk his own life and the lives of thousands of his men fighting for a worthless 'patch of ground' in Poland causes Hamlet to feel guilty and ashamed about his own inaction. Hamlet has far more compelling reasons to act ('a father killed, a mother stained'), but has done nothing. While this attack on Poland is further evidence of a rash streak in Fortinbras' character, his bold action pricks Hamlet's conscience, prompting him to re-dedicate himself to the business of gaining revenge: 'O from this time forth, my thoughts be bloody or be nothing worth!'

Ultimately, it falls to Fortinbras to restore order to the Danish state. Hamlet clearly admires and respects this bold man of action and gives him his blessing as the next king of Denmark: 'I do prophesy the election lights on Fortinbras. He has my dying voice'.

Pyrrhus

Pyrrhus is not a character in the play, only featuring in a speech delivered by the First Player. However, Pyrrhus also acts as a foil to Hamlet. Like Laertes and Fortinbras, Pyrrhus has lost a father and has compelling reasons for seeking revenge. Similar to Hamlet in the Prayer Scene, Pyrrhus briefly hesitates to gain revenge as his sword is suspended over the head of old Priam. However, while Hamlet draws back from killing Claudius, 'aroused vengeance' prompts Pyrrhus to bring his sword down on Priam with the force of 'the Cyclops hammers'. The act of revenge is graphically described as Pyrrhus hacks the old king to death. **In contrast to Hamlet who constantly wrestles with his conscience, Laertes, Fortinbras and Pyrrhus have no moral qualms about gaining revenge.**

12. *The Themes of Corruption, Hypocrisy and False Appearances*

On the surface, the Danish court is a world of nobility and dignity. In reality, it is a world of moral and political corruption, a world where people and situations are rarely what they seem to be. The fact that most people wear a mask of some sort and pretend to be something they are not inevitably makes for a great deal of hypocrisy. Hamlet rejects the hypocrisy of court life, and works to remove the false appearances hiding the evil reality that lies at the very heart of Elsinore.

Claudius is the source of the moral and political corruption that infects the Danish court. He appears to be a good king, dignified and statesmanlike, but is, in reality, a murderer and a usurper. He killed his own brother so that he could have the crown and queen for himself. Hamlet bitterly describes Claudius as a 'smiling damned villain.' For all of his apparent pleasantness ('And now my cousin Hamlet and my son . . .', 'What wouldst thou have Laertes? What wouldst thou beg? Laertes?'; 'Good Rosencrantz', 'Gentle Guildenstern', etc.), Claudius is a ruthless villain and the source of the moral and political corruption that spreads like a contagious disease through the Danish court. Images of sickness and rottenness are symbolic of the corruption in the Danish court. Hamlet refers to Claudius as 'this canker of our nature', while the Danish court is 'an unweeded garden'. Claudius' soliloquy indicates that he is well aware of the corrupt nature of the court over which he presides: 'In the corrupted currents of this world, offence's gilded hand may shove by justice'.

Gertrude is another example of the contrast between appearance and reality. The ghost describes her as 'my most seeming virtuous queen'. Gertrude seemed to be devoted to King Hamlet. Hamlet says 'she would hang on him as if increase of appetite had grown by what it fed on'. In reality, she betrayed him in life and in death. The ghost accuses her of having been involved in an adulterous affair with Claudius, while she married with unseemly haste after his death. Gertrude seems to be deliberately blind to the corruption all around her, remaining loyal to Claudius even after Hamlet's dramatic revelations regarding Claudius' murder of his own brother.

Polonius epitomises the corruption, falseness and hypocrisy of the Danish court. He is a man devoid of any sense of morality. Spying and eavesdropping are his stock-in-trade. He sends Reynaldo to spy on Laertes, and involves the innocent Ophelia in his spying games, using her as 'bait' to trap Hamlet. In his all-consuming desire to ingratiate himself with the king by finding out 'where truth is hid', Polonius does not hesitate to listen in on what should be a private conversation between Hamlet and his mother. **Like Claudius, Polonius is outwardly pleasant and agreeable. However, in reality, he is a false and untrustworthy character who spends his time spying and fishing for information.** Hamlet sees through and ridicules his falseness in their conversation about the shape of the clouds. Polonius himself unintentionally underscores the falseness and duplicity of court life when he tells the king that a virtuous appearance can often hide evil: ''Tis too much proved that with devotion's visage and pious action we do sugar o'er the devil himself'. Polonius also exemplifies the contrast between appearance and reality in another sense – **he appears to be a devoted father** ('This above all, to thine own self be true'), **but in reality spies on his son and uses his daughter as a pawn in his spying games.**

Rosencrantz and Guildenstern also typify the double-dealing that characterises court life. While they pose as Hamlet's concerned friends, they are in fact spies in the pay of the king. Like Polonius, their sole aim is to win the king's favour, and they do not hesitate to betray an old friend. Hamlet sees through their false façade of friendship: 'I know you what you are'. He bluntly tells them: 'I know the good king and queen have sent for you'. He describes Rosencrantz and Guildenstern as 'adders fanged' (suggestive of sly and dangerous aspects to their characters) as well as 'sponges' that 'soak up' the king's favour.

Laertes is also infected by the contagious corruption that is such a marked feature of Claudius' reign. In his blind determination to be 'revenged most thoroughly' for his father's death, he allows himself to be 'ruled' and manipulated by the king. While Hamlet's procrastination owes much to the fact that he is a man of conscience, Laertes is determined that he will be in no way constrained by considerations of conscience: 'Conscience and grace to the profoundest pit'. Like Claudius, Laertes has no qualms about using the most underhanded (devious) methods to achieve his aims. His finer qualities (Hamlet describes him as 'a noble youth'), are corrupted by the intensity of his desire for revenge, and by the king's malign (evil) influence. Claudius incites Laertes, telling him that revenge 'should have no bounds'. The duel that appears to be a test of swordsmanship has in fact a far more sinister purpose. Yet Laertes leads Hamlet to believe that he has accepted his apology: 'I do receive your offered love like love, and will not wrong it'. Once again there is a marked contrast between appearance and reality. Laertes appears to be 'a noble youth' (in the words of Hamlet), but proves to be devious and utterly unscrupulous in his pursuit of revenge.

Even the innocent Ophelia is to some degree affected by this all-pervasive corruption. She seems to love Hamlet, yet she betrays him by allowing herself to be used by Claudius and Polonius as they try to get to the root of Hamlet's strange behaviour. In essence, she conspires with Hamlet's enemies against him, allowing them to spy on what should be a private conversation between Hamlet and herself.

It is a measure of the falseness of the Danish court that so many situations are not what they seem to be. An apparently routine visit to England to deal with some outstanding financial issues between the two countries is in fact an attempt to have Hamlet killed. A seemingly innocent duel between Hamlet and Laertes is in reality another attempt by Claudius to rid himself of his increasingly troublesome nephew. Hamlet's meetings with Ophelia and with his mother are not as innocent as they seem to be because these meetings have been organised by Polonius to facilitate his spying. Of course Hamlet himself is also forced to engage in deception in his battle of wits with Claudius. *The Mousetrap* is not an innocent piece of entertainment, but a clever ploy aimed at establishing the king's guilt beyond all doubt. The Prayer Scene presents us with one of the most interesting contrasts between appearance and reality. Claudius appears to be praying, but in reality is unable to pray for forgiveness because he is unwilling to give up all that he has gained through his crime. On this occasion Hamlet fails to see the reality behind the outward show.

The centrality of the contrast between appearance and reality is underlined by patterns of imagery. Images of clothing, painting and acting recur throughout the play. Polonius, a man who attaches great importance to appearance, tells Laertes: 'The apparel oft proclaims the man'. In reality, it is not possible to judge a person on the basis of their attire. Hamlet tells Gertrude that his grief is real and that his black clothing is a mere reflection of that heart-felt grief: 'These are but the trappings and the suits of woe'. Using an image from art, he angrily denounces women who display a false appearance to the world: 'I have heard of your paintings too, well enough. God hath given you one face and you make yourself another'. Of course the ease with which the visiting actors feign real passion further reminds us that appearances may be misleading. The actor who sheds tears for Hecuba, prompts Hamlet to ask himself: 'What's Hecuba to him or he to Hecuba that he should weep for her?'

Hamlet knows that he lives in a world of false appearances where dishonesty and duplicity are commonplace. He tells Polonius that 'to be honest as this world goes is to be one man picked out of ten thousand'. He is disgusted by the way people use flattery to advance themselves: 'Let the candied tongue lick absurd pomp, and crook the pregnant hinges of the knee where thrift may follow fawning.' Those people who once regarded Claudius with disdain now buy miniature portraits of him. **In this world of** false appearances, Hamlet also wears a mask, adopting 'an antic disposition'** to confuse his adversary, Claudius. Hamlet continually strives to remove the false appearances that disguise the evil and corruption at the heart of the Danish court. He tells the actors that the purpose of playing is 'to hold, as 'twere, the mirror up to nature'. The play within the play highlights this idea of false appearances. **While almost all of the other characters unquestioningly accept the world as they find it, Hamlet rejects and battles against the falseness and hypocrisy of the Danish court, eventually succeeding in revealing and removing Elsinore's rotten core.**

13. *The Theme of Love*

There are different kinds of love in the play. There is romantic love and family love. However, love (regardless of its nature and context) is generally seen in a negative light in this play, with many of the characters being disloyal, insensitive or cruel to those they profess to love. The actions of the central characters are rarely driven by love. While Hamlet is a notable exception in that his actions are motivated by love for and loyalty to his dead father, he is extremely cruel to Ophelia in the Nunnery Scene.

Relationships based on romantic love include those between Gertrude and King Hamlet, Gertrude and Claudius and, finally, Ophelia and Hamlet. All of these relationships end unhappily. **The relationship between Gertrude and King Hamlet seemed to be a strong one.** Hamlet tells us that Gertrude appeared to be totally devoted to his father: 'Why, she would hang on him as if increase of appetite had grown by what it fed on'. **However, Gertrude was disloyal to the memory of King Hamlet when she married so soon after his death.** Hamlet bitterly declares that 'A beast that wants discourse of reason would have mourned longer'. **Not only did Gertrude betray King Hamlet in death, it seems she also betrayed him in life.** The Ghost claims that Gertrude was involved in an adulterous affair with Claudius. He describes Gertrude as 'my most seeming-virtuous queen'. The ghost is deeply pained by Gertrude's betrayal as is Hamlet. The queen's behaviour causes Hamlet to lose faith in all women ('Frailty thy name is woman') and leads to him regarding all relationships with deep disgust.

The relationship between Gertrude and Claudius also appeared to be a loving one. However, in the dramatic closing scene the self-centred Claudius puts himself before the woman he claims to love. He tells Laertes that he cannot arrest Hamlet for the murder of Polonius because of his love for Gertrude: 'She is so conjunctive to my life and soul that as the star moves not but in his sphere I could not but by her'. Of course the audience's view of this relationship is strongly coloured by the views of both Hamlet and the Ghost. The Ghost believes that the relationship between Gertrude and Claudius is based on lust: 'So lust though to a radiant angel linked, will sate itself in a celestial bed and prey on garbage'. Hamlet also characterises this relationship as something disgusting, comparing Gertrude and Claudius to pigs 'honeying and making love over the nasty sty'. Hamlet believes that, in addition to the lust factor, this is a marriage of convenience. The Player Queen declares that, 'The instances that second marriage move are base respects of thrift and none of love'. While Claudius claims to love Gertrude, his actions at the close of the play suggest that he is motivated primarily by self-love. Afraid of pointing to his own guilt, Claudius makes only a half-hearted attempt to prevent Gertrude from drinking the poisoned wine. The queen dies as a result of the treachery of the man who claims to love her. We are not surprised that Claudius' 'love' for Gertrude does not survive this 'acid test'. Claudius earlier told Laertes that love was ultimately self-consuming and self-destructive: 'Time qualifies the spark and fire of it. There lives within the spark and fire of love a kind of wick or snuff that will abate it'. Certainly, the king's actions in the closing scene indicate that his love for Gertrude does not endure.

The relationship between Hamlet and Ophelia also ends badly. What seemed to be a genuinely loving relationship ends up being strangled by the weeds of corruption that spread throughout the Danish court during Claudius' reign. Ophelia is manipulated into conspiring with the king and her father against Hamlet. In the Nunnery Scene she is used as 'bait' to 'trap' Hamlet. It seems that Hamlet knew that he was being spied upon and this, combined with his loss of faith in women in general, prompts him to launch a bitter attack on Ophelia: 'Get thee to a nunnery. Why, wouldst thou be a breeder of sinners?' The fact that the insane Ophelia sings songs of unrequited love suggests that her madness is caused not only by the death of her father, but also by the unhappy ending of her relationship with Hamlet. Despite his cruelty towards her, Hamlet stresses the depth of his love for the dead Ophelia in the Graveyard Scene: 'I loved Ophelia. Forty thousand brothers could not, with all their quantity of love, make up my sum'. **Tragically, the love between Hamlet and Ophelia could not survive in the corrupt world of the Danish court.**

Family love, like romantic love, is generally portrayed in a pessimistic light in the play. It is impossible to respect Polonius as a father because he betrays both Laertes and Ophelia in different ways. For her part Gertrude is far from an ideal mother to Hamlet. **Polonius is a deeply cynical character who does not trust his own children. He sends Reynaldo to Paris to spy on Laertes. Not only that, he encourages his servant to lie about his son in the hope of getting at the truth of his behaviour:** 'And I believe it is a fetch of warrant you laying these slight sullies on my son'. Polonius believes that the end justifies the means. He tells Reynaldo: 'Your bait of falsehood take this carp of truth'. **Polonius shows no regard for Ophelia's feelings. He dismisses any possibility that Hamlet might genuinely love his daughter:** 'You speak like a green girl'. He encourages her not to believe Hamlet's declarations of love: 'Do not believe his vows'. He does not hesitate to use his daughter in his spying games: 'At such a time I'll loose my daughter to him . . .'. Little wonder that Hamlet addresses him as 'old Jephthah', an Old Testament figure who was willing to sacrifice his daughter because he believed it would please God.

Gertrude is deeply insensitive to Hamlet's feelings when she marries Claudius within a few weeks of King Hamlet's death. She seems to regard Hamlet's grieving as something of an irritation, urging him to cast aside his mourning clothes: 'Good Hamlet, cast thy nighted colour off'. Gertrude is a weak woman who unrealistically hopes that her son will get along with her new husband. She angers Hamlet when she asks him why he 'seems' to be mourning so deeply: 'Why seems it so particular with thee?' Hamlet's anger with his mother explodes in the Closet Scene when he makes her aware of her wrongdoing: 'You go not till I set you up a glass where you may see the inmost part of you'. To be fair to Gertrude she shows her loyalty to Hamlet when she never reveals the truth about his 'antic disposition' to Claudius: 'I have no life to breathe what thou hast said to me'. She also tries to protect him from blame by attributing his killing of Polonius to his madness: 'Hamlet in madness hath Polonius slain'.

The one example of strong family love is Hamlet's love for and loyalty to his dead father. Hamlet idealises his dead father: 'A combination and a form indeed where every god did seem to set his seal to give the world assurance of a man'. He believes that his father was the perfect husband, the perfect king and the complete man. Speaking of his father, Hamlet tells Horatio: 'I shall not look upon his like again'. It is Hamlet's loyalty and sense of duty to his father that spurs him on to gain revenge. **The audience admires Hamlet's devotion to his father's memory. The protagonist's love for his father is untarnished by the corruption of the Danish court.**

In conclusion, love is, in the main, portrayed in a negative light in the play *Hamlet*. The actions of most of the major characters are driven not by love, but by the desire for self-advancement (e.g. Claudius, Polonius, Rosencrantz and Guildenstern) or by the desire for revenge (e.g. Laertes, Fortinbras). Love – whether romantic love or family love – is often flawed, tarnished or simply less than what it should be. The quality of personal relationships within the play is, in many cases, adversely affected by the dishonesty and corruption of court life.

14. *The Themes of Loyalty and Betrayal*

Loyalty and betrayal are important, indeed central themes in the play *Hamlet*. It is Claudius' betrayal of King Hamlet that sets the action of the play in motion, while Gertrude's betrayal of her husband dominates Hamlet's mind, filling him with a sense of revulsion. More generally, the Danish court is full of false characters who do not hesitate to betray friends or family. Loyalty is another key concept in the play. Hamlet, Laertes and Fortinbras are all driven on to gain revenge by their loyalty to their respective dead fathers. While Horatio is a shining example of loyalty (to his best friend, Hamlet), there is a less admirable type of loyalty among those who serve the king – such loyalty is motivated by self-interest. Ultimately the play boils down to a struggle between Claudius, who is guilty of the most grave act of betrayal and Hamlet, whose actions are motivated by loyalty to the memory of the father he idolised.

Claudius is guilty of the most serious act of betrayal when he kills his own brother in order to gain both his crown and his queen. This act of betrayal puts a corrupt usurper on the Danish throne and drives Hamlet on to avenge his father's murder. Claudius is an utterly unprincipled character whose corruption spreads through the Danish court like a contagious disease. He surrounds himself with similarly false people (such as Polonius) who do not hesitate to betray friends or family.

Gertrude betrays King Hamlet in life and in death. She betrayed him when he was alive by having an illicit affair with Claudius (according to the Ghost), and subsequently betrayed his memory by remarrying with unseemly haste after his death. Disgust at his mother's betrayal of his father dominates Hamlet's mind ('O most wicked speed, to post with such dexterity to incestuous sheets! It is not, nor it cannot come to good . . .'), and significantly colours his attitude towards all women.

Polonius betrays Laertes by sending Reynaldo to Paris to spy on him. Not only that, he encourages Reynaldo to slander his son's character in order to elicit (draw out) any incriminating information about him. Polonius' willingness to betray his own son suggests that he is unquestionably devoid of integrity or any sense of honour: 'I believe it is a fetch of warrant, you laying these slight sullies on my son . . .' This incident alone indicates that Polonius is well-suited to working with Claudius, a man of even lower moral character. **Polonius is unwaveringly loyal to Claudius.** His loyalty to the king and willingness to plumb any moral depths is motivated by self-interest.

Rosencrantz and Guildenstern betray Hamlet when, posing as his friends, act as spies for the king and try to discover the cause of Hamlet's strange behaviour. Like Polonius, Rosencrantz and Guildenstern are shallow, two-faced characters only interested in self-advancement. When they continue with their efforts to understand his erratic actions, Hamlet cannot contain his anger: ''Sblood, do you think I am easier to be played on than a pipe?' He contemptuously dismisses Rosencrantz as a sponge 'that soaks up the king's countenance, his rewards, his authorities.'

It can be said that Ophelia betrays Hamlet by allowing herself to be used as 'bait' to trap him so that Claudius and Polonius may spy on him. **Laertes later betrays Hamlet when, having seemingly accepted his apology for Hamlet's unseemly behaviour at Ophelia's graveside ('I do receive your offered love, and will not wrong it'), pretends to engage him in a fair duel.** In reality, Laertes plans to use a sharpened, poisoned foil to gain revenge on Hamlet.

Loyalty is an important driving force in the play. Laertes, Fortinbras and, of course, Hamlet are, in their entirety, driven to avenge their fathers' deaths out of loyalty to their respective memories. **Gertrude remains loyal to Claudius even after Hamlet's dramatic revelations** regarding Claudius' deeply serious wrongdoing. Her loyalty to this usurper and murderer is essentially down to her own weakness of character – she seems to be incapable of an independent existence.

The most admirable character in the play is also the most loyal. Horatio's loyalty to Hamlet is such that he is willing to take his own life when he sees that Hamlet is close to death: 'I am more an antique Roman than a Dane'. In ancient times, a Roman officer was prepared to take his own life if he had seen his good friend die bravely for his country. Horatio is an inspiring example of loyalty.

15. *A Dramatic Scene in the play* Hamlet

Act 3 Scene 4 is one of the most dramatic scenes in the play. This is a scene full of conflict, tension and dramatic incident. In this scene Hamlet angrily confronts Gertrude and rashly kills Polonius. The death of Polonius subsequently proves to have a very significant influence on the course of events in the play. The appearance of the ghost adds to the drama of this memorable scene.

Hamlet does not suspect that his meeting with his mother has been planned by Polonius so as to facilitate his spying. The fact that we are aware of Polonius' presence, while Hamlet is not, adds to the dramatic tension. In this scene Hamlet's deep resentment of his mother's behaviour explodes in a violent rage. **Hamlet is loud, aggressive and threatening** as he tells his mother that he wants her to examine her conscience: 'You go not till I set you up a glass where you may see the inmost part of you'. **The audience is taken aback by Hamlet's aggression and Gertrude is genuinely frightened.** Kenneth Branagh's *Hamlet* was especially menacing in this scene. When Gertrude

cries out for help the foolish Polonius echoes her cries, prompting Hamlet to impulsively run his rapier through the arras (curtain).

The killing of Polonius is one of the most dramatic moments in the play. It is particularly shocking because Hamlet – a man seemingly paralysed by indecision – acts on the spur of the moment. Hamlet apparently believed that it was Claudius who was hiding behind the curtain: 'I took thee for thy better'. From this we can conclude that Hamlet is in fact capable of killing the king in the heat of the moment.

Not alone are we shocked by his killing of Polonius, we are also taken aback by Hamlet's complete lack of remorse for what the queen describes as 'this rash and bloody deed'. Hamlet treats the dead Polonius with total contempt, coldly dismissing him as a 'wretched rash intruding fool' and as a 'foolish, prating knave'. Hamlet's behaviour in this scene is not what we would expect from a noble protagonist. While Polonius is a false, immoral, devious character, he did not deserve to die in this manner – however poetically just it might seem for him to have met his end as a result of his unprincipled behaviour.

The tension in this scene barely slackens for a moment because, at this point, Hamlet levels his most serious accusation at his mother. When she expresses her horror at his killing of Polonius, Hamlet replies: 'A bloody deed – almost as bad, good mother, as kill a king and marry with his brother'. Gertrude's shocked response ('As kill a king?') suggests that she had no knowledge of King Hamlet's murder.

Hamlet dramatically contrasts his father with Claudius. He describes his father as a perfect, complete man: 'a combination and a form indeed where every god did seem to set his seal'. In sharp contrast, Claudius is described as an infected ear of corn that spreads the disease of corruption throughout the Danish court: 'Here is your husband, like a mildewed ear blasting his wholesome brother'. The imagery here is particularly powerful, effectively evoking the contagious and devastating effect of corruption.

Hamlet angrily demands that his mother look deep into her own soul, repeatedly asking her: 'Have you eyes?' **In a dramatic moment of self-awareness, Gertrude acknowledges her sinful state:** 'Thou turn'st mine eyes into my very soul, and there I see such black and grained spots as will not leave their tinct'.

One of the reasons that this scene is so dramatic is that Hamlet treats Gertrude so severely. He portrays her relationship with Claudius as something utterly repulsive, comparing the two of them to pigs 'honeying and making love over the nasty sty'. **Hamlet does not simply make his mother more self-aware in this memorably dramatic scene – his harsh treatment of her amounts to a form of mental torture.** Gertrude begs Hamlet to stop tormenting her: 'These words like daggers enter in my ears. No more, sweet Hamlet'. However, Hamlet remorselessly hammers home his message, demanding that she end her physical relationship with Claudius: '. . . by no means that I bid you do, let the bloat king tempt you again to bed'.

The appearance of the Ghost is another particularly dramatic moment in a scene that has the audience on the edge of their seats throughout. The Ghost reminds the indecisive Hamlet of his duty to gain revenge: 'This visitation is but to whet thy almost blunted purpose'. The fact that Gertrude cannot see the apparition (perhaps because she is in a state of sin) further adds to the drama because she believes that her son is hallucinating: 'This is the very coinage of your brain'.

The audience is rather surprised that Hamlet admits to his mother that his madness is simply an act: 'I essentially am not in madness, but mad in craft'. **This is yet another dramatic moment in a scene full of dramatic incident.**

At the close of this scene, we are left anticipating Hamlet's plans for Rosencrantz and Guildenstern. Describing them as 'adders fanged', he tells his mother that he is confident of out-witting them: 'But I will delve one yard below their mines, and blow them at the moon'.

---

16. *Account for the enduring popularity of the play* Hamlet

Hamlet continues to entertain and fascinate audiences for a variety of reasons. It offers us a compelling plot with betrayal, murder, corruption, revenge, a supernatural dimension and a particularly dramatic ending. We are intrigued by the struggle between Hamlet and Claudius because they are two shrewd, well-matched adversaries. Their struggle is an interesting battle of wits, as well as a classic conflict between good and evil. We can relate to many of the themes of the play. For example, the corruption of the Danish court has an obvious relevance for a modern-day audience accustomed to regarding politics with a cynical eye. The play also offers us interesting insights into the Elizabethan world, particularly into the role and status of women. In addition, *Hamlet* offers us a rich variety of characters: in contrast to the falseness, corruption and cynicism of Claudius and his minions we have the innocence of Ophelia and the inspiring loyalty and nobility of Horatio. **The enduring appeal of the play may be attributed to the protagonist, Hamlet, one of the most complex and fascinating characters in English literature. Similar to all of the Shakespearian tragic heroes, Hamlet has a fatal flaw – that of indecision.** Finally, **the richness of the play's language and imagery also heightens its appeal.**

From the opening lines of the play, the audience is drawn into the fascinating plot. Adultery, betrayal, murder and revenge are among the elements that make this play compelling viewing. **This is a play full of dramatic incident.** The Nunnery Scene, the Prayer Scene and the Closet Scene all stand out in the memory. **The play opens in a very dramatic manner. The appearance of the ghost is regarded as a sign that all is not well in the Danish court. This supernatural element increases the dramatic appeal of the play.** The ghost fills Horatio 'with fear and wonder', with the latter believing that it 'bodes some strange eruption to our state'. Horatio regards the spirit of the dead king as a sign pointing to the future (a 'harbinger' and 'omen'), while Barnardo describes it in similar terms ('this portentous figure'). Barnardo, Marcellus and Horatio share a strong sense of foreboding, believing that some disaster is about to befall the Danish state. **Hamlet's encounter with the ghost is one of those events that keeps the audience on the edge of their seats. The ghost's revelations are particularly dramatic:** Hamlet learns that his father's murderer is his uncle / stepfather – the man now sitting on the Danish throne! **To add to the drama, Hamlet is charged with avenging his father's murder:** 'Revenge his foul and most unnatural murder!' **The stage is now set for an intriguing battle of wits between Hamlet and Claudius, which may also be seen as a classic struggle between good and evil.**

Conflict lies at the heart of all good drama. The struggle between Hamlet and Claudius is a fascinating one because they are two well-matched adversaries, and the outcome hangs in the balance until the very end of the play. Hamlet's antagonism towards Claudius is clear from the opening scenes. While all around him celebrate the king's recent marriage, Hamlet is brooding and resentful, set apart from everyone else in the Danish court by his black clothing and black mood. He promises the ghost that he will 'fly' to his revenge. **We are fascinated by Hamlet's adoption of 'an antic disposition' to confuse and gain an advantage over the king. We also marvel at his cleverness in devising 'The Mousetrap' to test the king's guilt.** However, the perceptive Claudius is a formidable villain. **The king's use of spies adds to the intrigue.** He does not hesitate to use Polonius, Rosencrantz and Guildenstern to spy on Hamlet, while manipulating others, especially Laertes, with consummate ease. **It is again apparent that Hamlet and Claudius are two suited antagonists. Hamlet perceives his former school-friends, Rosencrantz and Guildenstern for the 'adders fanged' that they are, and always sees through Polonius' falseness:** 'These tedious old fools!' He even seems to sense that Polonius is eavesdropping on his conversation with Ophelia: 'Let the doors be shut upon him that he may play the fool nowhere but in his own house.' **Hamlet's rash killing of Polonius is, of course, one of the most dramatic moments in the play.** It also makes Claudius aware of the serious threat that Hamlet poses not only to his kingship, but to his life. **The closing scene of the play is especially dramatic: the duel between Hamlet and Laertes is very tense because, unlike Hamlet, we are aware of the poisoned sword and the poisoned wine. This dramatic irony adds to the sense of tension. Ultimately, the king, the queen, Laertes, and Hamlet himself die in the play's violent denouement.** The manner in which Hamlet finally gains revenge is dramatic and very appropriate: Claudius is stabbed with the venomous sword and forced to drink the poisoned wine he had prepared for his nephew.

Many of the play's themes have a timeless and universal relevance. The struggle between good and evil is obviously a theme with an

enduring appeal, as is the contrast between appearance and reality. **The corruption of the Danish court has an obvious relevance for a modern audience all too familiar with false, two-faced politicians.** Claudius is the classic corrupt politician. He seems to be statesmanlike, but is in fact a 'smiling damned villain'. Claudius is the source of the dishonesty that spreads like a weed throughout the Danish court. The servile Polonius and the sycophantic Osric epitomise the falseness of court life, only saying what Hamlet wants to hear (as we see in their respective conversations with Hamlet about the shape of the clouds and the weather).

The play *Hamlet* offers us a range of interesting insights into life in Elizabethan times. A modern audience is particularly struck by the passive, subservient role played by women at that time. The women in the play are in effect second-class citizens whose lives are ruled by the men in their lives. Gertrude never emerges from the shadow of two kings, and seems to be incapable of an independent existence, remaining loyal to Claudius even after Hamlet's dramatic revelations. Ophelia is lectured by her brother ('Be wary then, best safety lies in fear'), used by her father ('Ophelia, walk you here . . .') and the king, and abused by the man she loves ('Get thee to a nunnery . . .'). Elsinore is a male-dominated world, devoid of strong women.

The richness and variety of the play's language and imagery also add to its appeal. Images of weeds ('. . . 'tis an unweeded garden that grows to seed') and sickness/disease (Claudius is 'a mildewed ear blasting his wholesome brother') effectively suggest the idea of a type of creeping, contagious corruption. In contrast, the flower imagery associated with Ophelia underscores her innocence ('. . . from her fair and unpolluted flesh may violets spring').

The appeal of the play also lies in the variety of its characters. To concentrate entirely on the theme of corruption, and on the falseness of Claudius, Polonius, et al would be an injustice to the spirit of the play because *Hamlet* is not entirely bleak in outlook. For example, the cynicism of Polonius contrasts with the innocence of Ophelia, while Horatio is a strikingly noble figure. Horatio is an inspiring example of loyalty and the one person in the Danish court in whom Hamlet can confide. His loyalty to Hamlet is such that he is prepared to take his own life when he realises that his friend is close to death: 'I am more an antique Roman than a Dane.'

While all of the foregoing points help to explain the enduring popularity of *Hamlet*, its timeless appeal is perhaps primarily attributable to its tragic hero. Hamlet is the most complex of all of Shakespeare's tragic heroes, and one of the most fascinating characters in English literature. Even more interesting than the conflict between Hamlet and Claudius is Hamlet's internal conflict. Events conspire to cast Hamlet in a role to which he is temperamentally unsuited. He must play the part of an avenger even though he is essentially a thinker rather than a man of action. He despises Claudius, but draws back from the idea of gaining revenge: 'O cursed spite that ever I was born to set it right!' His failure to act is the result of 'thinking too precisely on the event'. Despite regularly and passionately re-dedicating himself to the task of gaining revenge ('Now could I drink hot blood . . . ', 'O from this time forth my thoughts be bloody or be nothing worth!'), Hamlet continually procrastinates. He fascinates us because we wonder if he will ever act! Before he can hope to defeat Claudius, Hamlet must conquer his own indecision. We are also fascinated by Hamlet's unpredictability. In Acts 1-4 Hamlet generally thinks too much and does nothing (e.g.: the Prayer Scene), yet on occasions he acts rashly (e.g.: the killing of Polonius). We wonder which Hamlet we will see in any given scene. However, the Hamlet who returns from the voyage to England is a new man: balanced, composed, decisive and finally capable of gaining revenge. The total and dramatic nature of Hamlet's transformation that is apparent in the final act is particularly intriguing.

17. *Comic Aspects of the play* Hamlet

While *Hamlet* is obviously a tragedy, **the play has comic moments**. Hamlet's sharp wit and dark humour provide some light relief. Characters such as Polonius and Osric are unintentionally funny, while we are also entertained by the behaviour of the gravediggers in the Graveyard Scene.

Hamlet's punning is clever and witty, although there is always a sharp edge to his wit. When Claudius addresses Hamlet as 'my cousin Hamlet and my son', Hamlet cleverly replies: 'A little more than kin and less than kind'. When the king asks him why the clouds still 'hang' on him, Hamlet answers: 'Not so my lord. I am too much in the sun'. While such puns are certainly witty, the tone of their delivery is bitter. We also see Hamlet's clever word play in his exchanges with Polonius. When Polonius remarks that he played the part of Julius Caesar in a university play and that Brutus killed him, Hamlet replies: 'It was a brute part of him to kill so capital a calf there.'

The pompous, blustering Polonius is an unintentional source of humour. In a typically longwinded speech to Claudius and Gertrude, Polonius ironically observes that 'brevity is the soul of wit'. In reality, no character loves the sound of his own voice more than Polonius. Little wonder that the frustrated queen demands that he get to the point: 'More matter with less art'.

Hamlet's ridiculing of Polonius is another source of humour in the play. Hamlet highlights Polonius' falseness in the course of their conversation about the shape of the clouds. When Hamlet observes that the cloud is 'in the shape of a camel', Polonius agrees. When Hamlet subsequently suggests that the cloud resembles 'a weasel' and 'a whale', Polonius immediately changes his mind. In an aside, the frustrated Hamlet remarks: 'They fool me to the top of my bent'.

Hamlet's ridiculing of Osric is similarly entertaining. When Hamlet observes that the weather is cold, Osric agrees. When Hamlet subsequently suggests that the weather is in fact 'very sultry and hot', the servile Osric immediately changes his mind. Osric comes to inform Hamlet about the wager that the king has made on the upcoming duel between Hamlet and Laertes. Instead of coming straight to the point, Osric indulges in flattery, speaking in affected jargon. Hamlet's responses to the foolish young courtier are couched in similarly artificial language, but Osric is too dim-witted to realise that Hamlet is poking fun at him. Robin Williams plays the part of the unctuous Osric to perfection in Kenneth Branagh's production of the play.

Hamlet's wit is also to be seen in his conversations with Rosencrantz and Guildenstern. He describes Rosencrantz as 'a sponge' that 'soaks up the king's countenance, his rewards, his authorities'. He makes little of Claudius' kingship when he tells Rosencrantz: '. . . your fat king and your lean beggar are but variable service: two dishes but to one table, that's the end'.

We again see Hamlet's black humour in his conversation with Claudius about the whereabouts of Polonius' body. He tells the king: 'You will nose him as you go up the stairs into the lobby'. As the attendants rush off, Hamlet tells them that there is no need to rush: 'He will stay till you come'.

The Graveyard Scene provides some light relief before the play's dramatic and violent climax. The two gravediggers' jokes and antics bring a smile to our faces. They discuss Ophelia's death in the most casual, indifferent manner. The First Gravedigger likes to speak in riddles: 'What is he that build stronger than either the mason, the shipwright, or the carpenter?' The response is witty: 'A grave-maker – the houses he makes last till doomsday'. As Hamlet approaches, he is shocked to hear the gravedigger singing. However, while the exchanges are humorous, the graveyard scene also has a serious side to it, prompting Hamlet to reflect on the inevitability of death. The sight of the gravediggers casually throwing up skulls is quite funny on one level, but again serves to underline the grim reality of the grave.

---

18. *The Importance of Soliloquys in the play* Hamlet

Soliloquys fulfil a number of important functions in the play. Firstly, and most importantly, they provide us with important insights into Hamlet's state of mind at different stages of the play. It is only in his soliloquys and in his conversations with Horatio that we see the real Hamlet. **Hamlet's soliloquys ensure than the audience is sympathetic towards him by portraying his inner torment. They also inform us of Hamlet's plans. The soliloquys create a sense of dramatic irony and add to the dramatic tension because the audience knows more about the character who delivers them than the other characters in the play.** The only other character to deliver a number of soliloquys is Claudius. Since he is so adept at disguising his real self, **the king's soliloquys are very important because they reveal a side to his character that would otherwise remain hidden. They also inform us of his plans for Hamlet.**

Hamlet's opening soliloquy in Act 1 Scene 2 helps us to understand his hostility towards both Claudius and Gertrude. This soliloquy illustrates the depth of Hamlet's disillusionment with life. In it he describes the world as 'weary, stale, flat and unprofitable'. **This soliloquy reveals Hamlet's love for his dead father and his hatred of his uncle, Claudius:** 'So excellent a king that was to this Hyperion to a satyr'. **Hamlet goes on to express his disgust at his mother's behaviour:** '. . . a beast that wants discourse of reason would have mourned longer'. We see how Hamlet's disgust at his mother's behaviour now colours his attitude towards women in general: '. . . frailty, thy name is woman'.

Hamlet's next soliloquy comes at the close of Act 1 Scene 2. Horatio has just informed Hamlet of the appearance of his father's ghost. We see that Hamlet is immediately suspicious:

'My father's spirit in arms? I doubt some foul play.' He cannot wait for night to come so that he can see the ghost for himself: 'Till then sit still my soul'. **This soliloquy adds to the dramatic tension.**

At the end of Act 2 Scene 2 Hamlet delivers another soliloquy after seeing the players perform. This soliloquy again enables us to see Hamlet's innermost thoughts. In it he reproaches himself over his failure to act. The player has just delivered a passionate performance in which he shed tears for Hecuba, yet Hamlet, with real reasons to be passionate, seemingly lacks the passion to act. Hamlet concludes that he is a coward: 'It cannot be but I am pigeon-livered and lack gall'. **This soliloquy helps to create a sense of dramatic irony because Hamlet declares his intention of staging a play to test the king's guilt.** While Claudius expects *The Mousetrap* to be a piece of innocent entertainment, we know that it means much more than that to Hamlet: '. . . the play's the thing wherein I'll catch the conscience of the king'.

Hamlet's most famous soliloquy is delivered in Act 3 Scene 1. This is where we see Hamlet at his most philosophical as he wonders whether he should 'take arms against a sea of troubles'. **This soliloquy is important because it helps us to understand the essence of Hamlet's personality – we see that he is essentially a thinker rather than a man of action.** This soliloquy is also important because Hamlet identifies the key reason for his inaction: 'Thus conscience does make cowards of us all, and thus the native hue of resolution is sicklied o'er with the pale cast of thought.' In this soliloquy, Hamlet now confirms what we already suspected – the more he thinks, the less likely he is to act.

Hamlet's next soliloquy follows *The*

Mousetrap, the play (within the play) which confirms the king's guilt. This soliloquy seems to suggest that Hamlet is finally poised to act: 'Now could I drink hot blood and do such bitter business as the day would quake to look on'. It is here that we also learn of Hamlet's plan to confront his mother and 'speak daggers' to her.

We again see Hamlet's reflective nature in his soliloquy in the Prayer Scene. Hamlet now has concrete proof of the king's guilt when he comes upon him praying. However, he once again procrastinates, claiming that to kill Claudius when he is in prayer would be to send the villain to heaven. The audience suspects that Hamlet is simply drawing back from the idea of cold-blooded revenge.

The sight of Fortinbras boldly marching through Denmark on his way to Poland prompts Hamlet's next soliloquy. Again we get important insights into the protagonist's state of mind. Hamlet wonders if his failure to act is the result of cowardice or caused by 'thinking too precisely on the event'. Once again we see his guilt and anger at his own inaction. In contrast to Fortinbras (who is prepared to risk everything for a worthless 'patch of ground'), Hamlet, with far more compelling reasons to act ('a father killed, a mother stained'), seems to be incapable of acting. Self-disgust leads to another passionate outburst as Hamlet re-dedicates himself to gaining revenge: 'O from

this time forth my thought be bloody or be nothing worth!'

Claudius also has a number of soliloquys, the most important of which is delivered in the Prayer Scene. This soliloquy is important because it reveals a side to the king that we had not seen up to this point. Claudius is painfully aware of the enormity of his crime and is filled with guilt: 'O my offence is rank, it smells to heaven'. We see his inner torment as he longs to pray for forgiveness, but is unable to because he is unwilling to give up all that he has gained through his crime, notably the crown and the queen: 'My words fly up, my thoughts remain below. Words without thoughts never to heaven go.' Claudius knows that while he may avoid justice on earth, he will ultimately face divine justice: 'But 'tis not so above, there is no shuffling, there the action in his true nature'. This soliloquy is important because we now see Claudius as a more rounded, more credible character – he is a villain with a conscience.

Claudius' soliloquy at the close of Act 4 Scene 3 is important because it reveals his plan to have Hamlet killed in England: 'Do it England for like the hectic in my blood he rages . . .' This soliloquy creates a sense of dramatic irony because we know more than the unsuspecting Hamlet, who does not think twice about Claudius' instruction to go to England to collect monies owed.

19. *Imagery and Symbolism*

The images that recur in the play help to convey major themes and establish the distinctive atmosphere of the tragedy.

Images of Sickness and Disease

Disease imagery recurs throughout the play and is symbolic of the corruption of the Danish court. Hamlet believes that the Danish body politic is suffering from a disease and that Claudius is the source of this moral infection. Having literally poisoned King Hamlet with 'the leprous distilment', Claudius morally poisons

the Danish court. Hamlet describes Claudius as 'this canker of our nature'. He believes that his uncle spreads evil and corruption 'like a mildewed ear blasting his wholesome brother'. The queen admits to her sinful state when she speaks of her 'sick soul', while Laertes refers to his grief over his father's death as 'the very sickness of my heart". Ironically, given that it is he who is the source of the moral corruption in the Danish court, Claudius uses disease imagery to describe Hamlet. He believes that the disease that Hamlet's very presence represents requires a desperate remedy:

'Diseases desperate grown by desperate remedy are relieved or not at all'. Claudius compares himself to 'the owner of a foul disease'. After Claudius has ordered his nephew to England, he looks forward to the English putting Hamlet to death 'for like the hectic in my blood he rages.'

Weed Imagery

Weed imagery also suggests the idea of corruption. In his opening soliloquy Hamlet compares the moral condition of Denmark under Claudius' evil reign to a garden whose plants have been choked by ugly, repulsive weeds: '. . . 'tis an unweeded garden that grows to seed, things rank and gross in nature possess it merely'. When Hamlet urges Gertrude to end her relationship with Claudius, he uses an image that vividly reflects his profound sense of disgust: '. . . do not spread the compost on the weeds to make them ranker'.

Images of Rottenness and Decay

These images also suggest the moral decay of the Danish court under Claudius' evil rule. Marcellus declares: 'Something is rotten in the state of Denmark.' The repulsive image of the sun breeding maggots in a dead dog powerfully conveys the profound sense of disgust with which Hamlet now regards all human relationships. The guilty Claudius admits: 'O, my offence is rank, it smells to heaven'.

Animal Imagery

Images of lust highlight Hamlet's feelings of revulsion at the adulterous, incestuous relationship between his mother and his uncle. The bestial nature of their relationship is emphasised through a series of animal images. In his opening soliloquy the disgusted Hamlet declares that an animal lacking the power of reason would have mourned longer for its mate than Gertrude did for her dead husband: 'O God, a beast that wants discourse of reason would have mourned longer'. Hamlet compares Gertrude and Claudius to pigs 'honeying and making love over the nasty sty'. Polonius' use of animal imagery reflects his cynical view of love. He tells Ophelia that Hamlet walks 'with a larger tether' than she does, later telling Claudius that he will 'loose' Ophelia to Hamlet.

Flower Imagery

Ophelia is associated with flower imagery that underlines her innocence and purity – such imagery clearly contrasts with the weed imagery symbolic of the corruption of the Danish court. In her insanity, Ophelia wears garlands of flowers. When Ophelia dies, Gertrude says: 'I thought thy bride bed to have decked sweet maid, and not have strewed thy grave'. At her graveside, Laertes hopes that violets will spring 'from her fair and unpolluted flesh'.

Images of False Appearance

Images of clothing, painting and acting suggest the contrast between appearance and reality. Polonius tells Laertes that 'the apparel oft proclaims the man', but in reality it is not possible to judge a person simply on the basis of their clothing. Angry at his mother for urging him to dispense with his black mourning clothes, Hamlet tells her that these are only the outward expression of his grief: 'the trappings and the suits of woe'. Hamlet tells Ophelia that women often disguise their true selves: 'I have heard of your paintings too well enough. God hath given you one face and you make yourself another'. The passionate performance of the actor who cries for Hecuba further suggests the idea of false appearance.

The Characters: *Hamlet*

HAMLET

How should we regard Hamlet as a character? Is he essentially noble and admirable or is he more anti-hero than hero? Hamlet himself admits to a number of weaknesses when, speaking to Ophelia, he says: 'I am proud, revengeful, ambitious, with more offences at my beck than I have thoughts to put them in . . .' Any analysis of Hamlet's character must take cognisance (account) of some disturbing features in his outlook and behaviour. **He rashly slays Polonius and shows no remorse afterwards. He torments both his mother and Ophelia. He dispatches Rosencrantz and Guildenstern to their deaths in England without giving them an opportunity to have their sins forgiven. At Ophelia's burial scene** he appears to resent Laertes for endeavouring to attract attention to his grief **and behaves in an utterly inappropriate manner. His obsession with the 'incestuous' relationship between Gertrude and Claudius is both bizarre (strange) and unhealthy.** However, these unappealing aspects of Hamlet's character can be explained, if not excused. **Hamlet is essentially a noble-minded young man whose innate (natural) idealism is deeply undermined by a series of traumatic events.** Also, while there is little evidence of Hamlet's noble-mindedness for much of the play and while he at times comes close to alienating (losing the sympathy of) the audience, **our final impression of Hamlet is a positive one. It is significant that in the course of the play a succession of characters testify to the noble nature that had so endeared Hamlet to the people of Denmark and that his finer qualities are particularly in evidence in the final scene.**

Hamlet's disillusionment with life is expressed in a very direct manner in the opening scenes when he declares: 'How weary, state, flat and unprofitable / Seem to me all the uses of this world.' The image of 'an unweeded garden' conveys his vision of a coarse, corrupt world.

He places no value on his own life: 'I do not set my life at a pin's fee.' Later, he describes the earth as 'a sterile promontory' and 'a foul and pestilent congregation of vapours', dismissing man as a worthless 'quintessence of dust.'

Gertrude accurately identifies the roots of Hamlet's profound disillusionment with life when she says: 'I doubt it is no other but the main / His father's death and our o'er hasty marriage'. Speaking to Horatio of his dead father, Hamlet says, 'He was a man, take him for all in all / I shall not look upon his like again.' Hamlet bitterly highlights how closely his mother's marriage followed on his father's funeral when he tells Horatio that 'the funeral baked meats / Did coldly furnish forth the marriage tables'. He is utterly disgusted by his mother's unseemly haste in entering a new and, as he sees it, 'incestuous' relationship, describing her as 'pernicious' (malicious). He is bitterly disillusioned that his father's place has been usurped by a 'smiling damned villain'. **Hamlet is shaken to the core of his moral being by a rapid succession of traumatic experiences: the death of his adored father, his mother's indecently hasty marriage to his hated uncle and the ghost's revelation that his mother is married to his father's murderer. Furthermore, Hamlet is obliged to gain revenge on his uncle – a task for which he is temperamentally unsuited.**

Hamlet's treatment of his mother is cruel and unfeeling. Overcome once more by his passion, Hamlet is determined to make his mother aware of her weaknesses and wrongdoing: '. . . set you up a glass / Where you many see the inmost part of you'. The imagery Hamlet uses to characterise this marriage is repulsive: '. . . to live in the rank sweat of an unseamed bed / Stew'd in corruption, honeying and making love over the nasty sty.' His obsession with what he perceives to be the wholly lustful relationship between Gertrude and Claudius and his crude and cynical depiction of human relationships ('... the sun breeds maggots in a dead dog') highlights the less attractive side to his character. Gertrude begs Hamlet to 'sprinkle cool patience' on the 'heat and flame' of his anger and bitterness, finally proclaiming: 'O Hamlet! Thou hast cleft my heart in twain.'

Hamlet's treatment of Ophelia is similarly callous. Bitterly disillusioned by his mother's behaviour, he loses faith in all women: '. . . marry a fool, for wise men know well enough what monsters you make of them.' While Hamlet's unfeeling behaviour towards Ophelia can perhaps be explained in part by his awareness that both Polonius ('Let the doors be shut upon him, that he may play the fool nowhere but in his own house') and Claudius ('. . . we will have no more marriages; those that are married already, all but one, shall live') are spying on him with Ophelia's co-operation, his cruelty amounts to mental and emotional torture ('Get thee to a nunnery: why wouldst thou be a breeder of sinners?') and cannot be justified. **The audience is shocked by Hamlet's harsh and pitiless treatment of the innocent Ophelia.**

Hamlet's killing of Polonius is rightly described by Gertrude as 'a rash and bloody deed'. While Polonius is a thoroughly unappealing character who typifies the falseness of court life, Hamlet's impulsive action cannot be justified. **Hamlet's treatment of the old courtier unsurprisingly alienates much of the audience.** Having rashly killed Polonius in a fit of passion, he heartlessly dismisses him as a 'wretched, rash, intruding fool'. Hamlet's final comment on Polonius is utterly contemptuous ('a foolish, prating knave'), while his lifeless body is treated like that of a dead animal: 'I'll lug the guts into the neighbour room'.

The cold-hearted manner in which Hamlet sends Rosencrantz and Guildenstern to their deaths may be seen as further evidence of his cruel nature. Hamlet intercepts the letter ordering his own death and alters it so that his former school friends are instead executed. Hamlet tells Horatio that they are not even to be allowed to make an Act of Contrition: 'He should the bearers put to sudden death, not shriving-time allowed'.

Neither does Hamlet's over-the-top behaviour during Ophelia's burial scene do him any credit. He appears to resent what he sees as Laertes' attempts to out-do him in his expression of grief: 'Dost thou come here to whine? / To outface me with leaping in her grave?' We do not expect a supposedly noble hero to behave in such a disrespectful manner at the funeral of the woman he professed to love.

While Hamlet must, as a tragic hero, retain the sympathy of the audience, his thinking and behaviour are often far from noble. However, it is Hamlet's basic decency and idealism, which are at the root of his popularity continuing to exist in Denmark. Ironically, it is Claudius, Hamlet's arch-enemy, who observes that Hamlet is 'loved by the distracted multitude', testifying to his nobility once again when telling Laertes that he will not wish to examine the swords for what should be, but is not, an innocent duel ('being remiss / Most generous and free from all contriving'). **It is also significant that virtually all of the major characters at some point pay tribute to Hamlet's nobility.** Confronted by Hamlet's ferocious outburst of cruelty and cynicism, Ophelia bears eloquent testimony to his noble nature: 'O! What a noble mind is here o'erthrown / The courtier's, soldier's, scholar's eye, tongue, sword / The expectancy and rose of the fair state.'

Hamlet is essentially a man of conscience and it is this, which causes his indecision and procrastination: 'Thus conscience does make cowards of us all'. Hamlet's finer qualities are to be seen in his expert knowledge and enjoyment of drama. The noble Hamlet is especially evident in the final scene when he apologises to Laertes ('Give me your pardon, sir. I have done you wrong') and prevents Horatio from committing suicide. Horatio's absolute loyalty is in itself a powerful testimony to Hamlet's noble nature and to his capacity to inspire total devotion.

Notwithstanding (despite) his unappealing qualities, Hamlet never entirely loses our sympathy. While not excusing Hamlet's worst excesses, we can understand why he behaves as he does. We can see how his idealism and nobility are twisted by the pressurised situation in which he finds himself. Significantly, our final impression of Hamlet is a positive one as his finer qualities come to the fore towards the close of the play. **Ultimately, we see Hamlet as an imperfect, but essentially noble hero. When he realises that Claudius has already killed Gertrude and has also poisoned him after conspiring against him, the only person left for him to kill is the former, his uncle who usurped the kingship.**

Hamlet's finer qualities are particularly emphasised in the closing scene. Laertes exchanges forgiveness with 'noble Hamlet' and Horatio pays him a moving tribute: 'Now cracks a noble heart. Good night, sweet Prince / And flights of angels sing thee to thy rest.' The final word on Hamlet is left to Fortinbras who suggests that he possessed the qualities of a king: 'For he was likely, had he been put on / To have proved most royal.'

KEY ADJECTIVES

- complex character who grows on a personal level in the course of the play
- displays emotional extremes for the first four acts – wavering between the paralysis of excessive thought in the Prayer Scene, and rash, unthinking action in the killing of Polonius
- can be intolerant of and harsh on a range of characters he believes to have betrayed his father
- noble and idealistic in the eyes and words of many Danes
- undergoes significant personal growth – displays a balanced, decisive personality after returning from the voyage to England
- final scene portrays him as a noble figure possessed of royal-like qualities

CLAUDIUS

Our initial impression of Claudius is largely positive – we admire him for his efficient, business-like manner and because he seems anxious to please. As the play progresses we realise that he is a murderer, a usurper, and a hypocrite: 'a smiling damned villain'. **Claudius is no lightweight villain; he is shrewd, manipulative, and ruthless. Neither is he a stereotypical villain** – Claudius is painfully aware of the enormity of his crime and is tormented by his conscience. **It is this complexity which makes him such a credible character.** Shakespeare's skilful, convincing portrayal of Claudius reminds us of the delicate balance between good and evil that lies in the heart of every man.

When we first meet Claudius as a new king, he appears to be a comfortable and capable monarch, perfectly composed in the execution of his royal duties. He demonstrates considerable diplomatic skill in the manner in which he responds to the military threat posed by Fortinbras. He sends ambassadors to the old King of Norway to inform him of his nephew's plans to launch an attack on Denmark and to request that he suppress Fortinbras' military activities. The instructions which Claudius gives to the ambassadors are clear, precise and limited in their power and focus.

The opening scenes also seem to suggest that Claudius is kind and anxious to please: '. . . what is't Laertes . . . what wouldst thou beg Laertes? What would'st thou have Laertes?' However, his courtesy is exaggerated and hints at insincerity. Claudius is extremely anxious to put Hamlet at ease and to make him feel at home in the Danish court: 'But now, my cousin Hamlet, and my son … And we beseech you, bend you to remain / Here, in the cheer and comfort our eye, / Our chiefest courtier, cousin, and our son'. Claudius reminds Hamlet that he is heir to the throne: 'You are the most immediate to our throne.' Again, it is difficult to avoid the suspicion that his kindness is overstated (exaggerated) but that kind manner is sustained throughout the conversation. Even when Hamlet responds to him in a hostile way, Claudius does his best to placate him: '. . . 'tis a loving and a fair reply.'

Hamlet regards his uncle with contempt and ignores his blandishments (requests) to cast off the clouds that 'still hang' on him. Hamlet's worst suspicions are confirmed by the ghost's revelations: 'The serpent that did sting thy father's life / Now wears his crown . . . that incestuous, that adulterate beast.' Hamlet's anger at the hypocrisy of Claudius' earlier expression of grief and sorrow at his brother's death now becomes clear: 'O villain, villain, smiling, damned villain.'

Claudius deftly (skilfully) manipulates people for his own ends. He uses the terms 'dear Rosencrantz' and 'gentle Guildenstern' to 'glean' as much information as possible from Hamlet. Polonius sets out to find 'where truth is hid', anxious to justify Claudius' description of him as 'a man faithful and honourable.' Claudius' manipulative ability is particularly evident in the way he deals with Laertes. He allows 'good Laertes' to vent his anger after he breaks into the throne room, telling Gertrude to, 'Let him demand his fill.' Afterwards, Claudius skilfully converts a dangerous enemy into a useful ally and instrument of his own ends.

Claudius is shrewd and perceptive. His spying on Hamlet's meeting with Ophelia leaves him doubtful that his nephew is genuinely mad: 'Nor what he spoke, though it lacked form a little / Was not like madness.' **He is quick to recognise the danger to his kingship which Hamlet represents:** 'Madness in great ones must not unwatched go'. He understands the significance of Hamlet's killing of Polonius: 'It had been so with us had we been there / His liberty is full of threats to us all.'

Claudius is devoid of scruples. He callously poured a 'leprous distilment' in his brother's ear. The tormented ghost emphasises the enormity of this crime: 'Thus was I, sleeping, by a brother's hand, / Of life, of crown, of queen, at once dispatched; / Cut off even in blossoms of my sin.' Neither has Claudius any reservations about sending Hamlet to meet his death in England: 'Do it England; / For like the hectic in my blood he rages.' Claudius' encouragement of Laertes to use poison underlines his evil, devious nature. His lack of integrity is strikingly evident in his wide range of spying and eavesdropping. He eavesdrops with Polonius on the meeting between Ophelia and Hamlet and allows Polonius to spy from behind the curtain in the queen's bedroom.

Claudius is completely self-absorbed. He is generally unmoved by Polonius' death, and seems to be equally indifferent to the death of Ophelia. His selfishness reaches new depths when he allows Gertrude to drink from the poisoned chalice. Claudius subsequently admits that he does not believe in the permanence of love: 'There lives within the very flame of love / A kind of wick or snuff that will abate it.' Interested in nothing other than preserving his own life, Claudius makes only a half-hearted effort to save Gertrude: 'Gertrude, do not drink'.

Hamlet describes Claudius as a 'remorseless, treacherous, lecherous, kindless villain' and 'an incestuous, murderous, damned Dane.' **Perhaps the most interesting aspect of Shakespeare's portrayal of this 'smiling, damned villain' is that he is himself aware of the gravity of his offence:** 'O! my offence is rank, it smells to heaven; / It hath the primal eldest curse upon't / A brother's murder.' Claudius is unable to pray for forgiveness because he is unwilling to give up all that he has gained through his crime: 'My crown, mine own ambition, and my queen. / May one be pardoned and retain the offence?' Conscience-stricken, he realises that ultimately he cannot escape divine justice: 'In the corrupted currents of this world / offence's gilded hand may shove by justice . . . but 'tis not so above / There is no shuffling, there the action lies in his true nature'. This scene confirms that Claudius, the evil villain of the play, is not without humanity. Claudius is profoundly disturbed ('marvellous distempered') by *The Mousetrap* (the play within the play) and subsequently wrestles with his conscience in the Prayer Scene.

The fact that Claudius has a troubled conscience does not detract (take) from the enormity of his crime, but, by humanising him, Shakespeare makes him a more complex and hence more credible and interesting character.

KEY ADJECTIVES

- self-absorbed, selfish
- sly, two-faced, deceptive, scheming
- appears to be devoid of scruples, without morals – but his troubled conscience indicates his humaniity
- shrewd, astute, perceptive, sharp
- manipulative of others
- unwilling to give up all that he has gained from his initial usurping of his brother's throne

GERTRUDE

Gertrude is not an evil woman and there is no definite evidence that she was personally involved in the murder of King Hamlet. While the ghost suggests that Gertrude was unfaithful to him while he lived, there is no evidence, other than the queen's own later feelings of guilt, to confirm the truth of this accusation. At the very least, she remarried with unseemly haste and was disloyal to the dead king's memory. It must, however, be remembered that the old King Hamlet was a military man and very experienced in warfare. Marcellus refers to the ghost as wearing 'the very armour...When he the ambitious Norway combatted' and refers to another occasion when 'He smote the sledged Polacks on the ice'. Horatio confirms this image of the former king when he recalls earlier battles won by 'our valiant Hamlet'. There can therefore be little doubt that the sudden death of her husband would have created a political dilemma for Gertrude. Her son is clearly distraught by his father's death and in no emotional state to assume the responsibility of a king whose country is being threatened by Norway. The citizens are working day and night to prepare for what appears to be an imminent major military confrontation. In addition, Hamlet has spent some time away at the university in Wittenberg and, as the rest of the play illustrates, is given to thinking 'too precisely' on events. Claudius, in true Machiavellian style, seizes the opportunity to convince the Council of State that in such an emergency he is better suited to rule in his brother's stead. One must bear in mind that a marriage between a woman and her brother-in-law would be seen as adulterous at the time, so very good reason must have been put forward to convince the entire council to allow the marriage to take place and to go 'with this affair along'. Ironically, once the marriage has taken place, the threat from Norway is quite simply and diplomatically resolved by means of a letter to the Norwegian king!

Gertrude undoubtedly has no initial sense of personal guilt or shame concerning her sudden marriage to Claudius which lends credibility to the fact that her motivation may have had an element of acting in the national interest and of allowing her son some time before he has to step into the role of a 'warlike' king. She herself is clearly in no position to assume the burdens of state. Throughout the play we never see her interfere in military decisions or affairs but willingly leaves everything to Claudius.

Gertrude loves her son and has his best interests at heart when she encourages him to 'cast [his] nighted colour off'. She is anxious that Rosencrantz and Guildenstern should assist in drawing her 'too much changed son' out of his depression. **Gertrude is, however, a weak character, who is easily manipulated by the cunning Claudius. While she plays a very passive role in the play's action, it is clear that her 'sin', whatever its precise nature, dominates Hamlet's mind, profoundly affecting his outlook on life.**

Her desire to avoid trouble is evident in the early scenes of the play where she tries, without success, to promote harmony between the two people she loves most by encouraging Hamlet to 'look like a friend on Denmark'. She seems rather insensitive to Hamlet's grief and loss, wondering why he appears to be so deeply affected by his father's death: 'Why seems it so particular with thee?' However, this apparent insensitivity could also reveal a certain pragmatism and there is much common sense in Gertrude's advice. Death is a part of life and must be accepted as such. However, despite her best intentions, she merely succeeds in antagonising Hamlet further, unwittingly drawing upon herself his bitter cynicism and resentment.

The precise nature of Gertrude's wrongdoing is rather unclear. There is no evidence that she was involved in or knew about the murder. Indeed, her lack of reaction to both the dumb show and *The Mousetrap* suggests that she certainly knew nothing about the murder of her former husband. She seems to be genuinely shocked by Hamlet's revelations in this regard. By calling Claudius 'that adulterate beast', the ghost, by implication, accuses Gertrude of committing adultery. However, there is no evidence to substantiate this accusation. Certainly, Gertrude married with unseemly haste and the ghost is pained by the disloyalty of his 'seeming virtuous queen'. One must bear in mind, however, that the ghost arises from purgatory and, because he is aware that he was murdered by his brother, is quite justified in claiming that the marriage to Gertrude is, in fact, adulterous. However, he makes no allegation of actual adultery against Gertrude and this is an important distinction. Her lack of virtue may be more related to her weakness and capacity to be manipulated.

Hamlet is disgusted and profoundly disillusioned by his mother's behaviour: 'Frailty, thy name is woman … a beast, that wants discourse of reason / would have mourned longer'. His sense of revulsion at Gertrude's 'incestuous' relationship with Claudius dominates his mind. Indeed it might be said that Hamlet is unhealthily obsessed by this relationship. Hamlet's disgust at his mother's weakness of character extends to include all women, notably Ophelia. He accuses Gertrude of 'an act that blurs the grace and blush of modesty / calls virtue hypocrite, takes off the rose / From the fair forehead of an innocent love / And sets a blister there'.

However, Gertrude does have the capacity to recognise her own wrongdoing (although the exact nature of her 'sin' remains unclear). Hamlet sets out to make his mother aware of her moral failings: 'You go not, till I set you up a glass / Where you may see the inmost part of you'. Hamlet's bitter words force Gertrude to look into her very soul where she sees 'such black and grained spots as will not leave their tinct'. Her anguish is clear: 'O Hamlet! Thou has cleft my heart in twain'. Later, when she is about to speak to the distracted Ophelia, Gertrude makes a remark which suggests that she has something to answer for and **acknowledges her own spiritual sickness**: 'To my sick soul as sin's true nature is / Each toy seems prologue to some great amiss'. She evidently accepts that her marriage to Claudius was carried out with unseemly haste and has deeply disturbed her son. Nevertheless, one cannot accuse her with certainty of anything more serious.

Gertrude's most obvious redeeming feature

is her love for her son. She understands her son better than anyone else when she suggests to Claudius that the cause of Hamlet's 'distemper' is 'no other but the main; / His father's death and our o'er hasty marriage'. (Notice that it is not the marriage itself, so much as its overly-hasty aspect). Later, she expresses the hope that it is Ophelia's 'good beauties' which 'be the happy cause of Hamlet's wildness' and that her 'virtues' will bring her son back to his usual self. When Hamlet tells Gertrude that he is 'essentially . . . not in madness but mad in craft', she promises not to reveal anything of his admission to the king: 'I have no life to breathe what thou hast said to me'. When she tells Claudius of Polonius' death, she emphasises that the act was the result of insanity – 'mad as the sea and the wind', and that he killed Polonius 'in his lawless fit'. This is not a mere effort to excuse her son for the murder but a genuine belief that Hamlet is indeed mad. One must bear in mind that Gertrude does not see the ghost but sees Hamlet's reactions to it. After the murder of Polonius, Hamlet does indeed act like a lunatic by dragging away the body and refusing to reveal its whereabouts.

Gertrude is delighted by Hamlet's success in the fencing match and it is in drinking to his success ('The Queen carouses to thy fortune Hamlet.') that she dies. Of great importance here is the fact that as soon as Gertrude realises that the cup is poisoned, she uses her dying breaths to warn Hamlet of Claudius' treachery. Only then, perhaps, does she see the true nature of a man whom she trusted without question.

Gertrude possesses an interesting personality. She can appear weak and dull-witted rather than evil. It seems that she loved King Hamlet ('… she would hang on him … ') but is disloyal to his memory because she needs a man's strength to rely upon. Not possessing sufficient mental and emotional resources within herself, she is dependent on others for her security and happiness. Where the men in her life are concerned, Gertrude is submissive and dependent. She lives in the shadow of Claudius as she had probably lived in the shadow of King Hamlet. Her main concern is to avoid trouble at any cost and to preserve her comfortable, insular world from disturbance of any kind. However, we also see her capacity to be assertive when she reprimands Hamlet for his rudeness to her and again when she refuses to obey Claudius when he tells her not to drink a toast to Hamlet at the fencing match. Ultimately, the reality, which she is either unwilling or unable to see, intrudes dramatically on her unreal world and she dies a victim of Claudius' treachery.

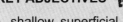

KEY ADJECTIVES

- shallow, superficial
- dependent, weak, subservient
- morally blind in her inability to initially see Claudius for the villain that he is
- very knowledgeable regarding Hamlet
- loyal to Hamlet (maternal love for him remains intact)
- deeply saddened by Ophelia's death

OPHELIA

Ophelia is the epitome of sweetness and gentleness. Young and innocent, she is easily dominated by the men in her life. She is lectured by her brother, manipulated by her father, used by the king and abused by the man she loves. The flower imagery with which she is associated sharply contrasts with the weed imagery symbolic of the corruption of the Danish court. **Her death highlights the play's tragic dimension.**

When we first meet Ophelia, she is at the receiving end of a lecture from Laertes who warns her that Hamlet's love for her will not last. He describes Hamlet's love for her as 'forward, not permanent, sweet, not lasting'. Laertes believes that since Hamlet is heir to the throne, he will not be free to choose his own wife: '. . . his will is not his own, for he himself is subject to his birth'. He urges his sister not to be 'too credent' (too trusting) and to guard her virtue: 'Be wary then, best safety lies in fear'. Basically, Laertes fears that Ophelia is no more than a plaything for Hamlet. Ophelia listens politely to her brother's moral lecture, but shows some spirit when she suggests that Laertes should not preach to her about the importance of virtue and self-restraint while following the 'path of dalliance' himself.

Ophelia is a dutiful daughter who obeys her father without question. This is unsurprising since in Elizabethan times fathers had absolute control over their daughters. She is also lectured by Polonius who dismisses her as 'a green girl' when she speaks of how Hamlet has expressed his affection for her. Polonius tells his daughter not to believe Hamlet's promises of love: 'Do not believe his vows'. Ophelia agrees to be guided by her father: 'I shall obey, my lord'. She subsequently returns Hamlet's letters and refuses to see him, heightening his sense of isolation in the Danish court.

Ophelia is manipulated and exploited by Polonius and Claudius who use her as bait to trap Hamlet in Act 1 Scene 3. The king wants to get to the root of Hamlet's 'dangerous and turbulent lunacy' and has no qualms about spying on his nephew. By allowing Claudius and her father to eavesdrop on her private conversation with Hamlet, Ophelia becomes enmeshed in the deception and double-dealing that is endemic (rife, widespread) in the Danish court. Polonius directs his daughter as a director might an actress: 'Ophelia, walk you here . . . Read on this book'.

Ophelia becomes the focus of Hamlet's profound disgust with love, marriage and procreation: 'Get thee to a nunnery. Why wouldst thou be a breeder of sinners?' Hamlet bitterly rejects Ophelia because he associates her with his mother. Gertrude's weakness influences his attitude towards all women. His condemnation of women is harsh and brutal: '. . . you jig, you amble and you lisp, and nickname God's creatures, and you make your wantonness your ignorance'. The audience feels great sympathy for Ophelia who does not understand or deserve this tirade (long, angry speech). Ophelia is deeply affected by Hamlet's apparent insanity: 'O what a noble mind is here o'erthrown! The courtier's, scholar's, soldier's eye, tongue, sword . . .' As Ophelia laments the apparent madness of the man she loves, she highlights Hamlet's admirable qualities, informing the audience of the kind of man he was before being so profoundly shaken by a series of traumatic events. Ophelia lovingly portrays Hamlet as the finest example of young Danish manhood.

Ophelia is too sweet and gentle to cope with the harshness of the world that she inhabits. The death of her father at the hands of the man she loves proves too much for her sensitive mind, ultimately causing her insanity. The songs that she sings in her disturbed state are concerned with unrequited love, suggesting that Hamlet's unrequited love for her is partly responsible for her breakdown. Ophelia is a pitiable figure at this point: 'She is importunate, indeed distract. Her mood will needs be pitied.'

Ophelia is the personification of sweetness and innocence. The flowers that surround her during her madness symbolise her beauty and purity. At her graveside, Laertes hopes that violets will spring from her 'fair and unpolluted flesh', and refers to her as 'Rose of May'. Ultimately, Ophelia is too sensitive and innocent to survive in the cruel, corrupt, patriarchal (male-dominated) world of Elsinore.

Ophelia's death highlights the play's tragic dimension. More than any other character in the play, Ophelia stirs our feelings of pity. She is the classic example of the innocent tragic victim. Her death is not the result of any personal flaw or wrongdoing. She is the pathetic victim of forces beyond her control and of events over which she has no influence. Ophelia is the guiltless victim of the evil that pervades the Danish court, enduring bereavement and insanity, and ultimately taking her own life.

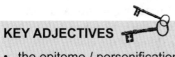

KEY ADJECTIVES

- the epitome / personification / embodiment of innocence
- a tragic character who represents the play's tragic dimension
- easily dominated by the men in her life – becomes enmeshed in the false, deceptive web of men that is now (with the usurper, Claudius, as king) a striking feature of life in the Danish court
- largely weak and passive (like Gertrude)

POLONIUS

The central characters of the play hold contrasting views of Polonius. Claudius describes him as 'a man faithful and honourable', while Gertrude refers to him (after his death) as 'the unseen good old man'. In striking contrast, Hamlet regards Polonius with undisguised contempt, describing him as 'a foolish prating knave' and as 'a wretched, rash intruding fool'. **The audience is inclined to agree with Hamlet's sceptical view of the king's chief adviser, seeing few, if any, redeeming features in the character of Polonius.** Our impression of him is almost entirely negative.

Claudius' positive view of Polonius is easily explained. A dutiful courtier who is unwaveringly loyal to the throne, Polonius is prepared to do anything to ingratiate himself with the king (win the king's favour). He is wholly devoted to serving Claudius: 'I hold my duty as I hold my soul, both to my god and to my gracious king'. Polonius promises Claudius that he will discover the cause of Hamlet's strange behaviour: 'I will find where truth is hid'.

The advice which Polonius gives Laertes shows him to be cautious, practical and shallow: 'Give every man thine ear but few thy voice . . . the apparel oft proclaims the man . . . Neither a borrower nor a lender be'. While the final piece of advice which he offers to his son sounds idealistic ('This above all, to thine own self be true'), we quickly see that there is nothing idealistic or noble about Polonius.

Polonius' cynicism is evident in his advice to Ophelia. While his advice may be inspired by parental concern, it reflects **an utterly cynical view of life and human relationships** (A cynic is someone who thinks the worst, someone devoid of idealism). Polonius dismisses any possibility that Hamlet's expressions of love for Ophelia might be genuine: '. . . you speak like a green girl . . . you have ta'en these tenders for true love which are not sterling'. **He is incapable of believing in Hamlet's decency or sincerity:** 'Do not believe his vows'. Polonius does not believe in the concept of romantic love. By instructing Ophelia to return Hamlet's letters and to deny him access to her, he disregards his daughter's feelings and sacrifices her possible happiness. **His profoundly (deeply) pessimistic outlook on loving relationships is reflected in the animal imagery that he uses to portray young people.** He says that Hamlet 'walks with a larger tether' than Ophelia, later telling Claudius that he will 'loose' his daughter to Hamlet. **Polonius reduces love to the level of lust and young people to the level of farmyard animals.**

Polonius' cynical, unscrupulous character is strikingly evident when he sends his servant, Reynaldo, to Paris to spy on Laertes. It is clear that Polonius does not trust his own son. **A Machiavellian character** (one who believes that the end justifies the means), he instructs Reynaldo to tarnish Laertes' reputation with a view to dredging up whatever incriminating material may exist in relation to his own son: '. . . put on him what forgeries you please . . . I believe it is a fetch of warrant you laying these slight sullies on my son . . . Your bait of falsehood take this carp of truth.' **Polonius is a devious (sly) and deeply unpleasant character.**

Polonius manipulates Ophelia for his own selfish ends, using her as a piece in his spying games: 'Ophelia, walk you here . . . Read on this book.' We should not be surprised that he displays little concern for his daughter's feelings since **his primary concern at all times is to advance his own position in the Danish court.** Hamlet compares Polonius to 'old Jephthah', an Old Testament figure who thought he was pleasing God by sacrificing his own daughter. Polonius is prepared to do something similar to please Claudius.

Polonius is pretentious and self-important. He likes to appear knowledgeable, especially in front of the king. He asserts that he has found 'the very cause of Hamlet's lunacy', insisting that Hamlet is mad because of his unrequited (unreturned) love for Ophelia (having earlier scoffed at his daughter's suggestion that Hamlet had been 'honourable' in his expressions of love for her) . . . **Polonius' longwinded speeches lack substance**, his verbosity prompting Gertrude to demand 'more matter with less art'. He pretends to be knowledgeable about acting, telling Hamlet that he was regarded as a good actor, yet the only comment he can make on the First Player's speech is that it is 'too long'. Hamlet contemptuously

dismisses Polonius as one of 'these tedious old fools'. Aware that Polonius is eavesdropping on his conversation with Ophelia, Hamlet declares that he should 'play the fool nowhere but in his own house'. **Hamlet highlights and ridicules Polonius' lack of sincerity when he speaks to him about the shape of the cloud,** Polonius by turns agreeing that it looks 'like a camel . . . like a weasel . . . like a whale'.

Polonius' willingness to spy on a private meeting between Hamlet and Gertrude underscores his low moral standards. Ever anxious to curry favour with the king, he unscrupulously and insensitively listens in on what should be a private conversation between mother and son. He tells Claudius that he will 'be placed . . . in the ear of all their conference'. Of course, the audience is not surprised by Polonius' lack of morality. **Devious behaviour comes naturally to this underhanded, immoral character. Ultimately, he dies a victim of his own underhanded scheming.**

Polonius typifies the falseness and artificiality of court life. He consistently tries to ingratiate himself with the king and is prepared to do whatever is necessary to advance his own position in the Danish court. **He does not hesitate to eavesdrop or spy and has no sense of morality.** He trusts his own children so little that he sends his servant to spy on his son and spies on his daughter himself. He instructs his servant to tell lies about Laertes, while coldly manipulating Ophelia for his own devious ends and showing no regard for her feelings. He sees people as puppets and has no respect for the privacy of others. **Self-absorbed, cynical, unscrupulous and devious, Polonius is an innately (naturally) unattractive character.**

KEY ADJECTIVES

- self-centred, self-absorbed
- cynical, sceptical
- false, insincere, hypocritical
- sly, devious, scheming, underhanded

- unscrupulous, ruthless
- immoral, unprincipled, Machiavellian
- manipulative

LAERTES

Laertes acts as a foil (contrast) to Hamlet. The similarities between the two are obvious: both Hamlet and Laertes are young man driven by a desire to avenge the deaths of their respective fathers. Speaking to Horatio about Laertes, Hamlet observes: '. . . by the image of my cause, I see the portraiture of his.' **However, while they share a common cause, there are fundamental differences between these two young men.** While Hamlet is deeply reflective and prone to procrastination (postponing action), **Laertes is inclined to act on impulse.** Also, (a related point) while Hamlet is essentially a man of conscience, **Laertes displays a lack of morality;** indeed such is the intensity of the latter's desire for revenge that he deliberately represses (restrains, bottles up) his conscience.

We first encounter Laertes in Act 1 Scene 2 when he dutifully returns to the Danish court to attend Claudius' coronation. **Like his father, Polonius, Laertes likes to moralise, offering Ophelia advice about her relationship with Hamlet.** While his advice to his sister is well meant, he basically talks down to her, warning her not to be 'too credent' (too trusting) and to guard her virtue. He believes that Hamlet, as heir to the throne, will not be free to choose his own wife and that his love for Ophelia is 'forward not permanent, sweet, not lasting'. He advises Ophelia to 'be wary'. However, Ophelia's response suggests that Laertes is unlikely to follow his own moral advice – according to her he 'recks not his own reed'. **Laertes' propensity for lecturing (tendency to lecture) his sister while following 'the path of dalliance' himself suggests that he is a shallow, hypocritical character.**

When Laertes learns of his father's death, he immediately returns to Denmark, determined to gain revenge. **We see how Laertes' impetuosity (impulsiveness) contrasts with Hamlet's indecision** when he angrily bursts into the throne room at the head of a mob, holding the king responsible for Polonius' death ('. . . young Laertes in a riotous head o'erbears your officers'). Unlike Hamlet, Laertes does not want proof of who is to blame for his father's death. All considerations of conscience are to be set aside in his quest for vengeance: 'To hell allegiance, vows to the blackest devil, conscience and grace to the profoundest pit!' Here again the contrast between Hamlet and Laertes is sharply clear. **While Hamlet admits that his failure to act has much to do with his conscience ('. . . conscience doth make cowards of us all'), Laertes is determined that nothing will prevent him from being 'revenged most thoroughly' for his father.**

Laertes' impulsiveness and lack of morality are skilfully exploited by the devious Claudius. The king manipulates Laertes with consummate (expert) ease, quickly winning this pliable (easily manipulated) young man round to his way of thinking through a combination of flattery and a false display of sympathy. **Laertes is a weak character who foolishly allows himself to be 'ruled' by Claudius.** He rises to the king's clever challenge to his pride ('What would you undertake to prove yourself your father's son in deed more than in words?'), by declaring his willingness to cut Hamlet's throat 'i' the church'. Here we clearly see the lengths to which Laertes will go to gain revenge. His willingness to kill Hamlet in the church contrasts with the inability of the latter to kill Claudius when he appears to be praying. **While Hamlet is restrained by his conscience, for much of the play, Laertes is determined that his conscience will not stand between him and the revenge that he craves.** He has no sense of morality where gaining revenge is concerned.

Laertes foolishly allows himself to become involved in a treacherous partnership with Claudius and is even willing to use poison to ensure Hamlet's death '. . . I'll anoint my sword: I bought an unction of a mountebank'. While Hamlet is not always admirable, it is impossible to imagine him being as devious (underhanded) and as unscrupulous as Laertes in his pursuit of revenge.

Ophelia's insanity and subsequent suicide give a further edge to Laertes' desire for revenge. He is deeply moved by the sight of Ophelia singing in her insanity: 'Hadst thou thy wits, and didst persuade revenge, it could not move thus.' **Laertes' shallowness is apparent at Ophelia's burial when he puts on an exaggerated display of grief.**

While Laertes feels a twinge of conscience in the course of his duel with Hamlet ('And yet it is almost against my conscience'), he still carries out the king's treacherous plan. **There is little to admire in the character of this weak, shallow young man.**

Laertes redeems himself to some extent before he dies. When he is mortally wounded, he accepts the justice of his own death ('I am justly killed with mine own treachery'). He identifies Claudius as the chief villain ('The king, the king's to blame') and asks Hamlet's forgiveness: 'Exchange forgiveness with me noble Hamlet. Mine and my father's death come not upon thee, nor thine on me.'

KEY ADJECTIVES

- impulsive, impetuous
- tends to be didactic (moralising) towards Ophelia regarding her relationship with Hamlet
- immoral, unprincipled, unethical
- pliable (easily manipulated by Claudius), malleable
- ultimately displays some redeeming qualities, showing himself to be conscience-troubled

HORATIO

Although Horatio does not do anything particularly memorable, or say something deeply meaningful, he nonetheless emerges as a character of considerable substance. He is **a patriot and a scholar, a man respected for his knowledge, judgement and good sense.** He is also to be **admired for his honesty and loyalty.** Horatio fulfils a number of **important dramatic functions**. It is he who **informs Hamlet about the appearance of the ghost. He is Hamlet's confidant and friend**, the one person with whom Hamlet can be open and honest. Horatio is **the personification of the balanced personality that Hamlet so admires**. He also acts as **a spokesman or commentator on Danish affairs**. Honest and true, he **is a symbol of loyalty and integrity** in the world of corruption and double-dealing that is the Danish court. Finally, at the close of the play when the royal family has been wiped out, **Horatio lives on and is trusted by Hamlet to tell the Danish prince's story.**

We meet Horatio before we meet Hamlet. **He is a key witness in identifying the ghost as the late king of Denmark.** As a respected scholar, Horatio is asked by Marcellus to address the ghost: 'Thou art a scholar, speak to it Horatio'. Initially sceptical, Horatio accepts the evidence of his own eyes, admitting to being filled 'with fear and wonder' at the appearance of the ghost in the likeness of the dead king. We see Horatio's **concern for his country** when he asks the ghost to share with him whatever knowledge he may have of any impending disaster for Denmark. **He suggests that the appearance of the ghost is a sign pointing to some violent disruption of the Danish state:** 'But in the gross and scope of my opinion, this bodes some strange eruption to our state'. **It is Horatio who informs Hamlet of the appearance of the ghost:** 'Let us impart what we have seen tonight unto young Hamlet'.

Horatio is Hamlet's friend and confidant. He is the one person in the Danish court in whom Hamlet can trust and confide. We only see the 'real' Hamlet in his soliloquys and in his conversations with Horatio. Hamlet speaks his mind to Horatio. He tells Horatio of his anger at his mother's hasty marriage: 'The funeral baked meats did coldly furnish forth the marriage tables'. He tells Horatio of his plans to test the king's guilt, and asks him to also observe Claudius' reaction to *The Mousetrap*: 'And after we will both our judgements join in censure of his seeming'. After observing the king's reaction to the play within the play, Hamlet tells Horatio that he is now convinced of the king's guilt: 'O good Horatio, I'll take the ghost's word for a thousand pound'. It is through his conversation with Horatio in Act 5 Scene 2 that we become aware of the dramatic development of Hamlet's character in the latter stages of the play. We see the new, decisive Hamlet in his account to Horatio of the dramatic happenings that occurred during the course of the voyage to England – he tells Horatio of how he did not hesitate to send Rosencrantz and Guildenstern to their deaths.

Horatio personifies the balanced personality that Hamlet so admires. Horatio is not a slave to his passion or his conscience. He possesses the correct temperamental balance between passion and reason (reflection): '. . . blest are those whose blood (passion) and judgement (reason) are so well comeddled.' The Hamlet we see in Acts 1 – 4 lacks Horatio's balanced personality, either thinking too much and doing nothing (e.g. the Prayer Scene) or else acting without thinking at all (e.g. the killing of Polonius in the Closet Scene). Hamlet openly expresses his admiration for Horatio's balanced personality: 'Give me that man that is not passion's slave, and I will wear him in my heart's core, ay in my heart of hearts, as I do thee.'

Horatio acts as a commentator or spokesman on Danish affairs. In the opening scene he shows his expert knowledge of Danish history. He recognises the armour worn by the ghost as that of the dead king. Through Horatio's conversation with Marcellus and Barnardo, the audience gets a detailed account of recent Danish history, particularly of the rivalry between the Danish and Norwegian kings which resulted in the death of King Fortinbras of Norway and in the loss of Norwegian territory to Denmark. In this way we are made aware of the reasons why young Fortinbras now threatens the security of the Danish state. Horatio provides us with important background information

Horatio is a symbol of loyalty and integrity in the corrupt and dishonest Danish court. His fundamental honesty and decency sharply contrast with the falseness of such characters as Rosencrantz and Guildenstern, so-called friends of Hamlet. He carries the banner of truth and honesty through the sea of corruption that is Elsinore. Horatio's loyalty to Hamlet never wavers. He tries to prevent Hamlet from taking part in the fencing contest with Laertes when Hamlet tells him of his sense of foreboding (sense that something bad is going to happen). His loyalty to Hamlet is such that he is even prepared to take his own life when he sees that his good friend is about to die: 'I am more an antique Roman than a Dane.'

Horatio survives the carnage at the close of the play. He is there to the end and is the one person who can tell all. **Hamlet charges Horatio with the responsibility for telling his story to the world:** 'Horatio, I am dead, thou livest, report me and my cause aright to the unsatisfied'. As a confidant of Hamlet's and as a respected figure in the Danish court, Horatio is ideally qualified to fulfil Hamlet's final request.

At the close of the play Horatio pays a moving tribute to Hamlet, reminding the audience of Hamlet's nobility: 'Good night sweet prince, and flights of angels sing thee to thy rest'.

KEY ADJECTIVES

- important primarily for his role / function
- patriotic and scholarly
- symbolic of loyalty and integrity (truth)
- informative – tells Hamlet of his encounter with the ghost
- trustworthy, honourable – the one person in the Danish court in whom Hamlet trusts and confides, with Hamlet ultimately asking him to tell the world the story of his life
- balanced in terms of his personality (unlike Hamlet, not given to either indecision or rashness)
- generous in spirit – pays tribute to Hamlet, accentuating (emphasising) the latter's nobility

ROSENCRANTZ and GUILDENSTERN

Rosencrantz and Guildenstern are former school friends of Hamlet. Claudius is very much aware of this and plans to exploit their friendship with Hamlet for his own deceptive purposes. **Rosencrantz and Guildenstern are not developed as individual characters, acting as one and making it virtually impossible to identify one from the other.** Their primary dramatic function is to act as spies for the king. They remind us that in the Danish court falseness is pervasive. They also advance the plot by being willing tools in the hands of Claudius and unquestioningly doing his bidding.

When Claudius greets Rosencrantz and Guildenstern, he expresses his concern at Hamlet's 'transformation' and asks them to use their friendship with Hamlet to get close to him. **Claudius wants them to probe Hamlet's troubled mind and get to the root of his strange behaviour. His treatment of Rosencrantz and Guildenstern illustrates the king's skill at manipulating people for his own devious ends.** Claudius addresses them as 'dear Rosencrantz' and 'gentle Guildenstern', his exaggerated politeness once again pointing to his falseness. Since Rosencrantz and Guildenstern are only interested in winning the king's favour, they are willing to do the most unpleasant things to demonstrate their loyalty. **They are compliant and servile (anxious to please) and do the king's bidding obediently and enthusiastically.** Betraying their personal friendship with Hamlet does not seem to concern them. They present themselves as Hamlet's friends, but are basically spies in the pay of the king. **They are shallow, two-faced characters who also typify the falseness of court life.**

Rosencrantz and Guildenstern are not convincing actors. Hamlet immediately sees through their façade of friendship: 'There is a kind of confession in your looks…' He bluntly tells them, 'I know the good king and queen have sent for you'. Lacking the guile (cleverness) to brazen it out, they confess the truth: 'We were sent for'. Following this admission, their mission to discover the cause of Hamlet's strange behaviour is doomed to failure. They are practically useless as spies, having nothing of any substance to report back to Claudius.

Hamlet does not respect his so-called friends, treating them with visible contempt. He resents their transparent attempts to get to the root of his strange behaviour, just as he disdains Polonius' efforts to impress the king. He avoids answering their questions whenever they attempt to probe his mind, leaving them confused by his 'crafty madness'. **When they continue with their efforts to discover the cause of his erratic behaviour, Hamlet cannot contain his anger:** 'You would play upon me, you would seem to know my stops, you would pluck out the heart of my mystery . . . 'Sblood, do you think I am easier to be played on than a pipe?' He contemptuously dismisses Rosencrantz as a sponge 'that soaks up the king's countenance, his rewards, his authorities.'

Hamlet naturally distrusts Rosencrantz and Guildenstern, describing them as 'adders fanged'. He knows that they are deceitful and hypocritical. He is always on his guard in their company and knows that they are keeping him under surveillance. However, he is confident that he can outwit them: 'But I will delve one yard below their mines, and blow them at the moon.'

Claudius uses Rosencrantz and Guildenstern to remove Hamlet from the Danish court. They accompany Hamlet on his voyage to England, the ostensible reason for which is the collection of monies owed to Denmark by England. There is no evidence to suggest that Rosencrantz and Guildenstern knew of the king's plot to kill Hamlet. **However, the fact that they act as spies and agents for Claudius means that Hamlet has no qualms about sending them to their deaths:** 'They are not near my conscience, their defeat does by their own insinuation grow'. In sending his former schoolmates to their deaths in England, Hamlet reveals a new, decisive quality to his character. They are to be killed without being given the chance to make their peace with God ('not shriving time allowed').

Rosencrantz and Guildenstern are shallow, self-seeking, uninteresting characters. Like Polonius, they represent the falseness of court life. Like him, they pay a high price for their servile obedience to a corrupt king.

KEY ADJECTIVES

- false, hypocritical
- shallow, superficial
- servile, fawning, obsequious
- selfish, self-seeking, self-absorbed, self-interested
- so similar to each other that they are virtually impossible to identify and discuss as individuals

FORTINBRAS

Fortinbras is not really developed as a character in his own right. However, he fulfils a number of dramatic functions in the play. He acts as a foil or contrast to Hamlet and, at the close of the play, **emerges as the man who will succeed Claudius** and restore order to Denmark.

In the opening scene Horatio presents us with a clear picture of Fortinbras, as a young man determined to avenge his father's death. He is also anxious to regain lands lost by Norway to Denmark. From Horatio we learn that Fortinbras has gathered together an army of desperate adventurers ('lawless resolutes'), and is now poised to attack Denmark. He acts without the permission of his elderly uncle, the King of Norway. Horatio describes Fortinbras as something of a hothead: a young man 'of unimproved mettle, hot and full.'

The contrast between Hamlet and Fortinbras is clearly drawn. While both share a common purpose in avenging the killing of a father,

these two young men are **very different in terms of their temperaments. While Hamlet is essentially a thinker, Fortinbras is very much a man of action.** While Hamlet hesitates to avenge his father's death, Fortinbras takes immediate action to redress what he perceives to be the wrong done to his father. Fortinbras's willingness to act decisively contrasts with and highlights Hamlet's inaction. When Hamlet watches Fortinbras marching through Denmark to fight for 'a little patch of ground' in Poland, he feels guilty about his own failure to act: 'How all occasions do inform against me and spur my dull revenge! . . . O from this time forth my thoughts be bloody or be nothing worth!' However, Fortinbras can hardly be admired for risking the lives of twenty thousand men for no important reason. **From a moral standpoint, he is rather reckless in his actions, giving little thought to the right or wrong of his cause.**

Hamlet and Fortinbras differ in the sense that while Hamlet is a man of conscience, Fortinbras shows himself to be quite unscrupulous. He is prepared to attack Denmark in defiance of a legally binding agreement. His war on Poland also seems to be one of aggression. **While Fortinbras has a sense of purpose and the capacity to act boldly, it is apparent that he lacks Hamlet's sense of morality.**

Hamlet admires Fortinbras as a bold man of action and, at the close of the play, gives his blessing to him as the next king of Denmark: 'I do prophesy the election lights on Fortinbras. He has my dying voice'. Hamlet and Fortinbras regard each other with mutual respect. Fortinbras has the final word on Hamlet when he describes him as having had the qualities of a king: 'For he was likely, had he been put on, to have proved most royal.'

KEY ADJECTIVES

- different attitude from Hamlet in terms of his attitude towards their shared purpose (avenging a father's death).
- bold and daring
- unscrupulous, immoral
- ultimately respected by Hamlet (who sees him as the next king of Denmark)

Comparative Study

Texts

- *The Plough and the Stars*
- *The King's Speech*
- *Foster*

Modes of Comparison

A. Theme or Issue: Complex Relationships

The Plough and the Stars

The exploration of the theme of Relationships, particularly those which are complex in nature, adds greatly to our understanding and interpretation of a text.

The Plough and the Stars by Sean O'Casey presents the audience with several examples of complex relationships which have an enormous impact on the lives of those personally involved in them and also on the community in which they live.

One such relationship is that which exists between Nora and Jack Clitheroe.

From the opening scene of the play, there is a suggestion that Nora's relationship with her husband, Jack, contains conflicting elements. Mrs Gogan's reference to the 'kissin' an' cuddlin' and the 'billin' an' cooin'' of the young couple is quickly followed by hints that the love between them may be waning. Speaking no doubt from a bitter perspective, she grimly concludes that 'afther a month or two, th' wondher of a woman wears off'. Fluther, the tenement philosopher, notices that the couple 'seem to get on well together' but adds his own whimsical realism by suggesting that if a man's love for a woman dies 'it's usually beginnin' to live in another'. The fact that O'Casey opens the play with such a strong emphasis on this apparently contradictory, complex relationship between the Clitheroes is an indication of its importance in the play as a whole.

The Clitheroes' relationship is later shown to be complicated by the conflict between their opposing value systems. Despite Jack's spirited defence of Nora when Bessie Burgess attacks her, Nora is clearly resentful of his desire to attend the meetings of the Citizen Army. Jack's own resentment at what he considers to be her controlling behaviour is vehemently expressed in his claim that Nora was 'always' at him to give up the Citizen Army and that he had given it up for her. However, Nora is quite well aware

that Jack only gave it up because he was not appointed Captain: 'It wasn't for my sake, Jack'. Although this brief argument resolves amicably, with Jack singing a love song for his wife, the tension escalates when he learns about the letter concerning his military promotion which she withheld from him and destroyed. Nora's rage as she defends her actions is extremely telling: 'Is your home goin' to be only a place to rest in? Am I goin' to be only somethin' to provide merry-makin' at night for you?' When Jack angrily leaves, telling her not to wait up for him, her retort: 'I don't care if you never come back!' is more an expression of her frustration than any real desire to be separated from her husband.

It is in this exchange that we see O'Casey emphasising one of the major issues of the play which relates to the importance of the home and the marital relationship as opposed to war and destruction. Jack is attracted by war, associating it with heroism and glory, whereas Nora seeks an escape from the poverty of the tenements in order to establish what she considers to be a respectable home for a family.

As the play progresses, the relationship of the Clitheroes becomes even more complex. Nora refuses to let go of Jack or of her dreams for the future and, defying the obvious danger, follows her husband to bring him home. She cannot accept that any woman willingly sacrifices her husband: '. . . if they say it, they're lyin', against God, Nature, an' against themselves!' Although her courage in risking her life to bring Jack home may be seen as evidence of love, there is also an element of possessiveness and a stubborn refusal to accept Jack's decision to fight with his comrades for an ideal in which he believes. Nora claims that 'Jack is more coward than hero'. He and his comrades are, according to her, 'afraid to say they're afraid'.

Despite this criticism, however, there is no doubt that she is deeply conflicted. She later vows to remember only what was pleasant in her marriage: 'only th' blossoms that grew out of our lives are before me now'. War has deprived her of 'th' little happiness life had to spare for me'. There is something profoundly poignant and disturbing in seeing this once vibrant, ambitious woman descend to the level of hysteria, eventually losing not only her husband but her unborn baby and her mind.

Jack Clitheroe is profoundly conflicted when he is placed in a situation of having to choose between what he perceives to be his military duty and his relationship with his wife . There is no doubt that his vanity, which Nora tells him will be the 'ruin' of both of them, propels him to choose his role of captain over that of a husband. Earlier in the play, Mrs Gogan reveals that Jack only left the army because he was not appointed to the role of captain: 'He wasn't goin' to be in anything where he couldn't be conspishuous'. At the meeting, Jack, along with Brennan and Langon, becomes mesmerised by the speeches and proclaims that 'Ireland is greater than a wife'. However, his words in Act III when he meets Nora after Langon has been wounded, show his growing disillusionment: 'I wish to God I'd never left you,' he claims in this key scene. Unfortunately, his vanity surfaces once more when he is taunted by Brennan who orders him to either leave his wife or 'go up an' sit on her lap'. Despite Nora's pleading that she is his 'dearest comrade', Jack cannot tolerate the mockery of Brennan or that of Bessie Burgess who asserts that 'General Clitheroe'd rather be unlacin' his wife's bodice than standin' at a barricade'. He roughly pushes his wife away. Vanity has triumphed again and, as Nora so accurately predicted, ruins their relationship and happiness.

Bessie Burgess is an example of an individual who has a very complex relationship with her neighbours. She is clearly regarded by them as a troublemaker who exults in antagonising the other tenement dwellers. Her treatment of Nora in Act I is threatening in nature, making Nora genuinely afraid of her. In addition, she takes delight in insulting and provoking Mrs Gogan in the pub, causing both of them to be ejected by the landlord. An outsider because of her religion and politics, she is preoccupied with Britain's role in the war. She sees the men who are fighting for Irish independence as being no more than traitors and parasites: 'There's the men [referring to the soldiers going to fight in the Great War] marchin' out into the dhread dimness o' danger, while the lice is crawlin' about feedin' on th' fatness o' the land'. The apparent callousness of Bessie's character can be seen most clearly in Act III when she expresses delight at the bloodshed and suffering of the wounded men. Fluther calls her 'an ignorant oul' throllope' while Brennan responds to her taunts with 'Shut up y'oul hag'.

Yet it is Bessie who secretly slips a mug of milk to the dying Mollser and who risks her life to fetch a doctor for Nora when she has a miscarriage. This humanity continues in her tender care of Nora after the loss of the baby. She stays up all night with her and finally risks and loses her own life in an effort to save Nora from a sniper's bullet. A different aspect of Bessie's relationship with her neighbours emerges as Mrs Gogan thanks her for her 'well chronicled' kindnesses to Mollser and Fluther says that he 'always knew there was never anything really derogatory wrong with poor oul' Bessie'. After her death, Mrs Gogan describes her as 'th' poor inoffensive woman' – an ironical description given the insults and threats of physical assault during the pub scene!

O'Casey, therefore, presents Bessie as a mass of contradictions which cannot be fully reconciled. Although heroic, she is no saint. She boasts about her own morality but has no hesitation in looting when the opportunity presents itself. Although she has taunted the political ideals of her neighbours, it is to her room they run for refuge when the fighting is at its most violent. She dies cursing Nora for being the cause of her death. All of these contradictions make Bessie a complex but very credible character. Despite her apparent contempt for the other characters in the play, she is nevertheless accepted for what she is and accepts others in return. **Her character demonstrates the fact that personal humanity is capable of transcending the petty quarrels** and differences which can complicate personal relationships.

Both of the most complex relationships in the play – that of the Clitheroes' marriage and that of Bessie Burgess' relationship with her neighbours – end in tragedy without any resolution of previous conflicts. Brennan's report of Jack's alleged last words are an attempt to assist Nora in accepting his death: 'Tell Nora to be brave . . . an' that I'm proud to die for Ireland'. Totally ignoring the deep division in the marriage relationship caused by Jack's desertion of Nora for a vain political 'ideal', Brennan hopes that 'Mrs Clitheroe's grief will be a joy when she realises that she has had a hero for a husband'. The reality, however, is that Nora's life has been ruined by Jack's decision to fight with the rebels rather than to stay with and protect his wife. On the other hand, Nora's own alienation of Jack by her obsessive desire to control him, her burning of his letter of commission and her public shaming of him by hysterical demonstrations of her love also contributed to the devastating outcome for both of them. At the end of the play there is no possibility of a resolution of the conflicts which spoilt and complicated their relationship.

Although Bessie's relationship with her neighbours in the tenement building seems to have changed by the end of the play, it cannot be claimed that tensions have completely resolved and that, had she lived, the complex factors which differentiated her from others would have changed. In a key moment just before her death she informs Corporal Stoddart that she is 'no Shinner, an' never had no thruck with anything spotted be th' fingers o' th' Fenians . . . ' She is faithful to her Protestant religion and there is no suggestion that she intends to change her habit of going to church to hear 'God Save the King' being sung at the end of the service. Bessie's isolation in death reminds the audience of her fundamental isolation in the tenements. She dies alone, singing one of the hymns which were, earlier, a source of great antagonism for her neighbours. **It is realistic to believe that, had she not been shot, Bessie would have maintained a complex relationship with her neighbours based on the conflicting beliefs and value systems which originally divided them.**

KEY POINTS

- The play presents the audience with examples of complex relationships which have an enormous impact on the lives of those personally involved in them and also on the community in which they live.

- From the opening scene of the play, there is a suggestion that Nora's relationship with her husband, Jack, contains conflicting elements.

- The Clitheroes' relationship is shown to be complicated by the conflict between their opposing value systems. O'Casey emphasises one of the major issues of the play which relates to the importance of the home and the marital relationship as opposed to war and destruction.

- As the play progresses, the relationship of the Clitheroes becomes even more complex. Jack Clitheroe is profoundly conflicted when he is placed in a situation of having to choose between what he perceives to be his military duty and his relationship with his wife .

- Bessie Burgess is an example of an individual who has a very complex relationship with her neighbours. This complexity arises also from a conflict of values and personal beliefs. As a Protestant and a Unionist, Bessie is alienated from her Catholic, predominantly Nationalist neighbours.

- In spite of the conflicts with her neighbours, Bessie's character demonstrates the fact that personal humanity is capable of transcending the petty quarrels and differences which can complicate personal relationships.
- Both of the most complex relationships in the play – that of the Clitheroes' marriage and that of Bessie Burgess' relationship with her neighbours – end in tragedy, without any resolution of previous conflicts.
- Although Bessie's relationship with her neighbours in the tenement building seems to have changed by the end of the play, it cannot be claimed that tensions have completely resolved and that, had she lived, the complex factors which differentiated her from others would have changed. It is realistic to believe that, had she not been shot, Bessie would have maintained a complex relationship with her neighbours based on the conflicting beliefs and value systems which originally divided them.

The King's Speech and *The Plough and the Stars*

The King's Speech, directed by Tom Hooper, also presents audiences with relationships which are very complex in nature. The conflicts which arise between key characters add tension to the narrative as a whole and illustrate the importance such relationships can have on individuals, communities and even the future history of a nation.

Unlike the Clitheroes in *The Plough and the Stars*, the relationship between husband and wife is more harmonious and supportive in *The King's Speech*. Elizabeth endures agony as she watches Bertie (later to become King George VI) stutter and stumble during his address to the nation at Wembley Stadium. She later becomes frustrated at the futile, and at times nonsensical, treatments which he undergoes at the hands of pompous and incompetent speech consultants. However, it soon becomes apparent from the dialogue that Elizabeth herself has been instrumental in engaging these experts to help cure her husband's speech defect. After one particularly trying scene in which he is asked to speak with a mouthful of marbles, Bertie storms out of the room and begs Elizabeth to cease her efforts to find a cure: 'Promise me: no more.' **A major difference in this relationship compared to that of the Clitheroes is that there is no evidence of any bitterness or resentment. Bertie knows that Elizabeth's insistence on finding a cure is in his own interests. Like Jack**

Clitheroe, who is outraged by Nora's burning of his letter, Bertie does object to his wife's attempt to take matters into her own hands by suggesting yet another therapist.** Although not as physically aggressive as Jack is with Nora, he becomes **similarly** assertive and angry when he says that his wife's proposals are 'Out of the question. I'm not having this conversation again. The matter's settled'. **Unlike Jack, Bertie is, however, a man who is capable of seeing reason when his anger abates.** The next time we see him and Elizabeth together they are in the tiny elevator on their way to Logue's consulting rooms. **The minor conflicts evident in this relationship are not on the same scale as those which beset the Clitheroes. There is far more trust and no bitterness between them because the ultimate goal they seek is a common goal. This relationship therefore lacks the complexity of that seen in *The Plough and the Stars* where Jack and Nora are divided by their opposing value systems and ideals.**

The first truly complex relationship in the film is that which exists between Bertie and Lionel Logue. Their first encounter is laden with tension which is generated by Bertie's frustration, his distrust of Logue's methods and his sense that he is not being treated with the respect due to a member of the royal family. The informality and lack of deference at this meeting astounds Bertie who hardly knows how to react to Logue's claim that 'In here, it's better if we're equals'. One could claim that the desire to be treated as superior arises from Bertie's vanity and creates an immediate barrier between himself and Logue. **This would suggest a parallel situation to that observed in O'Casey's play in which Jack Clitheroe seeks to be distinguished from his fellow rebels by being appointed captain in the Citizen Army.** However, Bertie's need for respect and deference is linked more to his own poor self-image coupled with an upbringing in which he was taught to expect that he should be treated differently to 'commoners'. **In contrast to Clitheroe, who seeks status, Bertie's status has been imposed on him and creates a social barrier during his first interview with Lionel Logue.** He leaves the consulting room having informed Logue that the methods used are not suitable for his needs. **Unlike the conflicts observed between Jack and Nora, the conflicts in this relationship are generated by one party and arise not from an incompatibility of desires or ambitions, but from an inability to adjust to an erosion of class distinctions.**

As the film progresses, the relationship between Logue and his royal client becomes more amicable. When Bertie hears himself speak without faltering on the recording made by Logue at the first consultation, he returns, in desperation, to avail of the therapist's services. There is nothing humble or apologetic in his demeanour as he instructs Logue to keep their relationship 'Strictly business. No personal nonsense'. But his attitude softens as Logue explains the need to go below the surface of the problem and both agree that Logue will assist Bertie by offering 'assistance in coping with a minor event'. Bertie even goes so far as to enquire if Logue finds this arrangement 'agreeable' and is shocked at his therapist's intention to see him 'every day'. What is evident in this key scene is the fact that both individuals are willing to engage in some degree of compromise in order to achieve a mutual goal; Bertie wishes to be cured of his speech defect and Logue wishes to cure him. **No such common purpose is apparent between Jack and Nora Clitheroe,**

making compromise an impossibility and increasing the conflict between them. A new understanding emerges between both men who relate to each other more as equals. Both men become closer when Bertie visits Lionel after the death of King George V. He confides intimate details of his childhood and his relationship with others, particularly his strained relationship with his father. 'You know, Lionel, you're the first ordinary Englishman . . . I've ever really spoken to,' he tells Lionel, admitting that he has never had a real friend or been able to express his innermost feelings to anybody.

Although Bertie and Logue appear to form a more amicable relationship in the therapy sessions, not everything runs smoothly. In the same way as fear and tension build between Jack and Nora, so the relationship between the two men becomes more complex and distant when Logue attempts to reassure Bertie that he has the capacity to be king if the situation should arise. During a key scene, when both men go for a walk together in the park, tensions rise and reach a climax when Bertie accuses Logue of 'treason' and of using 'poisonous words'. He insults him by saying he is no more than '. . . the disappointing son of a brewer! A jumped-up jackaroo from the outback!' Both men are angry as the camera captures their moving apart in the cold wintry landscape, the ground mist rising around them. **A similar scene of two people being driven apart by fear and tension can be seen in *The Plough and the Stars*.** In Act III Nora speaks her mind to Jack who, incensed with anger, retorts: 'What way d'ye think I'll feel when I'm told my wife was bawlin' for me at th' barricades? What are you more than any other woman?' Realising that she has worsened the situation, Nora tries to remedy it by saying '. . . I didn't mean any harm . . . I couldn't help it . . . I shouldn't have told you . . . ' **We are reminded here of Logue, accused of interference, attempting to justify his words: 'I'm just saying you *could* be king . . . I'm trying to get you to realise you need not be governed by fear.' There is a clear echo here of Nora urging Jack to recognise '. . . 'th' same fear that is in your own heart'. Both Nora and Logue fail in their efforts and both**

become further estranged in their respective relationships. Bertie walks angrily away from Logue and Jack 'roughly loosens (Nora's) grip, and pushes her away from him'.

A complex relationship can also be observed between David (King Edward VIII) and his lover Wallis Simpson. King George V rants with rage at David's choice of being in a relationship with 'a woman with two husbands living!' Like Bessie Burgess, Wallis Simpson is an outsider, but for very different reasons. She is not only unacceptable to the royal family because of her complicated marital history but also because of her personality and manners. She appears to have an extraordinary control over David's emotions to the point that he feels the need to apologise to her for spending time with his dying father. She antagonises Elizabeth by felling 'five hundred year old oaks . . . to improve the view!' Like Bessie, she seems to take pleasure in insulting others but does so in less direct ways. She describes the Scottish Royal Estate as 'our little country shack' and openly disrespects her lover, now King Edward VIII, by tapping her champagne glass and insisting that he fetch her drink from the cellar rather than allow a footman to do so. Churchill refers to her as 'a commoner' and both he and Elizabeth wonder about the 'hold' she has over the King. David's obsession with Wallis is not only apparent in his obsequious behaviour in her presence. When Bertie privately challenges him for 'laying off seventy staff at Sandringham and buying yet more pearls for Wallis while there are people marching across Europe singing 'The Red Flag'', he merely scoffs at the notion of duty and concentrates on pleasing 'Wally', who 'likes the very best'. An additional complexity in the relationship between Wallis and David lies in the fact that the King, being head of a church which forbids divorce, intends to marry the woman he loves – even if that means abdicating as king. He is clearly prepared to sacrifice everything for this unusual relationship prompting Baldwin to enquire: 'Does the King do what he wants, or does he do what his people expect him to do?' Unlike poor Bessie Burgess who sacrifices her only son to a war and who is unflinching in

her loyalty to king and country, both Edward VIII and Wallis Simpson put their own relationship and happiness before that of any other person or cause. Although Bessie may share some of the features of Wallis Simpson by being a source of irritation and an outsider, she exhibits a greater humanity and a finer sense of duty than this rich, spoilt woman who is far removed from the realities of existence due to her privileged position.

The relationship between David and Wallis can also be seen as a reversal of that between Jack and Nora Clitheroe. Jack makes his duty to his country greater than any wife and abandons Nora in order to fulfil his political ambitions. David does the reverse. Both relationships are thus complex and essentially destructive. At the end of *The King's Speech*, David and Wallis are seen listening dolefully in a villa in the South of France while Bertie addresses the nation. Their facial expressions and general demeanour do not suggest that their relationship has necessarily brought fulfilment or happiness to either one of them.

Whereas the outcome of the complex relationship between the Clitheroes ends in devastation, the relationship between Lionel Logue and his king grows in strength and understanding. Although there are still several scenes which show conflict and animosity – such as that immediately prior to Bertie's coronation, where he accuses Logue of being a cheat and an imposter – the final outcome is very positive. Bertie fully realises that Lionel has gone beyond the bounds of mere duty in order to help him find his true voice. Just before he delivers his speech, he acknowledges the debt he owes to his 'friend': 'No matter how this turns out, I don't know how to thank you for what you've done'. At the end of the film we are informed that 'Lionel and Bertie remained friends for the rest of their lives'. No such happy ending for any of the central relationships is evident in *The Plough and the Stars*, where most of the main characters suffer death, defeat or the loss of the potential happiness which good relationships can bring.

KEY POINTS

- Unlike the Clitheroes in *The Plough and the Stars*, the relationship between husband and wife is more harmonious and supportive in *The King's Speech*. A major difference in this relationship compared to that of the Clitheroes is that there is no evidence of any bitterness or resentment because both share a common goal of curing Bertie's speech impediment.

- The first truly complex relationship in the film is that which exists between Bertie and Lionel Logue. Unlike the conflicts observed between Jack and Nora, the conflicts in this relationship are generated by one party and arise, not from an incompatibility of desires or ambitions, but from an inability to adjust to an erosion of class distinctions.

- In contrast to Clitheroe, who seeks status, Bertie's status has been imposed on him and creates a social barrier during his first interview with Lionel Logue.

- As the film progresses, the relationship between Logue and his royal client becomes more amicable. Unlike the Clitheroes, both individuals are willing to engage in some degree of compromise in order to achieve a mutual goal; Bertie wishes to be cured of his speech defect and Logue wishes to cure him. No such common goal unites Jack and Nora, who have very different personal agendas which guide their behaviour.

- Although Bertie and Logue appear to form a more amicable relationship in the therapy sessions, not everything runs smoothly. Fear and tension enter the relationship in the same way as it does in *The Plough and the Stars*. Both Nora and Logue fail in their efforts to exert influence and both become further estranged in their respective relationships. Bertie walks angrily away from Logue and Jack 'roughly loosens (Nora's) grip, and pushes her away from him'.

- A complex relationship can also be observed between David (King Edward VIII) and his lover Wallis Simpson. Like Bessie Burgess, Wallis Simpson is an outsider, but for very different reasons. Like Bessie, she seems to take pleasure in insulting others but does so in less direct ways.

- Unlike poor Bessie Burgess who sacrifices her only son to a war and who is unflinching in her loyalty to king and country, both Edward VIII and Wallis Simpson put their own relationship and happiness before that of any other person or cause.

- Although Bessie may share some of the features of Wallis Simpson by being a source of irritation to her neighbours and an outsider, she exhibits a greater humanity and a finer sense of duty than this rich, spoilt woman who is far removed from the realities of existence due to her privileged position.

- The relationship between David and Wallis can also be seen as a reversal of that between Jack and Nora Clitheroe. Jack makes his duty to his country greater than any wife and abandons Nora in order to fulfil his political ambitions. David does the reverse. Both relationships are thus complex and essentially destructive, but for different reasons.

- Whereas the outcome of the complex relationship between the Clitheroes ends in devastation, the relationship between Lionel Logue and his king grows in strength and understanding. At the end of the film we are informed that 'Lionel and Bertie remained friends for the rest of their lives'. No such happy outcome of any central relationship is evident in *The Plough and the Stars*.

Foster, *The King's Speech* and *The Plough and the Stars*

Foster by Claire Keegan presents various complex relationships in a subtle, understated way because the story is told by a child narrator who does not fully understand the dynamics of such relationships. The fact that the viewpoint is First Person (as opposed to the multiple viewpoints of both *The Plough and the Stars* and *The King's Speech*) serves to add emphasis to the positive or negative impact of key relationships on individuals.

From the outset, it is apparent that the child narrator in *Foster* has a distant relationship with her father. Although she is being taken to foster parents for an undetermined length of time, her father does not engage with his child in any meaningful way. They drive in almost complete silence to the Kinsella's house. The child has many questions running through her head about the place she is going to but does not question her father or seek any reassurances from him. The reader is immediately aware that communication is lacking in what should be a close and affectionate relationship. **This aspect of their relationship is quite the opposite of that which exists between Jack and Nora Clitheroe, who despite some obvious resentments, engage in very lively, spirited dialogue. It is also different to the more reserved but open discussions between Bertie and Elizabeth which we see at the beginning of *The King's Speech*.** This lack of meaningful dialogue between Dan and his daughter prepares the reader for what is to come later in the narrative as we witness what is, effectively, a complete rejection of her father by the girl.

In common with the resentment Jack feels towards Nora for her deception concerning the burning of his letter in O'Casey's play, the child also resents her father's tendency to be dishonest. Although her father has done nothing about cutting or saving the hay, he claims that his loft is 'full to capacity' and that he nearly split his head on the rafters 'pitching it in'. **Unlike Jack, who confronts Nora about her deception, the child is powerless to contradict her father.** She wonders instead why her father 'is given to lying about things that would be nice, if they were true'. Her conflicted emotional state is apparent when she reflects on her situation: 'Part of me wants my father to leave me here while another wants him to take me back, to what I know.'

The lack of affection, intimacy and trust marks this relationship as being quite different to the loving, open one which is apparent between Bertie and Elizabeth and particularly between Bertie and his own children. While a father/child relationship is naturally different from that of adult couples, one nevertheless expects some indication of care or affection – particularly in a parental relationship with a child! Unfortunately, this is almost absent in Dan's treatment of his daughter. He tells the Kinsellas that they can 'work her' and leaves her with a warning: 'Try not to fall into the fire, you'. He does not say goodbye to his child but leaves abruptly, forgetting to leave the clothes her mother had packed for her. The hurt of the girl is palpable as she watches him reverse and drive away: 'Why did he leave without so much as a goodbye or even mentioning when he would come back for me?' **In many ways this relationship is the most complex in any of the three texts due to its unnatural, almost incomprehensible nature.** Many questions are left unanswered in the mind of the reader, who struggles to make sense of the situation or find any explanation for Dan's conduct.

The relationship between the girl's parents, Dan and his wife, Mary, is also seen as dysfunctional and lacking in any real love. **Dan, like Jack Clitheroe, tends to put personal vanity before the welfare of his wife.** When Mrs Kinsella asks if the child's mother would mind if she sent her some money, the child knowingly replies that 'She wouldn't, but Da would.' In a key moment, the child reflects on the kind of life her mother has with Dan. She is pregnant with a child she does not want. Her life is 'all work'. Apart from the 'butter-making, the dinners, the washing-up and getting up and getting ready for Mass and

89

school, weaning calves...', she is also burdened with having to employ men to do the work her husband should be doing: 'hiring men to plough and harrow the fields, stretching the money and setting the alarm for a time before the sun rises'. Earlier, we learn that Dan gambled a heifer to pay for his drinking and smoking habits. **There is no doubt that the marital relationship between the child's parents is not one of mutual respect and support, such as we see in *The King's Speech*. Likewise, in O'Casey's play, Nora's hard work to create a decent home for herself, her husband and the family she hopes to have can be compared with Mary's only insofar as Nora works hard, keeping lodgers in her home to expand the family finances. However, she does this in order to satisfy her own ambitions, unlike Mary, who seems powerless, overwhelmed and exploited in her relationship with Dan.** The impact on the child of her parents' loveless marriage is evident in her reluctance to leave the Kinsella's loving environment for the emotionally barren home of her parents. The conflict in Mary and Dan's marriage, (which is more implied than openly stated), resembles the conflict which is very apparent in the Clitheroes' marriage and which arises from their opposing value systems. **Neither Nora nor Mary is fulfilled or happy in marriage because of the conduct of their husbands who neglect their responsibilities towards their wives and the needs of the home. This lack of a shared goal is the complete opposite of the bond between Bertie and Elizabeth in *The King's Speech*.**

The relationship which develops between the child narrator and John Kinsella is complex in many ways. Kinsella reveals the love and care which one expects from a father towards a young daughter. **Like Lionel Logue who worked tirelessly to improve Bertie's confidence, Kinsella works tirelessly to build up the child's self-confidence by encouraging her to run timed races to the post box and using her progress as a motivation to try even harder to achieve her goals.** One could argue that Kinsella is, perhaps subconsciously, trying to replace the child whom he has lost. 'Petal', as he affectionately nicknames her, certainly seems to fill an emotional void in his life. However, as the narrative progresses, there are moments when his inner conflicts become apparent to the reader. At times his sharpness shocks and disturbs the girl. As they are preparing to go into Gorey, Kinsella sharply says 'You should wash your hands and face before you go to town . . . Didn't your father even bother to teach you that much?' The child responds by freezing in the chair, 'waiting for something much worse to happen'. There is no explanation for Kinsella's attitude here, but one senses the disrespect he feels for Dan and his disgust that the girl is not being properly cherished. In general though the relationship is very positive. In a key moment, when both of them go for a walk on the beach, we see the growing father/child relationship. The child initially feels uncomfortable when Kinsella holds her hand because her father has never done this. The scene culminates in Kinsella gathering the child into his arms as though she were his. The complexity of this relationship is apparent to the reader, who knows that it must, inevitably, come to an end. The growing closeness of the child to her foster father adds to a sense of foreboding concerning the coming separation.

The differences in social status which can affect relationships negatively and which are apparent in the early relationship between Bertie and Logue in *The King's Speech* also play a part in *Foster*. There is none of the division created by the clash between royalty and commoner in this text, but the impact of poverty versus relative wealth colours the child's attitude to her own home life. She is instantly conscious of the fact that the Kinsellas are wealthy people with 'money to spare'. When she later returns to her home she is uncomfortably conscious of the difference between her parents and the Kinsellas and between herself and her siblings. **Although she has not quite developed the 'notions of upperosity' which Mrs Gogan accuses Nora of, she is clearly feeling like an outsider and the reader is left wondering whether such feelings will have a lasting impact on her relationships with her family members.**

In the same way as tensions become characteristic of Nora's relationship with Jack and Bertie's relationship with Logue, so fear enters into Kinsella's relationship with the foster child. Knowing that she must return to her parents, Kinsella attempts to 'walk away' from the situation by immersing himself in his work but he is unable to detach himself from the child. The last moments of the novel illustrate the powerful bond which has developed between them.

A further complex relationship arises between the child and her mother in *Foster*, which has some parallels with the relationship between Mrs Gogan and Mollser in *The Plough and the Stars*. There is no doubt that the child has an understanding and sympathy for her mother but the relationships are flawed in both texts by the effects of poverty. Poverty affects these relationships as both mothers have to balance the needs of their children with the need to work and survive. Mollser makes no demands on her mother, constantly assuring her that she is alright when she is clearly dying of consumption. Likewise, the child in *Foster* seems protective of her mother but denies 'anything happened', keeping the incident of her own near drowning a secret from her mother: 'This is my mother I am speaking to but I have learned enough, grown enough, to know that what happened is not something I need ever mention'.

In all three texts there are characters who are hostile in their relationships with their neighbours or who create family tensions. Bessie Burgess is such a character in *The Plough and the Stars*, as is Wallis Simpson in *The King's Speech*. Both of these characters, in different ways, create discomfort and antagonism in their respective communities. A similar person in *Foster* is the interfering busybody Mildred. It is she who questions the child about the business of the Kinsellas, exhibiting a nasty envy in her desire to know the details of their financial and domestic circumstances. In the same way as Bessie and Wallis create discord and unease, so Mildred succeeds in upsetting the child by telling her the secret about the Kinsella's loss of their child. She does not do this with any hint of compassion or sensitivity but appears to stir up suspicion that the Kinsellas have not been fully truthful about the circumstances of the boy's death. Her mockery of the child's new clothes and her remarks about the girl wearing a dead child's clothing to Mass is calculated to create unease between the Kinsellas and their foster child who is traumatised by the revelation of this secret. A major difference in the complex relationships with others, exhibited by each of these three controversial characters (Bessie, Wallis Simpson, Mildred), is related to the motivation of each of them. Bessie is sincere in her religious and political beliefs but is also influenced by her overindulgence in alcohol; Wallis is deliberately irritating and obnoxious to the members of the royal family as a result of her background, complicated former relationships with men and a clear awareness that she, not being a member of the British aristocracy, is an unwelcome outsider at court. Mildred, however, acts out of envy, spite and ignorance, using a vulnerable child to strike a blow at her kindly neighbours. In all three texts, only Bessie emerges as a more noble character than her earlier actions may have suggested and enters into a more positive, supportive relationship with her neighbours in the tenement building.

Each of the three texts depicts certain family relationships as being essentially destructive in quality. Jack abandons Nora to follow his ambitions, David abandons his country by abdicating at a time of national crisis and Dan abandons his insecure and confused child when she most needs his loving support. Dan also abandons his responsibility to his wife and other children, creating misery and hardship in all of their lives. His behaviour is fundamentally selfish and irresponsible. All three men are willing to sacrifice their family relationships in order to pursue their own vision of what is best for themselves. What is very apparent to a careful observer is the fact that each one of these men either deludes themselves as to their true motivations or attempts to conceal it from themselves and others.

It is more difficult in *Foster* than in the other two texts to identify the outcome of the complex relationships which have been explored in the text. Whereas *The Plough and the Stars* ends in the destruction of central relationships through death, *Foster* has a more uncertain conclusion and differs from the positive conclusion of *The King's Speech*, in which Bertie and Logue not only resolve the conflicts which arose between them but become lifelong friends. There is an awkward moment at the end of *Foster* when the child races after the departing Kinsella, throwing herself into his arms, unwilling to let go of a man whom she has grown to regard as her true 'Daddy'. One cannot but remember the equally anguished final parting of Nora from Jack in *The Plough and the Stars*, where in spite of their love and need for each other, the relationship is destroyed by the inevitability of their separation. Kinsella knows that he must let the child go back to her family and accept the reality that she is not his and never can be. Like Nora, at some deep level he convinced himself that he could hold on to her. Now he must accept the reality of their separation. The narrative ends on a poignant note as both Kinsella and the child embrace: 'For a long stretch he holds me tight,' she says, and refers to something deep within her which 'keeps me there holding on'. The complex relationship which has evolved between Kinsella and the girl is heightened by the fact that the reader is left uncertain as to whether her reference to her 'Daddy' is to Kinsella or to her own father who is coming towards them.

Complex relationships are apparent in each of these comparative texts but the ending of *Foster,* unlike the play and film, raises more questions than it answers.

KEY POINTS

- *Foster* by Claire Keegan presents various complex relationships in a subtle, understated way because the story is told by a child narrator who does not fully understand the dynamics of such relationships. This is a major difference to both of the other two texts.

- From the outset, it is apparent that the child narrator in *Foster* has a distant relationship with her father. They hardly communicate at all with each other. This is quite the opposite of Jack and Nora Clitheroe who engage in very lively, spirited dialogue. It is also different to the more reserved but open discussions between Bertie and Elizabeth which we see at the beginning of *The King's Speech*.

- In common with the resentment Jack feels towards Nora for her deception concerning the burning of his letter in O'Casey's play, the child also resents her father's tendency to be dishonest.

- The lack of affection, intimacy and trust marks this relationship as being quite different to the loving, open one which is apparent between Bertie and Elizabeth and particularly between Bertie and his own children. In many ways this relationship (between Dan and his daughter) is the most complex in any of the three texts due to its unnatural, almost incomprehensible nature. Many questions are left unanswered in the mind of the reader, who struggles to make sense of the situation or find any explanation for Dan's conduct.

- The relationship between the girl's parents, Dan and his wife Mary, is also seen as dysfunctional and lacking in any real love. This is unlike what we see in *The King's Speech*. In O'Casey' play, Nora's hard work to create a decent home can be compared with Mary's only insofar as Nora works hard, keeping lodgers in her home to expand the family finances. Neither Nora nor Mary is fulfilled or happy in marriage because of the conduct of their husbands who neglect their responsibilities towards their wives and the needs of the home.

- The relationship in *Foster* which develops between the child narrator and John Kinsella is complex in many ways. Like Lionel Logue who worked tirelessly to improve Bertie's confidence, Kinsella works tirelessly to build up the child's self-confidence. At times, however, his sharpness shocks and disturbs the girl.

- The differences in social status which can affect relationships negatively and which are apparent in the early relationship between Bertie and Logue in *The King's Speech* also play a part in *Foster*. The child is instantly conscious of the fact that the Kinsellas are wealthy people. When she later returns to her home she is uncomfortably conscious of the difference. Although she has not quite developed the 'notions of upperosity' which Mrs Gogan accuses Nora of, she is clearly feeling like an outsider and the reader is left wondering whether such feelings will have a lasting impact on her relationships with her family members.

- In the same way as fear enters Nora's relationship with Jack and Bertie's relationship with Logue, so fear enters into Kinsella's relationship with the foster child.

- A further complex relationship arises between the child and her mother, which has some parallels with the relationship between Mrs Gogan and Mollser in *The Plough and the Stars*. Poverty influences both mothers who have to balance the needs of their children with the need to work and survive.

- In all three texts there are characters who are hostile in their relationships with their neighbours or who create family tensions. A major difference in the complex relationships with others, exhibited by Bessie Burgess, Wallis Simpson and Mildred, is related to the motivation of each. In the three texts, only Bessie emerges as a more noble character than her earlier actions may have suggested.

- Each of the three texts depicts certain family relationships as being essentially destructive in quality. Jack abandons Nora to follow his ambitions, David abandons his country by abdicating at a time of national crisis and Dan abandons his insecure and confused child when she most needs his loving support. All three men are willing to sacrifice their family relationships in order to pursue their own vision of what is best for themselves. What is very apparent to a careful observer is the fact that each one of these men either delude themselves as to their true motivations or attempt to conceal it from themselves and others.

- It is more difficult in *Foster* than in the other two texts to identify the outcome of the complex relationships which have been explored in the text. Whereas *The Plough and the Stars* ends in the destruction of central relationships through death, *Foster* has a more uncertain conclusion and differs from the positive conclusion of *The King's Speech*, where Bertie and Logue not only resolve any conflicts which arose between them but become lifelong friends.

- Complex relationships are apparent in each of these comparative texts but the ending of *Foster*, unlike the play and film, raises more questions than it answers.

Sample Answer

A. THEME OR ISSUE: COMPLEX RELATIONSHIPS

'The exploration of a central theme adds greatly to our understanding and interpretation of a text'.

Discuss this view with reference to the texts which you have studied for your comparative course.

The exploration of a central relationship in a text, particularly those which are unusually complex in nature, adds greatly to our understanding and interpretation of a narrative.

For my comparative study I have chosen *The Plough and the Stars* by Sean O'Casey, *The King's Speech* directed by Tom Hooper and *Foster* by Claire Keegan. In each of these texts, key relationships are explored revealing conflicts and complexities that are essential aspects of the narrative itself and which play a crucial part in determining the outcome. For purposes of comparison, I am limiting myself to the exploration of one major relationship from each of the texts.

The Plough and the Stars by Sean O'Casey presents the audience with several examples of complex relationships which have an enormous impact on the lives of those personally involved in them and also on the community in which they live. One such relationship is that which exists between Nora and Jack Clitheroe. Likewise, the relationship between King George VI and his speech therapist, Lionel Logue, in *The King's Speech* transforms the King, who must have a 'voice' in order to serve his people at a time of crisis. *Foster*, on the other hand, depicts a dysfunctional child / father relationship which has a transforming effect on the child at a crucial stage in her personal development. Her attachment to her uncle, John Kinsella, fills an emotional void created by the distance her father, Dan, displays in his interactions with her. All three texts can be better understood and interpreted by an analysis of the dynamics in these central relationships.

From the opening scene of O'Casey's play, there is a suggestion that Nora's relationship with her husband, Jack, contains conflicting elements. Mrs Gogan's reference to the 'kissin' an' cuddlin'' and the 'billin' an' cooin'' of the young couple is quickly followed by hints that the love between them may be waning. She cynically remarks that 'afther a month or two, th' wondher of a woman wears off'. The fact that O'Casey opens the play with such a strong emphasis on the conflicts in the relationship between the Clitheroes is an indication of its importance to the interpretation of the play as a whole. The Clitheroes' relationship, like the political issues of the time, is complicated by the conflict between their opposing value systems. Nora is clearly resentful of Jack's military ambitions while Jack is equally resentful at what he considers to be his wife's controlling behaviour. Tension escalates when he learns about the letter concerning his military promotion in the Citizen Army, a letter that Nora withheld from him and destroyed. Nora's rage as she defends her actions is extremely telling: 'Is your home goin' to be only a place to rest in? Am I goin' to be only somethin' to provide merry-makin' at night for you?' When Jack angrily leaves, telling her not to wait up for him, her retort: 'I don't care if you never come back!' is more an expression of her frustration than any real desire to be separated from her husband. It is in this exchange that we see O'Casey emphasising one of the major issues of the play which is necessary to both understanding and interpretation. This issue relates to the importance of the home and the marital relationship as opposed to war and destruction. Jack is attracted by war, associating it with heroism and glory, whereas Nora seeks an escape from the poverty of the tenements in order to establish what she considers to be a respectable home for a family. The worsening conflict between the young couple has major implications later in the play.

Unlike the marital relationship in *The Plough and the Stars*, the first truly complex relationship in *The King's Speech* is that which exists between relative strangers, Bertie (King George VI) and Lionel Logue. Their first encounter is laden with similar tension which is generated by Bertie's frustration, his distrust of Logue's methods and his sense that he is not being treated with the respect due to a member of the royal family. The informality and lack of deference at this meeting astounds Bertie who hardly knows how to react to Logue's claim that 'In here, it's better if we're equals'. One could claim that the desire to be treated as superior arises from Bertie's vanity and creates an immediate barrier between himself and Logue. This would suggest a parallel situation to that observed in O'Casey's play, where Jack Clitheroe seeks to be distinguished from his fellow rebels by being appointed captain in the Citizen Army. However, Bertie's need for respect and deference is linked more to his own poor self-image coupled with an upbringing that led him to expect that he should be treated differently to 'commoners'. This is an important factor in our understanding of his character and dilemma. In contrast to Clitheroe, who actively seeks status, Bertie's status has been imposed on him and creates a social barrier during his first interview with Lionel Logue. Unlike the conflicts observed between Jack and Nora, the conflicts in this relationship are generated by one party and arise, not from an incompatibility of desires or ambitions, but from an inability to adjust to an erosion of class distinctions.

Conflict in a key relationship is also apparent in *Foster*, where the child narrator lacks any real communication with her father. She is being taken to foster parents for an undetermined length of time, but on the journey to her new foster home her father does not explain the reasons or make any effort to allay her anxiety about this situation. Unlike Jack and Nora Clitheroe, who engage in very lively, spirited dialogue, they drive in almost complete silence to the Kinsellas' house. This lack of engagement between Dan and his daughter prepares the reader for what is to come later in the narrative as we witness what is, effectively, a complete rejection of her father by the girl. By carefully examining the child's comments about Dan, the reader moves closer to an understanding of the entire narrative. In common with the resentment Jack feels towards Nora for her deception concerning the burning of his letter, the child also resents her father's tendency to be dishonest. Although her father has done nothing about cutting or saving the hay, he claims that his loft is 'full to capacity' and that he nearly split his head on the rafters 'pitching it in'. Unlike Jack, who confronts Nora about her deception, the child is powerless to contradict her father. She wonders instead why her father 'is given to lying about things that would be nice, if they were true'. Her conflicted emotional state is apparent when she reflects on her situation: 'Part of me wants my father to leave me here while another wants him to take me back, to what I know.' This comment is very revealing as regards the child's emotional state and assists the reader in understanding why she later develops such close bonds with John Kinsella. It highlights the need to love and be loved – especially by a parent.

All three narratives, therefore, exhibit relationships which have important consequences in the narratives as a whole. By exploring the reasons for the conflicts which arise, the reader is assisted in the broader understanding and interpretation of the texts.

As *The Plough and the Stars* progresses, the relationship of the Clitheroes becomes even more complex. Nora refuses to let go of Jack or of her dreams for the future. Although her courage in risking her life to bring Jack home may be seen as evidence of love, there is also an element of possessiveness and a stubborn refusal to accept his decision to fight with his comrades for an ideal in which he believes. Jack Clitheroe himself is deeply conflicted when he is placed in a situation of having to choose between, what he perceives as being his military duty and his relationship with his wife. There is no doubt that his vanity, which Nora tells him will be the 'ruin' of both of them, propels him to choose his role of captain over that of a husband. Earlier in the play, Mrs Gogan reveals that Jack only left the army because he was not appointed to the role of captain: 'He wasn't goin' to be in anything where he couldn't be conspishuous'. Although he later admits to Nora 'I wish to God I'd never left you', Jack cannot tolerate the mockery of Bessie Burgess who asserts that 'General Clitheroe'd rather be unlacin' his wife's bodice than standin' at a barricade'. Vanity triumphs again as he pushes Nora away from him in an effort to save face with his comrades.

A contrast to the worsening rift between Nora and Jack Clitheroe can be observed in the interactions between Logue and his royal client in *The King's Speech*. Here, both men develop a more amicable relationship – at least temporarily. When Bertie hears himself speak without faltering on the recording made by Logue, he returns in desperation to avail of the therapist's services. There is nothing humble or apologetic in his demeanour as he instructs Logue to keep their relationship 'Strictly business. No personal nonsense'. But his attitude softens as Logue explains the need to go below the surface of the speech problem. What is evident in this key scene is the fact that both individuals are willing to engage in some degree of compromise in order to achieve a mutual goal; Bertie wishes to be cured of his speech defect and Logue wishes to cure him. No such common purpose, as we have noted, is apparent between Jack and Nora Clitheroe, which makes compromise an impossibility and increases the conflict between them. Both Bertie and Lionel, by contrast, become closer. After the death of King George V, Bertie's changed attitude becomes more obvious as he confides intimate details of his experiences in childhood to his new 'friend'. Such sharing of traumatic memories helps the reader to understand why Bertie has such low self-esteem and assists how we interpret the narrative. It becomes the story of a man's triumph over adversity and the drastic consequences of wounds inflicted at a very early age.

A similar understanding of the child in *Foster* can be gleaned from her disintegrating regard for her father. The lack of affection, intimacy and trust between Dan and his daughter marks this relationship as being quite different to the loving, open one which is apparent between Bertie and his own children in *The King's Speech*. In a father/child relationship, one expects some indication of care or affection. Unfortunately, this is almost absent in Dan's treatment of his daughter. He tells the Kinsellas that they can 'work her' and leaves her with a warning: 'Try not to fall into the fire, you'. He does not say goodbye to his child but leaves abruptly, forgetting to leave the clothes her mother had packed for her. The hurt of the girl is palpable as she watches him reverse and drive away: 'Why did he leave without so much as a goodbye or even mentioning when he would come back for me?' In many ways this relationship is the most complex in any of the three texts due to its unnatural, almost incomprehensible nature. While the conflict between Nora and Jack in *The Plough and the Stars* can be understood to some extent, as can the tensions between Bertie and Logue in *The King's Speech*, the conflict in *Foster* between Dan and his child leaves many questions unanswered in the mind of the reader, who struggles to make sense of the situation or find any explanation for Dan's conduct. One could even go so far as to claim that an understanding of this central relationship is essential to an understanding of the emerging bond which the child forms with Kinsella and to the interpretation of the whole narrative.

The most complex relationship in O'Casey's play – that of the Clitheroes' marriage – ends in tragedy without any resolution of their previous conflicts. Brennan's report of Jack's alleged last words are an attempt to assist Nora in accepting his death: 'Tell Nora to be brave . . . an' that I'm proud to die for Ireland'. Totally ignoring the deep division in the marriage relationship caused by Jack's desertion of Nora for a vain political 'ideal', Brennan hopes that 'Mrs Clitheroe's grief will be a joy when she realises that she has had a hero for a husband'. The reality, however, is that Nora's life has been ruined by Jack's decision to fight with the rebels rather than to stay with and protect his wife. On the other hand, Nora's own alienation of Jack by her obsessive desire to control him, her burning of his letter of commission and her public shaming of him by hysterical demonstrations of her love also contributed to the devastating outcome for both of them. Through an exploration of this relationship, the reader is enabled to understand and interpret the wider vision of the playwright. O'Casey is clearly demonstrating the destructive impact of a futile war on the lives of ordinary people. The clash of values between the Clitheroes represents the clash of different ideologies which can be destructive of an entire society.

Whereas the outcome of the complex relationship between the Clitheroes ends in devastation, the relationship between Lionel Logue and his king results in triumph. Although there are still several scenes which show conflict and animosity – such as that immediately prior to Bertie's coronation, where Logue is accused of being a cheat and an imposter – the final outcome is very positive. Bertie fully realises that Lionel has gone beyond the bounds of mere duty in order to help him find his true voice. Just before he delivers his speech, he acknowledges the debt he owes to his 'friend': 'No matter how this turns out, I don't know how to thank you for what you've done'. At the end of the film we are informed that 'Lionel and Bertie remained friends for the rest of their lives'. No such happy ending for any relationship is evident in *The Plough and the Stars*, where most of the main characters suffer death, defeat or the loss of potential happiness. Our understanding and interpretation of *The King's Speech* is therefore closely connected to, if not dependent on, the extraordinary, and at times conflicted, relationship between the king and his therapist. Bertie's success was not just the story of one man's determination and courage – it was the story of the courage of two men who were capable of transcending differences in search of a common goal. Their triumph had an impact, not only on themselves but on the entire society.

It is more difficult in *Foster* than in the other two texts to identify the outcome of the complex relationship which has been explored in the text. Whereas *The Plough and the Stars* ends in the destruction of central relationships through death, *Foster* has a more uncertain conclusion which lacks the positive conclusion of *The King's Speech*. There is an awkward moment at the end of *Foster* when the child races after the departing Kinsella, throwing herself into his arms, unwilling to let go of a man whom she has grown to regard as her true 'Daddy'. One cannot but remember the equally anguished final parting of Nora from Jack in *The Plough and the Stars*, where in spite of their love and need for each other the relationship is destroyed by the inevitability of their separation. Kinsella knows that he must let the child go back to her family and accept the reality that she is not his and never can be. Like Nora, at some deep level he convinced himself that he could hold on to her. Now he must accept the reality of their separation. The narrative ends on a poignant note as both Kinsella and the child embrace: 'For a long stretch he holds me tight', she says, and refers to something deep within her which 'keeps me there holding on'. The complex relationship which has evolved between Kinsella and the girl is heightened by the fact that the reader is left uncertain as to whether her reference to her 'Daddy' is to Kinsella or to her own father who is coming towards them. Complex relationships are apparent in each of these comparative texts, but the ending of *Foster*, unlike the play and film, raises more questions than it answers. The reader is left wondering if the child can ever really adapt to life without the Kinsellas or ever form a meaningful relationship with her biological father.

Each of the three texts provides the reader with several other interesting and revealing relationships. For example the relationship between Bessie Burgess and her neighbours in *The Plough and the Stars* is both fascinating and illuminating. Similarly, David's relationship with Wallis Simpson which leads to his abdication, acts as a foil to the supportive, dutiful relationship between Bertie and Elizabeth in *The King's Speech*. Dan's relationship with his wife Mary in *Foster* highlights his irresponsibility and is strongly contrasted with the marital harmony which exists between the Kinsellas. All of these relationships also aid in our understanding and interpretation of the texts.

However, the more central relationships which I have discussed throughout this essay are not only interesting but absolutely crucial in achieving understanding. The exploration of the conflicts and complexities of these relationships certainly helped to guide me in forming a personal interpretation of the authors' intentions.

B. General Vision and Viewpoint

The Plough and the Stars

The general vision or viewpoint of a text relates to the authorial/directorial outlook on life. This viewpoint inevitably influences our perspective on the text and on the world in which it is set. The vision of an author can be conveyed through his/her attitude towards significant events in the political or social background of a society, through key characters and relationships and also through language and imagery. Often, the dominant viewpoint of a text can be reflected in a key moment.

O'Casey's viewpoint concerning the power of politics to divide a society and bring about destruction and desolation is essentially negative. The play is set in 1916 in the Dublin tenements when people were rebelling against Ireland's status as a British colony and against poverty and deprivation. A people without a voice easily adopt patriotic slogans and catchwords which can lead to destructive consequences for those influenced by the rhetoric of others. The hero-worship of dead patriots and the linking of politics with religion had the potential at that time to make impoverished people believe that they also could become martyrs in the cause of an Irish Republic. In Act II, the Voice of the Man, an unnamed character who delivers passionate speeches on the glory of bloodshed during war to his listeners during this Act, declares that war is 'the Angel of God'. Suffering, bloodshed and death are seen as 'a cleansing and sanctifying thing'. The death of Jack Clitheroe, a key character in the play, is depicted as being a 'gleam of glory' and Nora, his widow, is expected to experience 'a joy when she realises that she has had a hero for a husband'. This empty rhetoric is in marked contrast to the reality of the situation.

Jack Clitheroe sees himself and his fellow nationalists in the Citizen Army (an organisation set up to prepare to fight for Ireland's independence from Britain) as being true freedom fighters who take inspiration from the sacrifices being made in World War I, which is taking place in Europe at the same time. He, Langan and Brennan (fellow Citizen Army members) openly state their willingness to die, if necessary, to set Ireland free from British rule. They perceive themselves to be patriots and soldiers but their slogans and fine words reverberate with hollowness, 'Ireland is greater than a mother…greater than a wife'. They claim to welcome and embrace 'Imprisonment…wounds…death' for Ireland but their apparent loyalty is depicted as being not only misguided but really a proclamation of their own intense vanity. Nora, in Act I, angrily expresses this when she asks Jack 'Is General Connolly an' th' Citizen Army goin' to be your only care? Is your home only goin' to be a place to rest in? Am I goin' to be only somethin' to provide merry-making at night for you? Your vanity'll be the ruin of you an' me yet'. Although many may claim that O'Casey's view is very negative towards men like Jack Clitheroe, who were genuine in wanting to make the sacrifices that they made, the reality is that many people suffered death and desolation as a result of the actions of the men of 1916 and this is not something of which O'Casey approves.

In direct contrast to the nationalists in the play, Bessie Burgess, a resident of the tenement building in which the Clitheroes live, is a staunch loyalist who believes that those involved in the uprising are traitors. Her son, whom she sees as a true hero, is serving with the Dublin Fusiliers in World War I in France. She angrily attacks those who have not joined the British Army to fight in the World War, 'There's th' men marchin' out into the dhread dimness o' danger, while th' lice is crawlin' about feedin' on the fatness o' th' land'. Bessie's singing of 'Rule Britannia' is meant to inflame the men whom she declares are 'all nicely shanghaied [tricked into an action] now' when the rebellion is brutally quashed. There is something profoundly sad in the fact that Bessie will not be able to 'Keep the home fires burning' for her only son, as she loses her life later in the play.

The Young Covey, Jack's cousin who lives with the couple, is also extremely hostile to the Citizen Army but for different reasons to those of Bessie. He believes that the men should be fighting for social justice rather than political freedom, 'There's only one freedom for the workin' man'. He creates conflict by arguing with Fluther and Peter, other tenement residents, about the links between religion and politics. He is deeply critical of the use of the flag of the Plough and the Stars by nationalists, an act which he considers a betrayal of the working classes whom the flag is meant to represent: 'it's a Labour flag an' was never meant for politics' he tells Jack. He refers to the nationalists as 'th' mugs' who have to 'renew their political baptismal vows' in order to be loyal to their Republican ideals. He claims that 'There's no such thing as an Irishman, or an Englishman, or a German or a Turk; we're all only human bein's'. This attitude of The Young Covey causes uproar with Fluther who describes his neighbour as 'a word-weavin' little ignorant yahoo of a red flag socialist'.

From the above examples and from many other moments in the play, it is clear that O'Casey has a profoundly negative attitude towards the power of political divisions to destroy a community. We see the illogical pointlessness of the struggle at the end when Bessie Burgess is shot by the British soldiers whom she was so loudly praising earlier. Many of the nationalists have also been killed and wounded without achieving the freedom of their ideals. Mollser, a teenage girl dying of tuberculosis in the tenement, sums up the attitude of the playwright himself when she asks Nora, 'Is there anybody goin', Mrs Clitheroe, with a titther o' sense?'

O'Casey, while admiring to some extent the courage of the men who fought and died in 1916, is clearly disillusioned by nationalism. He is outraged by the deflection of the labour cause and socialist ideals into nationalistic politics. He is both critical and condemnatory, using the full range of rhetoric, colloquialisms,

irony and caricature to highlight the tragic forces at play and the futility and waste of life and effort. The general vision and viewpoint of his play is thus essentially dark and pessimistic.

O'Casey's ironic view of posturing and cowardice is revealed in the course of the play and adds to the pervading negativity. Several of the men in the play are depicted as weak and inadequate. Some characters engage in absurd posturing. This is particularly true of The Young Covey and Peter, Nora's uncle. The Young Covey proclaims himself to be a socialist and enjoys displaying his knowledge and understanding of 'Jenersky's Thesis'. There is no doubt that he has a point in his objections to nationalism and its effect on the community. However, he is not as humane as he claims to be as can be seen when he attacks Rosie Redmond, another neighbour, and belittles her by calling her a prostitute. Later, he is more than willing to engage in looting, hurrying Fluther on with the words, 'Come on then, or there won't be anything left to save'. Peter also engages in self-delusion, proudly dressing himself in his Foresters' uniform, even though the society's only function seems to be an annual march to Wolfe Tone's grave. Fluther boasts that he has not missed a 'pilgrimage to Bodenstown' in 25 years and never failed to 'pluck a leaf off Tone's grave'. Although he claims during the patriotic speech in Act II that he is 'burnin'' to draw me sword, an' wave, an' wave it over me', his heroism is merely a façade. The only reason he does not go looting with the others is because he is afraid of being shot. Defeated by his own cowardice, he sanctimoniously condemns the looters, 'Makin' a shame an' a sin o' the cause that good men are fightin' for'. With his gaudy uniform of the Foresters and his loud declarations of valour, he represents very little that is truly admirable. His appalling self-centredness is shown when, hearing the sound of rifle shots, he tries to shut the door against Bessie and Mrs Gogan before they can get to safety. Bessie sums him up well when she describes him as 'a little sermonising, little yella-faced, little consequential, little pudgy, little bum...'. Despite the humour of the dialogue and characterisation, there is no doubt that the playwright is highlighting the hypocrisy and shallowness of certain characters who profess the highest ideals.

The extreme poverty of the Dublin City tenements strikes a note of gloom from the outset of the play. O'Casey refers to the tenement building as being originally a fine building but now 'struggling for life against the assault of time, and the more savage assaults of the tenants'. Because Nora is attempting to upgrade her accommodation, she is accused by Mrs Gogan of having 'notions of upperosity' and of being 'able to make a shillin' go where another would have to spend a pound'. Bessie Burgess's words are indicative of the poor condition of the tenements when she accuses Nora of putting a lock on her door for fear ' her poor neighbours ud break through an' steal'. Such comments reveal the claustrophobic intimacy of life in the tenement building where everybody knows and comments on the business of everybody else and where poverty abounds. In addition, in order to make ends meet, Nora has to share her home with Uncle Peter and The Young Covey which leaves very little privacy for her marriage and relationship with Jack Clitheroe. Rosie Redmond seems to have been driven into prostitution by poverty and the need to survive. Perhaps Mollser, the malnourished and dying child, most embodies the poverty and deprivation of the time. The Young Covey highlights this when he says of Mollser, 'Sure she never got any care. How could she get it, an' the mother out day an' night lookin' for work, an' her consumptive husband leavin' her with a baby to be born before he died'. Not only is Mollser a victim of the hideous poverty of the tenements but a victim of sickness and lack of proper care. The depiction of such harshnesss of daily life in the tenements creates a dark and depressing atmosphere throughout.

The extent to which comedy is used serves to intensify and exacerbate the tragic vision which lies at the heart of the play. Sean O'Casey described the play as being 'A Tragedy in Four Acts', despite the presence of many comic elements. In Act I, the snooping, nosy nature of Mrs Gogan and her comments on Nora's new hat, which she furtively tries on, initially create a light-hearted, humorous atmosphere. Further humour is introduced by Fluther and Uncle Peter. Both men are comic creations. Fluther, who is attempting to give up drinking alcohol, constantly misuses the word 'derogatory' assuring Mrs Gogan that there 'is nothing derogatory wrong with me' when she comments on his cough. However, Mrs Gogan's anecdote about the woman who died of a 'tickle in her throat', gives rise to a comical panic attack in Fluther who instantly believes that his cough is getting worse and that he is beginning to feel dizzy: 'I hope that I didn't give up th' beer too soon'. Peter, with his face 'shaped like a lozenge' adds an extra element of farce with his childish obsession concerning his Forester's uniform which, according to Mrs Gogan, makes him look 'like somethin' you'd pick off a Christmas tree'. However, although the audience may succumb to laughter at the clownish antics and the comic dialogue, a more fitting response to the general vision of the play would be anger at the political beliefs and at the effects of poverty which destroyed people like the Clitheroes, Bessie and Mollser.

The poignant loss of the happiness that Jack and Nora once experienced in their marriage adds a further negative tone to the play. Mrs Gogan seems to have insight into the nature of Nora and Jack Clitheroes' relationship when she says of Jack that 'the mystery of havin' a woman's a mystery no longer ' and that Nora is like a 'clockin' hen if he [Jack] leaves her sight for a minute'. Mrs Gogan is a comical character but these remarks flag the importance of the Clitheroes' relationship to the central tragedy. The opening act reveals that the source of this conflict is related to Jack's membership of the revolutionary Citizen Army. When General Connolly sends Captain Brennan with battle orders to Jack Clitheroe he is engaging in the destruction of the domestic order that Nora strives so hard to maintain. After a touching love scene between husband and wife, in which Jack sings Nora a love song, calamity strikes. An officer arrives with orders for Jack to actively engage in combat. Nora's desperate plea to her husband to 'Pretend we're not in… don't break our happiness', falls on deaf ears as Jack, enraged that she has deceived him by hiding a letter which appointed him as a Commandant in the Citizen Army, storms out of the room, declaring that he will be home very late and that she needn't wait up for him. Nora's bitter response – 'I don't care if you never come back' – sums up the despair she feels when her husband makes his political ambition and vanity more important than his marriage. This disintegration of what was once a loving relationship casts a gloom over this section of the play. Although he has effectively abandoned her, Nora's love for Jack is unshakeable. It is beyond her comprehension that any woman would willingly sacrifice her husband to a political ideal: 'If they say it, they're lyin', against God, Nature an' against themselves'. Her cursing of the rebels and her broken-hearted cry that war has 'dhriven' away th' little happiness life had to spare for me' is profoundly upsetting and true. Later, when Jack briefly returns, only to desert her again, she cries pathetically 'Oh Jack, I gave you everything you asked of me'. Nora then descends quickly into insanity under the pressure of her loss and suffers a miscarriage. Bessie Burgess, filled now with compassion for Nora's sad state, remarks that 'her eyes have a hauntin' way of lookin' in instead of lookin' out'. Indeed, O'Casey's general vision and viewpoint is summed up by Bessie when she exclaims: 'Blessing o' God on us, isn't this pitiful'.

Despite the predominantly pessimistic vision there are moments when O'Casey celebrates the human spirit. Bessie not only supports Nora when Jack deserts her, she also risks her own life by going for a doctor when Nora has her miscarriage. This courage is all the more impressive when one remembers the conflict between them earlier, when she flew at Nora 'like a tiger' and attempted to 'guzzle' her. Bessie also displays a tremendous compassion and humanity in her kindness towards Mollser. Mrs Gogan appreciates Bessie's generosity to her daughter. She thanks Bessie for 'all your gentle hurryin's to me little Mollser . . . never passin'

her without liftin' up her heart with a delicate word o' kindness'. We learn that Bessie offered food to Mollser at a time when food was in very short supply and to do so would be a genuine personal sacrifice. Fluther Good also reveals a courageous and compassionate nature when he risks his own life bringing Nora back from the barricades. These acts of humanity and courage affirm the audience's belief that human beings can rise above self-interest and become heroic in spite of the human failings which they inevitably possess.

A significant event that shows the dominant vision of the play occurs in the final act. Bessie's sterling quality (i.e. of the highest quality), which is celebrated by O'Casey in his portrayal of women in the play, adds to the horror and shock of her death. She is shot by British soldiers as she is trying to protect the hysterical Nora from dangerously approaching the window during a gun battle. O'Casey builds up the tension skilfully. First we hear a burst of rifle fire and rapid shots from a machine gun. The distraught Nora, crying for her husband and her miscarried baby, wakens the sleeping Bessie, who rushes forward to protect her from a window that she has opened. Frantically Bessie drags Nora, pleading with her, 'Come away, come away woman, from that window!' The strength she used forces her to stagger against the window herself. The stage directions tell us that 'Bessie jerks her body convulsively; stands stiffly for a moment, a look of agonised astonishment on her face . . .'. Her screams of fear and pain make a tremendous impact on the audience who, in disbelief, realise that she is critically injured, 'I'm shot, I'm shot, I'm shot! . . . Th' life's pourin' out o' me'. Her death is one of the darkest and most moving moments in the play; she cries out as she is dying: 'Jesus Christ, me sight's goin'! It's all dark, dark! Nora, hold me hand!' This event, which effectively marks the end of the play, leaves no doubt that O'Casey's general vision and viewpoint is profoundly pessimistic. Hopes and ideals have been extinguished and lives have been destroyed in so many diverse ways throughout the entire play.

KEY POINTS

- O'Casey's viewpoint concerning the power of politics to divide a society and bring about destruction and desolation is essentially negative.
- The playwright's negative, ironic view of posturing and cowardice is revealed through the characterisation. Many of the men in the play are depicted as weak and inadequate. They engage in hollow rhetoric and self-delusion.
- The extreme poverty of the Dublin City tenements strikes a note of gloom from the outset. Poverty can be seen as a tragic force which drives individuals to desperate lengths to survive and which is also partially responsible for the deaths of Mollser and her father from tuberculosis, a disease which was rampant at the time and most easily spread in crowded tenement dwellings.
- The extent to which comedy is used serves to intensify and exacerbate the tragic vision which lies at the heart of the play.
- The poignant loss of the happiness that Jack and Nora once experienced in their marriage adds a further negative tone to the play.
- Despite the predominantly pessimistic vision there are moments when O'Casey celebrates the human spirit. This is most evident in the unexpected heroism and humanity of Bessie Burgess and Fluther Good.
- The death of Bessie, which effectively brings the play to a close, emphasises the darkness of the overall vision.

The King's Speech and *The Plough and the Stars*

The general vision and viewpoint of *The King's Speech*, directed by Tom Hooper, is essentially positive and optimistic.

Unlike O'Casey's *The Plough and the Stars* which depicts the power of politics to divide a society and bring about destruction and desolation, *The King's Speech* shows how, with courageous and dedicated leadership, a society can act together in the fight for freedom and democracy.

The film deals with the emergence of King George VI in Britain as a figurehead who is capable of inspiring his people and uniting them during the lead-up to and duration of World War II, a time of political upheaval and conflict. Insofar as it deals with an inspirational speech, it could be said that both O'Casey's play and this film acknowledge the powerful influence a rousing political speech can have

in rallying people to a cause. In *The Plough and the Stars*, the Voice of the Man delivers a stirring, persuasive call to arms, which makes a huge impact on many of the listeners and further inspires men like Jack Clitheroe, Langan and Brennan to resolve to die in the cause of Republicanism. The Voice speaks with determination and authority, 'We must accustom ourselves to the thought of arms, we must accustom ourselves to the sight of arms, we must accustom ourselves to the use of arms . . .' However, in spite of such powerful rhetoric and fine appeals to patriotic fervour, there is no doubt that the playwright's point of view is essentially critical and disapproving of such sentiments. The viewpoint of *The King's Speech* is quite different. The plot culminates in King George VI's first wartime Christmas address of 1939. Backed by swelling music, there are repeated cuts from the radio studio, where the King is

103

broadcasting, to the rapt faces of listeners in homes and factories across his kingdom. These crowds of ordinary citizens listen with respectful attention and without any of the farcical posturing of men like Fluther or Peter in O'Casey's play who engage in hysterical fits of boasting and proclamations of potential heroism. King George's speech is far more measured in tone than that of the Voice of the Man and appeals to reason to explain why a nation should engage in a war, 'We have been forced into a conflict. For we are called, with our allies, to meet the challenge of a principle, which, if it were to prevail, would be fatal to any civilised order in the world. Such a principle, stripped of all disguise, is surely the mere primitive doctrine that might is right'. Unlike the Voice of the Man in *The Plough and the Stars* who rejoices in the exhilaration of 'this bloody war' and declares that it is 'not an evil thing', King George acknowledges that men can only 'do the right as we see the right and reverently commit ourselves to God'. The point of view revealed in the film's screenplay and directing is clearly one of admiration for a man of peace, who has no desire to embroil his people in military combat but understands the absolute need to do so in the particular political situation. When he finishes his speech, King George and his family go onto the balcony of Buckingham Palace, where they are met by cheers of approval and acceptance by their subjects. There are no signs of the divisions and conflicts such as those witnessed between The Young Covey and his neighbours. War is thus seen as an unwelcome but necessary thing in the film, where a nation is portrayed as being united, whereas it is seen as disruptive, unnecessary and futile in O'Casey's play. In addition, the audience is fully aware in advance that the 1916 Rising will be suppressed, whereas the Allies were successful in winning World War II. This prior knowledge contributes to the understanding of the general vision and viewpoint of each text.

It is important to bear in mind that the viewpoint of the film as regards political situations and war is far more limited than that which is evident in *The Plough and the Stars*. It is also important to remember that

film-makers can take liberties with historical accuracy. This film is not a documentary and there are several points which do not correspond to historical fact. This is particularly true of the role played by Winston Churchill, a man who openly supported King Edward VIII, rather than being one of his major critics as the film suggests.

In contrast to *The Plough and the Stars* where we see the playwright's open disapproval of social revolution, *The King's Speech* engages in a more positive view through oblique references to the same danger. There are occasional hints at the real concerns involved. Just before King George V's death, Bertie and his father discuss the pressing political issues. His father poses the question of a potential war when he says 'Who will stand between us, the jackboots [thugs – in this case, Germany], and the proletarian abyss [Russia]?' The threats from Hitler and Stalin are thus acknowledged. Later, after his father's death, Bertie discusses the unfolding political situation with the new king, his brother Edward VIII, warning him of the revolutionary threats that are facing the royal families of Europe. Edward offhandedly says that he has been terribly busy 'kinging', a comment which suggests that considering such political issues is not of much importance to him as king. **'Really? Kinging? Kinging is a precarious business,' replies Bertie, appalled by his brother's apparent indifference to the political threats.** Such oblique references to the danger of social revolution are, however, as far as the film goes in offering a viewpoint on the merits of war.

In common with *The Plough and the Stars*, *The King's Speech* is negative in its depiction of certain characters. The reason that Bertie ascended to the throne of England was due to the fact that his older brother, David (Edward VIII), decided to abdicate so that he could marry an American divorcee by the name of Wallis Simpson. In the film, Edward VIII is presented as childish and cruel to his brother, mocking his stutter, 'That's the scoop around town. Yearning for a larger audience are we, B-b-b-Bertie?'

He is also presented as having, like many of O'Casey's characters, shallow political views. He is disinterested in Bertie's genuine concerns about 'people marching across Europe singing The Red Flag' and makes a foolish comment about the Nazis, 'Stop your worrying. Herr Hitler will sort that lot out.' (The film does not mention that Edward VIII was actually an ardent admirer of Hitler and of fascism). Edward is thus presented as being little more than a ridiculous, selfish and self-indulgent individual who concentrates on the woman he loves at the expense of the welfare of his country and its people. His reaction to being made king after the death of his father is to fall into his mother's arms, sobbing pitifully, before he runs from the room. Mistaking his brother's reaction as grief, Bertie attempts to comfort him only to discover that the grief is all for David himself and Wallis, 'Poor Wallis. Now I'm trapped'. The abdication speech made by Edward VIII reminds us of some of the self-deluding hollow rhetoric observed in *The Plough and the Stars*. Particularly obnoxious is his claim that he is abdicating in the common interest rather than his own. He would find it 'impossible' to 'discharge [his] duties as king' he tells the nation, unless he has the 'help and support' of Wallis Simpson. His praise of Bertie's ability to discharge the same duties seems insincere when one considers his earlier derogatory remarks about, and treatment of, his brother. Now, when it suits him, he can describe Bertie as a man with 'fine qualities' who will be able to ascend the throne 'without interruption or injury to the life and progress of the empire'.

Wallis Simpson, in direct contrast to a character like Bessie Burgess in *The Plough and the Stars*, also emerges as a shallow, self-obsessed character. Her selfishness is blatantly obvious during a scene in which David is having a telephone conversation with her while his father is dying. Instead of offering support and comfort to her lover, Wallis apparently focuses on the fact that she misses David 'terribly'. He needs to placate her by acknowledging this fact, 'I know, darling, a talk, even a lovely long talk, is a poor substitute for holding tight and making drowsy'. When David becomes Edward VIII, she becomes

even more insufferable. Bertie's wife, Elizabeth, is aware that she is referred to by Mrs Simpson as 'The fat Scottish cook'. One of Wallis's first actions is to fell trees at a royal Scottish estate in order to improve her view of the surrounding countryside. Bertie and Elizabeth are aghast at this action with Elizabeth exclaiming in horror, 'Five hundred year old oaks . . . to improve the view!' When we actually see Wallis herself, she is dripping in jewellery, clinging to David's arm and condescendingly inviting her royal visitors to 'our little country shack'. Her control of the new king is apparent when she imperiously taps her champagne glass, waves off a footman who hastens to serve her and waits rather impatiently while her lover springs into action. As he hunts for the particular champagne which 'Wally likes the best', David is heard calling to her, 'Just be a sec, darling!'

Not only is Wallis a controlling mistress where David is concerned, she is also presented as being somewhat liberal and experienced in her relationships with men. This contrasts with the genuine love of Nora for Jack. Although Nora does stoop to deception by burning Jack's letter of commission, she does so out of genuine love and in an effort to keep him with her. She certainly lacks the 'skills' of a woman like Wallis Simpson. When Winston Churchill wonders what 'hold' Wallis has on David, Elizabeth responds by saying 'Apparently she has certain . . . skills, which she learnt in an establishment in Shanghai'. One could imagine that Elizabeth is exaggerating or joking here were it not for the fact that the Prime Minister, Stanley Baldwin has been informed by Scotland Yard that 'the King does not possess exclusive rights to Mrs Simpson's favours and affections, sharing them with a married used car salesman, a certain Mr Guy Trundle'.

It is profoundly ironic that a woman who was not only twice a divorcee but a 'commoner' in the eyes of the British Royal Family should have so much control and power over the new king. At no stage does she oppose his decision to abdicate in order to marry her, probably considering his action as being totally appropriate in the circumstances. Her small-minded attitude, exploitation of power over her lover and disregard for the needs of others make her a pathetic figure who lacks the humanity and selflessness of some of the poorest characters from O'Casey's Dublin tenements. That a king should abdicate his throne for such a creature is one of the major ironies and indeed, puzzling questions of *The King's Speech*.

The last we see of Edward and Wallis in the film is when they listen dolefully to Bertie's speech from a villa somewhere in the South of France. The clear implication is that their actions and decisions have not delivered the happiness they expected.

The Plough and the Stars and *The King's Speech* are both texts which present a vision of the damage which can be inflicted on individuals or societies by the thoughtless, selfish actions and aspirations of others.

Poverty is not as influential in creating a negative atmosphere in *The King's Speech* as it is in O'Casey's play. It would be true to say that there is actually no depiction of the crippling type of poverty experienced by the tenement dwellers of Dublin in 1916. Lionel Logue, Bertie's Australian speech therapist, is not, however, a wealthy man. His consultation rooms are, according to the screenplay, in 'the least attractive and most ill-maintained of the Georgian terraced houses' in Harley Street. He cannot afford to employ a receptionist and lives with his family in a modest London flat. He is a failed actor who strives unsuccessfully to audition for a part in a Shakespearean play. Although he does not suffer devastating poverty, the splendour and wealth of the royal palaces highlight his relatively humble circumstances. Unlike the inhabitants of the Dublin tenements in O'Casey's play, the Logue family enjoy privacy in their home and are happy with the simple things of life. Lionel's eldest son, Laurie, drives his parents around in a well-used Morris Oxford which sounds quite old and battered and the other Logue children play with simple, home-made toys. Books, however, are in fine supply and highlight Logue's love of learning and literature.

The atmosphere is not one of deprivation but of a contented though simple family lifestyle.

The director's vision of happiness as not being linked to or dependent on wealth is apparent when one hears the details of Bertie's privileged yet unhappy childhood as a young prince. Although he does not suffer from material poverty, there is an emotional poverty which casts a shadow over the film. Bertie confides in Lionel, telling him about his harsh upbringing where his siblings were encouraged by their father to tease him whenever he stuttered. His father's philosophy on child-rearing was cold and callous, 'I was afraid of my father, and my children are damn well going to be afraid of me'. He was cared for by a sadistic nanny who pinched him so that he'd cry during the 'daily viewing' sessions with his parents. Not only was he distanced emotionally from his parents but was forced, though naturally left-handed, to write with his right hand – an imposition which accounted in part for the development of his stutter. The Logue children, being 'commoners', are far better off than the young princes of the realm. They enjoy a normal, happy family life with parents who clearly love and care for them. It is refreshing also to observe the tender affection which Bertie has for his young daughters, Elizabeth and Margaret. It appears that Bertie has managed to set aside the practices of an earlier age and form close bonds with his own children. This creates a very positive viewpoint, which is further enhanced by Bertie's triumph over his speech impediment.

When we observe the lives of the tenement dwellers in *The Plough and the Stars* there is no doubt that their extreme poverty accounts for much of the play's pessimism and despair. O'Casey has a dark vision of life whereas *The King's Speech* shows that human happiness is not so much due to wealth and status as to acceptance and love.

Both texts have many comic moments which often serve to intensify and exacerbate that which is serious or even, at times, tragic. In common with *The Plough and the Stars, The King's Speech* is a powerful and deeply moving story told against the backdrop of a critical juncture in history. Both texts employ the use of humour to highlight their respective viewpoints. Both texts also succeed in transforming history into an approachable blend of drama and wit.

Whereas O'Casey's play opens with broad humour as Mrs Gogan tries on Nora's new hat and scares the wits out of Fluther with a story about a woman who died of a cough, *The King's Speech* **immediately plunges the audience into a tense situation as Bertie, the stuttering Duke of York, faces the daunting prospect of giving his 'inaugural broadcast to the nation and the world'.** There is no use of humour as the tension builds unbearably. Bertie approaches the microphone, his eyes widen in terror, the lights blink four times, turn solid and he is 'live' on air. Nervous glances are exchanged by BBC technicians as they stare at dials and listen to the hiss of silence. The discomfort grows in the listening crowds at Wembley Stadium, as Bertie, his voice quivering, attempts to speak, 'I have received from his Majesty the K-K-K . . .' The film then cuts to a new scene and the atmosphere changes from tragedy to comedy as we see the posturing of Sir Blandine-Bentham, an elderly, obsequious (fawning, servile) physician, who is attempting to cure Bertie of his speech impediment. One cannot but laugh at the farcical manner in which he uses forceps to deliver five 'sterilised' marbles into his patient's hand with the instruction that he place them in his mouth. After attempting to speak, Bertie spits the marbles out exclaiming that he 'nearly swallowed the damn things'. In a fit of rage he tells his wife that the doctor can 'insert his own bloody marbles . . .' Both texts use humour to highlight the actual tragedy of the situations. Fluther's terror of his cough worsening has a rational basis in the prevalence of tuberculosis and the speed with which people succumbed to it. This was particularly true of the poor who had to live in close proximity with other sufferers in the tenements. Likewise, in spite of the humour in the ridiculous 'treatments' being offered to Bertie, there is a tragedy in the spectacle of a vulnerable man being humiliated by his own inability to speak.

Tremendous humour is later created, as it is in O'Casey's play, from the clash of differing personalities. The confident outspoken Lionel Logue refuses to engage in any obsequiousness with the temperamental, snobbish but stuttering Royal. Logue's bizarre treatments are designed to shock his patient, whom he impertinently insists on calling 'Bertie'. He makes him lie on the floor, doing exercises to strengthen his diaphragm while his wife, Elizabeth, perches on his chest and asks 'Are you alright, Bertie?' before telling him that 'This is actually quite good fun'. And, in a key moment, Logue succeeds in getting him to swear. 'Say the 'F' word," he commands. 'Fornication?' howls Bertie, before escalating to a chorus of 'shits', 'buggers' and 'fucks'. However, despite the humour and the tension which laughter relieves, this moment couldn't be more tender or uplifting as it shows, for the first time, that Bertie is indeed capable of expressing himself openly and is becoming liberated by doing so.

The role of humour serves to underscore and highlight the human suffering and darkness at the heart of both texts. *The Plough and the Stars* deals with the suffering of ordinary people attempting to cope with the circumstances in which they find themselves. In a similar way, *The King's Speech* shows an individual attempting to cope and survive in the circumstances in which he finds himself. The film is not actually about fixing Bertie's voice, but fixing a mind bullied by a father and brother since boyhood, a soul imprisoned by the burden of unwanted kingship. The director plays on the idea of a traumatic childhood as Bertie begins to open up to Logue while gently completing a model plane. The tragedy is that he never had a childhood. Friendship is a voyage into the unknown for Bertie. Logue is, metaphorically, glueing him together by helping him to find his voice. Despite the use of humour in each text, the tragedy of personal experience surfaces and adds a dark note to the general vision of each narrative.

The texts differ in their viewpoints concerning fidelity in love and marriage. The poignant loss and destruction of the Clitheroes' relationship in O'Casey's play contributes to the general pessimistic vision. By contrast, marriage is seen in both positive and negative lights in *The King's Speech*. Jack Clitheroe abandons his fidelity to Nora, deserting his wife and unborn child in order to fulfil a political ambition and satisfy his own vanity. He engages in the Easter Rising of 1916 without fully considering the consequences of his actions on his own family. This sacrifice of wife and child to apparently serve Mother Ireland is clearly disapproved of by O'Casey and contributes to the overall vision of despair and gloom. In complete contrast to this viewpoint, *The King's Speech* pours scorn on King Edward VIII who abdicated his role as his country's leader in order to marry Wallis Simpson. Some would claim that Edward did the honourable and noble thing by giving up his throne for the woman he loved. At one point in the play he tells Bertie that Wallis is '. . . not just some woman I am carrying on with. This is the woman I intend to marry'. He refuses to simply have her as a 'mistress' or to 'just give her a nice house and a title'. Unlike Jack Clitheroe, he is not tempted to abandon his relationship for a title or a political principle. However, Edward VIII is not portrayed as a sympathetic or admirable character for his fidelity to Wallis Simpson. His story is not one about tremendous love but rather a story about tremendous selfishness. Instead of doing his duty by unifying and leading his country in a time of threatened war, he abdicated, thereby placing the burden on a brother whom he knew never wanted to be king and who, because of his speech impediment, was ill-suited to that role. His actions are seen as self-serving despite his attempts to assure his countrymen that he is acting in their best interests because he would be 'unable to discharge [his] duties as king without the help and support' of the woman he loved. Given the negative portrayal of David before he became Edward VIII and his shallowness and cruelty towards his brother, the audience is not convinced. His abdication is viewed as an act of supreme selfishness, almost amounting to treason. The viewpoint here is essentially negative towards Edward and suggests that

public duty takes precedence over affairs of the heart – especially in times of social upheaval or conflict. George V, the father of David and Bertie, also presents a negative attitude to marriage in his comments about the acceptance of adultery in relationships. Love and fidelity are seemingly of little importance to him.

On the other hand, there are two very positive depictions of marital relationships in the film. Bertie's marriage to Elizabeth is portrayed as being supportive and loving as is the relationship between Lionel Logue and his wife. Happiness is seen as possible in both of these households and creates a positive vision of marriage and family life.

As in *The Plough and the Stars*, there are moments in which the portrayal of the human spirit in a positive light adds to our understanding of the general vision and viewpoint. In O'Casey's play we see heroism in the actions of individuals like Bessie Burgess and, to a lesser extent, Fluther Good. These characters are not without their human faults and failings but it is their ability to rise above such limitations which inspires our admiration and affirms our belief in human nature. King George VI illustrates this uplifting aspect of the human spirit in *The King's Speech*. His struggle against his speech impediment boosts our appreciation of the human capacity to become the best one can be and to rise to even the most daunting challenge. As the writer David Seidler said in the introduction to his screenplay for the film: 'Bertie never thought he would be king – he wasn't meant to be king, wasn't trained to be king, nor with his stutter was he suited to be king. But when he had to be king, he came to the fore and did his job'. This coming to the fore was far from easy. With his self-confidence in shreds as a result of a harsh childhood where he was bullied, mocked and degraded, he had to face the expectations of a nation on the brink of war. He had to become king. At one stage, when confronted by his domineering father and ordered to speak into the microphone, he could only manage to stutter out, 'D-d-don't thu-thu-think I c-c-can'. The camera shots show us a pathetic figure breathing quickly with his neck muscles in spasm. He is far from a perfect character and, like Bessie Burgess, can explode in fits of rage and ill-temper. He turns savagely on Lionel Logue at another point in the film telling him to 'Bugger off!' and later accuses him of 'ensnaring a star patient you knew you couldn't possibly assist!' However, he is aware that his temper gets the better of him, struggles to succeed and is genuinely grateful to Lionel for his service to him. A wonderful moment comes when he shouts at Lionel saying 'I HAVE A VOICE!!!' to which Lionel calmly responds, 'Yes you do. You have such perseverance Bertie, you're the bravest man I know, and you'll make a bloody good king'.

A significant event which determines the film's general vision and viewpoint comes at the end. In direct contrast to the descent into madness of Nora and the harrowing death of Bessie Burgess in O'Casey's play, *The King's Speech* ends on a note of triumph over adversity.

After war has been declared by Chamberlain, Bertie faces the prospect of having to make a key address to the nation. His old terrors surface as he nervously practises with Logue, who gently and calmly guides him to 'turn the hesitations into pauses'. As Bertie insists 'I cannot do this', his therapist, who has now become his friend, reassures him, 'Bertie, you can

do this!' The practice session takes the audience once more through the singing, stammering, cursing techniques with which we have become familiar. Tension rises as Bertie makes his way through the palace, towards the microphone. If Bertie stumbles and fails to deliver the speech, his efforts and struggles, like those of O'Casey's patriots, will be seen to be in vain. An exquisite scene follows in which we see the king deliver a fluent and persuasive speech to an amazed but delighted audience. This performance of, literally, the king's speech consolidates the dominant optimistic vision of the entire film, which is not really about the outbreak of war but about the war a man waged with himself, and won!

All that remains is for the King to step out onto the balcony of Buckingham Palace to be cheered by an ecstatic crowd. He, his wife and their children wave to the crowds, accepting their adulation and love. The film ends with Lionel happily observing the scene from the shadows. An onscreen card tells us that 'Lionel was with the King for every wartime speech' and that 'George VI became a symbol of national resistance'. The audience is aware, of course, that the war was won. This outcome establishes the general vision and viewpoint as being immensely positive, affirming the belief that courage can prevail against even the most difficult obstacles.

KEY POINTS

- The attitude to political power as seen in *The King's Speech* is essentially positive and realistic. War is acknowledged as a necessary evil, whereas in O'Casey's play, politics is depicted as a power which divides a society and brings about destruction and desolation. This vision is essentially negative.

- As in O'Casey's play, *The King's Speech* depicts characters whose posturing and selfishness cause suffering and grief for others. In both texts, the viewpoints of the author and the director are revealed through the characterisation. Edward VIII is depicted, like many of O'Casey's characters, as being weak and inadequate. His abdication speech is an example of hollow rhetoric and self-delusion. Wallis Simpson also emerges as a shallow, rather crude individual who exploits the affections of her lover with no regard for the consequences of her power over him.

- The extreme poverty of the Dublin City tenements is not paralleled in *The King's Speech*.

In O'Casey's play, poverty can be seen as a tragic force which drives desperate individuals to desperate lengths in order to survive. It is therefore part of the playwright's negative vision. Emotional poverty and deprivation cast a similar gloom in *The King's Speech* but in this film we see an individual rising above such deprivation and achieving happiness. The vision is thus more positive and optimistic.

- Both texts have many comic moments which often serve to intensify and exacerbate that which is serious or even, at times, tragic.

- The texts differ in their presentations of love and marriage. The poignant loss and destruction of the Clitheroes' marriage in O'Casey's play contributes to the general pessimistic vision. No presentation of a successful marriage relationship is depicted or suggested. By contrast, marriage is seen in both positive and negative lights in *The King's Speech*. George VI is happily married, as is Lionel Logue. Edward VIII's marriage to Wallis Simpson is very negatively presented, as is George V's apparent acceptance of adulterous relationships.

- As in *The Plough and the Stars*, *The King's Speech* celebrates the capacity of the human spirit to achieve greatness. This is most evident in the struggle and success of Bertie in overcoming his speech impediment.

- A significant event in the final scene of both texts establishes the dominant general vision and viewpoint. O'Casey's dark, pessimistic vision in the circumstances surrounding Bessie's death contrasts with the triumph and optimism of *The King's Speech*.

Foster, The Plough and the Stars and The King's Speech

The author Claire Keegan has referred to *Foster* as her 'long short story'. This story is not quite as clear-cut in its general vision and viewpoint as *The Plough and the Stars* and *The King's Speech*. The reason for this is related to the fact that, unlike these other texts, which have multiple viewpoints, the viewpoint of *Foster* is that of a young child thrown into an unusual fostering situation in circumstances which she does not fully comprehend. We see and experience everything through the eyes of this child, who is never actually named in the narrative.

Unlike O'Casey's play and *The King's Speech*, political turmoil, war and the desolation these entail are not major factors in establishing the overall atmosphere of this text. Instead it's a timeless tale of rural Irish life in which the influences of the outside world are somewhat downplayed. Nevertheless, given her sparse style of writing, the fact that the

hunger strikes of the 1980s Northern Ireland are even mentioned confers on them some importance and significance. As the Kinsellas eat a meal they discuss the hunger strikes, where men are deliberately dying for a cause in which they passionately believe. This has much resonance with both of the other texts and serves to cast a gloom over the narrative at this stage by reminding the reader of civil unrest, violence and the ultimate sacrifices people are ready to make in the cause of nationalism or love of country. The starving 'strikers' are recalled as John Kinsella butters his bread, 'The butter is soft, slipping off the knife, spreading easily'. The conversation between the adults barely raises the political issues of the time and establishes a distance, as well-fed people discuss a man who starved to death:

'They said on the early news that another striker is dead.'

'Not another?'

'Aye. He passed during the night, poor man. Isn't it a terrible state of affairs?' 'God rest him,' the woman says. 'It's no way to die.'

This conversation is an arresting moment that makes the story seem suddenly more ominous.

One could claim that this political situation forms a type of backdrop to the narrative, highlighting the horror of the hunger striker's predicament by contrasting it with the peace and plenty of the Kinsella household. Later, as the child eats five Weetabix in succession, there is yet another mention of the hunger strike, 'I eat five in all during the nine o'clock news while they show the mother of the dead striker, a riot, then the Taoiseach and then foreign people out in Africa, starving to death, and then the weather forecast, which says the days are to be fine for another week or so'. The child, innocently detaches herself from the suffering around her, but the effect on the reader is to create a sense of gloom and foreboding very similar to the impact of the political and social issues in the other two texts.

In common with the other two texts, *Foster* **depicts characters whose posturing and selfishness cause suffering and grief for others.** The major character for such posturing and selfishness in *Foster* is the character of Dan, the child's father. Through her creation of this character, Keegan reveals a negative vision of parenthood. The little girl is treated by her father with the same emotional neglect that Bertie refers to when confiding in Lionel about his troubled childhood in *The King's Speech*. From the very opening of the narrative, Dan appears to have little or no interest in his child and makes no attempt to talk to her on the journey to the Kinsellas' house. Small hints are dropped into the narrative which alert us to the type of man Dan is: 'my father lost our red shorthorn in a game of forty-five,' the child says, indicating her father's reckless irresponsibility. She remembers an overheard conversation when her parents were discussing her departure. Dan's irritated wife, Mary, angrily responds to his questions as to what he should say to the Kinsellas by telling him to 'Say what you like. Isn't it what you

always do.' Later, Dan lies about the amount of work he has done on the farm, which provokes his child to wonder 'why my father lies about the hay. He is given to lying about things that would be nice, if they were true.' There is absolutely no doubt in the reader's mind that this man falls very short of Keegan's vision of what a father should be. His callous indifference to his child's welfare is further emphasised when he states that 'She'll ate but you can work her' and having 'eaten his fill' is anxious to leave her in the care of people who are strangers to her. His last words to his daughter as he departs lack any affection or sensitivity: 'Try not to fall into the fire, you'. Throughout the rest of the story, dogs, not human beings, are addressed as 'you', which makes this choice of word very telling. The child wonders, 'Why did he leave without so much as a goodbye or ever mentioning when he would come back for me?' A final cruelty occurs when the child discovers that her father hasn't even cared to ensure that he left her bag of clothing in her new home.

The darkness of this vision of failed parenting is highlighted by the relationship which grows between John Kinsella and the child. In one key moment the reader sees the extent of the distance between the child and her father when she is walking at night with Kinsella, 'There's a big moon shining on the yard . . . Kinsella takes my hand in his. As soon as he takes it, I realise my father has never once held my hand, and some part of me wants Kinsella to let me go so I won't have to feel this. It's a hard feeling but as we walk along I begin to settle and let the difference between my life at home and the one I have here be'. Although Mrs Gogan in *The Plough and the Stars* is neglectful of her dying daughter Mollser, who fears being left alone and who relies on the neighbours for company, one notices that this neglect is more dictated by the necessity of trying to find work to survive. Mrs Gogan is affectionate in the way she speaks about her child, 'me little Mollser', and shows gratitude to those who looked after her. These traits are not apparent in the behaviour of Dan in *Foster*.

Another character who reveals a dark and negative side to human nature is the neighbour, Mildred, who reveals the Kinsellas' 'secret' to the child. Like Uncle Peter and The Young Covey in *The Plough and the Stars,* she is a short-tempered, shallow individual who engages in pretence and deception. She seems to be kindly when she offers to take the child away, ' Mine'd be a bit of company for her. Can't they play away out the back?' and assures Edna that the child is 'Not a bother'. Her real attitude however is cold and callous as she questions the girl about the lifestyle and habits of her foster parents. It is not merely her blunt nosiness which creates concern here but the manner in which she talks about the drowning of the Kinsellas' only child. There is no pity or sensitivity in her account of the young boy's tragic death, 'Sure, didn't he follow that auld hound of theirs into the slurry tank and drown? That's what they say happened anyhow'. She calls the child a 'dope' for not realising that she was wearing the 'dead's clothes'. The impact of her words on the girl are devastating – 'I keep on walking and try not to think about what she has said, even though I can think of little else. The time for the sun to go down is hours from now but the day feels like it is ending'. This reflection adds a dark depressing note to the overall atmosphere. In all three texts, the portrayal of shallow, negative characters contributes to a vision of humanity which is pessimistic and dispiriting.

Foster, like *The Plough and the Stars,* shows poverty as a force which can impact negatively on human happiness and contentment. The emotional poverty and deprivation which casts a gloom in *The King's Speech* has a parallel here also, in the portrayal of the child's family life. There is little doubt that the child's mother has to struggle enormously to make ends meet and to support her expanding family. The fact that the child has to be sent away for a while, so that there is one less mouth to feed, provides evidence of this fact. The child comments on her mother's difficult life which is so unlike that of the Kinsellas when she says, 'With my mother it is all work . . . stretching the money and setting the alarm for a time before the sun rises. But this is a different type of house. Here there is room to think. There may even be money to spare.' One wonders what Dan is doing all day, other than smoking, gambling and enjoying a 'liquid supper' when his wife has to work so hard. We learn that there isn't enough money to pay a man to bring in the hay, 'She hasn't enough to pay the man. She only just paid him for last year.' Edna would like to assist by sending money but hesitates when told that while her sister Mary wouldn't be offended, her husband would. This effectively means that the child's mother is trapped in a marriage with a large family of children whom she struggles to rear without much help from her irresponsible husband. The poverty of their circumstances casts a dark shadow over the vision of their family life.

The description of the girl's home contrasts starkly with that of the spotless house belonging to the Kinsellas. 'Inside, the house feels damp and cold. The lino is tracked over with dirty footprints.' The young sisters of the narrator are thin and neglected in appearance, almost afraid to touch the fine clothing of their older sibling. The house is sparsely furnished as the Kinsellas are invited 'to sit down — if they can find a place to sit' while Mary 'fills the kettle from the bucket under the kitchen table'. Although we do not have anything like O'Casey's detailed stage directions to create the atmosphere of the poverty being experienced by this family, little hints in the narrative paint the picture. They have to 'move playthings off the car seat under the window' in order to sit down. Instead of the fine meal offered to Dan in the Kinsella's home, 'Mugs are taken off the dresser, a loaf of bread is sliced, butter and jam left out'. The warmth of a closely-knit family life such as that enjoyed by the Logue family in *The King's Speech* is missing here as we sense a tension in the air. The family do not communicate well and even the mother is not fully trusted by her own child who refuses to divulge the 'secret' of her accidental fall into the well on the Kinsella farm. The darkness of poverty, neglect and emotional distance creates a negative vision at this stage of the narrative. Because the child has thrived in the comfort of the Kinsellas' home, where she was cherished and encouraged to blossom, the reader has little doubt that the adjustment to her own home conditions will be very difficult, if not damaging, for her.

Humour is not used as much in *Foster* as it is in the other two texts. *The Plough and the Stars* and *The King's Speech* use humour to relieve tension in the audience and to act as a foil to the underlying serious issues raised in each text. In *Foster* the humour arises in part from the innocence of the child's perceptions and reflections on her experiences. Only in one key moment do we observe the use of laughter which helps to drown out sadness. Local people call to the Kinsellas' house to sell 'lines' for a raffle to put a new roof on the local school. Their slight embarrassment when they remember that John and Edna have lost their only child is soon relieved by Kinsella who generously contributes to their collection saying, 'Just 'cos I've none of my own doesn't mean I'd see the rain falling in on anyone else's'. It is a heart-breaking moment of an acknowledged loss which soon turns to broad comedy when a game of cards starts and, surprisingly, Edna is seen to have an ironic sense of fun, passing remarks about the poor skills of the competitors who react with witty dialogue:

'Oh, there's shots!'

'You have to listen to thunder.'

'Aisy knowing whose purse is running low.'

'It's ahead, I am,' she said. 'And it's ahead I'll be when it's over.'

The comedy increases when Ass Case begins to 'bray' with infectious laughter which spreads around the table until everybody joins in. The scene is brought to its conclusion when one of the men asks 'Is it a tittering match we have here or are we going to play cards?' which makes 'the Ass Casey bray once more, and it started all over again'. This moment of light relief, coming after the sadness associated with the childless state of the Kinsellas, serves to highlight the backdrop of suffering and loss which will be explained to the reader later in the story.

All three texts differ in their presentations of love and marriage. *Foster* presents us with a view of two quite different marriage relationships, one of which is more positive and loving than the other. The Kinsellas appear to have a loving understanding of each other and generally treat each other with respect and sympathy. The loss of their child does not divide them. At times, they differ regarding small details like suitable clothing for the girl or the appropriateness of a late night walk, but they are supportive of each other's difference of temperament and there is never any hint of animosity or intolerance. This is not true of the relationship between the narrator's parents. Without making any direct reference to her parents' marriage, the girl's words imply that her home lacks marital harmony. She can hardly believe the peace that she has found in her new home, 'I keep waiting for something to happen, for the ease I feel to end, but each day follows on much like the one before.' We learn that her pregnant mother did not want another baby and that the youngest child in the family is barely 'crawling'. The difference between her parents is also evident when she says of her father, 'Always, it's the same: he never stays in any place long after he's eaten, not like my mother, who would talk until it grew dark and light again. This, at least, is what my father says. I have never known it to happen'. The mother seems overburdened with the work of the household – '. . . us, the butter-making, the dinners, the washing up and getting up and getting ready for Mass and school, weaning calves, and hiring men to plough and harrow the fields . . .' However, what we hear of Dan is that he gambles, smokes, drinks, lies about his accomplishments and has very little time or concern for his own child, whom he treats with indifference. At the end of the story Kinsella asks Mary where her husband is. Instead of being there to meet the people who have cared for his child, he has absented himself, obviously for a reason unknown to his wife, ' "He went out there earlier, wherever he's gone," Ma says'. The silence between husband and wife is very telling when Dan eventually returns home. Neither one speaks directly to the other except for one brief moment when Mary reproaches her husband in a 'steel voice' for an insensitive comment about the difficulties of watching small children. This negative portrayal of married life echoes some of the tensions we observe between Nora and Jack Clitheroe. Like Dan, Jack is more concerned with his own self-importance and posturing than in pleasing and caring for his wife and unborn child. He puts his own political ambitions above the desires of Nora for a contented family life. Tensions exist in both of these texts which darken the vision of marriage. However, the relationship of the Kinsellas acts as a balance in *Foster,* a feature which is totally missing from *The Plough and the Stars*. The distancing of father and child in Keegan's narrative also recalls the gulf that existed between Bertie and his father in *The King's Speech*. The viewpoints expressed in each text are therefore, at times, quite negative as regards family life, love and marriage. The positive relationships observed between Bertie and Elizabeth and that of the Kinsellas act as foils to underscore this generally negative vision.

Both *The Plough and the Stars* and *The King's Speech* celebrate the capacity of the human spirit to achieve greatness. *Foster* does not deal with any such dramatic presentations. However, it does depict the growth and development of a child during one summer when she was loved, nurtured and encouraged to become her own person. Although more understated than the other texts, the vision is essentially positive and optimistic. As we read the story we see the child grow in self-confidence and awareness. She learns many things from her foster parents and understands that she has '. . . learned enough, grown enough, to know that what happened is not something I need ever mention. It is my perfect opportunity to say nothing'. From being a child who found it almost impossible to openly express her feelings, she now races towards the Kinsellas, 'My heart feels not so much in my chest as in my hands. I am carrying it along swiftly, as though I have become the messenger for what is going on inside me.' The final loving embrace of Kinsella, whom she now regards as 'Daddy' , constitutes a warning to her biological father that he has no automatic right to consider himself as her 'father' in anything but name. Her heart belongs in a special way to Kinsella because he has nurtured her growth as a person. He has taught her to believe in her own capabilities and has encouraged her to express herself while maintaining her ability to 'say nothing' if she so chooses. Despite the warmth and love evidenced in this moving moment, as the Kinsellas and child weep together before parting, the vision of the author seems to be ambiguous. Keegan leaves us wondering whether her viewpoint in this text is positive or negative. Will this child be able to thrive in her own parents' home or will she wilt without the presence and support of her foster parents? What will Dan make of his daughter's words to Kinsella? Or has the girl learnt enough to be able to deal with a changed outlook on life and on the differences which exist between people? Is her emotion one of gratitude and acceptance? The possibilities here are many and it is perhaps a pointless exercise to attempt to tie this significant ending to one dominant vision or viewpoint. This is in contrast to the more obvious darkness and pessimism of O'Casey's vision or the clear triumph and optimism of *The King's Speech*.

KEY POINTS

- Unlike the other two texts, *Foster* does not take place in a society disturbed and threatened by war. The reference to the hunger strikes in Northern Ireland does, however, form a type of backdrop to the narrative, highlighting that horror by contrasting it with the plenty of the Kinsella household. The idea of people being sacrificed or of offering their lives for political ideals is thus present in each text and casts a gloom over each.

- In common with the other two texts, *Foster* depicts characters whose posturing and selfishness cause suffering and grief for others. In each of the texts, the viewpoints of the authors and the director are revealed through the characterisation. The major character for such posturing and selfishness in *Foster* is Dan, the little girl's father. His portrayal reveals the author's viewpoint on the duty, responsibility and humanity expected from a parent towards a child.

- *Foster,* like *The Plough and the Stars,* shows poverty as a tragic force which impacts negatively on human happiness. It is therefore a feature of both Keegan's and O'Casey's general vision. The emotional poverty and deprivation which casts a gloom in *The King's Speech* has a parallel here also, in the portrayal of the child's family life.

- Each of the texts has comical moments which often serve to intensify and exacerbate that which is serious or even, at times, tragic. This is seen in the card game in *Foster,* just after Kinsella has made a donation to the local school.

- All three texts differ in their presentations of love and marriage. *Foster* presents us with a view of two quite different marriage relationships, one of which is more positive and loving than the other. Similarly, marriage is seen in both positive and negative lights in *The King's Speech.* By contrast, the poignant loss and destruction of the Clitheroes' marriage in O'Casey's play contributes to the general pessimistic vision. Unlike *Foster* no presentation of a successful marriage relationship is depicted or suggested in the play.

- Both *The Plough and the Stars* and *The King's Speech* celebrate the capacity of the human spirit to achieve greatness. *Foster* does not deal with any such dramatic presentations. However, it does depict the growth and development of a child during one summer when she was loved, nurtured and encouraged to become her own person. Although more understated than the other texts, the vision is essentially positive and optimistic.

- *Foster,* in common with each of the other texts, uses a significant event at the end of the narrative, which indicates the dominant general vision and viewpoint. However, the impact of this event where the child seems to acknowledge Kinsella as her 'real' father is slightly ambiguous. This is in contrast to the more obvious darkness and pessimism of O'Casey's vision or the clear triumph and optimism of *The King's Speech.*

Sample Answer

(a) How did you come to your understanding of the general vision and viewpoint in any one of the texts you read as part of your comparative course? (30)

(b) Write a comparison between two other texts on your course in the light of your understanding of the general vision and viewpoint in those texts. (40)

N.B. These answers are longer than what would be required under examination conditions. The purpose of this is to demonstrate the range of relevant points which could be explored.

(a) The general vision or viewpoint of a text relates to the authorial/directorial outlook on life which inevitably influences our perspective on the narrative and on the world in which it is set. From my reading of *The Plough and the Stars* by Seán O'Casey, I came to an understanding of his attitude towards political and social events in Dublin during the 1916 Rising. The playwright's presentation of key characters and relationships, his depiction of the impact of poverty on peoples' lives and his portrayal of unexpected heroism all contributed to my own feelings and helped shape my personal viewpoint towards these events. As in all texts, the dominant vision was most evident at the play's ending.

O'Casey's viewpoint concerning the power of political ideals to divide a society is essentially negative. The play is set in the Dublin tenements at a time when people were rebelling against Ireland's status as a British colony and against poverty and deprivation. O'Casey shows how the hero-worship of dead patriots and the linking of politics with religion have the potential to make an impoverished people believe that they are capable of dressing themselves in the costumes of heroism and the glorious robes of martyrs.

Jack Clitheroe, a key character in the play, sees himself and his fellow nationalists in the Citizen Army as being true freedom fighters. He and his companions openly state their willingness to die, if necessary, to set Ireland free from British rule. Their slogans and fine words reverberate with apparent heroism, 'Ireland is greater than a mother . . . greater than a wife', but their apparent loyalty is depicted as being not only misguided but really a proclamation of their own intense vanity. Nora, in Act I, angrily expresses this when she asks Jack, 'Is General Connolly an' th' Citizen Army goin' to be your only care? . . . Your vanity'll be the ruin of you an' me yet'.

On the other side of the political divide is Bessie Burgess, a resident of the tenement building in which the Clitheroes live. She is a staunch loyalist who believes that those involved in the uprising are traitors. She angrily attacks those who have not joined the British Army to fight in World War I, 'There's th' men marchin' out into the dhread dimness o' danger, while th' lice is crawlin' about feedin' on the fatness o' th' land'. The language and imagery here adds to the ugliness of the vision. The Young Covey, Jack's cousin who lives with the couple, is also extremely hostile to the Citizen Army. He is deeply critical of the use of the flag of the Plough and the Stars by nationalists, an act which he considers a betrayal of the working classes whom the flag is meant to represent: 'it's a Labour flag an' was never meant for politics,' he tells Jack. He refers to the nationalists as 'th' mugs' who have to 'renew their political baptismal vows' in order to be loyal to their Republican ideals. This attitude of The Young Covey causes uproar, with Fluther, another tenement resident, describing his neighbour as 'a word-weavin' little ignorant yahoo of a red flag socialist'.

From the above examples and from many other moments in the play, O'Casey's profoundly negative attitude towards the 1916 uprising becomes apparent. The illogical pointlessness of that struggle is seen when Bessie Burgess is shot by the British soldiers whom she was so loudly praising earlier in the play. Many of the nationalists are killed and wounded without achieving their ideals. I cannot but agree with Mollser, a teenage girl dying of tuberculosis in the tenement, who sums up the vision of the playwright himself, when she asks Nora, 'Is there anybody goin', Mrs Clitheroe, with a titther o' sense?'

O'Casey's vision of the shallow nature of some characters adds to the pervading negativity. Several of the men in the play are depicted as weak and inadequate, engaging in absurd posturing. This is particularly true of The Young Covey and Peter, Nora's uncle. The Young Covey proclaims himself to be a socialist and enjoys displaying his knowledge and understanding of 'Jenersky's Thesis'. There is no doubt that he has a valid point in his objections to nationalism and its effect on the community. However, he is not as civic-minded as he claims to be. I was shocked when this 'socialist' engaged in looting, hurrying Fluther on with the words, 'Come on then, or there won't be anything left to save'.

The character of Peter also adds to the vision of superficial posturing in the name of patriotic fervour. As a member of the Foresters, Peter boasts that he has not missed a 'pilgrimage to Bodenstown' in 25 years and never failed to 'pluck a leaf off Tone's grave'. His heroism, however, is merely a façade. The only reason he does not go looting with the others is because he is afraid of being shot. Defeated by his own cowardice, he sanctimoniously condemns the looters, 'Makin' a shame an' a sin o' the cause that good men are fightin' for'. Bessie sums him up well when she describes him as, 'a little sermonising, little yella-faced, little consequential, little pudgy, little bum...'. Despite the humour of this comment, there is no doubt that the playwright is using the comedy to highlight the hypocrisy of self-righteous individuals such as The Young Covey and Peter.

The description of the extreme poverty of the Dublin City tenements strikes a note of gloom from the outset. Even Nora's simple act of putting a lock on a door is regarded as having 'notions of upperosity' or having fears that 'poor neighbours ud break through an' steal'. In addition, in order to make ends meet, Nora has to share her home with Uncle Peter and The Young Covey which leaves very little privacy for her marriage and relationship with Jack Clitheroe. Rosie Redmond, another local, is driven into prostitution in order to survive while the dying, malnourished Mollser embodies the poverty and deprivation of the time. The Young Covey highlights this when he says of Mollser, 'Sure she never got any care. How could she get it, an' the mother out day an' night lookin' for work, an' her consumptive husband leavin' her with a baby to be born before he died'. The depiction of such poverty certainly left me with a dark and depressing vision of life at that time.

The poignant loss of the happiness which Jack and Nora once experienced in marriage adds a further negative tone to the play. When General Connolly sends Captain Brennan with battle orders to Jack Clitheroe, he is engaging in the destruction of the domestic order which Nora strives so hard to maintain. 'I don't care if you never come back,' she says as her husband makes his political ambition and vanity more important than his marriage. This disintegration of what was once a loving relationship casts a gloom over this section of the play. Later, when Jack briefly returns, only to desert her again, she cries pathetically, 'Oh Jack, I gave you everything you asked of me'. Nora then descends quickly into insanity under the pressure of her loss and suffers a miscarriage. Bessie Burgess, filled now with compassion for Nora's sad state, remarks that 'her eyes have a hauntin' way of lookin' in instead of lookin' out'. Indeed, O'Casey's general vision and viewpoint is summed up by Bessie when she exclaims: 'Blessing o' God on us, isn't this pitiful'.

Despite the predominantly pessimistic vision there are moments when O'Casey celebrates the human spirit. Bessie not only supports Nora when Jack deserts her, she also risks her own life by going for a doctor when Nora has her miscarriage. This courage is all the more impressive when one remembers the conflict between them earlier, when she flew at Nora 'like a tiger' and attempted to 'guzzle' her. Fluther Good reveals a courageous and compassionate nature when he risks his own life bringing Nora back from the barricades. These acts of humanity and courage affirm the audience's belief that human beings can rise above self-interest and become heroic in spite of the human failings which they inevitably possess.

The ending of any narrative plays a large part in determining its general vision and viewpoint. Bessie's generosity and kindness adds to the horror and shock of her death. She is shot by British soldiers as she tries to protect the hysterical Nora from dangerously approaching the window during a gun battle. This event, which effectively marks the end of the play, leaves no doubt that O'Casey's general vision is profoundly pessimistic. The negative portrayal of the political ideals which have not been realised, the creation of shallow, posturing characters, the deaths of innocents and the effects of extreme poverty all contribute to an overall picture of pessimism and gloom.

(b) Two other texts which I have studied for my comparative course are *Foster* by Claire Keegan and *The King's Speech* directed by Tom Hooper.

Foster is not quite as clear-cut in its general vision as is *The King's Speech*, which presents multiple viewpoints. The viewpoint in *Foster* is that of a young child thrown into an unusual fostering situation in circumstances which she does not fully comprehend. We see and experience everything through the eyes of this child, who is never actually named in the narrative. *The King's Speech,* however, allows us to look at events from several different angles.

The film is set in a time of political turmoil when the role of a king was of paramount importance for the morale of a nation – during the lead-up to and duration of World War II. Just before King George V's death, Bertie and his father discuss the pressing political issues. His father poses the question of a potential war when he says 'Who will stand between us, the jackboots, and the proletarian abyss?' The King is referring here to Germany as the jackboots and Russia as the proletarian abyss. The threats from Hitler and Stalin are thus openly acknowledged. *Foster,* on the other hand, is a timeless tale of rural Irish life in which the influences of the outside world are somewhat downplayed. Nevertheless, given Keegan's sparse style of writing, the fact that the hunger strikes of the 1980s Northern Ireland are even mentioned confers on them some importance and significance. The conversation between the Kinsellas barely raises the political issues of the time and establishes a distance, as well-fed people discuss a man who starved to death:

'They said on the early news that another striker is dead.'

'Not another?'

'Aye. He passed during the night, poor man. Isn't it a terrible state of affairs?'

'God rest him,' the woman says. 'It's no way to die.'

This conversation is an arresting moment that, for me, made the story seem suddenly more ominous. Unlike King George VI who must address the challenges posed by war, the child in *Foster* innocently detaches herself from the suffering around her. The effect on the reader is to create a sense of gloom and foreboding very similar to the impact of the political and social issues in *The King's Speech*.

Both texts create a gloomy vision of the damage caused to individuals by the selfishness of others. The major character for such posturing and selfishness in *Foster* is Dan, the child's father. Through her creation of this character, Keegan reveals a negative vision of parenthood. The little girl is treated by her father with the same emotional neglect that Bertie refers to when confiding in Lionel about his troubled childhood in *The King's Speech*. From the very opening of the narrative, Dan appears to have little or no interest in his child and makes no attempt to talk to her on the journey to the Kinsellas' house.

Small hints are dropped into the narrative which alert us to the type of man Dan is. 'My father lost our red shorthorn in a game of forty-five,' the child says, indicating her father's reckless irresponsibility. Later, Dan lies about the amount of work he has done on the farm, which provokes his child to wonder 'why my father lies about the hay. He is given to lying about things that would be nice, if they were true.' There is absolutely no doubt in the reader's mind that this man falls very short of Keegan's vision of what a father should be. His callous indifference to his child's welfare is further emphasised when the child wonders, 'Why did he leave without so much as a goodbye or ever mentioning when he would come back for me?' A final cruelty occurs when the child discovers that her father hasn't even cared to ensure that he left her bag of clothing in her new home.

Similarly, in *The King's Speech* we observe a father who is emotionally detached from his child. Bertie confides in Lionel, telling him about his harsh upbringing where his siblings were encouraged by their father to tease him whenever he stuttered. His father's philosophy to child-rearing was cold and callous: 'I was afraid of my father, and my children are damn well going to be afraid of me'. However, the major negative character portrayal is that of Edward VIII. In the film, Edward VIII is presented as childish and cruel to his brother, mocking his stutter, 'That's the scoop around town. Yearning for a larger audience are we, B-b-b-Bertie?' He is also presented as having, like many of O'Casey's characters, shallow political views. He is disinterested in Bertie's genuine concerns about 'people marching across Europe singing The Red Flag' and makes a foolish comment about the Nazis, 'Stop your worrying. Herr Hitler will sort that lot out'. Edward is thus presented as being little more than a ridiculous, selfish and self-indulgent individual who concentrates on the woman he loves at the expense of the welfare of his country and its people. The self-obsession and lack of sensitivity of such repellent characters in both texts contributes enormously to a reader's sense of disgust.

Foster shows poverty as a force that can impact negatively on human happiness and contentment. Although it is not the devastating poverty of *The Plough and the Stars,* there is little doubt that the child's mother has to struggle enormously to make ends meet and to support her expanding family. The child comments on her mother's difficult life when she says, 'With my mother it is all work . . . stretching the money and setting the alarm for a time before the sun rises. But this is a different type of house . . . There may even be money to spare.' One wonders what

Dan is doing all day, other than smoking, gambling and enjoying a 'liquid supper' while his wife has to work so hard. Descriptive techniques used by the writer subtly suggest poverty and deprivation. 'Inside, the house feels damp and cold. The lino is tracked over with dirty footprints.' Younger siblings are thin and neglected in appearance, almost afraid to touch the fine clothing of their older sister when she returns from her summer with the Kinsellas. The house is sparsely furnished as the Kinsellas are invited 'to sit down – if they can find a place to sit' while Mary 'fills the kettle from the bucket under the kitchen table'. The impact of such poverty, so opposite to the relative comfort of the Kinsellas' home, creates a negative vision in this narrative as the reader wonders how the narrator will be able to cope with the change back to her parents' home. By contrast, *The King's Speech* presents scenes of luxurious residences and fine palaces. However, the apparent comfort and the absence of poverty does nothing much to relieve the tension which pervades much of the atmosphere of the film. This tension does not arise so much from material as from emotional poverty. The family of Lionel Logue, although less well-off than the royals, live a contented, happy life compared to the children of George V who are 'presented' to their parents each evening by a seemingly sadistic nanny. What I learnt from my study of both texts is that poverty can create stress and deprivation but wealth does not compensate for the cold family relationships such as Bertie endures in his childhood. The presence of poverty, whether material or emotional in nature, casts a gloom over each of these texts.

Both *Foster* and *The King's Speech* offer positive and negative viewpoints on love and marriage. By using contrast, Keegan presents us with a view of two quite different marriage relationships. The Kinsellas appear to have a loving understanding of each other and generally treat each other with respect and sympathy. The loss of their child does not divide them. At times, they differ regarding small details like suitable clothing for the girl or the appropriateness of a late night walk, but they are supportive of each other and there is never any hint of animosity or intolerance. This is not true of the relationship between the narrator's parents. The writer does not make any direct reference to the marriage of Dan and Mary, but the narrator's words imply that her home lacks marital harmony. She can hardly believe the peace that she has found in her new home, 'I keep waiting for something to happen, for the ease I feel to end, but each day follows on much like the one before.' We learn that her pregnant mother did not want another baby and that the youngest child in the family is barely 'crawling'. The mother seems overburdened with the work of the household, while what we hear of Dan is that he gambles, smokes, drinks, lies about his work and leaves the burden of running the farm to his wife. The viewpoints expressed in these texts are therefore, at times, quite negative as regards love and marriage. Marriage is also negatively presented in the *The King's Speech* when Edward VIII abdicates the throne so that he can marry the American divorcee, Wallis Simpson. His relationship with this woman seems obsessive and even irrational. Wallis's control over the new king is apparent at a reception in their house when she imperiously taps her champagne glass, waves off a footman who hastens to serve her and waits rather impatiently while her lover springs into action. As he hunts for the particular champagne which 'Wally likes the best', we hear Edward calling to her, 'Just be a sec, darling!' This obsession with Wallis is made all the more negative when we are informed by the Prime Minister, Stanley Baldwin, that 'the King does not possess exclusive rights to Mrs Simpson's favours and affections, sharing them with a married used car salesman, a certain Mr Guy Trundle.' The vision of marriage is not, however, completely negative in either text given the positive marriage of the Kinsellas in *Foster* and that of Bertie's and Lionel Logue's marriages, respectively, in *The King's Speech*.

The King's Speech celebrates the capacity of the human spirit to achieve greatness and overcome obstacles. King George VI illustrates this uplifting aspect of the human spirit in the film. His struggle against his speech impediment boosted my appreciation of the human capacity to become the best one can be, and rise to meet even the most daunting challenge. As the writer, David Seidler said in the introduction to his screenplay: 'Bertie never thought he would be king – he wasn't meant to be king, wasn't trained to be king, nor with his stutter was he suited to be king. But when he had to be king, he came to the fore and did his job'. This coming to the fore was far from easy. With his self-confidence in shreds he had to face the expectations of a nation on the brink of war. He rose magnificently to this challenge. Claire Keegan in *Foster*, on the other hand, does not deal with any such dramatic presentations. Her story concentrates on the growth and development of a child during one summer when she was loved, nurtured and encouraged to become her own person. Although more understated than the other text, this aspect is also essentially positive and optimistic.

The general vision and viewpoint of a text is often made clear by the manner in which a narrative ends. *The King's Speech* ends on a note of triumph over adversity. After war has been declared by Chamberlain, Bertie faces the prospect of having to make a key address to the nation. Tension rises as he makes his way through the palace towards the microphone. If he stammers and fails to properly deliver the speech, his efforts, like those of O'Casey's patriots, will be seen to be in vain. An exquisite scene follows in which we see the king deliver a fluent and persuasive speech to an amazed but delighted audience. This performance of, literally, the king's speech consolidates the dominant optimistic vision of the entire film, which is not really about the outbreak of war but about the war a man waged with himself, and won! All he now has to do is to step out onto the balcony of Buckingham Palace with his family to be cheered by an ecstatic crowd. Before the credits roll, an onscreen card tells us that 'Lionel was with the King for every wartime speech' and that 'George VI became a symbol of national resistance'. The audience is aware, of course, that the Allies won World War II. This outcome establishes the general vision and viewpoint as being immensely positive, affirming the belief that courage can prevail against even the most difficult obstacles.

Foster does not deal with any such dramatic presentations. However, it does depict the growth and development of a child during one summer when she was loved, nurtured and encouraged to become her own person. As we read the story we see the child grow in self-confidence and awareness. She learns many things from her foster parents and understands that she has '. . . learned enough, grown enough, to know that what happened is not something I need ever mention. It is my perfect opportunity to say nothing'. From being a child who found it almost impossible to openly express her feelings, she now races towards the Kinsellas as they drive away from her home, 'My heart feels not so much in my chest as in my hands. I am carrying it along swiftly, as though I have become the messenger for what is going on inside me.' The final loving embrace of John Kinsella, whom she now regards as 'Daddy', constitutes a warning to her biological father that he has no automatic right to consider himself as her 'father' in anything but name. Her heart belongs in a special way to Kinsella because he has nurtured her growth as a person. He has taught her to believe in her own capabilities and has encouraged her to express herself while maintaining her ability to 'say nothing' if she so chooses. Despite the warmth and love evidenced in this moving moment, as the Kinsellas and child weep together before parting, the vision of the author seems to be ambiguous. Keegan leaves us wondering whether her viewpoint in this text is positive or negative. Will this child be able to thrive in her own parents' home or will she wilt without the presence and support of her foster parents? What will Dan make of his daughter's words to Kinsella? Or has the girl learnt enough to be able to deal with a changed outlook on life and the differences that exist between people? Is her emotion one of gratitude and acceptance? The possibilities here are many and it is perhaps a pointless exercise to attempt to tie this significant ending to one dominant vision or viewpoint. This is in contrast to the more obvious darkness and pessimism of O'Casey's vision in *The Plough and the Stars* or the clear triumph and optimism of *The King's Speech.*

From my reading of texts for the comparative study, I have become more aware of the often subtle techniques which authors and directors use to communicate their own vision and viewpoint while leaving the reader or audience free to experience the personal feelings which the narratives evoke.

C. Literary Genre

The Plough and the Stars

Literary genre refers to how an author tells his or her story. Plays, films, novels and short stories all differ from each other as regards the specific techniques employed by the authors/directors and an understanding of these techniques is important for any appreciation of a text.

The Plough and the Stars was described by Sean O'Casey himself as 'a tragedy in four acts'. The play is arranged in two halves: Acts I and II take place in November 1915 and Acts III and IV occur during Easter 1916. The first two acts make reference to World War I and to the simultaneous preparations by the Irish Citizen Army and the Irish Volunteers for revolution against Britain. These preparations involve organising public meetings and delivering rousing speeches in favour of a citizens' uprising against British rule over Ireland. The subsequent 1916 Rising is later suppressed. **In his play, O'Casey dramatises the effects of revolution on the lives of ordinary people who, willingly or unwillingly, get caught up in the conflict.**

The title of any text has an important function in stimulating reader/audience interest and in indicating a central issue or focus. *The Plough and the Stars* refers to the flag originally used by the Irish Citizen Army, a socialist, Republican movement. James Connolly, a co-founder of the movement, said that the flag symbolised a free Ireland in control of its own destiny. The flag depicted a plough surrounded by stars. O'Casey's play was written as a specific reaction against a play that Connolly had written and first staged in March 1916. Connolly's play was called *Under Which Flag?*, a title which posed a question as to which kind of banner Irish men and women ought to support: that is, whether to join Britain's wartime battle for the freedom of small nations (i.e. World War I), or whether instead to take the chance of striking out for an independent Ireland. At the end of Connolly's play the audience learns that the latter answer is the correct one. This simplistic moral infuriated

O'Casey. The title of *The Plough and the Stars*, therefore, acts as a response to Connolly's question by referring to the flag of the Labour movement. Perhaps, O'Casey suggests, Irishmen could rally behind these colours, but by the end of the play this emblem proves inadequate. **Fighting for any cause is portrayed as empty and dehumanising with political idealism drawing men away from life and from love.**

Although *The Plough and the Stars* **is described as being a tragedy by the playwright, it is difficult to identify any one character as being a tragic hero or heroine.** Some might consider that the revolutionaries who die fighting for freedom are heroes. Jack Clitheroe is described as a hero by the General who instructs Captain Brennan to tell Nora that 'Commandant Clitheroe's death was a gleam of glory'. Brennan himself adds that 'Mrs Clitheroe's grief will be a joy when she realises that she has had a hero for a husband'. However, it is very difficult for the audience to accept Jack as a true tragic hero given the weakness of his character. One senses that he is more motivated by vanity and a desire to command than by any real dedication to a political ideal. Mrs Gogan tells us that Jack 'Wasn't goin' to be in anything where he couldn't be conspishuous'. His desire to strut around in a Sam Browne belt looking for admiration seems more like the behaviour of a poseur than that of a hero. The other revolutionaries are also portrayed as men who imagine themselves as heroes without really understanding what war is all about.

The female characters whom we might consider as tragic heroines are Nora Clitheroe and Bessie Burgess but as with the male characters, there are reasons why it is hard to classify them as such. The intense possessiveness of Nora could be regarded as a tragic flaw which eventually leads to her own mental anguish and collapse when Jack leaves her to fight in the rebellion. Tragedy, however, demands that the tragic hero or heroine brings their disaster upon themselves by some action. Rather than causing Jack's death, Nora merely suffers the consequences of her husband's actions, so she cannot be considered a tragic heroine in any real sense. Bessie Burgess' death certainly is 'tragic' in the modern sense of the term but she cannot be considered a tragic heroine because she did not die as a result of any tragic flaw or action on her own part. She died accidentally while trying to drag Nora away from an open window. Her dying words leave no doubt that she had no intention of sacrificing her life. She calls Nora a 'bitch' and cries out: 'This is what's afther comin' on me for nursin' you day an' night . . . I was a fool, a fool, a fool!'

From a close examination of every character in the play, it becomes obvious that *The Plough and the Stars* is therefore not a tragedy in the classical sense. None of the characters gain tragic wisdom or insight from their suffering.

It is probably more accurate to classify the play as a tragi-comedy which combines elements of both tragedy and comedy without belonging fully to either genre. It is tragic because of the many deaths which occur and also because we see the devastating effects of war and poverty on the lives of ordinary human beings who struggle to survive in the most challenging of circumstances. Several forms of the comedy genre are contained in the play. Slapstick or clownish comedy can be observed in several scenes: Peter chases after The Young Covey with a sword; there are humorous quarrels between Bessie and Mrs Gogan and between Fluther and The Covey; the looting; there is an argument over a pram etc. Verbal comedy abounds through the use of repetition of phrases by Fluther, who consistently misuses the word 'derogatory' when expressing his opinions. A similar repetition can be seen in the long-winded title of a book by Jenersky, a political writer, which The Covey quotes to impress his listeners. Mispronunciation of words like 'conspishuous', 'wurum', 'mollycewels' etc. also create humour as do the long, lyrical speeches spoken by Bessie and Mrs Gogan in Act II.

Irony contributes to the comedy when Bessie

and Mrs Gogan aggressively defend their good names in the second act but have no problem joining forces when it comes to looting later on in the play. Likewise, the bragging of Peter and The Covey concerning their notions of honour and idealism are shown to be hollow and almost farcical when they are later revealed as cowards, both physically and morally. O'Casey uses the quarrels between these characters in Act II as a type of satirical (mocking) parody of the Rising where ordinary individuals wage their own personal battles while the Voice of the Man can be heard outside extolling the virtue of war. The fact that the whole scene takes place in a pub adds to the satirical effect.

In addition to the contrasting tragic and comic elements, O'Casey makes effective use of many other contrasts or juxtapositions to highlight serious issues in his play. Fluther's simple Catholicism is contrasted with The Covey's Marxism; Nora and The Covey's opposition to militarism contrasts with Peter's love of military uniforms and processions; Bessie's loyalism and Protestantism contrasts with the republican Catholicism of Mrs. Gogan, Jack Clitheroe and Captain Brennan; The Covey's academic socialist theories are contrasted with Rosie's practical attitudes to personal survival. A major juxtaposition (placing things side-by-side for contrast) is the speech made by the Voice of the Man, which is opposed to the reality we observe in the pub scene in Act II. Here, O'Casey moves rapidly from the outside Voice to the indoor ordinary people in such a way that the view advanced by the Voice as a sacred truth is shown as being false. O'Casey does not tell us that the Voice is speaking empty rhetoric but that implication is clear.

The play does not follow the conventional narrative format where a situation evolves as complications arise, builds to a climax and reaches a conclusion after a key, climactic scene. There is actually no single plot in this play, even though the Clitheroe couple seem to provide the main narrative thread. The play is structured around the development of a theme concerning the clash of opposing ideals

– the social cause of the Labour movement against the delusions of romantic Republican patriotism. **It is not that O'Casey wishes to attack the latter so much as that he wants to show that the wrong war was being fought. The real war, in the playwright's opinion, should have been that waged against poverty, disease and deprivation.** Act I is remarkable for its shapelessness, lack of significant incident and the wide variety of themes introduced. As the play develops through the next three acts, the audience's attention is focused on different characters at different times: Nora, Bessie, Fluther and the interactions between Peter and The Covey. Although Bessie's death is often considered to be the climax of the play, it does not function as such because it does not create any type of resolution. Rather than contriving a conventional form, O'Casey chose to allow events to develop as they would in real life. Exits, entrances and actions appear to be uncontrived – a technique known as 'Naturalism'.

Tension is used effectively at critical moments in the play. In Act I tension builds as Nora and Jack argue about Jack's membership of the Citizen Army. When Jack complains that Nora was '. . . always at me to give up th' Citizen Army, an' I gave it up; surely that ought to satisfy you', Nora angrily retorts 'Ay, you gave it up – because you got the sulks when they didn't make a Captain of you. It wasn't for my sake Jack'. This tension is slightly relieved by a romantic interlude but builds again steadily when Captain Brennan arrives to summon Jack to a meeting and the whole story of Nora's deception concerning the letter of commission is exposed. Jack's rough handling of his wife and her bitter comment that she doesn't care if he never returns from the meeting create tension in the audience and foreshadow another tense scene in Act IV when Jack and Nora engage in a similar exchange. The tension between Nora's desire to keep her husband by her side and Jack's fear that 'all the risks' he is taking will be turned into 'a laugh' is exacerbated by the fact that Lieutenant Langan is badly injured and Captain Brennan is taunting Jack because Nora refuses to let go of him. The scene reaches a climax with Jack roughly flinging his wife to the ground.

The tension in the scene where Bessie Burgess is shot is skilfully managed by the playwright. The audience is presented with the demented Nora, who has miscarried her child and is, as yet, unaware that Jack has been killed. The voices chanting 'Ambulance...lance! Ambu...lance! Red Cro...ss, Red Cro...ss' in a distant street are reminders of the bloodshed outside and are intermingled with Nora's gentle singing of a love song which is suddenly shattered with a burst of rifle fire. Bessie's efforts to pull Nora away from the open window reach a horrifying climax when Bessie stumbles and falls, two rifle shots ring out and Bessie realises that she has been shot. The convulsive jerking of her body, her futile cries for help and her pleading with Nora to fetch help mark what is probably the highest point of dramatic tension in the entire play.

Dialogue plays a crucial role in any play as it has the ability to anchor the narrative in a particular time and place. O'Casey succeeds in representing authentically the language and dialect of the tenement people in the early decades of the twentieth century. Their speech is vibrant, colloquial and wonderfully colourful. An example of this in Act II is when Bessie Burgess exclaims, 'There's a storm of anger tossin' in me heart, thinkin' of all th' poor Tommies, an' with them me own son, dhrenched in water an' soaked in blood, gropin' their way to a shatterin' death, in a shower o' shells!' There is a lyrical quality in this speech that indicates the depth of the speaker's emotion and compassionate attitude to those who suffer. Although she can be aggressive and argumentative, particularly when she is drunk, many of the things Bessie says indicate her true humanity and good nature.

Mrs Gogan's imaginatively embellished images create humour but also indicate a character who is morbidly obsessed with death. When she sees the ostrich plume on Peter's Foresters' uniform she links it to men hanging at the end of ropes, 'When yous are goin' along, an' I see them wavin' an' noddin' an' waggin', I seem to be lookin' at each of yous hangin' at the end of a rope, your eyes bulgin' and your legs twistin' an' jerkin', gaspin' an' gaspin' for air while yous are thryin' to die for Ireland'. The vivid, graphic details used by Mrs Gogan when she is discussing anything to do with death or dying reveals her as a character who has been deeply affected by the deaths of others close to her and by the impending death of her daughter Mollser. Her obsession with this subject is possibly the only way she can actually deal with it.

The socialist jargon used by The Young Covey is another example of language being used to define a type of character. He enjoys using words and phrases such as 'comrade' and 'th' emancipation of th' workers'. But his socialism is merely a façade or type of mask which he wears to conceal his real self-centredness and cowardice. These features of his character emerge later in the play.

The use of violent dialogue occurs frequently in the play and generally reflects the depth of feeling characters have on subjects ranging from politics to religion and social issues. Peter uses the language associated with 'fire and brimstone' sermons to describe his hopes for those who insist on tormenting him, 'I'll leave you to th' day when th' all-pitiful, all-merciful, all-lovin' God'll be handin' you to th' angels to be rievin' an' roastin' you, tearin' an' tormentin' you, burnin' and blastin' you!' The alliteration adds considerably to the venom of this comment, revealing Peter as a peevish and childish individual. Excellent examples of the use of violent language occur particularly in Act II where the tenement dwellers wage a war of words on a variety of subjects.

The Voice of the Man is extremely different in terms of the vocabulary and the phrases used from that of the other characters. The Voice incites the rebels: 'We must accustom ourselves to the thought of arms, we must accustom ourselves to the sight of arms, we must accustom ourselves to the use of arms . . . ' This language is rhetorical in nature with carefully balanced phrases, triadic patterns (groups of three) and repetition. However, there is an underlying violence in this language which is actually more threatening than that voiced by the uneducated people from the tenements who are usually merely venting frustration.

Stage directions (the descriptive text that appears within brackets) are an essential narrative technique in a dramatic text. They speak for the playwright when he is not there, providing details about how he has imagined the environment and atmosphere and describing critical physical aspects of the characters and settings. For example, the elaborate description of the tenement building at the start of the play not only indicates the setting but provides an insight into the efforts of Nora to provide a comfortable home in what is essentially a building which has been the object of 'savage assaults' by its tenants. The presence of Peter's military uniform hints at the military ideals which form so much of the play's meaning. Character is implied in the physical descriptions of characters. For example, Fluther's flashes of violent temper are excellently captured in the description of him as being 'harshly featured, under the left eye is a scar, and his nose is bent from a smashing blow received in a fistic battle long ago'. O'Casey's stage directions are also critical in dictating the intended tempo and rhythm of the piece, particularly in scenes of high suspense or tension such as the death of Bessie Burgess. One could say that they help tell the complete story that is in the playwright's mind.

Character creation is a technique at which O'Casey excels and one which is fundamental to all narrative texts. As already stated, the language used by the characters and the descriptions of these characters in stage directions give the audience great insight into their personalities and motives. We learn about them through what they say, what is said about them by others and how they act. Mrs Gogan provides an insight into the character of Nora in her comments to Fluther in the first scene. Before we even see her in person, we learn that Nora has 'notions of upperosity' and that her relationship with her husband is strained. Her obsessive nature is apparent in her efforts to control not only Jack but The Covey and Uncle Peter. When we actually see and hear Nora, these observations by her neighbour are shown to be quite accurate. Her words, as she attempts to separate her sparring lodgers reveal her personal determination and dominant motivation, 'Are you always goin' to be tearin' down th' little bit of respectability that a body's thryin' to build up? Am I always goin' to be havin' to nurse yous into th' hardy habit o' thryin' to keep up a little bit of appearance'.

Perhaps the finest example of O'Casey's skill in creating character is seen in his creation of Bessie Burgess. She is distinguished from the other characters by her religion, her politics and by the fact that she has a son fighting in a different war. O'Casey highlights her tremendous courage when he shows her hanging out a Union Jack and singing songs like 'Rule Brittania' to enrage her rebel neighbours. Although courageous and oftentimes aggressive, Bessie has a softer, more compassionate side which is hinted at in her subtle acts of kindness to Mollser and becomes more explicit in her compassionate care of Nora towards the end of the play. Bessie is not, however, a sentimental presentation of a heart of gold in a rough exterior. She curses Nora after she herself is shot, calling her a 'bitch'. By creating such a complex individual, O'Casey gives an additional sense of realism to the play.

Most of O'Casey's characters do not bring about changes in events. They are presented as being peripheral to what is going on around them. Although some – like Clitheroe, Langan and Brennan – do engage in the rebellion, they do not bring about any social or political change. What we see is the impact of poverty and low social status as well as the power of rhetoric to influence the uneducated. The characterisation is built around the differing efforts of individuals to cope with such forces.

Imagery and symbolism help to convey much of the play's meaning. Simple items like Nora's new hat and her efforts to furnish her rooms serve to symbolise her hopes of a better life beyond that of tenement living. The insertion of a lock on the door indicates the lack of privacy endured by the tenants generally and symbolises the need for an escape from the surrounding chaos of the building where children play on stairs and neighbours can enter another's room at will.

However, in the overall context of the play's meaning, these symbols are minor compared to those O'Casey employs to express his personal indignation. **The scene set in the pub while a political rally takes place outside is a key moment in *The Plough and the Stars*.** We see and hear the shadowy outline of the Voice like a ghost from the past imposing itself on the living as the workers are inflamed and incited to action by this speech. The pub scene symbolises the obscuring of reality. While Pádraig Pearse (symbolised by the Voice) praises the heroism of bloodshed, the intoxication this causes among those in the pub leads to a series of brawls.

A prominent presence in this scene is that of the prostitute Rosie Redmond who needs to sell her sexual favours in order to survive. The symbolism of this would have been unmistakable to O'Casey's audience, since the Anglo-Irish literary revival of the time often depicted Ireland or Irish nationalism as a woman (for instance in WB Yeats' play *Cathleen Ní Houlihan*). The revolutionaries consider Ireland to be greater than any wife or mother.

In Act IV, the men playing cards on the lid of Mollser's coffin create a metaphor for how the working people have become helpless pawns in the power struggles of political idealists. By failing to fight for their own interests (i.e., an end to the poverty they endured and their lack of access to education) they have lost even more. O'Casey's characters are thus seen as the victims, rather than the protagonists of the 1916 Rising.

KEY POINTS

- *The Plough and the Stars* was described by Sean O'Casey himself as 'a tragedy in four acts'. The play is arranged in two halves: Acts I and II take place in November 1915 and Acts III and IV at Easter 1916.

- The title of the text has an important function in stimulating audience interest and indicating a central issue or focus. The title here is drawn from the flag used by the Labour movement which O'Casey regards as being misused for a different political agenda.

- Although *The Plough and the Stars* is described as being a tragedy by the playwright, it is very difficult to identify any one character as being a tragic hero or heroine. It is not a tragedy in the classical sense as no wisdom or growth in awareness occurs. It could be more accurately described as a tragi-comedy, combining elements of both forms.

- Several forms of the comedy genre are contained in the play: slapstick, verbal comedy, comic repetitions, comic irony, parody and satirical parody.

- In addition to the contrasting tragic and comic elements, O'Casey makes effective use of many other contrasts or juxtapositions to highlight serious issues in his play.

- The play does not follow the conventional narrative format where a situation evolves as complications arise, builds to a climax and reaches a conclusion after a key, climactic scene. It is structured around the theme of opposing ideologies.

- Tension is used effectively at critical moments in the play.

- Dialogue plays a crucial role in any play. O'Casey succeeds in authentically representing the language and dialect of the characters.

- Stage directions (the descriptive text that appears within brackets in the text of the play) are an essential narrative technique in this text.

- Character creation is a technique at which O'Casey excels and one which is fundamental to all narrative texts.

- Imagery and symbolism help to convey much of the play's meaning.

The King's Speech and *The Plough and the Stars*

In O'Casey's play the narrative is arranged in four acts with a time lapse of some months between the first two acts and the last two acts. The dramatic action in the British film *The King's Speech* is carefully centred around four crucial incidents that evolve chronologically with no divisions. These events are: the death in 1936 of King George V, the first monarch to address his subjects via the radio; the accession to the throne of George's eldest son as King Edward VIII and his almost immediate abdication in order to marry the American divorcee Wallis Simpson;

the coronation of King George VI; and finally, in 1939, the outbreak of World War II which catapulted the royal family into immensely important figureheads of national significance during this dark period in world history.

In common with *The Plough and the Stars*, the title of *The King's Speech* is significant and creates a link to the central issues explored in the film. The title, although not symbolic, has a certain ambiguity in the fact that 'Speech' refers not only to the actual speech made by King

George VI (known in his family circle as Bertie) at the end of the film but also to the fact that he had a speech impediment or stutter which fuelled a personal sense of inadequacy and was, for him, a source of tremendous frustration. In the course of the film the director, Tom Hooper, sensitively portrays Bertie's battle and triumph over this obstacle and builds to a moment of climax: the impeccable speech the King publicly broadcasts at the outset of World War II.

***The Plough and the Stars* is inspired by the 1916 Rising. Similarly, *The King's Speech* draws its inspiration from actual historical events. A major genre difference, however, lies in the fact that the characters are fictitious creations in O'Casey's work but are not so in the film. It would therefore be inaccurate to describe this film as narrative fiction.**

In contrast to *The Plough and the Stars* which claims to be a tragedy, the film is the private story of a famous public man, King George VI (known in his family circle as Bertie). It has many common features of an historical film or what has popularly become known as 'heritage' film. A filmmaker dealing with historical events is confronted with certain tasks. Their work need not be literally true in every respect but it must have an underlying historical accuracy. While being true to history in general, *The King's Speech* is, however, a rather sanitised version of events. For example, one major inaccuracy is the depiction of the role played by Winston Churchill in King Edward VIII's abdication. In real life, Churchill was actually sympathetic to Edward and wanted him to retain his title. In the film, he is keen to see Edward's abdication. **By simplifying the rather more complex aspects of the political situation, the director Tom Hooper allows the focus of the film to remain firmly focused on Bertie's battle with his speech impediment and his emerging friendship with his speech therapist Lionel Logue. Both texts share the common feature of placing emphasis on the impact political events can have on ordinary people.**

A similarity between the two texts is the manner in which they avoid any hint of triumphalism or sentimentality. The film explores the nature of courage and public duty which allows it to transcend any political arguments about royalty and republicanism. **Unlike the play which explores the effects of war on ordinary people, The King's Speech is more concerned with one man's personal journey and ability to overcome a major obstacle than it is with considerations relating to ideologies or reflections on war.**

Comedy is effectively used in both texts but in very different ways. In *The King's Speech* there is very little use of the broad humour and slapstick used to almost pantomime effect in O'Casey's play. Some comic moments in the film are related to the techniques used by Sir Blandine-Bentham (the first speech therapist we see Bertie attending) and by Lionel Logue in their efforts to cure Bertie's speech impediment. There is an almost slapstick quality to watching Bertie fill his mouth with marbles at the bidding of the pompous Blandine-Bentham, whose meticulous sterilising and handling of the same marbles makes him appear little more than a clown. Lionel also engages Bertie in a series of wacky exercises, involving tongue twisters, shouting at the top of his lungs, swearing, rolling across the floor and having his wife sit on his stomach while she tentatively enquires if he is 'alright'. The humorous depiction of a member of a royal family undertaking such apparently ridiculous activities creates amusement but is not the only source of laughter. **In a similar manner to *The Plough and the Stars*, much of the film's humour involves witty banter.** The playwright creates sharp, humorous exchanges as Logue fearlessly barges through the pompous royal formality that is all part of the problem, cheerfully deriding Bertie's previous medical advisers: 'They're all idiots!' 'They've been knighted!' splutters Bertie. 'Makes it official then, doesn't it?' Logue replies. Another example shows Lionel who, in an effort to relax Bertie, asks him 'Do you know any jokes?' to which Bertie wittily replies 'Timing isn't my strong suit'. We see similar verbal humour in another question where Lionel asks Bertie if he knows the 'F' word. Bertie's stammering reply 'Fu…fu…fu…Fornication!' creates a moment of laughter in spite of the speaker's anguished attempts to get the word out. When Lionel tries to reassure Bertie that 'Pauses are fine, it shows solemnity', King George VI's response that he is 'the solemnest king in the world!' is poignantly funny. **Such witty exchanges add to the enjoyment of the audience in much the same way as the equally witty exchanges between the tenement dwellers adds to our enjoyment of *The Plough and the Stars*.**

O'Casey uses some ironic situation comedy which almost approaches farce and this technique is also evident in *The King's Speech*. We see examples of this in the scenes where Logue remarks that the King's doctors being knighted makes their being idiots 'official' but later asks for a knighthood for himself near the end of the film. At another point, the King and Queen visit Logue at home while his wife is out. Logue is encouraging Bertie to face his fears, but he himself hides in the corner when his own wife, Myrtle, unexpectedly walks in on them. Logue never told her he was treating a member of the Royal Family. Bertie tells him to stop being a coward and calmly steps out and greets Myrtle.

Several remarks can be seen as witty satirical comments on superficiality. When Lionel asks 'How do you feel?' just before the King makes his speech, Bertie replies that he is 'Full of hot air'. Logue's witty response, 'Isn't that what public speaking is all about?', adds a note of humour to what is a rather tense moment but also highlights the emptiness of mere rhetoric. In another scene, the King's angry reaction when he sees his tutor sitting on the coronation throne – 'Get up! You can't sit there! GET UP!' – is comically deflated by Logue's calm dismissal of royal pomp and circumstance, 'Why not? It's a chair'.

Although humour is used in different ways in each text, one common feature is that the comic serves to highlight that which is serious, or even tragic, in both texts.

The use of contrast as a powerfully dramatic technique is apparent in both texts. The contrast between the relatively comfortable rooms occupied by the Clitheroes in the tenement house highlights Nora's efforts to rise above her neighbours. On a grander scale, *The King's Speech* shifts between fine royal houses and palaces to the contrasting dullness of depression-scuffed 1930s' London. This contrast gives emphasis to the difference in social class between the Royal Family and the maverick Logue, who works in a plain, scruffy room, with dark wood and tatty furniture. The ornate state drawing room, adorned with gilt trellises and traceries, suits the logic of a film that deals with the pressures facing an intensely shy individual, hampered by a terrible stammer yet reluctantly having to become a public figure. It is interesting to note that much of his transformation will take place in Logue's contrastingly humble consulting room.

Contrast is also used in the depiction of the cold, wide-open space of Wembley Stadium with which the film opens and the small, draped room where King George VI makes his famous speech at the end of the film. Instead of the intimidating stares from the assembled crowds at Wembley, we have the friendly face of Lionel Logue as he encourages his pupil with gentle words and warm smiles. By use of this contrast, Hooper is showing us how much Bertie has changed in the course of the film, how comfortable and supported he now feels and how much he has progressed since that initial cold day in Wembley. The close-up shots reveal the difference in Bertie as he delivers his address with new-found confidence to the nation. It is significant that Logue stops conducting him halfway through the speech, to further acknowledge that the King can do it by himself.

Another contrast to the uncomfortable, tense atmosphere evident in the opening scene can be seen in the shots of the enormous crowds of people cheering on the Royal Family when they step onto the balcony in Buckingham Palace after the speech. While it is still a lot of pressure to be looking at so many people all of whom are depending on you, the cheers and waves from the crowd underline the new hope and confidence the people now have in their king. This is in sharp contrast to the silence and discomfort evident in the crowd during Bertie's speech at Wembley in the opening scene.

O'Casey makes effective use of contrasts or juxtapositions to highlight serious issues in his play, and *The King's Speech* makes use of similar juxtapositions. The character of the dutiful Bertie is in strong contrast to the self-centred, rather petulant David who, as King Edward VIII, abdicates the throne; the loving, supportive wives of both Bertie and Lionel Logue are complete contrasts to the more superficial, egotistical Wallis Simpson, David's partner; the unhappy childhood of Bertie under a bullying father are juxtaposed with the warm, family lives of the young princesses and the Logue children; the formality and snobbery of the royals is contrasted with the down-to-earth practical informality of Lionel Logue, who engages in no pretentious behaviour whatsoever. By use of this technique of creating sharp contrast or juxtapositions, Hooper, like O'Casey, draws out the main themes of the narrative.

The narrative structure of *The King's Speech* is typically chronological with a clear beginning, complication, moment of climax or crisis and a final resolution. O'Casey's play, by contrast, is less conventionally structured as it is built around the theme of opposing ideologies. The first stage or opening section of the film introduces the main conflict immediately as we observe the fiasco of Bertie's first speech at Wembley Stadium. This becomes an obstacle which requires a solution as David, Bertie's older brother, is seen by their father, King George V, as an unsuitable candidate for kingship, thereby placing the responsibility for leadership squarely on Bertie's shoulders. Lionel Logue creates a turning point or catalyst in the action as he is the only person who appears capable of truly assisting the stammering prince. A second stage of development occurs when, after the death of his father, David becomes King Edward VIII and shortly after abdicates in order to marry Wallis Simpson. Bertie then becomes King George VI just as World War II is breaking out in Europe. Tension builds as the King questions his therapist's qualifications and blames Lionel Logue for leaving the nation with a 'voiceless king'. A high point is reached in this development section when King George shouts 'I

have a voice', and the belief that he can overcome his impediment is seen. The third section of the film brings the narrative to a climax as the King delivers his first wartime speech successfully, after which a resolution is reached as is clear from the delight of his family, his court and the applause of his subjects. When Bertie thanks his 'friend' and Logue responds by calling him 'Your Majesty', we know that resolution has been attained and all conflict in the relationship resolved.

The creation of tension is effectively managed at critical moments in each of the texts. While it is quite easy to imagine a narrative about a civil uprising creating dramatic tension in *The Plough and the Stars*, it is more difficult to imagine suspense being created in a film which is mainly set in a room where two men talk to each other. The fact that the audience are familiar with the historical facts and know already that Bertie will deliver the important speech also adds to the difficulty faced by Hooper in this regard.

Like all good narratives *The King's Speech* exploits the importance of having high stakes. Given the historical circumstances, the stakes in the film are extremely high. The country has embarked on a war and needs a king who can speak to his nation and the world. Times have changed, as King George V tells Bertie, from the time when 'all a king had to do was look respectable in a uniform and not fall off his horse'. Now the 'devilish device' (the radio) provides an oral medium. George laments that the family must now become 'actors'. Bertie's stammer and lack of self-confidence appear to be totally resistant to cure but he must learn to speak fluently and reassuringly to his people. This situation provides the audience with high personal and public stakes. Very few people watching the film will be immune to the emotional importance of being able to overcome impediments which stand in the way of self-realisation. The screenwriter and director understand this fact and cleverly keep the audience on the edge of their seats, willing Bertie to succeed even though they already know that he will. The audience cringes as Bertie stammers his way through the speech at Wembley and they experience, with the help of some excellent close-up shots, his terror as he prepares at the end of the film to deliver his crucial speech. They will him to succeed because his success supports their own beliefs that they can overcome obstacles also – even if they are very different or of far less public importance.

Dialogue plays as crucial a role in *The King's Speech* as it does in O'Casey's play. Both texts succeed in authentically representing the language and dialect of the characters. One of the main functions of dialogue is to anchor a text in a certain time and place. From the outset of the film, the audience gets a sense of the 'world' of the narrative through the dialogue. The first voice we hear is that of a BBC newsreader who, according to the screenplay, speaks in 'flawless pear-shaped tones'. **The voice of Mrs Gogan establishes her social class and background in the opening lines of the play, and this voice, with its rounded vowels and clipped pronunciation, also creates a sense of context and class.** We learn that we are in 'Wembley Stadium for the closing ceremony of the second and final season of the Empire Exhibition'. The polished, confident and beautifully-paced elocution of the newsreader is replaced by the stammering, uncertain and almost embarrassing efforts of Bertie, the Duke of York, as he attempts to address the gathered crowds, 'I have received from his Majesty the K-K-K...the King, the following gracious message...' This opening sequence tells us where we are and the historical period we are in. It also introduces the main character along with the major conflict which he faces: his inability to speak fluently in a world which is fast becoming used to public broadcasts by members of the Royal Family.

Much of film dialogue, **like that of a stage play,** is to communicate the 'why?' and 'how?' and 'what next?' to the viewer. The 'what next' may be simply an indication of plot development such as that which takes place when Elizabeth visits the therapist Lionel Logue. After a stiff exchange of words between the formal, snobbish Elizabeth and the casual, off-hand Logue, the dialogue brings the scene to a climax which offers a glimpse of hope for a solution to Bertie's dilemma: Lionel confidently asserts, 'I can cure your husband. But for my method to work there must be trust and total equality in the safety of my consultation room. No exceptions'. Elizabeth's reaction to these conditions marks the beginning of a new direction for her husband. Somewhat taken aback by Logue's unexpected brusqueness she replies, 'Well then, . . . in that case . . .' she pauses dramatically before asking 'When can you start?' Here we see dialogue not only marking a turning point but also serving to highlight the clash of social classes which will be continued throughout the film.

Sometimes a simple statement by a character can mark a critical moment. **This is seen in *The Plough and the Stars* when Nora Clitheroe, after a row with Jack, shouts after her departing husband that she doesn't care if he never comes back (although she actually cares immensely) and ends up losing him to the revolutionary cause.** In *The King's Speech,* dialogue is used with a similar effect of marking a critical moment. A good example of this is seen in the scene in which Bertie, now King George VI, confronts Lionel Logue about what he perceives as a betrayal of trust. He believed that Logue was a qualified speech therapist which he is not. Bertie feels betrayed and is obviously worried that Logue's treatment is unlikely to work if he isn't qualified to work as a therapist in the first place. Bertie considers that his Empire has been saddled with 'a voiceless king' at a time when war is about to break out. Logue's calm, dignified explanation of his lack of qualifications leads Bertie to explode with rage, particularly when Logue sits on the coronation throne after offering his explanation. He bellows 'Listen to me...!' and is shocked at Logue's question, 'Why should I listen to you?' The next piece of dialogue marks the critical moment of the King's determination to succeed and his belief that he can. When Lionel asks by what right he should be heard, Bertie exclaims authoritatively that he is 'a man' and that he has 'A VOICE!' He does not stammer once during this outburst. A barrier has been overcome and, for the audience, the stage is set for the successful speech to take place.

As we have already seen in *The Plough and the Stars,* one of the most important functions of dialogue is that of character revelation. In real life we get to know people better by listening to them; obviously, dialogue helps audiences understand the characters' personalities and motivations. The compassionate nature of Lionel Logue is seen in his explanation to Bertie as to why he became a speech therapist. Referring to the traumatised soldiers returning from the trenches after World War I, he says, 'Those poor young blokes had cried out in fear, and no-one was listening to them. My job was to give them faith in their voice and let them know that a friend was listening'. The bullying nature of King George V is revealed earlier in the film by his unsympathetic tone when ordering Bertie to speak into a microphone, 'Sit up, straight back, face boldly up to the bloody thing and stare it square in the eye as you would any decent Englishman. Show who's in command'. We also see the selfish, self-obsessed nature of David. As his father, King George V, lies dying, David proclaims that 'The old bugger's doing this on purpose . . . Departing prematurely to complicate matters'. **The film, like O'Casey's play, abounds in examples of how dialogue reveals character and motivation.**

Dialogue plays a similar role in the film as it does in O'Casey's play insofar as it highlights the major themes. Putting thematic or moral messages in the mouths of their characters, as we see with the socialist opinions of The Covey in *The Plough and the Stars,* allows playwrights and filmmakers to talk to the audience. For example, Lionel Logue expresses the viewpoint of the film that personal experience is more crucially important when dealing with emotional or mental states than any letters after a name expressing academic qualifications. He tells Bertie, 'All I know I know by experience, and that war was some experience. My plaque says, "L. Logue, Speech Defects". No Dr . . . no letters after my name'. The point that experience trumps academic theory is thus succinctly made. One could also examine the speeches made by

Chamberlain, George V, Edward VIII and, of course, the King's wartime speech to explore how the spoken word can carry the film's messages to the audience.

The use of dialect exploits the resources of language in *The Plough and the Stars.* Likewise, *The King's Speech* makes full use of the dialogue and other sound effects to enhance the cinematic experience. After the era of silent movies when audiences for the first time could hear what characters were saying, cinema was offered infinite possibilities in terms of puns, jokes, misunderstandings, witticisms, metaphors, curses, whispers, screams, songs, poetry or storytelling. **It is interesting to compare how singing is used in both texts to convey theme or mood. The love song that Jack sings to Nora communicates better than any words the hopes of the young couple for their relationship and future. In the same way, the hymns of Bessie and songs of the soldiers express their beliefs and hopes.**

The songs that Bertie sings – at Lionel's request – in *The King's Speech* serve a different purpose as they enable Bertie to articulate that which he cannot speak. The cursing and swearing also give him the emotional outlet for his pent-up fury and reminds us of the outbursts which are so common in *The Plough and the Stars.*

O'Casey's use of stage directions to communicate his intentions to the audience in a theatre is replaced by cinematic techniques in *The King's Speech.* Film directors pay close attention to what is known as the point of view shot, or the POV. This refers to a technique where the view, through careful camera shots, enables the audience to see and hear what a character is seeing and hearing and to experience an event from their perspective (as if we for a moment are watching through their eyes). *The King's Speech* uses this technique to great effect by director Tom Hooper. There are many excellent examples of this in the film, so the opening scene will suffice to illustrate the power of the camera in this genre.

Shortly after the film begins, the audience sees Bertie looking profoundly nervous and glum as he makes his way through the tunnels of a concrete building and eventually comes to a flight of stairs. Already, the feeling has been created that he is reluctant to ascend the stairs ahead of him, but he continues this march to a destination unknown to the audience. The camera then cuts to a close-up shot of the stairs and pans the ascent of the Prince until he comes face to face with a microphone. At this point, the camera moves higher to reveal a stadium filled with thousands of people. The audience now realises that a public speech is about to be delivered, but as every single face in the crowd turns expectantly to face the Prince, a sudden feeling of terror is communicated by Bertie's expression. His face is filled with fear and discomfort. The little red light situated beside the microphone on the podium flashes three times and then the light remains steady, indicating the microphone is now live on air, a fact the audience is already aware of due to the POV shot. The use of these shots creates the sense of overwhelming pressure. When Bertie stumbles and stammers the audience understands his dilemma. This scene really sets the tone and solidifies our understanding of the enormity of the task that he faces in order to cure this impediment. By using the POV shot the audience sees how the Prince feels exposed, pressured and alone, regardless of the sympathetic presence of his wife next to him. The awkward, deafening silence in the stadium as he stammers through his speech sums up the void which Lionel Logue will strive to fill.

Imagery and symbolism help to focus the attention of the audience and to convey meaning in both texts. A major symbol in *The King's Speech* is that of the microphone. This 'devilish device' as George V calls it has a controlling influence on the narrative insofar as it symbolises everything most feared by Bertie. Most of the shots of the microphone are close-ups which give it a dominating status. Hooper cleverly uses the camera to look up at the microphone, making it a superior, threatening presence as it looms over the nervous Duke of York as he mounts the stairs at the exibition in Wembley.

The camera in the opening scene also reflects Bertie's psychological state through a series of silent, intense shots. Another important symbol is the long walk through the tunnel which Bertie makes in Wembley and again in London before he speaks to the nation as King George VI. This long, tortured walk represents the journey he has to undertake to overcome his speech impediment and his emergence into a new light of hope when he succeeds in addressing his subjects without stammering. It is interesting to note that his wife is by his side during each of these journeys to the microphone and Lionel Logue joins the King on the final walk. This clearly represents the support which Bertie drew from these two significant individuals in his journey to be a king with a voice.

Small details like the image of a father and his son in the crowds at Wembley foreshadow what we will later realise is the importance of the father/son relationship. Bertie's stammer was exacerbated by the stern relationship George V had with his children and particularly with Bertie because of his defective speech. The dark clouds and pea-soup fog of several outdoor scenes symbolise the depression and confusion in the mind of Bertie as he seeks a way to rid himself of his demons. Interestingly, the speech which Lionel recites at an acting audition begins with the lines: 'Now is the winter of our discontent / Made glorious summer by this sun of York'. These lines from Shakespere's play *Richard III* seem to sum up the major theme of a Duke of York becoming a king with a 'voice' after a long, cold journey towards that goal.

Such symbolic language whether spoken by characters or 'spoken' by the camera adds an extra, enriching dimension to the story in much the same way as the imagery in *The Plough and the Stars* adds depth to the play's themes.

KEY POINTS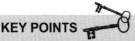

- In O'Casey's play the narrative is arranged in four acts with a time lapse of some months between the first two acts and the last two acts. The dramatic action in the *The King's Speech* is carefully centred around four crucial incidents which evolve chronologically with no such divisions.
- In common with *The Plough and the Stars*, the title of *The King's Speech* is significant and creates a link to the central issues explored in the film. It has a quality of ambiguity rather than a symbolic function such as *The Plough and the Stars*.
- In the same way as *The Plough and the Stars* is inspired by the 1916 Rising, so does *The King's Speech* draw its inspiration from actual historical events. A major genre difference, however, lies in the fact that the characters are fictitious creations in O'Casey's work but are not so in the film.
- In contrast to *The Plough and the Stars* which claims to be a tragedy, the film is the private story of a famous public man, King George VI (known in his family circle as Bertie). It has many common features of an historical/documentary film or what has become popularly known as a 'heritage' film.
- Unlike O'Casey's play which explores the effects of war on ordinary people, *The King's Speech* is more concerned with one man's personal journey and ability to overcome a major obstacle than it is with considerations relating to ideologies or reflections on war.
- Comedy is used in both texts but in very different ways. *The King's Speech* does not make as much use of broad slapstick humour but is more dependant on witty rejoinders and ironic comment. Although humour is used in different ways in each text, one common feature is that the comic serves to highlight that which is serious, or even tragic, in both narratives.
- The use of contrast as a powerfully dramatic technique is apparent in both texts.
- The narrative structure of *The King's Speech* is typically chronological with a clear beginning, complication, moment of climax or crisis and a resolution. O'Casey's play, by contrast, is less conventionally structured as it is built around the theme of opposing ideologies.
- The creation of tension is effectively managed at critical moments in each of the texts. While it is quite easy to imagine a narrative about a civil uprising creating dramatic tension in *The Plough and the Stars,* it is more difficult to imagine suspense being created in a film which is mainly set in a room where two men talk to each other. The tension is created in this text by the highlighting of the high stakes involved in Bertie overcoming his speech impediment.
- Dialogue plays as crucial a role in *The King's Speech* as it does in O'Casey's play. Both texts succeed in authentically representing the language and dialect of the characters.
- Stage directions (the descriptive text that appears within brackets in the text of the play) are an essential narrative technique in this text.
- Imagery and symbolism help to focus the attention of the audience and to convey meaning in both texts.

Foster, The Plough and The Stars and *The King's Speech*

The author Claire Keegan has described *Foster* as a 'long short story'. When asked in an interview whether it could be classed as a novella (a short novel), she emphatically stated that it was definitely <u>not</u> a novella as it does not have the pace of a novella. The narrative is arranged in eight chapters covering a mere 88 pages.

Set in the countryside of County Wexford, it is narrated by a young girl who is fostered out to another family, the Kinsellas, for the summer months while her mother is awaiting the birth of yet another child in an already large family. Due to the kindness of her foster parents, the child finds the space to develop and feel valued. The story has many features of a coming-of-age narrative but is too short to qualify as such. It is more accurate to describe it as a coming-of-awareness narrative which succeeds in illuminating the contrasting lives of the girl's struggling family with that of her well-off relatives.

In common with *The Plough and the Stars* and *The King's Speech*, *Foster* is told in a chronological manner. However, the viewpoint is totally different from that of the other texts as it is written as a first-person narrative. In *Foster,* the author shows us the world through the slanted gaze of a young girl, creating an emotionally complex story, full of anxiety and innocence. Keegan then leaves it to her readers to track the foreshadowing and carefully placed suggestions for ourselves – a technique which gives rise to many interpretations concerning the intention of the author and the meaning readers can draw from the narrative. 'I feel that every single story is completed by its reader, not by its writer', Keegan has said and this is certainly true of this story. The story is told with restraint, honesty and a sense of truth that is refreshing. The author does not intrude on the narrative with stylistic verbosity but simply lets the story unfold as it needs to. The characters and their world are allowed to live and breathe.

In the same way as the titles in the other two texts point to a major theme, the title *Foster* goes straight to the heart of the narrative. This is not only because the child is being physically fostered or cared for by the Kinsellas but because she is also being emotionally and psychologically fostered by them. Her sense of self-worth and self-belief are unexpectedly boosted by her stay in the foster home from which she emerges with a new vision and understanding. The choice of the one word *Foster* as a title, is, in itself, strange. Having read the story one could wonder why it was not called The Foster Child or The Foster Home. The word 'Foster' is neither a noun nor a verb in this context and leaves the reader asking questions as to why the author chose this particular title. **Unlike *The Plough and the Stars* or *The King's Speech,* the title of the story is vague as regards its exact meaning.**

Unlike O'Casey's play or Hooper's film, *Foster* is not profoundly influenced by the historical setting, although the writer does indicate that it takes place during the 1980s by reference to the hunger strikes in Northern Ireland. Although the narrator is unaware of the significance of the political situation in the North, the fact that it is mentioned at all adds a sense of reality to what is a fictitious story. **This is very like *The Plough and the Stars,* where a fictitious story is given a dimension of reality by its connection to actual historical events.**

***Foster* has a similarity with *The King's Speech* insofar as both explore the experience of an individual faced with obstacles that must be overcome before they can discover their own 'voice'.** The girl in *Foster* does not suffer from any speech impediment but her upbringing is in itself an impediment to her development and emotional well-being. Using the simple language of a child, the author manages to convey something of her father's cold attitude towards his little daughter. During the journey to the foster home, her father does not engage with her in any meaningful way, barely responding to her few questions and effectively ignoring her need to understand where she is going, who these people are and why she is being taken there. She only knows that her father wants to get away and leave her with strangers, 'Now that my father has delivered me and eaten his fill, he is anxious to light his fag and get away'. Later, she wonders, 'Why did he leave without so much as a goodbye or ever mentioning when he would come back for me?' By giving the child such questions, the author kindles our interest to know the answers also, a technique which sends us back repeatedly to the text searching for clues as to why this situation has arisen. The simple explanation that perhaps her family cannot afford to feed her seems shallow given that as the eldest child she could have been of most assistance to her pregnant mother around the house and farm and in helping with her younger siblings. The mystery deepens somewhat when the girl tells Edna, her foster mother, that her mother says '… you can keep me for as long as you like'. Such comments stir the imagination to the point that the reader is kept guessing about the real reason for the child's removal from her home. **Keegan does not fill in the gaps in the narrative which creates a totally different literary experience to either of the other two texts as they are both quite explicit in their meaning and in establishing a clear backdrop to the action.**

Unlike *The King's Speech* which follows the usual pattern of an opening, a complication which builds to a climax and a resolution, *Foster* dispenses with the usual conventions of a short story which makes it structurally more like *The Plough and the Stars.*

Foster abandons the well-worn route of taking a dilemma as a starting point with which to generate a series of dramatic incidents that would eventually lead to a climax and resolve shortly afterwards. For example, Keegan could have created a confrontation between the girl and her foster family perhaps or another crisis that would reveal some hidden reasons for her being sent away. Instead, the narrative turns inwards, extracting and exploiting the dramatic tensions that the situation evokes. For example, just before she leaves her home the girl overhears a conversation between her parents as to how long she will be staying with the foster family.

There seems to be no definite timescale involved which creates an added dimension of uncertainty for the child. The fostering arrangement is therefore indefinite, yet there is also something temporary about it. No significant dramatic event ever takes place in the course of the story and the ending is certainly not a resolution as it is deeply ambiguous when the child calls out to her 'Daddy' without identifying whether she is addressing Kinsella or her biological father. Although the secret of the child who drowned is indeed revealed, it is not a turning point in the story because nothing truly significant happens as a result of the child discovering that secret. In expressing admiration for *Foster,* one critic praised it as 'a highwire act of uncommon narrative virtuosity'. Its main attraction lies in a delicate balance between what we are told and what is left unsaid. **This distinguishes it in style from either of the other texts.**

Comedy is used sparingly in *Foster* compared to *The Plough and the Stars* or *The King's Speech.* This is largely due to the fact that a child is the narrator and therefore unaware of irony and incapable of seeing hypocrisy in human behaviour. She has not got the capacity to engage in witty repartee or to understand why other people laugh at things which she does not see as being funny. An example of this is when the Kinsellas both laugh heartily at Dan's mysterious words that 'There won't be a word about it this time twelve months'. However, the atmosphere of brooding tension which hangs over the story is relieved in one key moment when the locals call into the Kinsella household to play cards. The description of the braying laugh of the Ass Casey amidst the witty comments of the players creates humour and **has some similarity to the scene from O'Casey's play when the men sit playing cards in the middle of a tragedy which is unfolding around them.**

As with any good narrative, Keegan makes excellent use of contrast and juxtaposition to give depth to her story. In common with the other two texts much of this contrast is based on characterisation. The loving, supportive Kinsella is a sharp contrast to the reckless, distant

Dan; Edna Kinsella seems more practical in her acceptance of the child's return to her family compared to her husband who is deeply affected by it; the inquisitive, jealous neighbour Mildred is the opposite of the reserved and dignified Kinsellas. Juxtaposition is also used to highlight the comparative wealth of the Kinsellas to the poverty of the child's family, to emphasise the emotional warmth of the fostering environment to the cold distance of the girl's family life and to poignantly contrast the childlessness of the Kinsellas with the large family and partially 'unwanted' siblings of the young narrator.

Tension and conflict play a major part in *Foster* as they do in *The Plough and the Stars* and *The King's Speech*. The main source of tension in the story arises from the actual situation of the fostering arrangement and the child's sense of unease. At one point she says that, 'Part of me wants my father to leave me here while another wants him to take me back, to what I know. I am in a spot where I can neither be what I always am nor turn into what I could be'. When Edna tries to comfort her by telling her that there are things she does not understand because she is too young, the child reflects 'As she says this, I realise that she is just like everyone else, and I wish I was back at home so that the things that I do not understand could be the same as they always are'. Apart from the tension experienced by the child's lack of awareness of what is happening, there is also the tension created by the 'secret' of the drowned son which the neighbour Mildred reveals. The revelation of this secret appears to have more impact on the Kinsellas than it has on the child herself. They seem distraught that she knows and question her concerning every word spoken by Mildred. Perhaps the highest point of tension occurs when the narrator decides later to help Edna by fetching water from the well. The little girl's comment that 'It could be the last thing I do' strikes a note of terrified suspense in the reader who knows that a child has already died in an accidental drowning. For one irrational moment (given that the story is being told by the child), there is a sense of foreboding tension as the young girl, dressed in the clothing of the dead

child, makes her way to the well. A nightmarish description follows as the child, bending over with the bucket, feels 'another hand just like mine seems to come out of the water and pull me in'. The relief felt when she suffers no more than a heavy cold as a result of this experience has the effect of an anti-climax. However, the realisation of how close they came to experiencing a second tragedy deeply affects John and Edna Kinsella. At the end of the story, there is a new 'secret', this time concerning what could have been rather than what actually happened. The girl's mother is instinctively aware that something has happened but the girl refuses to tell. Edna's 'sobbing and crying, as though she is crying not for one now, but for two' suggests that she is releasing the terrible tension of knowing that two children could have been lost and that this journey home might never have taken place for the child whom she and her husband so lovingly fostered. The narrative ends on a tense note as the child, clinging tightly to Kinsella, sees her father coming towards them '…strong and steady, his walking stick in his hand'. Will there be an altercation? We never find out as the narrative ends on the tense, ambiguous cry, ' "Daddy", I keep calling him, keep warning him. "Daddy" '. The use of the word 'warning' here is open to several interpretations which leaves the narrative open-ended and uncertain. **Unlike the tension built up in *The King's Speech*, which ultimately resolves, there is no resolution of suspense in *Foster*.**

All three texts are successful in representing authentically the language and dialect of the characters. The dialect of the rural people is captured superbly just as the speech of the tenement dwellers is captured in *The Plough and the Stars*. Phrases like 'Have ye not the hay cut?' and 'Aren't ye late?' are typical of the manner of speaking of people from more rural areas. Kinsella greets Dan by asking 'What way are you?' and Edna asks the child what is 'ailing her' when she sees her discomfort at the shabby state of her clothing. Little words and phrases such as this, which are littered throughout the text, help to establish the rural Wexford dialect or manner of speaking and assist in adding realism to the story.

Dan is skilfully presented through the dialogue as being an insincere almost ignorant individual. He lies repeatedly about his work on the farm claiming that, 'The loft is full to capacity. I nearly split my head on the rafters pitching it in'. However, we later learn that it is the girl's mother who has to take over most of the responsibility for the work on the farm and pay men to take the hay in. **In this respect, Dan reminds us of several characters from *The Plough and the Stars*, who engage in bragging and lies to cover their own feelings of inadequacy.** Dan is more inclined to gamble, drink and satisfy his sexual appetite than to behave and speak like a loving father. He refers to the child as 'You', never mentioning her name or addressing her with respect or affection.

In complete contrast to the distant attitude of Dan, John Kinsella addresses the child by two nicknames. He refers to her as 'Long Legs' to celebrate her ability to run quickly and jokingly tells her that, 'By the time you're ready for home you're to be as fast as a reindeer, so there'll not be a man in the parish will catch you without a long-handled net and a racing bike'. He also calls her 'Petal', which is not her actual name but a form of endearment. It is remarkable that Keegan never actually reveals the child's name, the names of her siblings or the name of the Kinsellas' dead son. This may be because she is reflecting the relative anonymity of children in a society controlled by adults. The distance thus created also gives children an almost universal, symbolic quality as they represent the meaning and hope which a child can bring to a family and the emotional devastation when an only child is lost.

The dialogue between the narrator and Edna Kinsella is very revealing of both characters. Mrs Kinsella is presented as a reserved individual. Although she is very kind and caring towards her charge, she seems to maintain a more detached attitude towards her than that of her husband. She speaks in brief sentences to the child, asking questions, giving explanations of how jobs are done and commenting occasionally on the child's appearance, 'I think it's nearly time you had a bath', '"You have nice long toes," she says. "Nice feet."'. However, she never really converses with the girl as though she were in any way emotionally attached to her. This is possibly due to the fact that she has already accepted that the girl will go home eventually and she cannot bear to become too attached only to lose a child again. Many of her comments and questions concerning the girl's mother, her tactful handling of the wet mattress on the first night and her efforts to reassure the child that there are no secrets and no cause for shame reveal a loving, caring person who has been dealt a blow from which she can hardly recover.

Keegan's prose is stark and pared back to essentials but her use of dialogue has **the same impact on the reader's understanding of characters as that used in *The Plough and the Stars* and *The King's Speech*, adding realism by creating a sense of time, place, character and attitude.**

In common with O'Casey's play and Hooper's film, *Foster* makes effective use of symbolism and imagery. In one of her interviews Keegan said: 'It's essentially about trusting in the reader's intelligence rather than labouring a point. To work on the level of suggestion is what I aim for in all my writing'. This 'suggestion' is closely related to her use of symbol and image. The style of Keegan's writing is exquisitely simple yet it carries a depth of underlying emotion and meaning. She manages to capture the essence of rural Ireland and the story of the young girl's engagement with the world in very few words and through meaningful images. Take for example the passage describing Kinsella's preparation of a meal for the girl and her father, 'The kettle rumbles up to the boiling point, its steel lid clapping. Kinsella gets a stack of plates from the cupboard, opens a drawer and takes out knives and forks, teaspoons. He opens a jar of beetroot and puts it on a saucer with a little serving fork, leaves out sandwich spread and salad cream. Already there's a bowl of tomatoes and onions, chopped fine, a fresh loaf, ham, a block of red cheddar'. By means of this apparently simple description, Keegan manages to convey the comfortable lifestyle of the Kinsellas; their generosity and hospitality; the difference between her father who gives no assistance in the household and Kinsella who helps his wife by setting the table; the plentiful food which acts as a contrast to the hunger strikes taking place in Northern Ireland and the famines in Africa. The fine details used in the description of the food add a realism and authenticity to the experience as it makes its impact on the narrator. Food, which is always carefully prepared throughout this story, has this effect of representing peace, tranquillity, contentment and the satisfying of appetite – whether it is the appetite for physical or emotional nourishment.

The well is another important symbol in the text. Not long after the child arrives she is brought to see the well by Mrs Kinsella. 'There's not a finer well in the parish,' Edna claims, inviting the child to taste the water. The narrator's reaction to the water is symbolic of her sense that she has embarked on a cleaner, fresher way of life and that this water represents all that she thirsts for. 'This water is as cool and clean as anything I have ever tasted. I dip it again and lift it level with the sunlight. I drink six measures of water and wish, for now, that this place without shame or secrets could be my home.' The symbolism changes dramatically when the child almost drowns in the well later in the narrative. Now the well becomes symbolic of danger and death. The path is 'muddy and slippery in places' and the water level higher. The water, once so pure and fresh, appears to be 'sucking the edge of the step' before 'another hand' just like her own 'seems to come out of the water and pull [her] in'. The well and the danger it posed to the girl becomes a 'secret' between herself and the Kinsellas. It represents the change which has taken place in her since she left her home to live with her foster parents and the life-sustaining nature of their love towards her. It simultaneously represents the reality of the danger which this experience poses for her relationship with her own parents, particularly her relationship with her father.

When summoned home by her mother, she appears to drown in a well of sadness which sucks her deep down, almost to destruction, 'I stand there and stare at the fire, trying not to cry . . . I wake earlier than usual and look out at the wet fields, the dripping trees, the hills, which seem greener than they did when I came'.

The image of drowning but surviving the experience also occurs when Kinsella tells the child that fishermen sometimes find horses at sea, 'A man I know towed a colt in once and the horse lay down for a long time and then got up. And he was perfect'. This image is an attempt to reassure the girl that although 'a strange thing' has happened as a result of Mildred's revelation of the secret to her, she will survive that disturbing experience.

The image of the lost heifer also carries a symbolic meaning. The child's father lost 'a red heifer playing cards' which would have been a substantial financial loss for his family who struggle to survive. Here, the heifer symbolises the reckless gambling nature of Dan who seems incapable of accepting his responsibility as a husband and father. Further on, as the child walks to the wake with Edna, they see a lost heifer, 'At the first crossroads, we meet a heifer, who panics and races past us, lost'. Just after Mildred reveals the secret of the boy's death, the heifer is referred to again, 'Farther along, the same heifer is still lost, in a different part of the road'. Heifers are herd animals who panic when they become lost and alone. Symbolically, this could be read as an image of the child herself who needs to belong to a family which protects and cherishes her. The fact that the heifer is racing in her search for her herd links to the child racing towards the Kinsellas as they are departing from her and clinging to them in an effort to feel less 'lost'.

In common with *The Plough and the Stars* and *The King's Speech*, such use of imagery, along with the beautifully lyrical style of writing, enriches the text and adds to the depth of its meaning.

KEY POINTS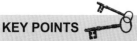

- The author Claire Keegan has described *Foster* as a 'long short story'. It is arranged in eight chapters and is the shortest of the three texts, being only 88 pages long.

- In common with *The Plough and the Stars* and *The King's Speech, Foster* is narrated in a chronological manner. However, the viewpoint is totally different from that of the other texts as it is written as a first person narrative.

- In the same way as the titles in the other two texts point to a major theme, the title *Foster* goes straight to the heart of the narrative but has a quality of uncertainty as to its exact meaning.

- Unlike O'Casey's play or Hooper's film, *Foster* is not profoundly influenced by the historical setting, although references to the hunger strikes in Northern Ireland clearly indicate that it takes place during the 1980s.

- *Foster* has a similarity with *The King's Speech* insofar as both texts explore the experience of an individual faced with obstacles which must be overcome before they can discover their own 'voice'.

- Keegan does not fill in the gaps in the narrative. This creates a totally different literary experience than either of the other two texts which are quite explicit in their meaning and in establishing a clear backdrop to the action.

- Unlike *The King's Speech* which follows the usual pattern of an opening, a complication which builds to a climax and a resolution, *Foster* dispenses with the usual conventions of a short story which makes it structurally more like *The Plough and the Stars.*

- Comedy is used sparingly in *Foster* compared to *The Plough and the Stars* or *The King's Speech*. This is largely due to the fact that a child is the narrator and therefore unaware of irony and incapable of seeing hypocrisy in human behaviour.

- As with any good narrative, Keegan makes excellent use of contrast and juxtaposition to give depth to her story. In common with the other two texts much of this contrast is based on characterisation.

- Tension and conflict play a major part in *Foster* as they do in *The Plough and the Stars* and *The King's Speech*. The main source of tension in the story arises from the actual situation of the fostering arrangement and the child's sense of unease. Unlike the tension built up in *The King's Speech,* which ultimately resolves, there is no resolution of suspense in *Foster.*

- All three texts are successful in authentically representing the language and dialect of the characters. The dialect of the local people is captured superbly just as the speech of the tenement dwellers is captured in *The Plough and the Stars.*

- Keegan's prose is stark and pared back to essentials but her use of dialogue has the same impact on the reader's understanding of characters as that used in *The Plough and the Stars* and *The King's Speech,* adding realism by creating a sense of time, place, character and attitude.

- In common with O'Casey's play and Hooper's film, *Foster* makes effective use of symbolism and imagery.

Sample Answer

C. LITERARY GENRE

'The creation of memorable characters is part of the art of good storytelling.'

Write an essay comparing the ways in which memorable characters were created and contributed to your enjoyment of the stories in the texts you have studied for your comparative course. It will be sufficient to refer to the creation of <u>one</u> character from each text.

In all texts the delineation of character is essential to establish the necessary illusion of credibility so that the reader or viewer can enter into the world of the narrative in a meaningful way. Unsophisticated narratives tend to have simple characters such as we read about in fairy tales, but quality storytelling demands more 'rounded' characters. Real people do not fall into simple categories of good or bad; they are not just the embodiments of recognisable qualities. They are complicated, even contradictory. Unlike the stock symbolic figures of simple narrative, they have some capacity to understand themselves. The creation of memorable characters in the texts which I studied for my course added greatly to my enjoyment and helped me to appreciate the skills of the storytellers.

The texts which I have studied for comparative purposes are the play *The Plough and the Stars* by Sean O'Casey, the film *The King's Speech* directed by Tom Hooper and the 'long short story' *Foster* by Claire Keegan. Each of these texts presents characters who are truly memorable and who are convincing mainly because of their complexity. For purposes of comparison, I have chosen Bessie Burgess from O'Casey's play, King George VI from *The King's Speech* and the child narrator from *Foster*.

Although *The Plough and the Stars* is described as being a tragedy by the playwright, it is very difficult to identify any one character as being a tragic hero or heroine. Bessie Burgess comes closest to the role and certainly is one of the most memorable characters in the play. Through his use of detailed stage directions, O'Casey introduces us to Bessie in Act I: 'She is a woman of forty, vigorously built. Her face is a dogged one, hardened by toil and a little coarsened by drink'. The detail of this description prepares us for the aggressive behaviour of Bessie in the play. Her lyrical use of language, snide comments and witty retorts when arguing her case with Mrs Gogan in Act II added great enjoyment to my experience of the play.

There is no doubt that like Bessie Burgess, King George VI, known as Bertie to his family, emerges as one of two outstanding characters in *The King's Speech*. Like Bessie, he is presented early on in the text although in this case it is not by stage directions but by the superb camera shots which open the narrative of the film. Shortly after the film opens, the audience sees Bertie looking profoundly nervous and glum as he makes his way through the concrete tunnels of an unknown building and eventually comes to a flight of stairs. The camera then cuts to a close-up shot of the stairs and pans the ascent of the Prince until he comes face to face with a microphone. At this point, the camera moves higher to reveal a stadium filled with thousands of people. The audience now realise that a public speech is about to be delivered, but as every single face in the crowd turns expectantly to face the Prince, a sudden feeling of terror is communicated by Bertie's expression. His face is filled with fear and discomfort. When he stumbles and stammers the audience understands his dilemma. By using the camera in such a creative way the director allows the audience to see how the Prince feels exposed, pressured and alone, regardless of the sympathetic presence of his wife next to him. In both texts, stage directions or skilful film directing allow us to form initial impressions of these major characters and to engage with them in a way which I found both interesting and enjoyable.

The child in *Foster* is presented to the reader in a far more subtle way. Because she is the narrator of the text and everything is seen through her eyes only, she is immediately present in the text, which is narrated in the present tense. I enjoyed the way the writer involves the reader by letting us see how events unfold from a young child's perspective. Unlike the characters in each of the other texts, we are not prepared in any way for the child's entry into the narrative and she is not even given a name. The author Claire Keegan allows the reader to form their own impression of the young girl by the manner in which she tells the story as it occurs. For example, in the opening paragraph, we can see that the child is sensitive to nature and extremely observant. She describes the 'hot August day, bright, with patches of shade and greenish sudden light along the road'. Her acute memory can be seen in her capacity to associate places with events such as her father losing 'our red shorthorn in a game of forty-five' and her imaginative, sensitive nature reveals itself in her concerns about the people she will be going to live with for an indefinite period, 'I see a tall woman standing over me, making me drink milk still hot from the cow. I see another, less likely version of her, in an apron, pouring pancake batter into a frying pan, asking would I like another, the way my mother sometimes does when she is in good humour. The man will be her size. He will take me to town on the tractor and buy me red lemonade and crisps. Or he'll make me clean out sheds and pick stones and pull ragweed and docks out of the fields'. From just this first paragraph, the reader gleans many points about the child which will become increasingly important as the narrative progresses.

All three texts therefore introduce memorable characters who immediately capture the imagination of the reader or viewer but do so in different ways according to their specific genres.

The development sections of each text give us further insight into these central characters. Not long after her initial introduction, we discover that Bessie Burgess is a Protestant woman, a supporter of British rule in Ireland and completely opposed to the rebellion of 1916. Most of what we discover about her background emerges from her own dialogue. She accuses the rebels of being 'lice' who 'crawl about feedin' on the fatness o' the land' and regards her own son, who is fighting in the trenches of World War I, as a true hero. Her passionate nature is shown when she says, 'There's a storm of anger tossin' in me heart, thinkin' of all the poor Tommies, an' with them me own son, dhrenched in water and soaked in blood, gropin' their way to a shatherin' death in a shower o' shells!' There is a lyrical quality in this speech which is indicative of the depth of the speaker's emotion and her compassionate attitude to those who suffer. Although she can be aggressive and argumentative, particularly when she is drunk, many of Bessie's actions indicate her true humanity and good nature and make her a more complex character. I enjoyed how O'Casey reveals her softer, more compassionate side by hinting at it in her subtle acts of kindness to the dying Mollser to whom she gives food and drink. When I first saw a production of this play, I formed the impression that Bessie was a thoroughly unlikeable individual until the moment when she quietly offered Mollser a drink of milk and I realised that her hard exterior might not be a true reflection of the real person.

In the same way as O'Casey develops the character of Bessie, the direction of *The King's Speech* also develops the character of Bertie through dialogue and background information. A key moment occurs in the scene where Bertie, who has a violent temper just like Bessie Burgess, confides in his therapist Lionel Logue. Up to this moment, Bertie has been a bit of an enigma for the audience as he seems to be able to speak quite fluently when he interacts with his wife or their children yet stammers or remains silent when in company. He has also developed an ability to speak to Lionel without too much difficulty but his terror at having to speak publicly remains. Shortly after his father's death, he reveals the source of his speech impediment. One can only feel immense pity for Bertie as he recounts the manner in which he was treated by his bullying father, ridiculed for his stammer by other family members, pinched and starved by a sadistic nanny and punished for being left-handed.

In addition to this psychological abuse, he had to endure the 'bloody agony' of wearing metal splints to correct knock-knees. The scene reaches a moment of intense poignancy when Bertie admits that Lionel is the first ordinary person he has ever spoken to. When Lionel asks him 'What're friends for?', he can only reply that he 'wouldn't know'. In both texts therefore, the audience experiences a warmth and affection for the central character despite the knowledge that they are deeply flawed human beings in other areas of their lives, given to violent outbursts of temper and even abusing others as a result of their own frustrations.

Claire Keegan in *Foster* also gives us a deeper insight into the character of the child by providing important background information on her family circumstances and through the use of her dialogue with the Kinsellas. The child is fully aware that her father is an irresponsible liar who does not play his part in the support of his family. 'I wonder why my father lies about the hay. He is given to lying about things that would be nice, if they were true' she thinks, after her father brags that he has been working hard at drawing in the hay. She is aware that he gambled away the family's heifer in a game of cards and that her mother is overburdened with the work of the farm. She tells Edna that the hay is not in because her mother could not afford to pay the labourers but when Edna asks if it would be offensive to send money she has no hesitation in replying that her father would resent it. Although it is, at times, heartbreaking in intensity, I enjoyed how the writer lets us piece together the picture for ourselves through subtle suggestion and as much by what is not spoken as that which is. In a key scene, the girl reveals her closeness to the affectionate Kinsella when they are walking to the shore. A moment of tremendous poignancy, similar to that when Bertie confides in Lionel, occurs when she says, 'Kinsella takes my hand in his. As he does it, I realise that my father has never once held my hand, and some part of me wants Kinsella to let me go, so that I won't have to think about this. It's a hard feeling but, as we walk along, I settle and let the difference between my life at home and the one I have here be'. Both she and Bertie have been, in their own respective ways, the victims of negligent, emotionally cold fathers who bear a great deal of responsibility for the suffering of their children. The beauty of Keegan's lyrical prose – its sparseness and simplicity – contributes greatly to the reader's enjoyment and the memorable quality of this key moment.

The development of the three characters, seen through background information offered in their dialogue, establishes each one of them as being in some way isolated and unhappy due to personal circumstances. Bessie is an outsider because of her politics and religion, Bertie feels isolated because of his speech impediment and the child in *Foster* has suffered unhappiness because she has been neglected and made to feel worthless by a drunken, irresponsible father. Their capacity to endure suffering and rise above it makes them not only admirable but immensely memorable in my opinion.

In each of the texts, the endings serve to consolidate the impressions made by the central characters up to this stage of the various plots. I was personally horrified at the manner in which Bessie Burgess met her death. The tension in the scene where she is shot is skilfully managed by the playwright. The audience is presented with the demented Nora, who has miscarried her child and is still unaware that Jack has been killed. The voices chanting 'Ambulance...lance! Ambu...lance! Red Cro...ss, Red Cro...ss' in a distant street are reminders of the bloodshed outside and are intermingled with Nora's gentle singing of a love song which is suddenly shattered with a burst of rifle fire. Bessie's efforts to pull Nora away from the open window reach a horrifying climax when Bessie stumbles and falls, two rifle shots ring out and Bessie realises that she has been shot. The convulsive jerking of her body, her futile cries for help and her pleading with Nora to fetch help mark what is probably the highest point of dramatic tension in the entire play. Because Bessie has changed from being an aggressive, drunken creature who enjoys haranguing her neighbours into a compassionate individual who supports a neighbour, her death is profoundly moving. Who could ever forget her pleas to Nora to fetch help or her anguished accusation of the 'bitch' who has caused her death? In this moment O'Casey does not sentimentalise Bessie but presents a woman who deserves our admiration because she allowed human compassion to rise above petty differences. I know I will always remember this complex character who is appropriately summed up by Fluther Good, 'I always knew there was never anything really derogatory wrong with poor oul' Bessie'.

The outcome of the plot for King George VI is quite different than that for Bessie Burgess in O'Casey's play. After a valiant battle to overcome his stammer and take on the public duties of a king, Bertie achieves what can only be described as a magnificent victory. His personal battle is presented in the film as having some degree of progress which is immediately offset by periods of regression and despair. The King argues with and blames his therapist for the fact that he is a 'voiceless' king, before he finally discovers his confidence and asserts that he is 'a man' who has a 'VOICE'. Although the audience have been aware all along that Bertie will triumph and deliver his address to the nation, the moment is superbly handled and deeply moving. The final scene is almost a replica of the initial walk through the dark tunnel towards the light, as George VI makes his way to the microphone. This time, however, the set is different. Instead of the intimidating crowds at Wembley Stadium, we see the King in a small room, alone with his therapist and friend who only needs to guide him for half of the speech because he is able to complete it on his own. The skilful camera work, perfect pacing and emotional intensity is absolutely memorable. I almost cheered myself with the crowd who acknowledged this courageous man as he stepped onto the balcony of Buckingham Palace having faced his worst fear and overcoming it.

The ending of *Foster* surprised me even more than the death of Bessie Burgess in *The Plough and the Stars*. Even though I knew that the girl would probably have to return to her family home, Keegan's writing created such a convincing case for her remaining with the Kinsellas that I believed the story might end on a happy note. It would seem to be the perfect ending for the Kinsellas who would have a child to love and cherish and for the child herself to continue to thrive physically and emotionally under their care. However, Keegan inserts an unexpected twist when the young girl, watching her foster parents depart, runs in a panic reminiscent of the lost heifer who seeks her herd, towards the only man she can recognise as fulfilling the role of a father. As she clings to him, she 'can feel him, the heat of him coming through his good clothes, can smell the soap on his neck'. I found this a beautiful moment which was only marred by the fact that as she clung to Kinsella, she could see her biological father coming towards them, bearing a walking stick. I found it difficult to interpret what exactly this meant. Was Dan going to attack Kinsella or the child for some reason? Or was he just coming to bring her home? When the child says that she kept 'calling him' and 'warning him' by using the word 'Daddy', I found it difficult to know whether she was speaking to Kinsella or to her own father and wondered what the 'warning' was about. It is an intriguing part of Keegan's style. Because of the weight of suggestion or insinuation with which the narrative is laden, the reader finds the need to go back and read the entire story again, seeking answers where none are really provided. I found myself wanting to know if the Kinsellas ever saw that child again, whether she settled back into her family life or whether she pined for the couple who had nourished her so lovingly. It is, in my opinion, the mark of a great writer that anyone reading their work wants more. This technique encouraged me to become an active reader, filling in the gaps for myself and working out my own ending for this memorable child narrator.

As can be seen from the above discussion, texts in different genres use specific techniques which not only result in enjoyable, memorable stories but in exceptionally memorable characters who linger in our imaginations long after their stories have been told.

Guidelines for Answering Exam Questions: Comparative Study

1   In the examination you are asked to compare the texts under one of three different modes of comparison. Two of these modes will appear on the paper and you will be asked to select one and discuss it in relation to the three texts you have studied. You should write for about 65 minutes. The modes are as follows.

        A.   **Theme or Issue:** Complex Relationships: This relates to the exploration of complex relationships that exist between certain characters and how it can add greatly to our understanding and interpretation of a text.

        B.   **The General Vision or Viewpoint:** This relates to the author's/director's outlook on life. Their viewpoint influences our perspective of the text and its setting.

        C.   **Genre:** This refers to the ways in which a story is told.

2   Comparison means both similarities and differences.

3   Texts must be discussed in relation to each other – identify and explore links between them.

4   Avoid summarising the stories of the texts that you have studied – your response should be analytical / discursive in approach.

5   There are two types of question – the single essay-type question and the two-part question.

6   The two-part question generally makes reference to a key moment / key moments. After you identify and describe a key moment, you may range through the text to establish the context and significance of this particular moment.

7   Where the essay-type question is concerned, address the question in your opening paragraph and outline your response to it.

8   Each paragraph in the essay-type answer should be based on one point of comparison between the texts. Aim to bring the different texts together in each paragraph with a view to producing a coherent comparative analysis.

9   The opening sentence in each paragraph should make the point of comparison.

10   Each point should be illustrated by relevant and accurate reference to (and possibly quotation from) the texts under discussion.

11   Refer back to the terms of the question at intervals to ensure that your response remains focused on the key issues.

12   As well as comparing the texts, show that you have engaged with them on a personal level – give your personal reaction to certain aspects of the texts that have come up for discussion in your response and that had an impact on you.

13   Write a brief conclusion.

14   Use the language of comparative analysis, e.g.:

- *I noticed in both Text A and Text B that . . .*
- *Text C differs from both Text A and Text B in that . . .*
- *While both Text A and Text B highlight this issue, they treat it in a different manner.*
- *In contrast to Text A, Text B . . .*
- *Only in Text C do we see . . .*
- *John in Text A reminds me of Peter in Text B because . . .*
- *The manner in which A is portrayed in this text differs from its portrayal in my two other comparative texts . . .*
- *I was struck by the sharp contrast between the responses of the protagonists when confronted by . . .*
- *The worlds of both Text A and Text B have a number of common features.*
- *The vision of society in Text A is much more positive than the vision of society in Text B.*

TAKE CARE OF YOURSELF!

Well-Being in Post-Primary Schools

Guidelines for Mental Health Promotion and Suicide Prevention

The Well-Being Guidelines are available to download at: **www.education.ie**

Looking after your well-being is one of the most important things you can do. If you have a problem don't be shy about asking for help. Everyone has difficult times - yes, everyone!

We all need a friend or adult we trust who accepts us and believes in us. Talk to someone: maybe a family member, friend, teacher or guidance counsellor. Don't struggle alone.

Help is there for you. Ask your teachers about the **Well-Being Guidelines for Post-Primary Schools.** They give lots of advice for your school on how to work together to make things better for everyone.

SOME USEFUL WEBSITES:

Spunout.ie
Reachout.ie
Letsomeoneknow.ie

This Well-Being campaign is supported by the Department of Education and Skills with the co-operation of the Irish Educational Publishers Association.

Poetry

Biography / Poetry / Sample Answers

John Donne

Biographical Note

John Donne (1572–1631) was born in London into a prosperous Catholic family. His father was a successful merchant but unfortunately died when John was only four years old. His mother was a grandniece of Sir Thomas More who had been executed by King Henry VIII in 1535 because he would not accept Henry as supreme head of the church. In a time of religious upheaval, the minority Catholic population suffered discrimination and persecution. Donne was educated at home (possibly by Jesuits), entering the University of Oxford at the age of twelve. Because he was a Catholic he was not allowed to receive a degree. He later attended Cambridge where he studied rhetoric and logic before going on to study law at Lincoln's Inn, London. It was during this period that much of Donne's early poetry was written. He is reported to have had an active social life in London. In 1595 Donne abandoned his allegiance to Catholicism and converted to Anglicanism (a branch of Protestantism).

Over the next couple of years Donne participated in two naval expeditions – one against Spain and the other to the Azores (islands off the coast of Portugal). When he returned he became personal secretary to Sir Thomas Egerton, a powerful lawyer who often acted as Queen Elizabeth's legal representative. With Egerton impressed by him, Donne's career prospects seemed to be promising. However, his decision to secretly marry Egerton's seventeen-year-old niece, Ann More, resulted in his brief imprisonment. A poorly paid job as a lawyer meant that Donne struggled to support his wife and the large family they went on to have together. Happily he was eventually reconciled with his father-in-law and Ann received a dowry that greatly improved their material circumstances.

In 1615 King James, impressed with Donne's religious writings, persuaded him to become an Anglican priest. In 1617 Donne's wife Ann died in childbirth. In 1620 Donne was appointed Dean of St. Paul's, going on to earn a reputation as the greatest preacher of that period. He died in 1631 and the first edition of his poems was published two years later.

Metaphysical Poetry

John Donne is one of a group of poets known as 'The Metaphysicals'. The term 'metaphysical' refers to a particular style of poetry which was written between 1590 and 1680. This period of history followed the Reformation and was a time of new scientific thinking and of intense questioning of traditional values. (Literally, the word 'metaphysical' describes that which transcends the physical).

The main stylistic features of metaphysical poetry are:

- Metaphysical poetry deals with **ideas and concepts**. These may be philosophical and are often related to the themes of **love** and **religion**.
- **Logical argumentation:** there is usually a debate going on, as in a law-court, in which a case is being made for or against somebody or something. Frequently the argument is with the poet's lover, with God or with himself.
- **An intellectual approach** to subject matter and themes, which gives the impression of the poet being somewhat detached. Despite their intellectual quality, most of the metaphysical poets were also **very passionate** but they managed to **combine intellect** and **emotion**.
- Clever, unusual figures of speech, known as **conceits**, which make startling comparisons between apparently totally dissimilar things.
- **Wit** or clever reasoning, using puns, conceits and paradoxes (apparent contradictions).

- The presence of a **strong, individual 'voice'**.
- **Conversational language** which gives a sense of realism and sincerity. This was a reaction to the more ornamental, polished language of earlier poetry.
- The best metaphysical poetry is **honest, unconventional** and reveals the poet's sense of the complexities and contradictions of life. It is intellectual, analytical and psychological. Frequently it is absorbed in thoughts of death, physical love and religious devotion.
- **Conciseness of expression**: an attempt to

communicate the maximum thought in the minimum of words.
- **Dramatic techniques** such as sudden, startling openings, rhetorical questions, variety of tone and mood etc.

Donne's poems on the syllabus can be divided into:

1. A series of early **love poems**.
2. The religious or **Holy Sonnets** revealing the poet's quest for spiritual meaning in his life. Donne wrote these poems later in his life.

The Sunne Rising

The whole of *The Sunne Rising* is a dramatic apostrophe (address) to the sun, which is personified throughout the poem. Donne uses the sun to represent different things. In the first stanza the sun marks the passing of hours and the changing of the seasons. Such a passage of time is seen as an enemy to the poet's love as he wishes to remain in this loving moment forever. The sun also represents power, strength and authority, calling all to work and duty. Rather than welcoming the sun as a source of life and light, Donne expresses a different attitude towards it, describing it in very disparaging (insulting) terms.

The poem opens in a wonderfully dramatic manner with the poet addressing the sun in a conversational voice, 'Busy old fool, unruly sun'. The rising sun is dismissed as an interfering busybody insensitively intruding into the lovers' intimate world. The poet questions the power of time over the lovers, 'Must to thy motions lovers' seasons run?' The sun is derided as 'a saucy pedantic wretch' foolishly obsessed with time. Donne directs the sun to awaken those who have duties to perform such as schoolboys, apprentices, courtiers and farmers. We can visualise the 'sour prentices' (apprentices) sullenly dragging

themselves from their beds, while the image of farmers as 'country ants' suggests the busy day that awaits them as they bring in the harvest. All are engaged with activities outside themselves, activities which they resent having to do but must. The poet confidently asserts that the lovers are not controlled by and can even transcend time: 'Love, all alike, no seasons knows, nor clime, / Nor hours, days, months, which are the rags of time'. Following a rhyming pattern of *abba* and *cdcd*, this rhyming couplet at the close of the first stanza underscores the poet's confident tone. The description of various units of time as 'rags' seems to diminish (belittle) the power of time.

The poet's attitude towards the sun appears to change at the start of stanza two. The earlier dismissive tone seems to be replaced by a new, respectful attitude, 'Thy beams so reverend, and strong'. However, the question that follows indicates that, in the poet's eyes, this is how the sun sees itself, 'Why shouldst thou think?' Donne irreverently claims that he 'could eclipse and cloud' such rays 'with a wink', but does not want to lose sight of his loved one, even for a moment. He goes on to suggest that his lover's bright eyes might blind the sun itself. He tells the sun to look at the world the following day and to tell him if everything and everyone is where he left them. Donne confidently claims the sun will discover that everything precious and wonderful ('th' Indias of spice and mine') and the most powerful of people ('kings') are to be found in the room he and his lover now occupy. Having already asserted that he and his lover are immune to time, he now insists that the vastness of the universe is contained within the lovers' world, 'All here in one bed lay'. In making such dramatic claims the poet attempts to convey the power and enormity of their love. In essence the lovers have become the world, the central point around which all else revolves. Having initially turned away from his lover to angrily take issue with the sun, the poet's attention gradually switches back to his lover and to the nature of their love. It is worth noting the way the poet employs vivid imagery to move fluidly from the intimacy of the bedroom to the outside world.

Donne's unshakeably confident tone continues into stanza three where he sees his lover and himself as a universe in themselves, 'She's all states, and all princes, I'. The repetition of 'all' suggests the idea of their total, all-sufficient love. Nothing exists outside of this love, 'Nothing else is'. If there is another world, it is no more than a pale imitation of their kingdom of love, 'Princes do but play us'. Every type of honour and wealth is meaningless by comparison with their complete love, 'All honour's mimic; all wealth alchemy'. Donne pities the sun because of its solitary existence, 'Thou, sun, art half as happy as we'. The poet now adopts a more respectful attitude towards the sun ('Thine age asks ease'), inviting him to enter their world of love. With amusing logic, he argues that since the sun's duty is to warm the world and since the lovers *are* the world, the sun will fulfil his duty 'in warming us'. In shining on the lovers, the sun will be shining 'everywhere'. The closing line suggests that the sun will take its place in the lovers' world in a natural, harmonious manner, 'This bed thy centre is, these walls, thy sphere'.

KEY POINTS

- A key theme is the lovers' complete, all-sufficient love, which is triumphant over time or place.
- Donne uses a dramatic setting and moment, using the natural rhythms of speech and conversational language to engage the reader in the situation. There is a sense of immediacy in the moment.
- Contrast is effectively used to differentiate the warm intimacy of the bedroom with the bustling, activity-ridden world outside.
- Excellent word choice captures the lives of the people outside the room. The schoolboys are 'late', the courtiers scurry to please the king, the farm workers are like 'country ants'. The rhythm of the lines captures the contrasts between the lovers and everybody else.
- Notice the sense of the poet challenging the light and power of the sun. He claims he could blot out its power by simply closing his eyes, but he wishes to see his beloved. Donne also declares that his lover's eyes are bright enough to blind the sun. This hyperbole emphasises the powerful impact of love on the poet.
- The poem revolves around the central image of the lovers being a world in themselves. This theme is drawn together in the final stanza of the poem where the poet declares that his lover is 'all states' and he is 'all princes'.
- Unlike the lovers, the sun is depicted as being lonely as it moves across the sky, whereas the poet has the intimacy of a relationship. In a humorous manner, Donne takes pity on

the sun, allowing it to enter their room and shine on a true world.

- The tone varies from the abrupt and dismissive in stanza one to the respectful, almost pitying tone in stanza three. The slowed rhythm in the final four lines marks the emotional change from an excited, exuberant confidence to a sympathetic attitude to the sun.

- Donne employs a playful kind of logic to suggest that in shining on them, the sun is fulfilling its duty to shine everywhere, since the lovers' world is a complete world of its own.

Song: Go and catch a falling star

This song is a light-hearted, witty joke aimed at women. It is, of course, very sexist, but it is most likely not meant to be taken seriously.

The poem opens dramatically with a series of explosive imperatives – 'Go', 'Get', 'Tell', 'Teach'. No one in particular is addressed, but Donne provides a strong sense of audience. These orders demand a series of impossible tasks: to catch a falling star, to cause a mandrake plant to become pregnant, to discover where all past years have gone, to find out who split the devil's hoof, and to teach the poet how to hear mermaids singing. The sixth line, however, takes on a more serious tone as the speaker mentions tasks that are more capable of fulfilment, but nevertheless extremely difficult to accomplish: to avoid envy of others and to reward honesty rather than hypocrisy.

In stanza two the poet imagines a person travelling the world in search of strange sights. He imagines this person devoting his life to this quest ('ten thousand days and nights') and growing old in the process ('Till age snow white

hairs on thee'). When this person returns home after travelling to the ends of the earth he will tell the poet of 'strange wonders', but will swear that 'No where / Lives a woman true, and fair'. The tone is extremely mocking and sarcastic which may suggest that Donne felt recently betrayed by a woman. Or perhaps it is meant to be taken as a harmless, although cynical joke. There is also the possibility that the speaker is an adopted persona and not Donne himself.

The cynical tone is sustained in stanza three. Allowing for the possibility that such a woman (true and fair) may exist (the use of the word 'pilgrimage' suggests that she would have to be a saintly figure), Donne claims she would have proved unfaithful by the time he might find her. The depth of the poet's cynicism is underlined when he claims that, even though he might have to travel no further than 'next door' to find this woman, she would still have lost her honour between the time the letter identifying her was sent and the poet's arrival, 'Yet she / Will be / False, ere I come, to two, or three'.

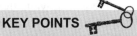

KEY POINTS

- A key theme is the poet's apparent lack of faith in the fidelity of women.

- The song has three nine-line stanzas, basically in tetrameters, but the seventh and eighth lines are actually half-lines. The triple rhymes falling close together at the end of each stanza produce quite a light-hearted ending each time.

- Woman's inconstancy is a traditional theme in Elizabethan literature. Donne here broadens the topic to women in general. At best, we could say Donne is a disillusioned idealist; at worst, a cynical young man.

- While one could argue that the sheer exaggeration and generalisations indicate that this poem was never meant to be taken seriously, it is difficult to avoid its cynical implications.
- The poet makes effective use of imagery ('envy's stinging', 'Till age snow white hairs on thee', etc.).

The Anniversarie

This poem is set on the first anniversary of the poet's meeting with his lover. Its idealistic, confident belief in the enduring power of love means that it has much in common with *The Sunne Rising*. Both poems are also alike in their dramatic nature (both are located in a specific place – a bedroom – at a specific time) and in their use of royal /courtly imagery.

The poem begins with a list of the powerful, the beautiful and the clever, 'All kings, and all their favourites, / All glory of honours, beauties, wits'. Donne lists the powerful and the admirable simply to point out that they are subject to the passage of time. The repetition of 'all' underlines the universal nature of the destruction wrought by time but is also evidence of sweeping generalisations. Donne goes on to point out that 'The sun itself.../ Is elder by a year, now, than it was / When thou and I first one another saw'. While all things inexorably draw closer 'to their destruction', the poet insists to his lover that their love is above time, 'Only our love hath no decay'. He portrays their love as timeless and everlasting, 'This, no tomorrow hath, nor yesterday'. Finally, Donne employs a memorable paradox to convey the permanence of their love, 'Running it never runs from us away'.

The poet's tone is not so assured at the start of stanza two. Donne reflects on how he and his lover will be separated in death, 'Two graves must hide thine and mine corse / If one might, death were no divorce'. Since Donne was not married to his lover, they could not be buried in the one grave. (This poem may relate to the early stages of his relationship with Ann More when their relationship was still a secret.) Again

depicting his lover and himself as royal figures who are a kingdom in themselves '(Who prince enough in one another be)', he considers how, along with 'other princes', they too must face death. Donne is filled with sadness when he reflects on the reality of death, 'Must leave at last in death, these eyes, and ears, / Oft fed with true oaths, and with sweet salt tears' (this is one of the few references that Donne makes to the physical aspects of love). However, the word 'But' signals a dramatic change in mood, with the poet confidently declaring that souls filled with love will be reunited beyond the grave. An interesting conceit (elaborate, unusual comparison) sees the lovers' souls as dwellings where love is the only tenant ('souls where nothing dwells but love'). Donne tries to further reassure his lover by claiming that their mutual love will be heightened in heaven ('a love increased there above'). The closing line in this stanza underlines Donne's certainty that the special love that he and his lover share will survive the end of physical life, 'When bodies to their graves, souls from their graves remove'.

The poet declares that he and his lover 'shall be thoroughly blessed' in heaven. However, in heaven everyone is equally blessed, 'But we no more, than all the rest'. In contrast, while they are on earth, they are special – rulers of their own unique kingdom, 'Here upon earth, we're kings, and none but we / Can be such kings'. While royal courts were filled with deception and intrigue, Donne and his lover have no fear of betrayal, 'Who is so safe as we? where none can do / Treason to us, except one of us two'. The poem closes with Donne declaring that he and his lover must love honourably and enjoy their earthly 'reign' to the full in the years ahead, 'Let us love nobly, and live, and add again / Years and years unto years'. He looks forward to them sharing 60 years together; 'till we attain / To write threescore, this is the second of our reign'.

KEY POINTS

- A key theme is the poet's belief in the power of love to transcend time.
- The poem presents us with a very idealistic view of love.
- Even though this is a passionate love poem, it has a logical structure because Donne is argumentative (regardless of the topic, Donne adopts an argumentative approach).
- In typical metaphysical fashion, Donne uses paradox to depict the nature of their love. It is 'running', but it 'never runs away'– this is because, although it exists in time, it will last forever. Another paradox can be seen when the poet declares that love 'truly keeps his first, last, everlasting day'– their love cannot be contained or limited by time.
- Note how the rhythm of the opening lines, broken into fragments, resembles the ticking of a clock. The lines flow more smoothly as the lovers are mentioned.
- The poem is based on the extended conceit of the lovers as royal figures. A further conceit is apparent in the description of the soul as a house where thoughts are merely lodgers, while true love 'dwells' there. Thoughts are therefore transient unlike the permanence and immortality of love.
- Tone changes occur frequently in the poem. The first verse reveals certainty that love will endure for eternity. However, the second verse acknowledges the reality of death and separation and is tinged with regret and sadness. The third verse resumes the celebration and joy of the opening as the lovers cherish their earthly experience of love before joining the blessed in heaven.
- In a way, this poem is an extension of the theme of the microcosm of the lovers' world boldly proclaimed in *The Sunne Rising*. If the lovers' world consists of only two inhabitants, then they are both royalty, the King and Queen of their own little universe.
- The repetition of 'we' and 'our' underscores the lovers' close union.

Song: Sweetest love, I do not goe

The poem opens in a typically dramatic manner. The poet and his beloved are engaged in a deep conversation about his imminent departure. The poet addresses his beloved in a tender manner ('Sweetest love') and attempts to reassure her in relation to his leaving. He insists that he is not leaving because he has grown tired of her ('I do not go, / For weariness of thee') or because he wishes to find a new lover ('A fitter love'). Donne argues that since he must die someday, he and his lover should use the pain of his leaving to prepare for the inevitability of his death, ''tis best, / To use myself in jest / Thus by feign'd deaths to die'.

In stanza two the poet continues with his efforts to comfort his beloved by speaking of how the sun goes and returns, 'Yesternight the sun went hence, / And yet is here today'. He tells her that he will return more speedily than the sun because, unlike the emotionless sun ('He hath no desire nor sense'), he will be driven by the desire to return to his beloved. Spurred on by this yearning for reunion and travelling on the wings of love, the poet promises to travel more quickly than the sun, 'I take / More wings and spurs than he'.

Stanza three is a general reflection on the way people respond to the vicissitudes (ups and downs) of life. While we tend to take the good times for granted and soon forget them ('Nor a lost hour recall!'), we have a propensity for dwelling on our misfortune ('bad chance'). Self-pity extends the duration of such misfortune and allows it to overwhelm us, '... we teach it art and length, / Itself o'er us to advance'. In essence, the poet is urging his lover to be strong and to not allow the 'bad chance' of his departure to make her miserable.

The philosophical musings of stanza three give way to a much more personal tone in stanza four. Donne's argument here is very clever. He tells his beloved that her excessive sighing (suggested by the repetition of 'sigh'st') and weeping affect him both spiritually ('When thou sigh'st, thou sigh'st.../...my soul away') and physically ('My life's blood doth decay'). He suggests that

the woman cannot really love him because in wasting her own life, she is also wasting his, 'It cannot be / That thou lov'st me, as thou say'st, / If in thine my life thou waste'. Basically this argument amounts to emotional blackmail – but of course it is emotional blackmail with a loving purpose. The final line in this stanza underlines the closeness of the lovers' union and the depth of the poet's love for this woman, 'That thou... art the best of me'.

In the closing stanza Donne pleads with his beloved not to imagine the bad things that might befall him in the course of his journey ('Let not thy divining heart / Forethink me any ill'), although he allows for the fact that they have no control over destiny. The poem ends with a tender, intimate image. The poet urges his partner to think of their separation as sleeping with their backs to each other, 'But think that we / Are but turn'd aside to sleep'. The poem concludes with Donne pointing out that people who love each other are never really parted, 'They who one another keep / Alive, ne'er parted be'.

KEY POINTS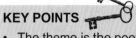

- The theme is the poet's deep love for his partner. He sees their loving relationship within the context of eventual death, wasting away and fear. However, all of this is dismissed in the last four lines, which could be interpreted as an assertion of love over the transience and suffering of life.

- The dramatic opening is typical of Donne's poems and immediately grabs the attention of the reader.

- Notice how the male speaker is empowered with 'wings and spurs', venturing out beyond the 'world' of the lovers as depicted in *The Sunne Rising*. The female figure appears to be a powerless stereotype of femininity. She has a 'divining heart'. However, she also has a certain power to emotionally control him which is revealed in the imagery of the poem.

- The tone is tender and affectionate but lacks the sparkling, witty humour of some of the other poems. The general impression is one of sincerity. The tone varies from simple sadness at the departure to serious reflections on life and death.

- This poem presents us with a very idealistic view of love.

- The poem is structured in five eight-line stanzas. This solid structure creates a contrast to the unpredictable outcome of the separation.

- Simple language is used. The diction of the poem is often monosyllabic, as can be seen in the opening four lines. Such simplicity characterises the relationship between the two lovers.

- Donne uses hyperbole to exaggerate the speed with which he will return. He claims that he will return quicker than the sun can rise because he has more motivation for speed.

The Dreame (Dear love, for nothing less than thee)

This poem describes the poet awaking to find the woman of whom he has been dreaming standing at his bedside. This is a challenging poem because it is difficult to know when the poet is asleep and dreaming or awake and describing reality. This poem, like so many other poems by Donne has a dramatic opening, with the poet addressing his lover. The conversational voice gives the opening a sense of immediacy.

Clearly untroubled at being awoken from his happy dream, the poet's tone is tender, 'Dear love, for nothing less than thee / Would I have broke this happy dream'. His dream was so realistic ('much too strong for fantasy') that it is more suited to the real world. Therefore, Donne tells his lover, she acted 'wisely' in waking him. He goes on to tell her that she did not break his dream, but rather continued it because she was at the centre of his fantasy and now she is with him in reality. His dream of her was so real ('so true') that it seemed to be 'truth'. The poet was so convinced of his lover's presence that he was virtually in the world of reality even before she woke him. The closing lines indicate that the dream was an erotic one as Donne now extends a sexual invitation to his lover, 'Enter these arms, for since thou thought'st it best, / Not to dream all my dream, let's act the rest'.

The intensely intimate mood is carried into the second stanza with Donne telling his lover that it was her bright eyes ('As lightning or a taper's light') and not some noise she made that woke him. He then tells her that he thought her 'an angel' upon first awakening. However, her ability to see into his heart and read his thoughts pointed to knowledge beyond that of an angel,

'But when I saw thou saw'st my heart, / And knew'st my thoughts, beyond an angel's art'. She knew what he was dreaming about and when 'excess of joy' would wake him. It was at this point that she came to him. These lines point to the lovers' intimate sexual relationship. The poet realises that he should not view the woman as an angel, but as the flesh and blood woman that she is – it would 'be / Profane, to think thee any thing but thee'.

There is a change of mood in stanza three which centres on the feelings evoked in the poet by the woman's leaving. Whereas the mood in stanzas one and two is pensive and romantic, there is a sense of doubt and uncertainty in the final stanza, 'Coming and staying show'd thee, thee, / But rising makes me doubt, that now, / Thou art not thou'. On the most obvious level, the poet, caught in that strange time between sleeping and waking, may be confused as to whether his beloved was actually there or not. On a deeper level, these lines may express the poet's doubts regarding his relationship with his lover. The fact that the woman came to him and stayed with him proved she was her true self, but now that she is no longer there he wonders about the nature of her love for him. He considers what mixture of emotions prompted his beloved to depart. Donne believes that love should be 'all spirit, pure and brave' and should not involve any feelings of fear or shame, 'That love is weak, where fear's as strong as he'. The poem ends on an optimistic note with the poet reflecting that his lover may only have left to come back to him again. She has lit the torch of his love and he looks forward to her re-lighting that torch.

KEY POINTS

- The poem, like many others by Donne, opens dramatically and engages the reader immediately. However, the drama does not depend so much on a startling statement as on a sense that we have captured a special, vulnerable moment where the speaker is caught between sleeping and waking.
- A key theme is the various emotions evoked in the poet by the arrival of his lover in the middle of his dream.
- Although the poet refers to his lover as an 'angel', he sees her literally as a real person and doesn't spiritualise her into a sacred object.
- The language is simple. The conversational voice gives the poem a sense of immediacy and credibility.
- The mood changes as the poem develops: pleasure, uncertainty, expectation. The ending reflects a complex emotional state as Donne wishes to return to 'dream that hope again', believing that he will die if he is denied such joy. Here, the poet admits to a dependence on the love of his partner, a need for her presence and the certainty of her love for him.

A Valediction: Forbidding Mourning

A valediction refers to a farewell speech. In this poem Donne is embarking on a journey and so must leave his beloved. As the title suggests, the poet does not want his departure to be a cause of sadness. Thematically, this poem is similar to *Song: Sweetest love, I do not goe.*

The opening stanza compares the lovers' separation to a death. It presents us with a deathbed scene in which a virtuous man is drawing his last. Having lived good lives, virtuous men 'pass mildly away'. They have no fear of death: 'And whisper to their souls, to go'. The atmosphere surrounding the death of such virtuous men is composed and dignified. Their passing is so tranquil that friends are unsure as to the exact moment of death, '... some of their sad friends do say, / The breath goes now, and some say, 'No''. This stanza implies that the poet wishes his departure to be as tranquil and as imperceptible as the passing of such a virtuous man.

Donne tells his beloved that he wishes them to quietly 'melt' away from each other. He wants no histrionics, no loud demonstration of grief,

'No tear-floods, nor sigh-tempests'. The poet's use of religious terminology ('profanation', 'laity') indicates that he views their relationship as something sacred. An ostentatious display of anguish would only tarnish their special love and perhaps cause neighbours to intrude into an intimate scene, ''Twere profanation of our joys / To tell the laity our love'.

Stanza three is dominated by a sense of movement. First there is an image of an earthquake that causes damage that men can measure ('Moving of th' earth brings harms and fears') and then a reference to the movement of the planets which causes no visible damage and seems to go unnoticed by man ('But trepidation of the spheres, / Though greater far, is innocent'). Earthquakes create consternation (feelings of anxiety or alarm) in people who seek to discover their cause, but far greater events, such as the movement of the spheres, are superior events which largely go unnoticed. The implied meaning is that any dramatic, showy form of leave-taking would debase their love, depriving it of its extraordinary, superior quality.

The astronomical imagery continues into stanza four when Donne speaks of 'Dull sublunary lovers' love'. The adjective 'dull' suggests that other loves pale by comparison with their shining love. The term 'sublunary' literally means 'under the moon', implying that this kind of love is subject to change. Such love cannot survive absence 'because it doth remove / Those things which elemented it'. Put simply, a love that is purely physical ('Whose soul is sense') cannot withstand physical separation.

From stanza five on, Donne focuses on the superiority of the love that he and his beloved share. Their love is pure ('so much refined') and complex. It has a mysterious quality that defies definition – the lovers themselves cannot articulate what makes it special ('... ourselves know not what it is'). The important thing is that this is a relationship based on mutual trust ('Inter-assured of the mind'). Since theirs is a love that is essentially spiritual, they do not care about the physical aspects of a relationship that so preoccupies other couples, 'Care less, eyes, lips, and hands to miss'.

Donne now suggests that since he and his lover have achieved spiritual union and share a single soul ('Our two souls ... are one'), physical separation will not lead to 'a breach' in their relationship. On the contrary, Donne asserts that it will lead to 'an expansion' of their love. This idea is conveyed by the image of gold being beaten into gold leaf, like gold to airy thinness beat. Gold imagery suggests the precious, enduring nature of their love.

The poet now considers the possibility that he and his lover have two separate souls – if this is the case, then their separate souls are closely connected and inter-dependent. He conveys this idea by means of an effective conceit, comparing his lover and himself to the two legs of a compass (a mathematical compass). The woman, who will remain at home and await his return, is the fixed leg of the compass, while the poet on his travels is the moving leg, 'Thy soul the fixed foot .../... when the other far doth roam'. While the two legs are separate, they are intimately linked and mutually dependent. The woman is the point around which the poet revolves – she is depicted as a point of stability in the poet's life. The image of the compass suggests that no matter where he travels, the poet and his lover will never be separated because of their intimate spiritual connection. The image of the compass drawing the circle implies that the poet will eventually return home to his beloved, 'Thy firmness makes my circle just, / And makes me end, where I begun'.

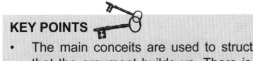

KEY POINTS

- The main conceits are used to structure this poem. It is also through the conceits that the argument builds up. There is a focus on scientific or mathematical images: earthquakes, compasses, the properties of gold.

- The conceits are contrasted with the traditional imagery of parting: sighs and tears, which are dismissed as 'tear-floods' and 'sigh-tempests'.

- The use of the term 'melt' suggests the perfect silence and tranquillity.

- The first image, the deathbed, is the only one that suggests moral quality. 'Virtuous men' have the power to pass gently into death and do it silently. Silence becomes a moral virtue.

- A key theme is the special nature of their love, which is depicted as being essentially spiritual. The poet urges his beloved not to be sad at his departure and contrasts the special love that he and his lover share with the ordinary loves of other lovers.

- The tone is tender and confident throughout.

The Flea

This is one of Donne's best known and most original poems. The poet builds a series of highly imaginative arguments around the image of the flea, which he uses as an image of the sexual union of a man and a woman. The object of this exercise is to win over his lover.

This poem opens in a dramatic manner with Donne addressing his lover in a sermonising tone. Repetition underlines the need for her to pay attention to what he is saying, 'Mark but this flea, and mark in this, / How little that which thou deny'st me is'. The poet yearns for physical intimacy with his lover. The flea has bitten both of them and consequently 'our two bloods mingled be'. At this time there was a mistaken belief that sexual intercourse literally involved the mingling of the lovers' blood. Donne asks his lover to admit that the flea's actions cannot be deemed wrong, 'Thou know'st that, this cannot be said / A sin, nor shame, nor loss of maidenhead'. Of course the implication of this argument is that if their bloods were to mingle that would not be wrong either. The poet points out the flea enjoys physical pleasure without having to engage in the courtship rituals that men must observe ('enjoys before it woo'). He envies the 'pampered' flea, 'And this, alas, is more than we would do'. This argument is really a form of emotional blackmail.

Stanza two begins with a dramatic plea as the poet asks his lover not to kill the flea, 'Oh stay, three lives in one flea spare, / Where we almost, nay more than married are'. Having sucked the blood of both the poet and his lover, the flea now represents three lives, 'This flea is you and I.' Donne uses religious language and imagery to depict the flea as something sacred, 'and this / Our marriage bed and marriage temple is'. The lovers have not married yet because of parental opposition and have not consummated their relationship because of the woman's reluctance. They are joined together only within the flea, 'Though parents grudge, and you, we are met, / And cloistered in these living walls of jet'. The term 'cloistered' reinforces the idea that the flea's body has become a sacred place. Taken together, all of the religious references suggest that Donne sees physical intimacy with his lover as something sacred. Stanza two concludes with the poet again urging his lover not to kill the flea. To do so, he argues, would be to commit three major offences. Firstly, she would be guilty of murder because part of him is within the flea. Secondly, she would be committing suicide because the flea also contains part of her. Finally, she would be committing sacrilege because the flea has become their holy 'marriage temple'.

At the beginning of stanza three we learn that the poet's lover has ignored his pleadings and killed the flea with her fingernail. This stanza opens dramatically with the woman's actions being described as 'Cruel and sudden'. Her nail is depicted as being 'purpled' with the 'blood of innocence'. Donne tells his lover that the flea was guilty only of sucking a 'drop' of blood from her. The woman seems to enjoy her triumph. Her action has effectively disproved the poet's argument. He had claimed that in killing the flea, she would be killing part of each of them, but neither of them is 'the weaker now'. In a last desperate bid to win her over, Donne now cleverly attempts to use his lover's argument against her, arguing that this episode has taught them 'how false, fears be' and that, just as the flea's death took no life from her, succumbing to his sexual desires will involve no loss of honour.

KEY POINTS

- This poem is an excellent example of a metaphysical poem. Donne compares human intimacy to the intimacy of the flea in a witty and outrageous attempt to persuade the woman to have sex with him.

- The poem is dominated by the flea conceit. It is through the image of the flea that Donne expresses his sexual longing.

- The poet puts forward a series of highly imaginative arguments in his efforts to seduce the woman. Many of these arguments are humorous and display the poet's wit.

- Note the use of hyperbole in the reference to the 'blood of innocence', a phrase which suggests a heartless crime but is, in reality, no more than the killing of a flea with a 'fingernail'. Donne's pretended horror and upset adds to the humorous exaggeration of the callous act. His linking of the flea to a 'temple' is yet another example of hyperbole.

- A key theme is the poet's desire to consummate his relationship with his lover. To achieve this aim he implies that such intimacy is quite harmless and all sense of morality totally irrelevant.

- The opening of the poem is dramatic. The poet instructs the woman to 'Mark' (notice) the flea and its activity. This sets the scene for what appears to be a moral lesson but is, in fact, an attempt to seduce the woman. The high moral tone is dramatically at odds with the intention of the speaker. Further drama is added with the use of such terms as 'alas' and 'Oh stay'.

Batter my heart

This poem is a prayer to God to enter the poet's life and deliver him from the power of Satan. What makes this poem remarkable is its urgent, demanding tone. The opening is particularly striking with the poet pleading with God to 'batter' his heart, 'Batter my heart, three-personed God'. We are startled by the violence of the poet's language. The phrase 'three-personed God' refers to the Holy Trinity. Donne seems to admonish (scold/rebuke) God for being too gentle with him, 'for you / As yet but knock, breathe, shine, and seek to mend'. Clearly Donne feels that his soul needs much more than a gentle polishing – it needs to be hammered into shape. There follows an interesting paradox – if Donne is to 'rise and stand', God must knock him down, overwhelm him, 'That I may rise and stand, o'erthrow me'. The emphasis on the necessity for God to be forceful is underscored by a series of energetic verbs, 'bend / Your force, to break, blow, burn, and make me new'.

In spiritual terms, the poet needs to be broken down and built anew. The loud alliterative 'b' sound accentuates the urgent, demanding tone.

The second quatrain is dominated by the image of a captured town. As Donne develops this image we get a wonderful example of his mastery of the metaphysical conceit, 'I, like an usurped town, to another due, / Labour to admit you, but oh, to no end'. Conquered by evil, the poet struggles in vain to let God into his life. Reason is God's 'viceroy' (representative) in him and should protect him from sin as the viceroy should protect the town. However, just as the viceroy fails in his duty, reason has failed to safeguard the poet from sin. Held captive by evil, reason has proven 'weak or untrue'. The most unusual image in the poem is to be found in the sestet where the poet compares himself to a woman who loves God and longs to be with him, 'Yet dearly I love you, and would be loved fain'. However, she is engaged to his enemy, 'But am betrothed unto your enemy'. The urgent tone with which the poem opens is once again evident as the poet pleads with God to sever his connection with the devil, 'Divorce me, untie or break that knot again'. He wants God to forcefully take control of his soul and free him from the bondage of sin, 'Take me to you, imprison me'. The poem concludes with two memorable paradoxes. Donne tells God that he will never be free unless God enslaves him, 'Except you enthral me, never shall be free'. The second paradox relates to the shame the woman feels at being intimately involved with God's enemy and is particularly daring. Donne declares that he will never be pure unless God ravishes (rapes/enraptures) him, 'Nor ever chaste, except you ravish me'.

KEY POINTS

- This poem is written in the form of a Petrarchan sonnet, with two quatrains (sets of four lines) and a sestet. The octet states the poet's dilemma. He is imprisoned by Satan and seeks deliverance. The sestet indicates how he can be saved by the power of God.

- A key theme is the poet's desperate longing for God to take possession of his soul and free him from his enslavement to sin.

- It is probably one of the best known of all Donne's religious poems due to its striking and dramatic imagery. Donne combines the language of violent sexuality with images of warfare to make an impassioned plea to God for some spiritual breakthrough. Just as in his love poetry, Donne desired intensity and a wholeness of experience.

- The poem has a very striking opening. The initial outburst reminds us of Donne's dramatic voice, also seen in so many of his other openings.

- The language used by Donne is highly dramatic. The monosyllabic verbs have a powerful impact as they are listed in quick succession: 'knock, breathe, shine' contrast with 'break, blow, burn'. This series of energetic verbs accentuates the need for God to take dramatic action to rescue the poet's soul ('Batter . . . o'erthrow . . . bend . . . break, blow, burn'). The alliterative 'b' sound is carried on from the opening 'Batter'. The pauses between the verbs mimic the repetitive strokes of the battering ram as it attacks the gates.

- The urgency is maintained through the number of run-on lines and the many lists of words which make for an interrupted and jerky reading, which of course, mirrors the poet's own state of mind.

- A dominant device is the use of violent imagery in a typical metaphysical fashion – unity with a tender God is achieved through violence.

- Notice the personification of reason, which should have protected the soul but has become weakened by being taken 'captive'.

- The tone of this poem is varied. It is essentially argumentative and witty. The opening lines are urgent, demanding and expressed through the use of imperatives. A tone of humility follows as Donne acknowledges that he is unworthy and weak. Great tenderness is evoked in the phrase 'Yet dearly I love you' before the poet returns to the violent, impassioned pleading of the opening. There is a curious tension between persistence and reverence.

- The poem contains some memorable conceits. The poet compares himself to a gate, an alchemist and a captured town. The last conceit where the poet compares himself to a woman, is quite shocking: 'Nor ever chaste, except you ravish me'.

- In typical metaphysical fashion, paradoxes enhance the wit of the poem: 'That I may rise, and stand, o'erthrow me'; 'imprison me, for I, / Except you enthral me, never shall be free / Nor ever chaste, except you ravish me'.
- In addition to the paradoxes, fine use is made of contrast. Reason is contrasted with passion and emotion. Religious concepts are expressed in secular terms.
- Donne speaks to God in an engagingly personal, direct manner throughout the poem.

At the round earth's imagined corners

Donne calls out in this poem for the world to come to an end, but later changes his mind, realising that he is not prepared to face judgement. This poem is written in the form of a Petrarchan sonnet, in the octet of which the poet envisions the Day of Judgement. The opening line of the poem is clearly inspired by the Book of Revelations, the final book of the Bible which describes the end of the world and speaks of 'four angels standing on the four corners of the earth'. The octet depicts a dramatic scene. Angels' trumpets call on the souls of the 'numberless' dead to rise up and rejoin their 'scattered bodies'. The placing of verbs at the end of lines ('blow...arise...go') and the repetition of 'arise' give lines 1–4 a sense of drama and urgency.

In lines 5–7 Donne employs a listing technique in an attempt to convey a sense of the vast numbers of people who have lived and died since time began. He solemnly enumerates the various ways in which people have met their end, 'All whom the flood did, and fire shall o'erthrow, / All whom war, dearth (famine), age, agues (diseases), tyrannies (cruel leaders), / Despair (suicide), law, chance (accidents), hath slain'. The repetition of 'All whom' accentuates the enormous number of the dead who will be summoned to arise by the angels' trumpeting. Finally, the poet mentions those still alive on the final day. Such people would see God without experiencing the sadness of death, 'you whose eyes, / Shall behold God, and never taste death's woe'. Coming at the end of the grim catalogue of different ways of dying, the reference to everyone meeting their maker on the last day offers hope.

There is a striking contrast in both rhythm and mood between the octet and the sestet. While lines 1–8 convey a sense of breathless excitement as well as a fearful and frantic energy (the only full stop in the octet occurs at the end of line 8), the pace of the poem becomes much gentler in the sestet. Having earlier felt sufficiently confident in his own spiritual state to call for the end of the world, Donne now expresses a more humble attitude. While the octet presents us with an awe-inspiring panoramic vision, the focus of the poem now narrows to a single individual – the poet. At this point Donne basically reconsiders his wish for the world to end. Fearing that he is spiritually unprepared to meet his maker, the poet asks God to let the dead sleep, 'But let them sleep, Lord, and me mourn a space'. Since it will be too late for him to repent on the Day of Judgement, he asks God to help him to repent while he is 'here on this lowly ground'. If God teaches him how to repent, Donne has no doubt about his salvation – it will be like a royal pardon sealed in God's blood ('for that's as good / As if thou hadst seal'd my pardon with Thy blood'). The poem closes with this striking image suggesting Donne's sense of certainty – with God to help him, he has nothing to fear.

KEY POINTS

- A key theme is the poet's relationship with God – more particularly, his awareness of his sinful state and of his need for repentance. This poem is one of a series of twenty poems by Donne known as the 'Holy Sonnets'.
- Written in the form of a Petrarchan sonnet. There is a sharp contrast in both mood and rhythm between octet and sestet.
- The octet is particularly dramatic – note the use of imperatives/commands ('Blow . . . arise . . . go'), repetition ('arise, arise').
- The list of various causes of death conveys some sense of the infinite number of the dead. It also emphasises that the manner of death is unimportant compared to the judgement day when all shall 'behold God'.
- The imagery is initially harsh and terrifying compared to the gentle meeting which the poet hopes to experience – 'you whose eyes / Shall behold God'.
- Donne's characteristic variety of tone is apparent in this sonnet. The repeated long 'o' sound contributes to the creation of the solemn tone ('blow . . . go . . . o'erthrow . . . woe . . . abound . . . ground', etc.).
- The poem closes with a memorable image which reveals the poet's firm belief in God's forgiveness as long as he repents of his sins.

Thou hast made me

This poem, along with *Batter my heart* and *At the round earth's imagined corners*, is yet another of the Holy Sonnets in which Donne reflects on and explores his relationship with God. The poem opens in a typically dramatic manner, with an angry Donne directly addressing God, asking why He created him, only to watch him decline, 'Thou hast made me, and shall Thy work decay?' He asks God to help him now that his life is drawing to a close. There is a sense of urgency in his pleading, 'Repair me now, for now mine end doth haste'. The personification of death adds to the dramatic nature of the poem, 'I run to death, and death meets me as fast'. Thoughts of death overshadow his life, causing life's pleasures to recede into memory, 'And all my pleasures are like yesterday'.

Donne is filled with a sense of despondency and dread, 'I dare not move my dim eyes any way'. If he looks back on his life, he is filled with despair; if he looks to the future, he can see only death, 'Despair behind, and death before doth cast /

Such terror'. Worst of all, enfeebled (weakened) by sin, the poet fears that he is doomed to hell: 'and my feebled flesh doth waste / By sin in it, which it towards hell doth weigh'. The mood of the octet is bleak. Note the series of negative terms: 'decay', 'death', 'dim', 'despair', 'terror', 'feeble', 'waste', 'hell'. The tone is despairing.

The sestet signals a dramatic change in the poet's mood. Only when Donne looks up towards heaven do his spirits rise, 'Only thou art above, and when towards thee / By thy leave I can look, I rise again'. Donne admits that he is susceptible to temptation and dependent on God to protect him from evil, 'But our old subtle foe so tempteth me / That not one hour I can myself sustain'. The use of 'our' suggests the poet's close relationship with God, while their common foe is Satan. The angry, demanding tone of the opening lines is now replaced by a sense of humility as Donne asks God to give him the grace to rise above the devil's clever scheming, 'Thy grace may wing me to prevent his art'. Here we see that grace is depicted as an angel that rescues the poet from evil. The poem ends with a memorable image of God drawing Donne's heart upwards away from earthly temptation and towards heavenly thoughts as surely as a magnet attracts iron, 'And Thou like adamant draw mine iron heart'. The poet speaks of his 'iron heart' because it is hardened by sin.

KEY POINTS

- A key theme is again the poet's relationship with God, specifically his dependence on God to protect him from evil.
- Again, Donne speaks to God in a direct, personal manner. The simplicity of the language is all the more remarkable for the fact that the poet is experiencing a complex spiritual struggle.
- The octet opens in a very dramatic manner as the poet asks the devastating question concerning his life's meaning. The sestet is more reflective.
- The alliterative 'd' sound helps to convey Donne's initial sense of gloom ('Despair behind, and death before doth cast /Such terror').
- The mood is initially one of despair and terror, but becomes more hopeful in the sestet.
- The poem ends with a powerful, memorable image which suggests a liberating ease and certainty. Despite the intellectual argument, faith is seen as essentially unscientific – even irrational!

Sample Answer

'John Donne, though a seventeenth-century poet, is well worth reading in the twenty-first century'. Do you agree with this statement?

The extraordinary appeal of the poetry of John Donne, a seventeenth-century poet, certainly surprises many modern readers. It certainly took me by surprise! Having read a selection of his poems, I can understand why Ben Jonson judged him: 'the first poet in the world in some things'. Despite the passage of centuries, his poems continue to engage and challenge readers who come to him afresh. Despite Donne's old-fashioned language, his ideas remain fresh, relevant and interesting.

Few other poets capture the range and complexity of the emotions associated with being in love as Donne does. *The Sunne Rising* is a wonderful evocation of a love that is timeless and self-sufficient. The opening of the poem is dramatic. Donne addresses the sun in a conversational, irreverent manner which takes the reader by surprise: 'Busy old fool, unruly sun'. The depiction of the rising sun as an interfering busybody insensitively intruding into the lovers' intimate world is both fresh and original. Donne confidently declares that the lovers transcend time, 'Love, all alike, no seasons knows, nor clime / Nor hours, days, months, which are the rags of time'. This leads him to assert that everything precious and wonderful ('th' Indias of spice and mine') and the most powerful of people ('kings') are to be found in the room he and his lover now occupy. The vastness of the universe is contained within the lovers' world, 'All here in one bed lay'. These dramatic claims effectively convey the power and enormity of the love that the poem celebrates – a theme of enormous appeal to a modern reader in a world where love is often trivialised.

Although Donne's love poetry was written nearly 400 years ago, another reason for its modern appeal is that it speaks to us as directly and urgently as if we are eavesdropping on a confidential conversation. Take for example *A Valediction: Forbidding Mourning*. This is an interesting poem which explores the spiritual aspect of Donne's relationship with his beloved. In this poem Donne is about to embark on a journey and wants his departure to be as tranquil as possible. He tells his lover that he wishes them to quietly 'melt' away from each other, with no loud expression of grief: 'No tear-floods, nor sigh-tempests'. The poet's use of religious terminology indicates that he sees their relationship as something sacred which would be tarnished by an ostentatious display of anguish, ''Twere profanation of our joys / To tell the laity our love'. Since he and his lover have achieved spiritual union ('Our two souls ... are one'), physical separation will not lead to a 'breach' in their relationship. The attitude to love expressed in both *The Sunne Rising* and *A Valediction: Forbidding Mourning* has an uplifting, almost spiritual quality which, in my opinion, makes them well worth reading and offers modern readers valuable insights into the nature of human love. They celebrate a mutual attachment between lovers that time and distance cannot diminish and which is relevant in any century.

Not all of Donne's love poems are quite so uplifting however! He has a wicked sense of humour which can be seen in *The Flea* – a clever, wonderfully original poem. Donne builds a series of highly imaginative arguments around the image of the flea which he uses as an image of the sexual union of a man and a woman. The object of this exercise in persuasion is to seduce his beloved. The poem opens in a typically dramatic manner, with Donne addressing his lover in a sermonising tone. Repetition emphasises the need for her to listen carefully to what he is saying, 'Mark but this flea, and mark in this, / How little that which thou deny'st me is'. The poet yearns for physical intimacy with his lover. The flea has bitten both of them and consequently 'our two bloods mingled be'. At this time it was believed that sexual intercourse literally involved the mingling of the lovers' blood.

Donne asks his lover to admit that the flea's actions cannot be deemed wrong, 'Thou know'st that this cannot be said / A sin, nor shame nor loss of maidenhead'. This argument cleverly implies that if their bloods were to mix, that would not be wrong either. The poet points out that the flea enjoys physical pleasure without having to engage in the courtship rituals that men are expected to observe ('Enjoys before it woo'). He envies the 'pampered' flea: 'And this, alas, is more than we would do'. While Donne is often inventive in his arguments, he is clearly not averse to employing some emotional blackmail in his attempts to seduce his lover. He pleads with her not to kill the flea, since, having sucked blood from both of them, it now represents three lives, 'This flea is you and I.' I really enjoyed how the woman, ignoring Donne, kills the flea. Her action effectively disproves the poet's arguments. He had claimed that in killing the flea the woman would be killing part of each of them, but neither of them is 'the weaker now'. One has to, however, admire Donne's cleverness in using his lover's argument against her. He argues that this episode has taught them 'how false, fears be' and that, just as the flea's death took no life from her, succumbing to his sexual desires will involve no loss of honour. This poem is well worth reading for the cleverness of its imagery, the tongue-in-cheek argument by which he attempts to satisfy his sexual desires by tricking his lover and the general originality and audaciousness of the tone. Most of my class enjoyed this poem immensely.

In addition to his love poems, Donne wrote many religious poems which still appeal to the reader and are worth reading in a modern age. Perhaps the most powerful of these is *Batter my heart*, a sonnet which is basically a prayer to God to enter his life and free him from his enslavement to sin. There is something profoundly moving in the way Donne speaks to God in an engagingly direct, personal manner. What makes this poem remarkable is its urgent, demanding tone. The poet dramatically pleads with God, 'Batter my heart, three-personed God'. I was taken aback to find Donne almost admonishing God for being too gentle with him: 'for You, / As yet but knock, breathe, shine and seek to mend'. The need for God to be more forceful with him is underlined by a series of energetic verbs, 'bend / Your force to break, blow, burn, and make me new'. The loud alliterative 'b' sound accentuates the urgent, demanding tone. The most unusual image in the poem, however, is to be found in the sestet where Donne compares himself to a woman who loves God and longs to be with him, 'Yet dearly I love You, and would be loved fain'. Donne declares that he will never be pure unless God ravishes him, 'Nor ever chaste, except You ravish me'. This image has an astonishing quality which almost seems irreverent, even in the twenty-first century which considers itself liberal compared to the seventeenth-century. I think that such shocks challenge the reader to consider the relationship between spiritual and human love in a novel, thought-provoking manner. This alone makes the poem relevant reading in any age.

Thou hast made me **is yet another appealing poem that highlights Donne's personal relationship with God**. It opens in the dramatic manner we expect of Donne. The angry poet directly addresses God and poses a question that crosses most people's minds at some point: why did God give him life, only to watch him decline? ('Thou hast made me, and shall Thy work decay?'). The personification of death adds to the dramatic nature of the poem, 'I run to death, and death meets me as fast'. As readers, we can identify with the fear and gloom, 'I dare not move my dim eyes any way'. If he looks back on his life he is filled with despair; if he looks to the future, he can see only death, 'Despair behind and death before doth cast / Such terror'. Worst of all, enfeebled by sin, the poet fears that he is doomed to hell, 'and my feebled flesh doth waste / By sin in it, which it towards hell doth weigh'. The poet's close relationship with God is appealing in its simplicity and trust despite the terror evoked in the sonnet. The poem ends with the uplifting image of God drawing Donne's thoughts heavenwards as surely as a magnet attracts iron. I think these religious poems have a timeless appeal because Donne's personal fears and insecurities are universal. The modern reader can identify with the questions posed and be impressed with the power of faith to provide hope and strength. Whether he is speaking to his lover or his God, Donne's poetry is intimate and immediate. The engagingly personal, direct poetic voice and his incisive awareness of spiritual realities make the poems act as contemplations which reward a thoughtful reading.

Finally, it is impossible not to be impressed with Donne's cleverness – strikingly evident in his vigorous arguments and original images. The sophistication of the metaphysical conceit is mainly due to the use of far-fetched imagery drawn from different fields of knowledge such as geometry, astronomy, chemistry, geography, philosophy and other sciences. Their extraordinary wittiness amazed me and exposed me to a new type of imaginative experience. To be effective, a conceit should be tied to a logical argument. In Donne's poetry the conceit and the logical argument can, almost always, be found together. The most striking conceit for me is that of the compasses in *A Valediction: Forbidding Mourning* where Donne goes to the extremes of using scientific imagery. Compasses had never been associated with the subject of romantic love before; they are used for drawing regular circles in geometry and have nothing to do with poetry or with lovers.

In conclusion, Donne's poetry is certainly still worth reading. His themes are universal and timeless, while the personal, direct manner in which he addresses both his lover and his God has an obvious appeal for the modern reader.

John Keats

Biographical Note

Keats (1795–1821) was born in Finsbury, close to London, England. He was the eldest of five children. He was educated in a small, private boarding school. In 1804 Keats' father was killed in a riding accident. While Keats' mother, Frances, married again, her second marriage was unhappy and the children were raised by their grandparents. His mother suffered from depression and later contracted tuberculosis, dying in 1810. Keats, who had devotedly nursed her through her illness, was devastated. At just fourteen years of age, he was parentless. In 1811 Keats left school to take up an apprenticeship as a surgeon. However, he never had any real interest in this work, eventually feeling repelled by it. Poetry was becoming increasingly important in his life, and in May 1816 he had his first poem published in the *Examiner*, a sonnet entitled *O Solitude! if I must with thee dwell*. Keats' first volume of poetry, *Poems*, was published in 1817. Later that year, he wrote a four thousand word epic poem, *Endymion: A Poetic Romance*. The opening line of this famous poem remains instantly recognisable: 'A thing of beauty is a joy forever.'

On a personal level, Keats' life involved a great deal of pain and loss. His brother Tom contracted tuberculosis, dying from the illness in 1818. From a young age, Keats was fearful for his own life, as we see in his sonnet *When I have fears that I may cease to be*. Keats' greatest fear was that he would die before he had expressed all of the ideas that were teeming in his fertile imagination.

Keats produced the bulk of his poetic work in a highly productive four-year period between 1817 and 1820. One of his most famous achievements was his development of his theory of Negative Capability. In essence this theory suggests that the poet may harbour doubts and uncertainties, and not feel compelled to reach definite conclusions. Keats himself explained this theory as 'when a man is capable of being in uncertainties, mysteries, doubts, without any irritable reaching after fact and reason'. Keats, of course, belonged to the Romantic Movement, which began in the early nineteenth century and ended some fifty years later. Central to the Romantics' beliefs were the power of the imagination to see truths, the importance of man as an individual rather than as a social being, the need for man to re-establish an intimate relationship with the natural world and the necessity of developing a new poetic language that was as close as possible to everyday speech.

In 1820 Keats started to cough up blood and, with his medical training, immediately understood its grave implications. For a time he was looked after by Frances (Fanny) Brawne, the great love of his life and the woman to whom he was engaged, and her mother in their home in Hampstead. His friends advised a spell in Italy, as it was widely believed at the time that tubercular patients would benefit from being in a warm climate. However, Keats did not improve and he died in Rome in 1821. He was, remarkably, only twenty-six years old. At his own request, the following epitaph was inscribed on his tombstone: 'Here lies one whose name was writ on water.'

To one who has been long in city pent

The opening lines of this Petrarchan sonnet convey the contrast between the confinement of the city and the vast expanse of the beautiful sky. The sky is personified, with Keats speaking of 'the fair / And open face of heaven' and 'the smile of the blue firmament'. The restorative powers of nature are conveyed by the image of the poet, fatigued from life in the city, happily relaxing in the pleasantly long grass, reading 'a gentle tale of love and languishment'.

The sestet is dominated by a sense of melancholy as the poet returns home in the evening. As he hears the song of the nightingale ('the notes of Philomel') and watches the clouds sail by, Keats 'mourns' the rapid passing of the day. The closing lines compare the passing of this uplifting day to the falling of an angel's tear from heaven to earth.

References to breathing a prayer (presumably in gratitude for the beauty of the sky), heaven and 'an angel's tear' suggest Keats' awareness of a divine power behind the beautiful countryside.

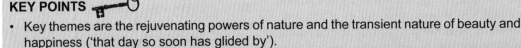

KEY POINTS

- Key themes are the rejuvenating powers of nature and the transient nature of beauty and happiness ('that day so soon has glided by').
- Effective use of metaphors and personification.

Ode to a Nightingale

In this poem we see Keats' deep desire to escape from the imperfect, transient physical world into the perfect, immortal world of the nightingale's song. For Keats the bird's song is a symbol of eternal beauty, happiness and freedom.

The opening stanza conveys the poet's gloom and lethargy: 'My heart aches and a drowsy numbness pains / My sense, as though of hemlock I had drunk.' Keats explains his feelings of despondency and inertia by means of a paradox: ''Tis not through envy of thy happy lot, / But being too happy in thine happiness'. The paradoxical notion that pain can be the result of excessive happiness startles and challenges the reader. The opening stanza contrasts the poet's melancholy with the joy and ease of the nightingale's song: the bird 'singest of summer in full-throated ease'.

The poet considers various avenues of escape from the grim world of reality. He considers the possibility of reaching the perfect world of the bird's song by means of alcohol: 'O for a draught of vintage!' The repetition of 'O' underscores his sense of longing. Keats describes the wine in the type of sensuous detail that is characteristic of his poetry. We can almost taste the wine, which has been 'cooled a long age in the deep-delved earth', and visualise 'the beaded bubbles winking at the brim'. The use of alliteration underlines the sensuous appeal of the wine by means of which the poet hopes 'to leave the world unseen' and fade away with the nightingale 'into the forest dim'.

The third stanza accentuates (emphasises) the pain and sorrow of the physical world from which Keats longs to escape. The poet thinks of physical life in terms of 'the weariness, the fever, and the fret'. The transience of life is vividly captured in a particularly grim image: 'Where youth grows pale and spectre-thin and dies.' The poet believes that Beauty and Love (their personification underlines their importance to

Keats) cannot survive in a world of transience: 'Where Beauty cannot keep her lustrous eyes, / Or new Love pine at them beyond tomorrow.'

In stanza four Keats emphatically dismisses the idea of using wine to reach the perfect world of the nightingale's song, proclaiming that he will instead access it through the power of the imagination: 'Away! away! for I will fly to thee, / Not charioted by Bacchus and his pards, / But on the viewless wings of Poesy.' Through the power of his imagination, Keats finds himself in the world of the nightingale: 'Already with thee!'

Stanza five depicts the ideal world of the nightingale's song. This is a world rich in sensuous appeal, a world of darkness and tranquillity where the poet can smell the 'soft incense' that 'hangs upon the boughs', taste the 'dewy wine' and hear 'the murmurous haunt of flies on summer eves.' While the references to 'embalmed darkness' and to flies are suggestive of death and decay, Keats does not view death as something threatening – indeed at the start of the next stanza he even admits to having been 'half in love with easeful Death'.

The poet has considered the possibility of escaping harsh, painful reality through death. The idea of dying when the nightingale is 'pouring forth' his soul 'in such an ecstasy' appeals to the poet. As in *Bright Star*, he longs to forever capture a moment of perfect joy by dying when he is at his happiest. Here Keats sees death as a means of achieving total happiness.

However, he realises that death is not the answer to his problems since it would deprive him of the perfect pleasure of the bird's song: 'To thy high requiem become a sod.'

In the seventh stanza Keats contrasts his own mortality with the immortality of the bird's song: 'Thou wast not born for death, immortal bird!' The beautiful song, which the poet has just enjoyed, has been experienced 'in ancient days by emperor and clown'. Keats suggests that the nightingale's song has had an uplifting and inspiring effect on people from ancient and biblical times through to the present. The song fires our imaginations, allowing us to experience a rare and special beauty: 'Charmed magic casements, opening on the foam of perilous seas, in faery lands forlorn.'

The word 'forlorn' acts as a reminder to the poet of the inescapable reality of loneliness and misery. It is like a tolling funeral bell signalling the end of the poet's imaginative experience. As the bird's 'plaintive anthem' fades, Keats realises that the imagination cannot offer him a lasting means of escape: 'Adieu! The fancy cannot cheat so well as she is famed to do'. The wonderful, magical experience stimulated by the bird's song is over and the poet returns to the world of reality. At the close of the poem Keats is back where he began, wondering if the power of his imagination has enabled him to experience a truly visionary moment or merely provided him with the means of temporarily escaping from reality: 'Was it a vision or a waking dream?'

KEY POINTS

- Key themes are the transience and pain of life and the poet's yearning to escape from reality into a world of lasting happiness and perfection.
- The contrast between the perfection and permanence of the bird's song and the imperfection and transience of real life is sharply drawn.
- Sensuous imagery – note stanzas 2 and 5 in particular.
- Symbolism: the bird's song is a symbol of lasting beauty and perfection.
- Sound effects: alliteration (e.g. 'Deep-delved', 'beaded bubbles'), assonance (e.g. 'blown . . . glooms'), sibilance (e.g. 'Singest of summer in full-throated ease'), etc.

On First Looking into Chapman's Homer

The reference to Homer in the title calls to mind his epic travel poems and, as we read into it, we see that this poem is dominated by images of travel and exploration. The 'realms of gold' in which Keats has travelled suggest the richness and power of the imagination. The 'many goodly states and kingdoms' and 'many western islands' he has seen represent the different poets whose work he has explored. Homer, whose wisdom is suggested by his 'deep brow', rules his own poetic realm, but Keats could never travel there because he did not understand Greek. However, Chapman's translation of Homer's classic opened the door to the latter's kingdom, enabling Keats to 'breathe in' its pure air: 'I heard Chapman speak out loud and bold'.

Keats draws an analogy between the excitement he felt on discovering Chapman's translation of Homer and that of an astronomer ('some watcher of the skies') on discovering a new planet ('When a new planet swims into his ken'). He also compares his feelings of elation to that felt by the Spanish explorer Cortes when he first set eyes on the Pacific Ocean. Like Cortes and his men staring silently and awestruck at this hitherto undiscovered vast expanse of water, Keats is moved beyond words by his own dramatic discovery of a whole new poetic world: 'and all his men / Look'd at each other with a wild surmise – / Silent, upon a peak in Darien'.

KEY POINTS

- Key theme is the excitement of reading poetry – this poem suggests that poetry opens up new worlds to the reader.
- The poem is dominated by metaphorical language of travel and exploration.
- Written in the form of a Petrarchan sonnet.

Ode on a Grecian Urn

This poem is similar in theme to *Ode to a Nightingale*. In both poems we see Keats' desire for permanence and immortality in a world of transience. The Grecian urn, like the nightingale's song, is a symbol of lasting perfection. However, in both poems Keats also acknowledges that he cannot remain forever in an ideal world conjured up by the imagination. In both poems he concludes that, having experienced perfect, timeless beauty, he must return to reality.

In the opening stanza Keats addresses the urn, which depicts pastoral (rural) scenes of a pagan festival. The metaphors of the 'still unravished bride of quietness' and 'foster child of silence' evoke the stillness and tranquillity of the urn. This sense of peace is reinforced by the sibilant

's' sound of the opening lines. Paradoxically, the silent urn can tell a tale more eloquently than the poet and his poem. There is a sense of excitement as Keats brings the lifeless urn to life by entering into the world of the story depicted on its sides: 'What men or gods are these? What maidens loth? / What mad pursuit? What struggle to escape?'

The second stanza opens with Keats asserting that art is superior to reality, that the world of the imagination is superior to the real world. He claims that the music that the piper on the urn is playing is more beautiful than real music because it appeals not to the ear but to the spirit or to the imagination: 'Heard melodies are sweet, but those unheard / Are sweeter.' He also suggests that the love depicted on the urn is superior to real love because it is forever beautiful and forever young. The 'bold lover' will never kiss the maiden he pursues (the repetition of 'never, never' is particularly emphatic) but, while he will never actually experience the 'bliss' of love, that love and her beauty will live eternally, untarnished by the harshness and disappointment of reality: 'For ever wilt thou love, and she be fair!'

The repetition of 'happy' (six times) and 'for ever' (five times) seems to underline the poet's belief in the superiority of art. We do however wonder if the poet is as convinced as he claims to be of the superiority of art over real life. As someone painfully aware of life's transience, Keats understandably delights in this vividly imagined world of eternal youth, timeless music and everlasting love. This perfect work of art has forever captured a variety of happy scenes, effectively freezing them in time. However, there is a suggestion that the love depicted on the urn lacks the vibrancy and warmth of real human passion: 'All breathing human passion far above that leaves a heart high-sorrowful and cloyed / A burning forehead, and a parching tongue.' While human love is subject to change and can involve sorrow and pain, Keats realises that art, although perfect and immortal, is also cold and lifeless.

In stanza four, Keats captures the ritual sacrifice of a heifer in a typically sensuous image: 'that heifer lowing at the skies, / and all her silken flanks with garlands dressed.' The image of the deserted, lifeless town reinforces the impression of the urn as a cold, lifeless object: 'And little town, thy streets for evermore will silent be.'

In the final stanza Keats moves from contemplating the scenes on the urn to reflecting on the urn itself. As he steps back and looks at the urn, he leaves the world of the imagination and returns to the world of reality. For all its timeless beauty, the urn is ultimately a lifeless artifact, as the poet's references to 'marble men and maidens', 'Thou, silent form' and 'Cold Pastoral!' clearly suggest. He admires the beauty of the urn and its capacity to 'tease us out of thought' (which is suggestive of its capacity to provoke an imaginative, as opposed to an intellectual or logical response). The urn remains 'a friend to man', reminding us that 'Beauty is truth, truth beauty'. While this equation of truth and beauty has provoked much controversy and debate, Keats seems to argue that what the imagination perceives as beauty must be truth.

As in *Ode to a Nightingale*, Keats accepts that he must return from a vividly imagined world of perfect, everlasting beauty to the world of imperfect, transient reality.

KEY POINTS

- Themes include Keats' desire to escape from transitory reality into a timeless world of enduring perfection.
- The contrast between art (perfect and everlasting, but cold) and reality (imperfect and transient, but living) lies at the heart of Keats' inner debate.
- Use of paradoxes, e.g. 'Heard melodies are sweet but those unheard are sweeter'.
- Memorable metaphors, e.g. 'unravished bride of silence', 'foster child of silence', etc.
- Sensuous imagery: e.g. Love is described as leaving 'a heart high-sorrowful and cloyed, / A burning forehead and a parching tongue'.
- The use of regular questions suggests the poet's imaginative engagement with the scenes depicted on the urn, e.g. 'What men or gods are these? What maidens loth?'
- Sound effects: alliteration (e.g. 'marble men and maidens', etc.), assonance (e.g. 'Sylvan historian', etc.).

When I have fears that I may cease to be

In this sonnet Keats reflects on poetry, love and the transience of life. The repetition of the words 'when' and 'before' reflect his keen awareness of the passage of time. The poet's great fear is that he will die before he has achieved poetic fame or experienced perfect love. While the title of the poem underlines the poet's fear of death, this sonnet also expresses Keats' ambition and love of life.

Keats fears that death will prevent him from giving expression to all of the ideas in his fertile mind, and from realising his full potential as a poet. The metaphor of the harvest suggests the richness and fertility of the poet's imagination. He fears that he may not live long enough to harvest or express all of the ideas in his 'teeming brain'.

The second quatrain develops the idea that Keats may die before he has written all that he hopes to write. He appreciates and wishes to capture the beauty and mystery of the world, symbolised by the personified night sky ('the night's starred face') in his verse. He also wishes to write about the 'high romance', symbolised by the stars. The phrase 'the magic hand of chance' suggests the mysterious nature of the creative process. The references to night and shadows evoke the idea of death.

In the third quatrain Keats considers the possibility of time preventing him from experiencing the magical power of perfect love: 'Never have relish in the fairy power of unreflecting love.' However, he is also sharply aware of the transience of human beauty and of life itself: 'Fair creature of an hour.'

The poem concludes in a despondent manner in the rhyming couplet. When Keats considers 'love and fame' in relation to time, he is filled with a sense of gloom which is reflected in the image of the poet standing alone 'on the shore of the wide world'. Love and fame fade into unimportance or 'nothingness' when they are set against the grim, inescapable reality of life's transience.

KEY POINTS

- Key theme is the insignificance of love and poetic fame when set against the grim reality of life's transience.
- Effective use of imagery (e.g. 'on the shore of the wide world I stand alone'), metaphor (e.g. harvest metaphor), personificaton (e.g. 'the night's starred face').
- Uses Shakespearian sonnet form.
- Sound effects: assonance (e.g. 'fears . . . cease . . . gleaned . . . teeming'), alliteration (e.g. 'wide world') and end-rhyme (e.g. 'brain / grain', 'more / shore') give the poem a musical quality.
- Uses a euphemism ('When I have fears that I may cease to be') when speaking of his own death.
- Tone is ultimately one of despair.

La Belle Dame sans Merci

This poem is written in the form of a medieval ballad. It tells a story that is full of mystery, drama and uncertainty. As in other Keats' poems there is a contrast between the harshness of the real world and an ideal world of beauty and happiness.

This ballad consists of a dialogue between the knight and an unknown speaker. Stanzas 1–3 are addressed to the knight, while stanzas 4–12 express his reply. As in other Keats' poems, the real world is seen as a place of suffering. The knight looks sickly ('With anguish moist and fever dew), despondent ('So haggard and so woe-begone') and bewildered ('Alone and palely loitering'). The autumnal setting underlines the sense of desolation: 'The sedge has withered from the lake and no birds sing.' Long vowel sounds reinforce the bleak mood ('Alone . . . palely . . . woe . . . fading', etc).

The knight's meeting with this supernatural beauty ('a fairy's child' with 'wild eyes') seems to have been accidental. Everything about her is beautiful and the knight seems to be instantly enchanted by her: 'Full beautiful . . . / Her hair was long, her foot was light.' He immediately starts to woo her with garlands and bracelets of flowers: 'I made a garland for her head and bracelets too'. He put her on his 'pacing steed' and watched her 'all day long'. Once again, this poem is rich in sensuous detail: 'She looked at me as she did love / And made sweet moan . . . She found me roots of relish sweet, / And honey wild and manna-dew.' This mysterious woman speaks a strange language, yet the knight seems to understand her: 'she said / I love thee true.' Later, she took the knight to her mysterious fairy cave. The happy mood is dispelled when this enigmatic beauty is inexplicably overcome by sorrow: 'And there she wept, and sigh'd full sore'. After the knight attempts to console her 'with kisses four', she lulls him asleep.

The knight's strange experience has a nightmarish dimension – he has a vision of 'death-pale' kings, princes and warriors who warn him that he, like them, has been enslaved by 'La Belle Dame Sans Merci'. The image of their 'starved lips . . . gaped wide' is particularly grotesque and frightening. The beautiful, bewitching enchantress is closely associated with death, and may even be the embodiment of death.

At the close of the poem, the knight is back in the real world: 'And I awoke and found me here / On the cold hill's side'. He seems to have escaped from the nightmare, yet he can never escape the inevitability of death. The mood at the close of the poem is particularly bleak, with the knight isolated and seemingly without purpose or direction ('Alone and palely loitering'). The absence of birdsong ('And no birds sing') suggests that the happiness associated with birds singing is no longer possible.

Once again we see the contrast between the ideal world of beauty and happiness that the knight briefly experiences and the harsh world of reality to which he returns at the close of the poem. For a brief time the knight (perhaps representative of Keats) is captivated by a vividly imagined experience of an ideal world. However, like Keats, in both *Ode to a Nightingale* and *Ode on a Grecian Urn*, the knight, too, inevitably returns to reality.

This poem is gloomy in outlook since it suggests that love and death are inseparable. It is similar to *Ode to a Nightingale* in that both poems suggest the impermanence of love ('Where Beauty cannot keep her lustrous eyes, / Or new Love pine at them beyond tomorrow'). It resembles *Ode on a Grecian Urn* in that both poems suggest that love inevitably involves pain ('A burning forehead and a parching tongue').

- Key theme is the contrast between the ideal beauty and happiness that the knight briefly experiences, and the harshness of the real world.
- A gloomy poem dominated by images and suggestions of death.
- The atmosphere of the poem is one of darkness and mystery.
- Vivid imagery.
- Repetition (e.g. first and last stanzas are largely similar).

To Autumn

While most poems on the subject of autumn tend to be largely gloomy reflections on death and decay, this poem celebrates the natural abundance of the autumn season. While there are suggestions of death and the passage of time, this is not a poem about life's transience; instead we see Keats delighting in the richness and beauty of the season. The sensuousness, which is a constant feature of Keats' verse, is strikingly evident in this poem. Each stanza deals with a different aspect of the autumnal world.

Stanza one opens with a wonderfully atmospheric description of autumn: 'Seasons of mists and mellow fruitfulness'. The alliterative 'm' ('mists . . . mellow . . . maturing') and repeated 'l' sounds ('mellow', 'apples', 'fill', 'shells', 'cells') suggest a sense of ease and harmony. Personified autumn is addressed in all three stanzas. In stanza one autumn is depicted as a co-conspirator with 'the maturing sun' in bringing about the seemingly unending fruitfulness of the season. Their shared work has an almost sacred quality as they 'load and bless / With fruit the vines that round the thatch-eves run'. Together, they are responsible for the weight of apples that bend the trees. The phrase 'budding more and still more' suggests unending abundance. Even the bees are deceived into thinking that this bountiful season will never end, with their hives full of honey ('For summer has o'er-brimmed their clammy cells'). Tactile imagery conveys the rich bounty of the season: autumn and the sun combine 'to swell the gourd, and plump the hazel shells'.

In the second stanza autumn is personified as various people engaged in the diverse activities of harvesting. She is, in turn, a granary worker, a reaper, a gleaner and finally a cider maker. Autumn is largely inactive in this section of the poem. The images in this stanza are mainly visual. We see autumn 'sitting careless on a granary floor' with her hair 'soft-lifted by the winnowing wind'. The gentle, alliterative 'w' and assonant 'i' sounds create the sense of autumn's hair being lightly lifted by the wind. The image of autumn asleep 'on a half-reaped furrow' evokes a sense of ease. She is in no rush to complete the reaping and harvesting. Her lethargy suggests a sense of fulfillment. A sensuous image suggests how she is drowsy 'with the fume of poppies'. As a cider maker, autumn patiently watches over the production of cider from the abundant apples that had caused the trees to bend in stanza one: 'thou watchest the last oozings hours by hours.' The sibilance of this line underlines the sense of ease and tranquillity. Time is moving on: in the first stanza we could almost touch the ripening fruit, while in the second we can visualise the harvesting and processing of these fruits.

In stanza three time has moved on further and the harvest is done; all that now remains of it is 'the stubble-plains with rosy hue'. While this is a tactile-visual image, the imagery in this stanza is mainly aural. The poet listens to the plaintive music of autumn, the various sounds combining to create a veritable symphony: '. . . in a wailful choir the small gnats mourn . . . lambs loud bleat . . . Hedge-crickets sing . . . The red-breast whistles . . . And gathering swallows twitter in the skies.' There is a clear suggestion of death in this stanza with references to 'the soft-dying day', 'a wailful choir', the mourning gnats and the robin – a bird traditionally associated with winter. Keats is not despondent; he seems to be accepting of this natural process. He does not dwell on life's transience, but instead celebrates the distinctive beauty of autumn.

KEY POINTS

- Key theme is the abundance and distinctive beauty of autumn.
- Sensuous imagery present throughout.
- Sound effects: alliteration (e.g. 'mists and mellow fruitfulness', 'winnowing wind'), assonance (e.g. 'mourn', 'bourn'), sibilance (e.g. 'Thou watchest the last oozings hours by hours'), etc.

Bright Star

In this sonnet Keats is attracted to the permanence ('would I were steadfast as thou art') and 'splendour' of the 'bright star'. However, he is not enamoured of its detached, isolated existence. Keats describes the star as being hermit-like in its solitude: 'Like nature's patient, sleepless eremite'. Here we again see Keats' tendency to give human qualities to the natural world. As the sonnet develops, the words 'not' and 'no' make clear the poet's rejection of the star.

The star is depicted as watching over the 'moving waters' below. The poet's imagination infuses these waters with 'priestlike' powers as they cleanse 'earth's human shores'. The freshness and purity of the natural world is evoked by metaphor of the 'soft-fallen mask / Of snow upon the mountains and the moors'. Here the alliterative and sibilant 's' sound suggests the tranquillity of this winter scene, while the alliterative 'm' sound adds to the poem's musical qualities.

While the star is 'still steadfast, still unchangeable', it is also cold and remote. Keats is instead drawn to the transitory (transient or passing) but warm and vibrant world of human passion. The poet's idea of perfect happiness would be to be forever 'Pillowed upon my fair love's ripening breast, / To feel forever its soft fall and swell'. This sensuous image with its soft alliterative and sibilant 's' sound conveys the warmth of shared human love which contrasts with and highlights the cold isolation of the star. If the poet cannot forever experience this intensely passionate moment, then he would choose to 'swoon to death'.

In much of Keats' verse we see the tension between the poet's yearning for permanence and immortality, and his desire to enjoy the warm pleasures of real love.

While the transient physical world is a place of sorrow and pain, it is also the realm of passionate experience.

This sonnet resembles both *Ode to a Nightingale* and *Ode on a Grecian Urn* in that in all three poems Keats is drawn to the idea of an unchanging ideal world, before accepting the need to return to reality. Ultimately, permanence is not enough for the poet. The enduring splendour of the cold star, like the timeless perfection of the cold Grecian urn, cannot ultimately satisfy Keats who longs to forever savour the 'sweet unrest' of passionate love.

KEY POINTS

- Key theme is the contrasting attractions of the constant but cold star and the transient but warm world of human passion.

- Contrasting imagery: coldness and isolation of the star ('in lone splendour hung aloft the night') contrasted with the shared experience of warm human love ('pillowed upon my fair love's ripening breast, / To feel forever its soft rise and fall').

- Personification of nature: the star is 'like nature's patient, sleepless eremite'.

- Sound effects: Alliterative and sibilant 's' sound evokes the sense of perfect peace and happiness that accompanies the shared experience of human love.

Sample Answer

Explain why the poetry of Keats did *or* did not appeal to you.

The poetry of Keats greatly appealed to me for a range of reasons. Purely on a descriptive level, I love the way he uses sensuous imagery to convey the beauty of the natural world.

Few poets appreciate and celebrate beauty like Keats. On a deeper level Keats grapples with some issues of universal relevance in his work, reflecting on such matters as mortality, the pain of life, the search for permanence in a world of change and the power of the imagination. At the heart of much of Keats' poetry are the conflicting attractions of art and reality. While art is perfect and timeless, it can also be cold and lifeless. In contrast, while reality is painful and transient, it can also be vibrant and passionate. We can all relate to Keats' inner struggles as the issues that preoccupy him are universal and timeless. In the context of these inner struggles, another quality I greatly admire about Keats strongly emerges – his realism. Finally, I was impressed with the various sound effects Keats so effectively employs in his verse.

A simple poem that I greatly enjoyed is *To one who has been long in city pent*. Weary of the confinement of the city, Keats is rejuvenated by the natural world as he lies back in the long grass reading 'a gentle tale of love and languishment'. I like the way Keats regularly gives human qualities to the natural world, in this poem personifying the sky with his reference to 'the smile of the blue firmament'. However, his realism expresses itself before the sonnet ends when he reminds us of the transience of this uplifting day by comparing its passing to the fall of an angel's tear from heaven to earth.

In *Bright Star* Keats is attracted to the permanence and 'splendour' of the 'bright star'. However, he is not attracted to its detached, isolated existence. Keats sees the star as being hermit-like in its solitude: 'Like nature's patient, sleepless eremite.' The beauty of nature in winter is captured in the memorable image of the 'soft-fallen mask / Of snow upon the mountains'. The alliterative and sibilant 's' sound evokes a sense of perfect peace. While the star is 'still steadfast, still unchangeable', Keats is drawn back to the real world. His idea of perfect happiness would be to be forever 'Pillowed upon my fair love's ripening breast, / To feel forever its soft fall and swell'. This beautiful sensuous image with its soft sibilant and alliterative 's' sound conveys the warmth of shared human love that is ultimately more appealing to the poet than the existence of the immortal, but cold, star. The tension between Keats' yearning for immortality and his desire to enjoy the passionate pleasures of real love is apparent in much of his verse.

I regard *Ode to a Nightingale* as one of the truly great poems. In this poem we see Keats' intense desire to escape from the painful, transient physical world into the perfect immortal world of the nightingale's song. Like many people at difficult moments in their lives, Keats considers alcohol as a possible avenue of escape. He describes the wine in sensuous detail – one of the features of his verse that I particularly enjoy. We can almost taste the wine that has been 'cooled a long age in the deep-delved earth' and visualise 'the beaded bubbles winking at the brim'. The alliterative 'd' and 'b' sounds underscore the sensuous appeal of the wine, by means of which Keats hopes to fade away with the nightingale 'into the forest dim'. When he dismisses the idea of using alcohol to reach the perfect world of the nightingale's song, the poet finally accesses it by means of his imagination, flying there on 'the viewless wings of Poesy'. The world of the nightingale's song is rich in sensuous appeal. Here Keats can smell the 'soft incense' that 'hangs upon the boughs', taste 'the dewy wine' and hear 'the murmurous haunt of flies on summer eves'. However, we can sense the poet's realism asserting itself in the suggestions of death and decay to be found in the references to the 'embalmed darkness' and the murmuring flies. Ultimately, Keats realises that the imagination cannot offer him a lasting means of escape: 'Adieu! adieu! The fancy cannot cheat so well / As she is famed to do'. The wonderful, magical journey inspired by the bird's song is over and the poet returns to the world of reality. I can certainly understand Keats' longing to escape life's problems and transience, but I am impressed with the realism that brings him back to the physical world.

In *Ode on a Grecian Urn* we again see Keats' desire for permanence in a world of transience. The Grecian urn, like the nightingale's song, is a symbol of lasting perfection. The metaphors of the 'still unravished bride of quietness' and 'foster child of silence' effectively evoke the stillness and tranquillity of the urn. In the early part of the poem Keats asserts that art (symbolic of the power of the imagination) is superior to reality when he claims that the music played by the piper in one of the pastoral scenes depicted on the urn is more beautiful than real music because it appeals, not to the ear, but to the spirit or the imagination: 'Heard melodies are sweet, but those unheard / Are sweeter . . .'

Keats also suggests that the everlasting love of the figures on the urn is superior to real human passion. However, we get the impression that he 'doth protest too much' with the repetition of 'happy' when describing this love: 'More happy love! more happy, happy love! / For ever happy and still to be enjoyed.' There is a clear suggestion that the love depicted on the urn lacks the vibrancy and warmth of real human passion: 'All breathing human passion far above, / That leaves a heart high sorrowful and cloy'd, / A burning forehead and a parching tongue.' While human love is subject to change and can involve disappointment and pain, Keats realises that art, although perfect and timeless, is also cold and lifeless. Moving on to another scene portrayed on the urn, the poet captures the ritual sacrifice of a heifer in a typically sensuous image: 'that heifer lowing at the skies, / And all her silken flanks with garlands dressed.' In the final stanza, the poet leaves the world of the imagination and returns to the world of reality. For all its perfection, the urn remains a cold artifact, a mere reflection of real life as Keats' references to 'marble men and maidens', 'thou silent form' and 'Cold Pastoral!' clearly suggest. Another aspect of this poem that I enjoyed is the manner in which Keats leaves us grappling with his controversial declaration that 'Beauty is truth, truth beauty'.

The Keats' poem that I most enjoyed was *To Autumn*. While the title leads us to expect a despondent reflection on transience and death, what we actually get is a wonderful description and celebration of the overflowing abundance of the season. The sensuousness that I particularly admire in Keats' verse is again strikingly evident in this poem. The poem opens with a wonderfully atmospheric description of autumn: 'Season of mists and mellow fruitfulness, / Close bosom-friend of the maturing sun.' The alliterative 'm' ('mists . . . mellow . . . maturing') and repeated 'i' sounds evoke a sense of ease and harmony. Tactile imagery conveys the rich bounty of the season as autumn and sun combine 'to swell the gourd, and plump the hazel shells'. Autumn is brought to life as Keats personifies her as a variety of workers involved in the diverse activities of harvesting. The images in the second stanza of the poem are mainly, but not entirely, visual. We see autumn 'sitting carelessly on a granary floor' with her hair 'soft-lifted by the winnowing wind'. The gentle, alliterative 'w' and assonant 'i' sounds create the sense of autumn's hair being lightly lifted by the wind. The image of autumn asleep 'on a half-reaped furrow' evokes a sense of ease. Another sensuous image portrays her as being drowsy 'with the fume of poppies'. In the final stanza, the harvesting has been completed and all that now remains of the harvest is 'the stubble-plains with rosy hue'. While this is a tactile-visual image, the images in this stanza are predominantly aural. Keats listens to the plaintive music of autumn: 'in a wailful choir the small gnats mourn . . . lambs loud bleat . . . Hedge-crickets sing . . . The red-breast whistles . . . And gathering swallows twitter in the skies.' While the references to 'the soft-dying day', mourning gnats and 'a wailful choir' evoke the idea of death, Keats is not despondent. He is accepting of this natural process and does not dwell on the passage of time, choosing instead to celebrate the unique beauty and richness of autumn.

In conclusion, I would only like to restate my great admiration for and genuine enjoyment of the work of John Keats, a truly great poet.

POETRY

Gerard Manley Hopkins

Biographical Note

Gerard Hopkins (1844–1889) was born to Manley and Catherine Hopkins. Gerard was the first of their nine children. Although he ultimately wrote no more than 40 mature poems, he is regarded as one of the major English poets. His parents were High Church Anglicans, and his father, a marine insurance adjuster, also published a volume of poetry. His talented family encouraged his artistic nature. In 1854 he entered Highgate School where he distinguished himself as a gifted student, winning a poetry prize after he began to write Keatsian nature poetry. He went on to win a scholarship to Balliol College, Oxford (1863-1867). At Oxford he searched for a religion that could speak with true authority – it was here that he came under the influence of John Henry Newman. In 1864 Hopkins was deeply moved by his reading of Newman's *Apologia Pro Vita Sua* which explained the reasons for his conversion to Catholicism. In 1866 Hopkins was received by Newman into the Catholic Church.

In 1868 Hopkins resolved to become a priest and he entered Manresa House, a Jesuit novitiate near London. Following three years of theological studies in St. Beuno's College in North Wales, Hopkins served as assistant to the parish priest in Sheffield, Oxford and London from 1877 until 1879 before going on to work as a parish priest in the slums of Manchester, Liverpool and Glasgow. Hopkins was appointed as Professor of Greek and Latin at University College Dublin in 1884. He taught there until he died of typhoid fever, after a long period of ill health, on 8 June 1889.

It is important to be aware of the unique features of Hopkins' style if his poetry is to be fully appreciated. Two key literary terms which Hopkins personally created must be understood. 'Inscape' refers to the essential inner nature of a person, an object, etc. For Hopkins, inscape is 'the species of individually distinctive beauty'. This term has also been defined as 'the revelation of God's energy to one's senses through nature'. The second poetic concept developed by Hopkins is 'sprung rhythm' which, in essence, relates to a new metre based on the counting of stresses rather than syllables.

God's Grandeur

Hopkins is a poet of intense emotions. This poem unifies feelings of both ecstasy and distress. Since this poem was composed in 1877, the year he was ordained as a priest, Hopkins is unsurprised that mankind may have disfigured and violated the earth, but contends that an unending freshness and a charged magnificence bring life to the natural world.

In the first quatrain of the octave in this sonnet, the poet portrays a natural world that is animated by God's existence. Similar to an electrical current, God's presence briefly develops into beams of light 'like shining from shook foil'. The poet goes on to compare the presence of God in the world to 'the ooze of oil /Crushed'. These clear and palpable demonstrations of God's existence in the world prompt the poet to pose a serious question which sees him wondering why we do not pay attention to God's authority, 'Why do men then not now reck his rod?'

Once again, the poet makes efficient and impressive use of both assonance ('ooze…oil') and alliteration ('reck his reed') – in this instance to underscore his serious, disheartened mood.

Onomatopoeia is also employed to good effect, with the repetition of 'trod' ('Generations have trod, have trod, have trod), conveying a sense of unending and tedious exertion.

This poem is written in the traditional form of

a Petrarchan sonnet, with the octave normally setting a question or a difficulty and the sestet offering a decision on these matters that resolves them.

The theme that dominates this poem is the deep connection between man, nature and God. A related theme is the freedom Hopkins felt to resolve his religious faith with his love of nature. Indeed his capacity to see God in nature is also an obvious theme in many of his poems. Another theme of this poem that Hopkins explores is the contrast between the everlasting newness of nature and the deterioration of the appearance of the earth because of human behaviour.

The sestet displays Hopkin's intense belief in nature's capacity to regenerate itself. It also demonstrates his deep religious beliefs. The regeneration of nature imagined by Hopkins is controlled by the Holy Ghost, pondering over the earth with 'warm breast' and 'bright wings' and guaranteeing its productivity. As Hopkins puts it, in spite of all the oppression and misuse of the earth by people, 'nature is never spent'.

The closing image is not readily visualised. The enormous world has developed into the bird's nest and the warmth and sparkling contained within the image is comforting and consoling. The everyday language in the final lines heightens the accessibility of the poem, 'Oh, morning at the brown brink eastward, springs - / Because the Holy Ghost over the bent / World broods with warm breast and with ah! bright wings'.

KEY POINTS

- This poem shows us that Hopkins is a poet of deep emotions, with this poem combining feelings of both elation and despondency.
- In the first quatrain of the octave in this sonnet, the poet portrays a natural world that is enlivened by God's existence.
- Once again, the poet makes efficient and impressive use of sound effects.
- This poem is composed in the conventional form of a Petrarchan sonnet.
- A variety of themes are identifiable in this poem, particularly the poet's ability to see God in nature.
- The sestet displays Hopkin's intense belief in nature's capacity to regenerate itself.
- The closing image is not readily visualised.
- The everyday language in the final lines heightens the accessibility of the poem.

Spring

This is one of Hopkins' most renowned poems. It commences with an authoritative, forceful declaration that is incontrovertibly true, 'Nothing is so beautiful as spring –'.

This is then supported by a myriad of examples of nature's beauty and richness, '. . . weeds, in wheels, shoot long and lovely and lush; / Thrush's eggs look little low heavens, and thrush / Through the echoing timber does so rinse and wring / The ear, it strikes like lightnings to hear him sing'. Hopkins' willingness to commemorate weeds rather than flowers, for example, highlights his ability to see beauty in the everyday world.

There is an elated tone throughout the octave. Hopkins' control of sound effects is both efficient and impressive, 'When weeds, in wheels, shoot long and lovely and lush'. The alliteration of 'w' and 'l' in addition to the assonance of 'ee' and 'o' enhance this depiction of rich growth. We can visualise the wild flowers growing as we observe them.

The vitality of the new plants is captured in the verb 'shoot'. The beauty of the natural world has much to do with its eye-catching combination of colours such as the speckled appearance of the thrush's eggs (which are so impressive, they 'look little low heavens') and the variegated (multicoloured) blue and white in the sky. Once again, Hopkins' use of sound effects proves particularly effective, with the alliterative 'b', 'r' and 'f' sounds ('The descending blue; that blue is all in a rush / With richness; the racing lambs too have fair their fling') helping to convey nature's unique beauty.

Similar to virtually all of Hopkins' other poems, the impetus behind this one is essentially religious. Heaven and earth are brought closer together here; it is almost as if heaven is on earth. The advent of spring sets Hopkins thinking about Adam and Eve's loss of the Garden of Eden following their loss of innocence.

As is always the case with a Petrarchan sonnet, the descriptive octave is followed by a reflective sestet that analyses the ideas raised earlier. Hopkins associates spring with the youthful freedom from sin. This is why he appeals to Christ to watch over the young and to protect their innocence, or else they will become 'sour with sinning'.

In the concluding line Hopkins pictures Christ as a boy and Mary as a young maid, 'Most, O maid's child, thy choice and worthy the winning'.

KEY POINTS

- Poem opens with a dramatic declaration of the beauty of spring.
- There is an elated tone throughout the octave.
- Hopkins' use of sound effects is both efficient and impressive.
- The impetus behind this poem is essentially religious.
- As is always the case with a Petrarchan sonnet, the descriptive octave leads on to a reflective sestet.
- Among the broad themes in which Hopkins is interested are innocence and the physical demonstration of God's beauty in the human and natural worlds.

As kingfishers catch fire, dragonflies draw flame

This is a poem which commemorates uniqueness. Every natural thing is distinctive. The poem begins with memorably graphic images, 'As kingfishers catch fire, dragonflies draw flame; / As tumbled over rim in roundy wells'. In these lines Hopkins portrays the flash of the sun on the wings of the kingfisher and the dragonfly.

The sonnet confirms the uniqueness of every created thing. Hopkins portrays everything in the world around him from birds (kingfishers), insects (dragonflies) and inanimate stones to human beings trying to declare their identity. In doing this, everything gives glory to God. It is important to remember what, for Hopkins, makes his poetry so distinctive and special in terms of God and nature. For the poet, inscape is 'the species of individually distinctive beauty'. This term has also been defined as 'the revelation of God's energy to one's senses through nature'.

Aural imagery presents us with a range of everyday sounds that help to convey the distinctiveness of our existence and to see the individuality of everything around us as a manifestation of God's greatness This is achieved through the use of onomatopoeia ('Stones ring') and, more particularly, alliteration ('fire... flame', 'rim... roundy... ring', 'tucked... tells', 'finds... fling', 'grace... goings graces', 'Lovely... lovely', 'Father... features... faces').

Once again, Hopkins employs the Petrarchan sonnet form. The theme of the poem is the physical demonstration of God's beauty in the human and natural worlds. At the heart of this poem is Hopkins' desire to give the reader a convincing example of his theory of inscape. He views God's sanctity (divinity) as the obvious and indisputable quintessence of His unique nature.

There is a striking contrast between the vividly descriptive octave and the reflective sestet. In the sestet of this sonnet Hopkins meditates on the distinctiveness of human beings. He believes that a human's most important quality is freedom of choice. They can select or reject the idea of giving glory to God. They communicate their individuality by complying with God's will, 'I say more; the just man justices; / Keeps grace; that keeps all his goings graces'. In agreeing with God's will, human beings make God present in the world.

KEY POINTS

- Key theme is the celebration of the uniqueness of every natural thing.
- Aural imagery provides us with a variety of everyday sounds that help to convey the uniqueness of our existence.
- Once again Hopkins uses the Petrarchan sonnet form, with the descriptive octave being followed by the reflective sestet.
- Hopkin's utilisation of sound effects (onomatopoeia and, more particularly, alliteration) proves to be highly effective.

The Windhover

The Windhover is a profoundly personal poem, with 'I' being the first word ('I caught this morning morning's minion') and 'my' featuring before the end of the octave ('My heart in hiding').

The opening line engages the reader's interest such is the sense of immediacy it creates '... this morning morning's minion...'). Hopkins is exhilarated and strikingly affected by his encounter with the bird ('My heart in hiding / Stirred for a bird...').

In this poem Hopkins commemorates the inimitable nature of the bird and the intensity of his relationship with 'Christ our Lord' (the poem's subtitle) – a relationship which develops through the poet's ability to see God in nature.

The bird's name derives from its habit of hovering in the air as it struggles to cope with the power of the wind, with its head in the wind. The windhover is a falcon which is likened to a knight. This image is developed by using the language of chivalry. The poet visualises the bird to be a knight on horseback fighting against the wind. The image of the windhover as a knight is also evocative of Christ, whom the poet names 'my chevalier', reflecting images of chivalry and knighthood.

This is certainly one of Hopkins' best-known, most discussed and best-loved poems. Hopkins himself described it as 'the best thing I ever wrote'. It is obviously open to a variety of interpretations, both literal and symbolic. There are even regular disagreements over the meaning of ambiguous words. One source of difficulty is Hopkins' use of the term 'Buckle!', the meaning of which is much debated – it could mean either 'collapse' or 'give way under pressure'. Another source of difficulty is the group of words 'To ring upon the rein', which may be a riding-school term, while 'to ring' is also a technical term of falconry.

The Windhover was written in Hopkins' final year of study in 1877 before being ordained as a priest. He expresses his respect and admiration for the beauty and wonder, strength and energy of the windhover, while also highlighting its praiseworthy individuality. The poem is dedicated to Christ, implying that while the poet is writing about nature, his primary theme is a spiritual one. This subtitle was added later with a view to accentuating the poem's religious importance.

Hopkins writes this poem in the form of a sonnet – a structure he commonly employs. He evokes the energy of the bird's movement by using alliteration and assonance, 'I caught this morning morning's minion, king- / dom of daylight's dauphin, dapple-dawn-drawn Falcon, in his riding / Of the rolling level underneath him steady air, and striding…'. The use of 'riding', 'rolling', 'striding' and 'wimpling' evoke the movement of the windhover in flight.

The vividly descriptive octave is followed by a discursive, analytical sestet. The falcon is juxtaposed to a knight. This image is advanced by using the language of chivalry. The poet pictures the bird as a knight on horseback fighting against the wind. The image of the windhover as a knight is also evocative of Christ whom the poet addresses as 'my chevalier'. Having portrayed the attractive nature of the bird's flight in the octave, Hopkins compares the beauty of the bird to that of Christ. He views Christ as 'a billion / Times told lovelier, more dangerous…' The image of the fire is indicative of Christ fighting against evil exactly as the bird fights against the wind. It is interesting to note that the octave may present the falcon as an emblem of Christ's sacrifice. The outstretched wings may symbolise the outstretched arms of Christ on the Cross.

In the sestet the fire image is introduced and continues to the final line. The embers appear lifeless, but when they collapse, the glowing heart of the fire is to be seen. The 'O my chevalier' develops into Christ in the hawk. In the concluding three lines the poet speaks of 'the sheer plod' of the religious life. The image of the ploughman showing the shine on the soil as he ploughs is comparable with the light which the demanding work of the religious brings to the poet. In the final two lines we have a suggestion of reward following labour as 'blue-bleak' develops into 'gold-vermilion'.

KEY POINTS

- A profoundly personal poem.
- The opening line engages the reader's interest, such is the sense of immediacy it creates.
- The intensity of the poet's relationship with God develops through his capacity to see God in nature.
- The poem is open to a variety of interpretations, both literal and symbolic.
- The poem is written in the form of a sonnet, with the vividly descriptive octave followed by the discursive and analytical sestet.
- The poem concludes on an optimistic note, with 'blue-bleak' being transformed into 'gold-vermilion'.

Pied Beauty

This is a shortened version of the conventional sonnet with ten and a half lines instead of the traditional fourteen. This is known as a curtailed sonnet form. In this poem man's presence is perceived to be in accord with God's creation. It starts and finishes with words of admiration, while advancing from the past ('brinded', 'plotted', 'pieced', 'freckled') to the present tense ('Who knows how?...Praise him').

Pied Beauty is a hymn of praise to God for the infinite diversity of nature. The opening line is filled with words of acclaim for God, 'Glory be to God for dappled things – '. This prayer-like beginning is then accompanied by a litany of vivid examples of the 'dappled' beauty to be located in the natural world. Hopkins includes the mottled blue and white colours of the sky, the 'brinded' (streaked) hide of a cow and the patches of contrasting colour on a trout. The chestnut presents us with a more complex and challenging image as we try to visualise its interior after it is compared to the coals in a fire ('Fresh-firecoal chestnut falls'), black on the outside and glowing within. The wings of finches are variegated, as is patchwork-like farmland. The final example is of the 'trades' (occupations) and activities of man, with their variety of materials and equipment, 'Fresh –firecoal chestnut-falls; finches' wings; /landscape plotted and pierced – fold, fallow and plough; /And all trades, their gear and tackle and trim'. Here we once again see Hopkins' effective use of alliteration enhancing the poem's musical qualities. More significantly, man is depicted as being in harmony with God's creation.

In the concluding five lines, Hopkins gives moral characteristics to the miscellaneous images on which he has expanded up to this point in terms of physical qualities. At this moment we are presented with a new idea or image: God is to be praised. Hopkins claims that the examples he has given are creations of God which highlight the unity and permanence of His power and inspire us to 'Praise Him'.

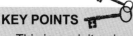

KEY POINTS

- This is a minituriased version of the conventional sonnet (also known as 'curtailed').
- It is a hymn of praise to God for the infinite diversity of nature.
- Effective use of alliteration.
- Man is portrayed as being in harmony with God's creation.
- God begins and ends this poem.

Felix Randal

This poem is written in the form of a Petrarchan sonnet and follows the traditional structure of this sonnet, with the descriptive octave followed by a reflective sestet.

Hopkins wrote this sonnet when he was working as a priest in Liverpool. This is one of the few poems in which he names an individual man and identifies his occupation, 'Felix Randal the farrier, O he is dead then? My duty all ended,'. The 'duty' to which the poet refers is the healing duty of the priest. In this poem, we see the ultimately fatal impact of a physical illness on the blacksmith, a strong, healthy man. The repetition of 'pining' evokes the gradual nature of this illness. Tragically, in addition to his physical decline, the poet's psychological health clearly deteriorated, '…watched his mould of man, big-boned and hardy–handsome / Pining, pining, till time when reason rambled in it…'. A combination of an unnamed four deadly ailments sadly caused the collapse of the blacksmith's balance of mind: '…and some / Fatal four disorders, fleshed there, all contended?'

Lines 5-9 open dramatically with the abrupt declaration, 'Sickness broke him'. The comfort that religion can bring is a significant feature of Hopkins' work. Perceiving himself to be primarily a priest in his poet-priest role, Hopkins recalls how he comforted and consoled the blacksmith, helping him to come to terms with the illness he had earlier cursed. He anointed Randal for the Last Rites before hearing his confession and giving him the Eucharist, '…I had our sweet reprieve and ransom / Tendered to him. Ah well, God rest him all road ever he offended!'

Following the traditional structure of the Petrarchan sonnet, the vividly descriptive octave is followed by the interesting observations of the sestet which focus on Hopkins' encounter with sickness and death. Tending the sick and looking after their needs encourages us to value them more. Hopkins recognises from his contact with Randal that there is a mutual exchange of love in hard times, with the terms 'touched', 'endures' and 'tears' conveying the profound nature of his emotions.

The poem concludes on an undeniably upbeat note with the underlying idea that Hopkins the priest becomes God's blacksmith, preparing shoes for the great dray horse for his journey into the next world. The final image of 'his bright and battering sandal!' is particularly optimistic, with the loud, alliterative 'b' sound suggestive of Hopkins' power and energy.

One of the most appealing features of this poem is the regular use of everyday language, 'Impatient he cursed at first, but mended / Being anointed and all, / Ah well, God rest him all road ever he offended!' Such colloquialisms ensure the accessibility of the content, themes and language of the poem.

KEY POINTS
- Written in the form of a Petrarchan sonnet.
- One of the few poems in which Hopkins names an individual man and identifies his profession.
- The poet suffers both physically and psychologically.
- Lines 5-9 open dramatically with the abrupt declaration, 'Sickness broke him'.
- Hopkins perceives himself to be primarily a priest in his poet-priest role.
- One of the most appealing features of this poem is the regular use of simple, everyday speech, which ensures it is readily accessible in terms of its content, themes and language.
- The poem concludes on an incontrovertibly optimistic note. The final image of 'his bright and battering sandal!' is particularly upbeat, with the loud, alliterative 'b' sound suggestive of Hopkins' power and energy.

Inversnaid

The inspiration for this poem originates in Hopkins' desire for the uncontrolled, tranquil and appealing world of the Scottish Highlands, where he sojourned only very briefly. The poem to some extent commemorates the unruly magnificence of the Scottish Highlands, a pleasing difference from the unattractive nature of such industrial cities as Liverpool and Glasgow where Hopkins served as a priest.

Hopkins' ability to see God in nature is an admirable feature of much of his verse. The poet tries to provide a precise portrayal of a highland stream, 'This darksome burn, horseback brown, / His rollrock highroad roaring down, / In coop and in comb the fleece of his foam / Flutes and low to the lake falls home'. Sadly, the poem's opening line evokes a similarly unappealing, disheartening world, with the dark water's implication of a polluted rural earth.

The effective use of alliteration evokes the speedy movement of the dark stream, '… burn… brown', 'rollrock… roaring', 'coop.,.. comb', 'fleece… foam…/ Flutes…. falls'. The employment of onomatopoeia ('roaring') is similarly efficient and impressive in that it creates an aural image that enables us to imagine the distinctive noise of the Highlands.

The Scots-English nature of the language roots this poem in a quickly identifiable world, and results in the type of colloquial expressions that are easily comprehensible. Examples of such distinctive terms include 'burn', 'in coop and in comb', 'flutes', 'twindles', 'degged', 'groins of the braes', 'heathpacks', 'beadbonny ash' etc.

KEY POINTS

- This poem celebrates the natural world but, unlike so many other poems, this poem celebrates its creation, without speaking of God.
- The poet's use of sound effects is once again efficient and impressive.
- The Scots-English nature of the language roots this poem in a quickly identifiable world, and results in the type of colloquial expressions that are easily comprehensible.

I wake and feel the fell of dark, not day

This is one of the three sonnets known as the 'terrible sonnets' in which Hopkins plumbs the depths of despair. There is general agreement that this is the darkest of the terrible sonnets. This sonnet provides us with disturbing insights into the poet's primary psychological problem of severe depression. This poem portrays an inner world of gloom and hopelessness. In many respects, this is the most vivid of the terrible sonnets. The imagery deftly reflects the anguish of awakening in a state of total hopelessness. The initial image is palpable in nature, with the poet claiming to 'feel the fell of dark'.

The opening lines portray an experience familiar to depressives, many of whom awaken long in advance of the sun rising and endure anguish revealed in this poem in a frightening recomposition of an arousal from sleep in the blackness of night. We also perceive the poet's sense of an unseen evil around him. In this context 'fell' is a central term, with a double meaning – it may be interpreted as threat/ blow and also as an animal's skin, a truly horrifying image.

This sonnet evokes a sense of prevalent darkness. The poet awakens, anticipating the light of day, but discovers that he is engulfed by darkness. He clearly perceives the seemingly endless nightfall to be a threat, 'I wake and feel the fell of dark, not day. / What hours, O what black hours we have spent / This night!' The darkness of the night is evocative of the darkness of Hopkins' soul. The dark hours seem never-ending, '...where I say / Hours I mean years, mean life'. His cries for God's assistance are compared to unanswered letters, making God appear remote and coldly indifferent to his plight, 'And my lament / Is cries countless, cries like dead letters sent / To dearest him that lives alas! away'.

The traditional symbolism of light and darkness is very prevalent in this sonnet. While darkness indicates spiritual despair, daylight implies hope and consolation which are sadly regarded as far away.

The theme of the poem may be the poet's sense of being abandoned by God and lacking support. It also depicts his sense of self-loathing: In the sestet Hopkins attempts to explain why God has forsaken him, 'I am gall, I am heartburn'. He employs the image of yeast souring 'the dull dough' to show how his failings have soured his soul and have undermined his spiritual relationship with God.

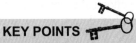

KEY POINTS

- The key theme of the poem is spiritual suffering.
- The poem provides us with insights into the psychological problem of severe depression.
- This sonnet evokes a sense of prevalent darkness.
- The traditional imagery of light and darkness is very common in the poem.
- The conclusion of the poem reveals the poet's sympathy for others.

No worst, there is none. Pitched past pitch of grief

The poem opens with one of the most profound declarations of suffering ever made by a poet, 'No worst, there is none'. The use of the superlative persuades us that this is no overstatement, but a direct expression of reality.

This is one of the most dismal of the 'terrible sonnets'. This is a cry of despondency and spiritual agony. Hopkins conveys profound torment, believing that God has forsaken him. In this sonnet he is plumbing the depths of mental distress. There is no optimism and no spiritual sustenance. His only consolation is that death will bring a conclusion to his inner pain, while sleep offers him a brief break from his suffering.

In a memorable opening the poet declares that suffering has no limit and that pain will inevitably be heightened, 'No worst, there is

none. Pitched past pitch of grief, / More pangs will, schooled at forepangs, wilder wring'. At this point Hopkins seeks assistance from the Holy Spirit, 'Comforter, where, where is your comforting?' The repetition of 'where' underscores his despondency and communicates a sense of total dependency.

The deep inner suffering which the poet endures is revealed through his use of frightening, horrifying metaphors. His mind is a fathomless pit. He resembles a climber hanging over the edge of the steep, sheer face of a cliff. Alliteration underscores his cries for assistance, 'My cries heave, herds-long; huddle in a main, a chief / Woe, world-sorrow...'. Hopkins' feeling of abandonment is underlined by his direct appeals to the Holy Ghost and to the Mother of God,

'Comforter, where, where is your comforting? / Mary, mother of us, where is your relief?' He communicates here the sense of a man who believes himself unfairly treated and forsaken.

The sestet is a reflection on what has passed. The image of the mountain with the frail figure clinging to it, buffeted by the gales, and tempted to release his hold is suggested by the 'mountains' and the 'cliffs of fall'. These also symbolise the ups and downs of the spiritual life of mankind.

In the most renowned passage of the poem ('O the mind, mind has mountains; cliffs of fall / Frightful, sheer, no-man-fathomed, Hold them cheap / May who ne'er hung there'), we have the presentation of a terrified, despairing mind in terms of a mountain climber falling into an abyss.

The sonnet concludes on a hint of hope. Death ends even the most dismal life and sleep ends the most gloomy day, '...all / Life death does end and each day dies with sleep'.

KEY POINTS

- The poem opens with one of the most intense declarations of suffering ever made by a poet.
- This is one of the most dismal of the terrible sonnets.
- Written in the traditional form of a Petrarchan sonnet, with the descriptive octave followed by a reflective sestet.
- The poem concludes in a slightly optimistic mood.
- Key themes are mental and spiritual suffering and abandonment by God.

Thou art indeed just, Lord, if I contend

Although Hopkins had a strong religious faith, in this sonnet he wonders why his goodness goes unrewarded. In the opening two lines he acknowledges the righteousness of God when he complains to Him ('if I contend'), but believes that his questioning of God's justice is justifiable, 'Why do sinners' ways prosper? And why must / Disappointment all I endeavour end?'

He addresses God as 'Lord', accepting that he is fair-minded. But if he is genuinely fair, why does he allow goodness to go unrewarded? The poet has dedicated his life to God, while those who are the 'sots and thralls of lust' appear to prosper unscrutinised. If God was his enemy, Hopkins could understand why He has not in some way honoured him. On the contrary, God is his friend.

He is clearly hurt that God permits the wicked to thrive, while God's servants suffer. While recognising God's justice, he declares the justice of his own cause. The case is put respectfully ('Sir'), with the formal language of the courtroom being employed to evoke a sense of fairness. The questions he poses in the first quatrain reflect his sense of frustration. The questions continue in the second quatrain. If God was his enemy, he could not hurt him more. The drunkards and 'the sots and thralls of lust' can at least enjoy their sins, while he seemingly has no reward for his life of service. It is sadly ironic that those who gratify their sensuous desires appear to thrive, while he himself, who dedicated his entire life to God, appears to encounter only frustration, 'Oh, the sots and thralls of lust / Do in spare hours more thrive than I that spend, / Sir, life upon thy cause'.

In the sestet the poet contrasts the productivity of nature with his own infertility. Effective use of imagery conveys the rich abundance of the natural world, 'See, banks and brakes / Now leaved how thick! Laced they are again / With fretty chervil…'

The alliterative sound effects enhance the musical quality of the sonnet. The images of life, the growing plants and the nest-building birds highlight and sharply contrast with his own creative sterility, '…birds build – but not I build; no, but strain, / Time's eunuch, and not breed one work that wakes'. The cruel self-image ('Time's eunuch') may indicate his inability to find inspiration to glorify God through his poetry.

While God was reverentially referred to as 'my chevalier' in *The Windhover*, here the poet addresses him formally as 'Lord' and 'Sir'.

We get the impression that Hopkins is placing himself at a distance from God.

There is a striking absence in this sonnet of Hopkins' positive spirituality as conveyed in his earlier poems. The image of the anvil contrasts with the use of a similar image in *Felix Randal*. In this poem there is the idea that the blacksmith is forging his soul into shape. Here, in contrast, Hopkins' soul is being battered on 'an age-old anvil'.

Although the poem may be interpreted as a complaint to God, it concludes in a serious prayer to God to make him fruitful, 'O thou lord of life, send my roots rain'. The image of a plant in need of rain is suggestive of Hopkins in need of creative sustenance.

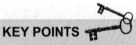

KEY POINTS

- A deeply personal poem.
- Written in the form of a Petrarchan sonnet.
- Key themes are intense psychological suffering and his wrestling with his religious faith.
- In the sestet, the poet contrasts the productivity of nature with his own infertility.
- Effective use of imagery throughout the poem.
- The alliterative sound effects enhance the musical quality of the poem.

Sample Answer

A Personal Response

Notwithstanding the fact that he was born and died in the nineteenth century, Hopkins' poetry retains its relevance for the twentieth century reader. I admire many aspects of his style, particularly his creation of the inscape literary theory which refers to the essential inner nature of a person. It is good to be reminded that we are all unique in our own way. For Hopkins, inscape is 'the species of individually distinctive beauty'. He also defined this term as 'the revelation of God's energy to one's senses through nature'.

I also like Hopkins' use of the Petrarchan sonnet because it ensures variety in the content of much of his poetry, with the vividly descriptive octave being followed by a reflective sestet. It is interesting to note the variety of moods in his poetry. While many of his poems are downbeat in mood given that they are concerned with exploring the theme of depression, other poems are strikingly more optimistic. Another appealing aspect of his verse is the regular use of everyday language that ensures the accessibility of its content and themes. A final feature of his poetry that impressed me is his efficient use of sound effects.

With *Felix Randal* following the traditional structure of the Petrarchan sonnet, the vividly descriptive octave is followed by the interesting observations of the sestet which focus on Hopkins' encounter with sickness and death. Tending the sick and looking after their needs encourages us to value them more, while assisting us to respect our own innate worth. Hopkins recognises from his contact with Randal that there is a mutual exchange of love in hard times, with the terms 'touched', 'endures' and 'tears' conveying the profound nature of his emotions.

The poem concludes on an undeniably upbeat note with the underlying idea that Hopkins the priest becomes God's blacksmith, preparing shoes for the great dray horse for his journey into the next world. The final image of 'his bright and battering sandal!' is particularly optimistic, with the loud, alliterative 'b' sound suggestive of Hopkins' power and energy.

One of the most appealing features of this poem is the regular use of everyday language, 'Impatient he cursed at first, but mended / Being anointed and all, / Ah well, God rest him all road ever he offended!'. Such colloquialisms ensure the accessibility of the content and themes of the poem.

The Windhover is certainly one of Hopkins' best-known, most discussed and best-loved poems. Hopkins himself described it as 'the best thing I ever wrote'. It is obviously open to a variety of interpretations, both literal and symbolic. There are even regular disagreements over the meaning of ambiguous words. One source of difficulty is Hopkins' use of the term 'Buckle!', the meaning of which is much debated – it could mean either 'collapse' or 'give way under pressure'. Another source of difficulty is the group of words 'To ring upon the rein' which may be a riding-school term, while 'to ring' is also a technical term of falconry.

The vividly descriptive octave is followed by a discursive, analytical sestet. The falcon is juxtaposed to a knight. This image is advanced by using the language of chivalry. Hopkins' use of imagery is very effective. He pictures the bird as a knight on horseback fighting against the wind. The image of the windhover as a knight is also evocative of Christ whom the poet addresses as 'my chevalier'. Having portrayed the attractive nature of the bird's flight in the octave, Hopkins compares the beauty of the bird to that of Christ. He views Christ as 'a billion / Times told lovelier, more dangerous…'. The image of the fire is indicative of Christ fighting against evil exactly as the bird fights against the wind.

I wake and feel the fell of dark, not day is one of the three sonnets known as the 'terrible sonnets' in which Hopkins plumbs the depths of despair. There is general agreement that this is the darkest of the terrible sonnets, providing us with disturbing insights into the poet's primary psychological problem of severe depression, which sadly has become an extremely common problem in today's world. This poem portrays a sense of gloom and hopelessness. In many respects, this is the most vivid of the terrible sonnets. The imagery deftly reflects the anguish of awakening in a state of total hopelessness. The initial image is palpable in nature, with the poet claiming to 'feel the fell of dark'.

The opening lines portray an experience familiar to depressives, many of whom awaken long in advance of the sun rising and endure anguish after being awakened from sleep in the blackness of night. We also perceive the poet's sense of an unseen evil around him. In this context 'fell' is a central term, with a double meaning – it may be interpreted as threat/blow and also as an animal's skin – a truly horrifying image.

Pied Beauty is a hymn of praise to God for the infinite diversity of nature. The opening line is filled with words of acclaim for God, 'Glory be to God for dappled things – '. This prayer-like beginning is then accompanied by a litany of vivid examples of the 'dappled' beauty to be located in the natural world. Hopkins includes the mottled blue and white colours of the sky, the 'brinded' (streaked) hide of a cow and the patches of contrasting colour on a trout. The chestnut presents us with a more complex and challenging image as we try to visualise its interior after it is compared to the coals in a fire, black on the outside and glowing within. The wings of finches are variegated, as is patchwork-like farmland. The final example is of the 'trades' (occupations) and activities of man, with their variety of materials and equipment, 'Fresh-firecoal chestnut-falls; finches' wings; /landscape plotted and pieced – fold, fallow and plough; /And all trades, their gear and tackle and trim'. Here we once again see Hopkins' effective use of alliteration enhancing the poem's musical qualities. More significantly, man is depicted as being in harmony with God's creation.

In the concluding five lines, Hopkins gives moral characteristics to the miscellaneous images on which he has expanded up to this point in terms of physical qualities. At this moment we are presented with a new idea or image: God is to be praised. Hopkins claims that the examples he has given are creations of God which highlight the unity and permanence of His power and inspire us to 'Praise Him'.

In conclusion, Hopkins' poetry remains relevant, ensuring that it continues to be well worth reading.

T.S. Eliot

Biographical Note

T.S. Eliot (1888–1965) remains one of the most celebrated and influential poets of the twentieth century. He was a leading member of the Modernist movement that revolutionised English literature in the early decades of the last century. Eliot was born into a prosperous family in St Louis, Missouri in 1888. As a child, Eliot attended a local school. He entered Harvard University in 1906 and, after taking both his BA and MA degrees, seemed set for an academic career. However, he had been writing poems during his early years in Harvard and decided to spend a year in Paris after college in pursuit of his poetic vocation. After spending some years in France and Germany, he moved to England shortly before the outbreak of the First World War in 1914. In 1915, one of Eliot's most famous poems, *The Love Song of J. Alfred Prufrock*, was published. In London he met Ezra Pound, a fellow American poet who was greatly impressed with *Prufrock*, telling Eliot, 'This is as good as anything I have ever seen'. Also in 1915, Eliot married Vivienne Haigh-Wood after a brief courtship. His impulsive marriage led to a major rift in his family. Vivienne's refusal to cross the Atlantic meant that Eliot remained in England, taking his place in literary London.

Marriage forced Eliot into taking a regular job and in 1917 he took up a post in the foreign department of Lloyds Bank in London, where he worked for eight years. The job gave him the financial security he needed to return to his poetry, and in 1917 he received a huge boost from the publication of his first book, *Prufrock and Other Observations*. Eliot's best-known work, *The Waste Land*, was first published in 1922 in a literary journal entitled *The Criterion*. Suffused with Eliot's horror of life, this poem reflects the deep disillusionment of the post-war generation. It would become one of the most important and most influential poems of the twentieth century. Publishing house Faber and Gwyer (later Faber and Faber) offered Eliot a job as literary editor, allowing him to escape from the demands of his job in the bank.

Many people were surprised that a man who had penned *The Waste Land*, a poem of philosophical despair depicting the spiritual barrenness of the modern era, was baptised into the Anglican Church in 1927. From this point on, Eliot's poetry addressed explicitly religious issues.

Eliot's reputation as a great poet saw him receive numerous literary awards. In 1926 he delivered the prestigious Clark lectures at Cambridge University, followed in 1932-1933 by the Norton Lectures at Harvard. He received every award the literary world had to offer, culminating in his receiving the Nobel Prize for Literature in 1948.

The Love Song of J. Alfred Prufrock

The epigraph with which the poem opens comes from Dante's *Inferno* (Canto 27, lines 61–66). The speaker is trapped in hell and filled with a sense of hopelessness. Prufrock is similarly trapped in his own private hell, a hell of endless indecision, low self-esteem and fear of rejection. The key themes of this poem are Prufrock's isolation and the difficulty he has in reconciling the needs of his romantic soul with the fears of his conventional and reserved outer self.

This poem is written in the form of a dramatic monologue that reflects Prufrock's stream of consciousness. It begins with Prufrock setting out on an imaginary journey in the course of which he struggles to resolve his inner conflict regarding asking an unnamed woman a significant, but unspecified, question: 'Let us go then, you and I . . .' The 'you' and 'I' refer to the two sides of Prufrock's character: the outer respectable and timid man and the inner suppressed and frustrated romantic. Eliot portrays the evening in a strikingly original manner, comparing it to a patient 'etherised upon a table'. This image suggests the speaker's feelings of vulnerability, while also evoking a lethargic atmosphere. From the beginning, there is a sense that Prufrock is not facing into this journey with any great energy or enthusiasm. The urban world is portrayed in a very unattractive manner, with Prufrock choosing to travel through the sleazy part of the city. There is a restless, sordid quality to the city ('muttering retreats . . . one-night cheap hotels'). The shabby streets will ultimately bring Prufrock to a room where he hopes to ask 'an overwhelming question'. This adjective suggests both the enormity of the question in the speaker's mind and its capacity to destroy his present lonely, frustrated existence. We do not know the nature of the question ('Oh, do not ask, "What is it?"'), but can assume it involves revealing some aspect of his hitherto hidden inner self. The room in which the question is to be asked seems to be located in a refined and sophisticated (or possibly shallow and pretentious) middle-class world: 'In the room the women come and go / Talking of Michelangelo.' The fact that the women 'come and go' suggests that this is a world of transient (passing, short-lived) relationships.

An extended metaphor compares the drifting of the fog and smoke through the city to the movements of a cat. The imagery in this section of the poem has a striking sensuous quality: 'The yellow fog that rubs its back upon the window-panes, / . . . Licked its tongue into the corners of the evening, / Lingered upon the pools that stand in drains . . .' It seems that the cat (fog) is going to make a decisive move ('Slipped by the terrace, made a sudden leap . . .'), but ends up falling asleep ('Curled once about the house, and fell asleep'). A seemingly decisive action that ultimately leads to nothing may suggest how Prufrock's journey will ultimately end.

The repetition of 'There will be time' reflects Prufrock's growing anxiety at the thought of asking his 'overwhelming question'. He tries to reassure himself that he has plenty of time to change his mind about asking a question that could profoundly disturb his personal universe. The world in which Prufrock moves is shallow and artificial – it is a world where he is almost certainly not alone in hiding his true, inner self behind a polite, refined exterior: ' . . .there will be time / To prepare a face to meet the faces that you meet . . .' While Prufrock's assertion that, 'There will be time to murder and create' would seem to be ironic and self-deprecating in that he will never possess the creative powers of a genius like Michelangelo, it also suggests that if Prufrock asks this question, he may well 'murder' his cautious and reserved outer self and 'create' a new, confident and expressive man. The tension mounts as Prufrock anticipates the disturbing impact of the question he plans to ask; he imagines it having the resounding effect of a piece of cutlery dropped on a plate ('Time for all the works and days of hands / That lift and drop a question on your plate. . .').

He comforts himself with the thought that his roundabout route through the seedy side of the city allows him time 'for a hundred indecisions, / And for a hundred visions and revisions . . .' The repetition of 'time' (it is mentioned eight times in the Fog Passage) reflects Prufrock's increasing anxiety. Prufrock is clearly afflicted by chronic indecision as he procrastinates endlessly about asking the question. The trivial, mundane nature of his world is conveyed by the reference to 'the taking of a toast and tea'.

The next section of the poem highlights Prufrock's timidity and extreme self-consciousness. His growing tension is evident as he wonders if he will have the courage to enter the room that is his destination: 'And indeed there will be time / To wonder, "Do I dare"? And, "Do I dare?"' He is painfully aware of how others view him as the repetition of 'They will say' indicates: 'They will say: "How his hair is growing thin!" . . . They will say: "But how his arms and legs are thin!"' Prufrock's preoccupation with his appearance is further evident in his desire to dress in a sedate manner: 'My necktie rich and modest, but asserted by a simple pin.' He wonders if he will have the courage to ask a question that would 'disturb the universe'.

Prufrock's life is one of unvarying, monotonous routine: 'For I have known them all already, known them all – / Have known the evenings, mornings, afternoons . . .' The trivial, measured nature of his existence is captured in the evocative image of his life being 'measured out . . . with coffee spoons . . .'

Prufrock is a prisoner of other peoples' perception of him – he has been fixed 'in a formulated phrase'. Society has labelled him and he is keenly conscious of people's expectations of him. His feelings of inadequacy and low self-esteem are very apparent when he pictures himself as a trapped insect 'pinned and wriggling on the wall . . .' At this point he wonders how he might approach the asking of this momentous question: 'Then how should I begin / To spit out the butt-ends of my days and ways?' This image suggests the distaste with which Prufrock views his life, while also suggesting that asking the critical question could mark the beginning of a new, fresh and meaningful life.

The sensuous image of the 'white and bare' arms that 'lie along a table, or wrap about a shawl' is a reminder of Prufrock's sensitive and romantic inner self – the hidden side to him that craves expression. He wonders if it is 'perfume from a dress' that caused him to 'digress' from his primary concern, before again asking himself how he should begin to ask this question: 'And should I then presume? / And how should I begin?' He asks himself if he should begin by describing his journey to this room during which he observed 'lonely men in shirt-sleeves, leaning out of windows'. Perhaps this evocation of the isolation and loneliness of modern urban life might serve as a means of approaching the matter of his personal loneliness and hidden passions?

Ultimately, Prufrock's torturous inner debate concludes with the question going unasked and his romantic inner self remaining suppressed. Prufrock is filled with fierce self-disgust at his timidity, seeing himself as 'a pair of ragged claws / Scuttling across the floors of silent seas.' This image of one of the lowest life forms 'scuttling' away from any possible danger powerfully conveys Prufrock's self-contempt. He remains locked by his fears into a 'silent' world where his true self will remain forever repressed.

After the critical moment has passed the tension slackens, and Prufrock succumbs to the lethargic atmosphere that envelops the personified day: 'And the afternoon, the evening, sleeps so peacefully! / Smoothed by long fingers, / Asleep . . . tired . . . or it malingers . . .' He sees himself in the room where 'tea and cake and ices' (another reminder of the triviality of the lives his class lead) are served and where he wondered if he would 'have the strength to force the moment to its crisis'. In the course of his anguished preparation ('wept and fasted, wept and prayed') for his ordeal, he had conjured up images of his social humiliation, imagining his balding head, in a figurative sense, 'brought in upon a platter' for all to scrutinise and ridicule. He had even imagined the footman 'snickering' at his degradation. Ultimately, Prufrock's dread of being a martyr to mockery is expressed simply: 'And in short, I was afraid.'

In attempting to justify his failure to himself, the emotionally inarticulate Prufrock wonders if revealing his inner romantic self 'would . . . have been worth it' if it had resulted in the embarrassment of being told: 'That is not what I meant at all, / That is not it, at all.' His intense anguish at not being able to express and share his deepest feelings is powerfully conveyed in his exclamation: 'It is impossible to say just what I mean!'

Prufrock mocks himself by comparing himself to a number of heroic figures from the Bible, history and literature. He is painfully aware of the sharp contrast between himself and a heroic figure such as John the Baptist: 'I am no prophet.' He similarly contrasts himself with Lazarus, but his inner self will never emerge Lazarus-like 'from the dead . . .'

We observe the steady collapse of Prufrock's self-esteem as he compares himself first to Hamlet, then to Polonius and finally to the Fool, a character from *King Lear*. Prufrock resembles

Hamlet in his indecision, but not in his ability to act decisively ultimately. He compares himself to the 'deferential' and 'cautious' Polonius who was always anxious to please, before finally likening himself to the Fool. However, while the Fool may have been regarded as a 'ridiculous' figure, he was, at heart, sensitive, caring and not without wisdom. Similarly, there is much more to Prufrock than his conventional outer self would suggest.

By the close of the poem, Prufrock accepts that he will never achieve the heroic status of Michelangelo, John the Baptist or Hamlet: 'I grow old . . . I grow old . . .' Having failed to ask the 'overwhelming question', Prufrock's life continues to revolve around trivialities: 'I shall wear the bottoms of my trousers rolled. Shall I part my hair behind? Do I dare to eat a peach?' He imagines himself walking on a beach and hearing 'the mermaids singing, each to each'. The line that follows stands alone for emphasis: 'I do not think they will sing to me.' This line poignantly evokes Prufrock's feelings of isolation and loneliness. The mermaids are associated with the sea which, for Prufrock, represents a world of beauty, romance, happiness and fulfilment. In this ideal world Prufrock's inner and outer selves are integrated: 'We have lingered in the chambers of the sea / By sea-girls wreathed with seaweed red and brown . . .' Sadly, Prufrock has 'lingered in the chambers of the sea' only in his dreams. Ultimately, reality, in the form of 'human voices' intrudes to awaken him from his dream world. The poem ends on a despairing note as Prufrock 'drowns' in a sea of loneliness and isolation, his inner self forever silenced by his extreme self-consciousness and fear of rejection.

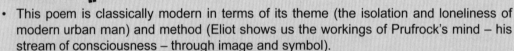

KEY POINTS

- This poem is classically modern in terms of its theme (the isolation and loneliness of modern urban man) and method (Eliot shows us the workings of Prufrock's mind – his stream of consciousness – through image and symbol).
- Prufrock's thought processes (which are often disjointed) are presented in the form of an internal monologue.
- This poem has strong dramatic qualities. Eliot presents us with a specific setting, characters, dialogue (internal), conflict and tension.
- The poem explores Prufrock's inner conflict between his romantic inner self's longing to find expression and his deeply conventional outer self's fear of rejection and humiliation.
- Many allusions to historical, literary and biblical figures.
- Contrast is regularly employed (Prufrock compares himself to a number of heroic figures) to highlight Prufrock's feelings of inadequacy.
- Repetition of key words and phrases gives emphasis to important ideas and evokes specific moods.
- While written in free verse form (closer to conversational speech patterns), Eliot makes regular use of rhyme.
- This poem is very pessimistic in outlook.

Preludes

This poem presents the reader with various aspects of the modern urban world. The first Prelude portrays the city in a grim light, using such negative adjectives as 'grimy', 'withered', 'vacant', 'broken' and 'lonely' to directly express a truly dark vision. Similar to *The Love Song of J. Alfred Prufock*, this poem is dramatic in style. We find ourselves in an urban backstreet on a winter evening without any visible human presence. However the 'smell of steaks' and the 'cab-horse' suggest human activity. The image of 'The burnt-out ends of smoky days' compares the end of the day to the butt-ends of cigarettes, suggesting the unpleasant and unhealthy nature of urban life. There is no escaping the pervasive gloom of the city as 'a gusty shower wraps / The grimy scraps / Of withered leaves about your feet'. The general sense of neglect ('broken blinds and chimney pots') adds to the despondent mood. Even the 'cab-horse' is described as 'lonely'. However, the lighting of the lamp holds out the possibility of hope – hope that the working people (perhaps symbolised by the horse) living in these backstreets may somehow transcend the grime and gloom of the city.

Just as the evening is personified in the first Prelude ('The winter evening settles down'), so is the morning personified in the second ('The morning comes to consciousness'). The second Prelude begins in the morning, a time often associated with freshness, hope and new beginnings. However, any sense of optimism we might feel is quickly dispelled as the personified morning wakes up to 'the faint stale smells of beer'. The negative portrayal of the city continues with the depressing image of 'the sawdust-trampled street / With all its muddy feet . . .' Perhaps the most dispiriting aspect of this section of the poem is the suggestion that urban life is essentially a series of 'masquerades' – in other words, a world of false appearances and deception where people are not always what they appear to be. Almost as disheartening is the reduction of city workers to the level of utilitarian 'hands' (a reminder of the Charles Dickens' novel *Hard Times* where workers are similarly dehumanised and similarly described). Eliot presents the reader with the image of 'all the hands / That are raising dingy shades / In a thousand furnished rooms'. This image also evokes the drab uniformity of urban life where there seems to be no place for individuality.

The third Prelude focuses on an individual woman – a welcome contrast to the mass portrayal of a thousand 'hands' in the second 'Prelude'. This woman appears to be restless and agitated as she 'tossed a blanket from the bed'. Lying on her back, she sees 'The thousand sordid images' that had contributed to the creation of her personality ('. . . of which your soul was constituted'). These images are 'flickering against the ceiling' as if on a cinema screen. As day dawns, the woman hears sparrows, but in this grim world even nature cannot inspire or elevate – we are told that the sparrows are 'in the gutters'. When morning arrives, it is apparent that this woman is not concerned about personal cleanliness: '. . . clasped the yellow soles of your feet / In the palms of both soiled hands.' These images of neglect highlight the woman's seedy existence, while also evoking the squalid nature of urban life in general. In this Prelude, as in the previous two, the mood is utterly bleak.

The fourth and final Prelude opens with the surreal image of a man's soul 'stretched tight across the skies / That fade behind a city block . . .' This is an image of spiritual suffering, as is the image of his soul 'trampled by insistent feet' – the latter image also being suggestive of the harshness of urban life. Just as the woman's soul will be forever marked by the many 'sordid images' she has absorbed, so is the male speaker's conscience 'blackened' by life in the city.

At this point, a speaker (perhaps the poet) interjects: 'I am moved by fancies that are curled / Around these images, and cling / The notion of some infinitely gentle / Infinitely suffering thing.' These lines would seem to suggest that the speaker is 'moved' to sympathise with the inhabitants of a world devoid of beauty and hope. What this 'infinitely gentle / Infinitely suffering thing' may be is unclear, but it evokes a sense of tenderness and concern against the background of an extremely bleak and depressing urban landscape.

The positive feeling prompted by these lines is very brief, with the final three lines presenting us with a deeply negative response to the misery and suffering of the urban world: 'Wipe your hand across your mouth, and laugh'. The gesture and laugh amount to a cynical dismissal of the grim lives depicted in the poem. *Preludes* concludes with a depressing, universal image of poverty and hardship: ' . . . ancient women / Gathering fuel in vacant lots.'

KEY POINTS

- Key theme is the dark, depressing nature of modern urban life.
- Objective description in the first two parts of the poem is followed by personal responses to life in the city in the third and fourth sections.
- This poem abounds with negative adjectives describing life in the city: 'burnt-out', 'withered', 'broken', 'lonely', 'stale', 'dingy', 'sordid', 'soiled', etc.
- Different periods of the day are personified in the first two parts of the poem.
- Images generally suggest the drab, dispiriting nature of urban life.
- The outlook in this poem is deeply pessimistic.

Aunt Helen

This poem opens in a coldly factual manner: 'Miss Helen Slingsby was my maiden aunt, / And lived in a small house near a fashionable square / Cared for by servants to the number of four.' There is not a hint of sentiment in lines that are purely informative. We learn that the poet's aunt had a privileged life with four servants tending to her every need. Her life is defined in terms of her unmarried status and her possessions. As a 'maiden aunt', it was likely that her life was devoid of romance and passion. There is no mention of friends or of any kind of meaningful relationship. Her death was greeted by 'silence in heaven / And silence at the end of the street.' It seems that her death does not register with anyone in an emotional sense. No tears are shed at her passing. The poet says nothing of his own feelings towards his aunt – we can assume that he was as detached and unemotional as the tone of the poem suggests. Following her death, the usual rituals were observed: 'The shutters were drawn and the undertaker wiped his feet – / He was aware that this sort of thing had occurred before.' This touch of humour lifts a lifeless poem. The fact that 'The dogs were handsomely provided for' further suggests Aunt Helen's lack of emotional ties with her relatives (including the poet presumably).

It is difficult to see the significance of the reference to the parrot's death. It sometimes happens that a husband or wife dies shortly after the passing of their lifelong partner – perhaps the parrot was the closest thing Aunt Helen had to a life partner! Here we are again reminded of the emptiness of her life. The fact that 'the Dresden clock continued ticking' suggests that life goes on.

The most memorable aspect of this poem is the description of the servants' behaviour after their employer's death: 'And the footman sat upon the dining table / Holding the second housemaid on his knees – / Who had always been so careful when her mistress lived.' The servants' bawdy behaviour, with its obvious sexual associations, sharply contrasts with the coldness and restraint of Aunt Helen's life. Of course, the upper class society of which she was a part attached great importance to 'civilized' and 'refined' behaviour, while disdaining the unrestrained expression of emotions which was commonly associated with their social 'inferiors'. With their mistress's passing, the servants are no longer slaves to Aunt Helen's standards of order and decorum and, delighting in their new-found freedom, engage in the type of behaviour they know she would have seen as base and despicable.

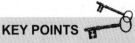

KEY POINTS

- This poem satirises (mocks) the poet's aunt and her way of life.
- The lifeless nature of the poem is suggestive of his aunt's lifeless existence.
- The poem contrasts the values of the upper and working classes.
- This poem has an unusual structure, being one line short of a sonnet – it would seem that Eliot did not think his aunt worthy of a poem written in this classic poetic form.
- Some touches of humour lift the mood of the poem.

II A Game of Chess (from *The Waste Land*)

A Game of Chess is the second part of *The Waste Land*, one of Eliot's most celebrated and influential works. This poem is also located in an urban landscape and, similar to *Prufrock*, portrays personal relationships in a very dark light. Written in 1922, it is commonly believed that this poem reflects the desolation of the post-World War era. This is a complex poem, replete with literary allusions. Even the title of the poem is taken from a play by Thomas Middleton entitled *Women beware Women* in which each move in a game of chess is closely associated with each step in the seduction of a young woman. This poem juxtaposes two very different worlds: one a world of wealth and privilege, and the other an everyday working-class world.

The opening scene in this poem takes place in the bedroom of a wealthy woman. The lady's ornate chair is compared to a highly polished throne. The phrase 'a burnished throne' is taken from Shakespeare's *Antony and Cleopatra* – a play whose themes of love, betrayal and tragedy are also apparent in this poem. Lines 1–20 portray this lady's luxurious bedroom in vivid detail: the marble floor, the ornamented mirror, the 'sevenbranched candlelabra' and her 'rich profusion' of jewels that spill out from her satin jewellery cases.

However, the atmosphere in this opulent room is not entirely pleasant. The verb 'lurked' suggests some hidden threatening presence ('In vials of ivory and coloured glass / Unstoppered, lurked her strange, synthetic perfumes'). The odour they release is almost suffocating in its intensity ('And drowned the sense in odours') and causes the senses to become 'troubled' and 'confused'. The air from the window enlivens the candle flame which sends smoke up to the panelled ceiling ('laquearia'). The flame of the fire is a strange 'green and orange' colour, creating a 'sad light'. Ordinarily, one would expect that the flame from the fireplace would be cheery and inviting. Above the antique mantelpiece hangs a painting depicting *The change of Philomel*. The mythical tale of Philomel's brutal rape at the hands of her brother-in-law, King Tereus, creates a disturbing change of tone. After the cruel rape, Tereus cut her tongue out so she could tell no one of his barbarous crime. Taking pity on Philomel, the gods turned her into a nightingale. While Philomel was violated in her human existence, her nightingale's song will be 'inviolable'. Sadly, she still feels pursued by the world: 'And still she cried, and still the world pursues'. When the poem states that various figures in paintings on the walls 'Leaned out, leaning, hushing the room enclosed', the atmosphere in the room becomes claustrophobic.

At this point, 'footsteps shuffled on the stair', and a man enters the ornate room where the woman has been sitting at her dressing table, brushing her hair. The 'dialogue' that follows reveals much about this woman's state of mind. But to what extent is it a dialogue, since the man's (probably her husband) responses are not placed in inverted commas? Are his responses simply unspoken thoughts? The woman is agitated: 'My nerves are bad tonight. Yes, bad.' Her mental distress is reflected in her desperate pleas not to be left on her own: 'Stay with me. Speak to me.' There is a serious communication problem between the two: 'Why do you never speak to me? . . . I never know what you are thinking.' The woman's disjointed speech ('Speak', 'What?' 'Think') further suggests that she is on the brink of a mental and emotional breakdown. The man's grim and disturbing response (seemingly kept within his head) would seem to indicate that he too is mentally distressed: 'I think we are in rats' alley / Where the dead men lost their bones.' His internal responses are completely unrelated to the woman's questions. Their disconnection seems total, their relationship non-existent.

As is commonly the case with people who are mentally disturbed, the woman finds harsh sounds difficult to bear: 'What is that noise? . . . What is that noise now?' Even the sound of the wind under the door unsettles her. The man's silence further agitates her: 'You know nothing? Do you see nothing? Do you remember / Nothing?' It seems that theirs has been a mutually destructive relationship, with the capitalisation of 'Nothing' suggesting what now connects them. The man appears to be unmoved by the woman's mental torment, attempting to drown out the sound of her increasingly anxious questions with a popular ragtime song, 'that Shakespeherian Rag'. The woman's anguish has now intensified to the point where a nervous breakdown seems imminent: 'I shall rush out as I am, and walk the street / With my hair down.' Her questions continue as she asks, 'What shall

we do tomorrow? / What shall we ever do?' The man's response underscores his bleak view of life: 'The hot water at ten. / And if it rains, a closed car at four. / And we shall play a game of chess, / Pressing lidless eyes and waiting for a knock upon the door.' These lines suggest his boredom with life's unvarying nature, with the reference to 'a closed car' evoking a sense of claustrophobic confinement. What is most disturbing is the horrific image of 'pressing lidless eyes' (presumably against the windows of the car). The literary allusion to 'a game of chess' (the title of a play by Thomas Middleton) suggests the idea of betrayal, manipulation and deceit.

The second section of the poem presents us with a very different setting, as the poem moves from the ornate bedroom of a wealthy woman to a working-class pub in the East End of London. A woman is gossiping with her friends about a couple named Lil and Albert, a soldier who has recently been 'demobbed' at the end of World War I. Her narrative is regularly interrupted by a barman shouting, 'Hurry up please its time'. The relationship between Lil and Albert seems to be strained, with the woman telling of how she advised Lil to make herself 'a bit smart'. It seems that Albert is no longer attracted to his wife, having told her to get 'a nice set' of teeth, before adding, 'I swear, I can't bear to look at you.' The woman reminds Lil that after four years of army service, Albert 'wants a good time', warning that if she doesn't 'give it to him, there's others will'. The fact that Lil resents the advice does not in any way discourage the woman from her withering criticism of her appearance: 'You ought to be ashamed, I said, to look so antique (And her only thirty-one.)' Lil's explanation shocks the reader as she explains that it was the pills she took to induce an abortion that aged her so dramatically: 'It's them pills I took, to bring it off, she said.' The harsh, depressing nature of Lil's life becomes clear when the gossiping woman refers to her five children ('and nearly died of young George.)' It is apparent that Albert attaches greater importance to his sexual pleasure than his wife's physical health, but there is little sympathy for Lil's plight: 'Well if Albert won't leave you alone, there it is, I said'. The barman's repeated announcement ('Hurry up please its time') may have another level of meaning beyond his anxiety to close the premises. It may suggest the inexorable passage of time and life's unending pressures.

Given its bleak tone throughout, this poem concludes in a predictably depressing manner, with the Cockney 'Goonight' recalling the final words of Ophelia (in Shakespeare's *Hamlet*) before she commits suicide: 'Good night , ladies, good night, sweet ladies, good night, good night.' The reference to Ophelia underscores the harshness of the world in which this poem is set. Ophelia was the epitome of beauty and innocence, but was ultimately crushed by the cruel nature of a male-dominated world.

KEY POINTS

- The key theme is the breakdown of relationships across all social classes.
- This poem is dramatic in form – specific settings, characters, dialogue, tension, etc.
- The poem is set in contrasting social settings: the ornate bedroom of a wealthy woman, and a working-class pub in the East End of London.
- A highly allusive poem – the numerous literary allusions challenge the reader.
- The modern urban world is portrayed in a very negative light.
- A relentlessly gloomy poem.

Journey of the Magi

In this poem Eliot imaginatively recreates the well-known story of the Magi or Three Wise Kings. The Magi's journey to Bethlehem was a lengthy and, as described in this poem, difficult one from their kingdoms in the exotic East. Similar to many of Eliot's poems, *Journey of the Magi* is presented in the form of a dramatic monologue, with one of the Three Wise Kings (we don't know which one) speaking directly to the reader.

This poem may also be read on a metaphorical level, with the Magi's journey to Bethlehem symbolising Eliot's spiritual voyage to the Anglican faith.

The poem begins with a quotation from a sermon delivered by Bishop Lancelot Andrews, a seventeenth century clergyman, on Christmas Day, 1622: 'A cold coming we had of it, / Just the worst time of year / For a journey, and such a long journey: / The ways deep and the weather sharp, / The very dead of winter.' These lines convey the arduous, demanding nature of the journey undertaken by the Magi, a journey that took its toll on man and animal alike. The disgruntled camel men were 'cursing and grumbling / And running away'. Such was the discomfort of the 'sore-footed' camels that they became unmanageable ('refractory'), stubbornly lying down in the snow rather than continuing on with their journey. The contrast between the world of warmth, ease and comfort the Magi had left behind ('The summer palaces on slopes, the terraces, / And the silken girls bringing sherbet.') and the cold, harsh, unwelcoming world they now travel through ('And the cities hostile and the towns unfriendly / And the villages dirty and charging high prices') is strikingly evident. Little wonder the speaker admits that they sometimes 'regretted' leaving their homeland. The repetition of 'and' creates a sense of memories tumbling through the speaker's mind. At this point, the difficulties of the Magi's journey are succinctly summed up: 'A hard time we had of it' (echoing the earlier, 'A cold coming we had of it'). Ultimately, they 'preferred to travel all night', snatching whatever sleep they could, all the time haunted by an inner voice telling them that their challenging journey 'was all folly' (foolishness).

There is a noticeable change of mood in stanza two as the Magi arrive in Bethlehem (although the town is never named). After travelling through harsh and arid terrain for so long, the Magi now find themselves in a very different world. Images of life and fertility ('a temperate valley' that is 'smelling of vegetation', 'a running stream and a water-mill') suggest how the birth of Jesus will impact on the world. However, the imagery that follows is more suggestive of Jesus' death on the cross than of his birth in a stable. The image of 'three trees on the low sky' is clearly symbolic of the three crosses on the hill of Calvary where Jesus endured horrific suffering before he finally died. In a similarly dark vein, the image of hands 'dicing for pieces of silver' evokes both the idea of the soldiers dicing for Jesus' clothing at the foot of the cross, and Judas' betrayal of Jesus for thirty pieces of silver. It seems that the old magus has premonitions of Jesus' suffering and death as he approaches the place of his birth. The Magi arrive 'not a moment too soon' to witness the birth of Jesus. The speaker's response to this momentous occasion is strangely subdued: ' . . . it was (you may say) satisfactory.' How do we account for his muted reaction? Perhaps his sense of awe at witnessing this momentous occasion prevented him from being more expressive, or perhaps his vision of the intense suffering involved in Jesus' destiny negated any sense of joy he may have felt.

The third stanza sees the old man in a reflective mood as he recalls the Magi's journey to Bethlehem ('All this was a long time ago'). He insists he would 'do it again', but struggles with a key question: ' . . . were we led all the way for / Birth or Death?' He acknowledges

that he unquestionably witnessed a birth: 'There was a Birth, certainly.' However, the power of Christianity derives from the death and subsequent resurrection of Jesus (Easter being the most important event in the Christian calendar). Before his life changing experience at Bethlehem, the speaker had thought that life and death 'were different'. However, this experience taught him that they are inextricably (inseparably) linked. He describes how the birth of Jesus was 'Hard and bitter agony for us, like Death, our death.' The birth of Jesus marked the birth of the Christian religion and a new era in the history of mankind. It also marked the painful spiritual re-birth of the Magi, the corollary (natural consequence of) being the death of their previous beliefs.

After returning to their kingdoms, the Magi find that they are 'no longer at ease' there, 'in the old dispensation' (religion). Their new religious beliefs meant that they now feel alienated from their own people. The poem concludes with the old magus expressing his desire for 'another death'. Having experienced the death of his old beliefs, he now looks forward to his actual death with a sense of acceptance, after witnessing the birth of Jesus and having had a revelation of Christianity. While he could no longer subscribe to his old pagan beliefs after his experience at Bethlehem, he cannot call himself a Christian because Christianity had not yet been founded, with Jesus yet to begin his teachings.

This poem is open to a metaphorical reading, with the arduous physical and spiritual journey of the Magi being a metaphor for Eliot's difficult spiritual voyage from Agnosticism to Christianity, or, more specifically, Anglicanism. Just as the Magi felt alienated in their own world after their spiritual rebirth, so did Eliot meet with an unsympathetic response from those close to him after his own spiritual voyage brought him to Christ.

KEY POINTS

- Key theme is the difficult, painful nature of spiritual rebirth.
- Similar to other Eliot poems such as Prufrock, this poem is written in the form of a dramatic monologue.
- This poem is open to a metaphorical reading, with the Magi's arduous journey to Bethlehem a metaphor for the poet's spiritual voyage to Christ.
- The poem is clearly structured, with its three sections describing the Magi's journey, their arrival in Bethlehem and the impact of witnessing the Nativity on their spiritual beliefs.
- The contrast between the luxurious lives the Magi have left behind and the arduous nature of their journey to Bethlehem is sharply drawn.
- This poem is rich in symbolism, e.g.: The 'three trees on the low sky' evoke the image of the crucifixion, with Christ's cross flanked by two others.
- While the Nativity is generally portrayed as a joyful event, this is a joyless poem, with images of suffering and death predominant.
- Once again, this is a highly allusive poem, with many biblical and some literary references.

III. Usk (from *Landscapes*)

This is one of a series of short lyric poems entitled *Landscapes*. This poem was inspired by his visit to Usk, a small town in South Wales. The two most significant features of Usk are its association with the legendary King Arthur, and its popularity in medieval times as a place of pilgrimage.

This poem consists of several pieces of advice regarding how to approach this area of the Welsh countryside. The first piece of advice is delivered in a commanding tone, instructing the reader not to 'suddenly break the branch' (presumably because this would be a destructive intrusion into the world of nature). With their references to 'lance' and 'Old enchantments', lines 1–5 evoke Usk's associations with the Arthurian legends. Eliot tells the reader not to expect to find 'the white hart behind the white well'. Harts (stags) are no longer to be found in the Welsh countryside and neither, obviously, are knights with lances. While Eliot sees nothing wrong with getting a sense of the wonderful, mysterious Arthurian tales, he urges the reader not to delve too deeply into their magical, mystical aspects ('old enchantments'): 'Let them sleep./ "Gently dip, but not too deep."'

(The words in double quotes are taken from a poem by the Elizabethan writer, George Peel).

Lines 7–11 offer advice that is more positive in nature: 'Lift your eyes / Where the roads dip and where the roads rise.' Eliot advises the reader to focus more on Usk's Christian tradition than on its mythological past if we 'seek' meaning or spiritual fulfilment in life: 'Seek only there / Where the grey light meets the green air / The hermit's chapel, the pilgrim's prayer.' If we focus on 'The hermit's chapel, the pilgrim's prayer', symbols of our Christian faith, we will be better able to 'lift' our eyes and see the presence of God in the undulating hills (suggested by the reference to roads that 'dip' and 'rise') of the Usk countryside ('Where the grey light meets the green air').

One of the most striking features of this poem is its musicality. This musical quality is created through the use of end rhyme ('well-spell', 'sleep-deep', etc.), repetition ('Where the roads dip and where the roads rise', etc.) and alliteration ('break the branch', 'dip . . . deep', etc.).

KEY POINTS

- Key theme is religion – Eliot's later poetry is clearly influenced by his conversion to Anglicanism.
- While many of Eliot's poems reflect his bleak perception of Christianity, lines 7–11 of this poem present us with a more positive attitude towards religion.
- This poem evokes the unique spirit of this area of the Welsh countryside through images associated with Arthurian legend and Christian tradition.
- A poem rich in musical qualities.

IV. Rannoch, by Glencoe (from Landscapes)

Similar to *Usk*, this poem is one of a series of poems entitled *Landscapes*. Some knowledge of the historical background to this poem is necessary if the reader is to fully appreciate its meaning. Glencoe was the location of a particularly barbaric and bloody massacre in 1692. Thirty-seven members of the MacDonald clan were surprised and butchered in their beds by forces loyal to the new king, William of Orange (whom the Catholic MacDonalds refused to recognise). Many women and children also died from exposure after their homes were razed to the ground.

The opening lines of this poem convey an image of a grim, forbidding world of death. The mood is dark and despondent: 'Here the crow starves, here the patient stag / Breeds for the rifle.' There is also a sense of claustrophobic confinement – there is 'scarcely room' for the stag to 'leap' or for the crow to 'soar'. The landscape appears to fall away before our very eyes: 'Substance crumbles'.

The terms 'listlessness' and 'languor' refer to a lack of energy ('Listlessness of ancient war, / Languor of broken steel'). It is almost as if the bloodbath that occurred centuries earlier has drained all life and energy from the landscape, leaving it appropriately silent ('apt / In silence'). In the next line, the poet points out that folk memory is strong, continuing to live on long after the bones of the dead have crumbled: 'Memory is strong / Beyond the bone.'

The closing lines suggest that the spirits of the defeated MacDonalds still haunt this area, anxious for revenge and intent on restoring their family's shattered pride. It is as if the spirits of the dead are still battling 'in the long pass', driven on by the long 'Shadow of pride'. Fighting to the death in life, the MacDonalds are unlikely to agree with their enemies in the after-life: 'No concurrence of bone.'

A series of negative words ('crumbles', 'broken', 'confused', 'snapped' etc.) reflect the poem's grim mood, while sound effects reinforce this dark atmosphere. The assonant long 'o' sound contributes to the poem's sombre tone ('crow', 'moor', 'cold', 'bone', etc.), while the repeated hard 'c' sound ('Clamour of confused wrong . . .') suggests the harshness of the slaughter that occurred so long ago.

KEY POINTS

- The key theme of this poem is the way in which important events of the past live on in the landscape where they took place.
- Imagery is striking and memorable, effectively suggesting the idea of violence and death.
- Sound effects reinforce the poem's dark atmosphere.

East Coker IV (from *The Four Quartets*)

In this poem Eliot portrays man's position in the world in allegorical terms (an allegory is a work that can be read both on a literal and symbolic level. The purpose of an allegory is often to highlight a moral or truth). This poem is based on the analogy (comparison between one thing and another) of the world as a hospital. The patients represent mankind and the surgeon is Christ.

The first stanza opens in a dramatic manner as we find ourselves in an operating theatre in the middle of a surgical procedure. 'The wounded surgeon' is Christ, his wounds evoking his suffering as he was nailed to the cross. His scalpel is used to investigate (or possibly remove) the diseased ('distempered') part of the patient. The patient is feverish (in a state of sin), but the surgeon is 'sharp' and compassionate. Employing 'the healer's art', he resolves the mystery ('enigma') of the patient's fever.

The second stanza begins with a paradox: 'Our only health is the disease / If we obey the dying nurse'. For Eliot, health and disease are inextricably bound up together. True spiritual health can only be achieved by the healing of the 'disease' that is original sin ('Adam's curse'). Eliot tells us that we must 'obey the dying nurse' (the Church) whose purpose 'is not to please', but to remind us 'that, to be restored, our sickness must grow worse.' Put simply, we must be prepared to endure suffering and death if we are to achieve healing and spiritual rebirth.

The third stanza opens with a startling metaphor: 'The whole world is our hospital.' This metaphor implies that every human being is spiritually sick from original sin. The idea of the hospital being 'endowed by the ruined millionaire' is paradoxical on two levels. A 'ruined millionaire' would not have the financial resources to endow a hospital. Secondly, such an act would be seen as an act of charitable goodness. However, 'the ruined millionaire' is Adam and his moral failings meant that he 'endowed' mankind with the stain of original skin. To 'do well' in this hospital is to die of 'the absolute paternal care' that we receive from God the Father. If man accepts this constant divine care he will be redeemed (saved).

Stanza four vividly describes the process of dying and the subsequent cleansing of the soul that takes place in purgatory. The sensuous imagery in this stanza contrasts with the more generalised expression of ideas in the earlier part of the poem. We can almost feel the coldness of death as it 'ascends from feet to knees'. There follows another paradoxical notion with the poet declaring that if he is to be warmed, he 'must freeze / And quake in frigid purgatorial fires'. The final line in this stanza is rather cryptic (mysterious): 'Of which the flame is roses, and the smoke is briars.' Roses are a symbol of love, so perhaps this line suggests that the flames of purgatory burn with divine love, while the reference to 'briars' evokes the image of the crucified Christ with his crown of thorns. The final line then reminds us of the depth of God's love for us (that he would undergo the agony of crucifixion that our souls might be saved). It also suggests the idea of God (on the cross) and man (in the flames of purgatory) united in suffering.

The final stanza again evokes the image of the crucified Christ, but this time in a more vivid, more powerful manner: 'The dripping blood our only drink, / The bloody flesh our only food.' These references to the flesh and blood of Christ clearly suggest how the Sacrament of Communion provides us with spiritual nourishment. The poem closes with the poet wondering how, in the light of Jesus' agonising death on the cross, we still refer to the day of his crucifixion as Good Friday: 'And, in spite of that, we call this Friday good.'

KEY POINTS

- Key theme is Eliot's grim view of Christianity – throughout this poem there is a strong emphasis on the idea of suffering and death (Christ on the cross and man in his everyday life) as the only path to salvation.
- As an allegory, this poem can obviously be read on a metaphorical level.
- This poem contains some interesting paradoxes.
- Imagery is, once again, striking and unusual.
- Tone is didactic (instructive, moralising), with Eliot tending to sermonise the reader.

Sample Answer

T.S. Eliot – A personal response

Support your point of view by reference and quotation.

I found Eliot's poetry challenging, but interesting and rewarding. Although his poems were written in the early part of the last century, his themes remain relevant to the modern day reader. He writes about the isolation of modern urban man, the shallowness of much social interaction, human relationships and his quest for meaning and spiritual fulfilment in life. I admire many aspects of Eliot's poetic style, particularly his use of the 'stream of consciousness' technique (which enables us to see the workings of a person's mind). I also admire the dramatic nature of many of his poems and his unusual and memorable imagery. While the range of his allusions is impressive, it can be difficult to see the meaning and significance of some of his more obscure references. Another aspect of his poetry I do not like is his consistently pessimistic outlook on life.

Notwithstanding the obscurity of the epigraph with which it opens and its pessimistic tone, *The Love Song of J. Alfred Prufrock* is my favourite Eliot poem because of the manner in which it depicts the doubts and uncertainties that afflict us all at different times in our lives, especially when it comes to revealing our innermost selves. This poem is written in the form of a dramatic monologue that reflects Prufrock's stream of consciousness. The opening line in the poem suggests the two sides to his personality: 'Let us go then, you and I . . .' as he sets off on his journey to a room where he hopes to ask an unnamed woman an unspecified question. The 'you' and 'I' represent the two different sides to Prufrock's personality. The dramatic tension in the poem is caused by the conflict between outer respectable and reserved man ('you') and the inner repressed and frustrated romantic ('I'). A strikingly original image ('Like a patient etherised upon a table') suggests Prufrock's feelings of vulnerability at the thought of revealing something of his inner self in asking this question. The artificiality of social interaction in Prufrock's middle-class world is suggested by his need 'To prepare a face to meet the faces that you meet', and by the pretentious conversation of the women who 'come and go / Talking of Michelangelo.' Prufrock's increasing anxiety as he nears his destination is evident in his stream of consciousness: 'Time for you and time for me, / And time yet for a hundred indecisions / And for a hundred visions and revisions.' Another memorable image conveys the trivial, measured nature of his existence: 'I have measured out my life with coffee spoons.' His feeling of self-disgust at failing to ask the question that might have changed his life is powerfully conveyed by the image of the fearful crab: 'I should have been a pair of ragged claws / Scuttling across the floors of silent seas.' A series of literary allusions underline the total collapse of Prufrock's self-esteem as he compares himself to Hamlet (the classic procrastinator), then to Polonius ('an attendant lord', always 'deferential'), before finally comparing himself to the Fool in *King Lear*. Prufrock's expression of frustration at being unable to ask his 'overwhelming question' is one that most of us can relate to, having also felt emotionally inarticulate at some point in our lives: 'It is impossible to say just what I mean!'

A Game of Chess is a poignant poem that powerfully conveys the despair wrought by the breakdown of (presumably) once loving relationships. This theme has an obvious relevance in today's world where marital breakdown continues to become ever more common. In this poem Eliot depicts the breakdown of relationships in two very different worlds, one a world of wealth and privilege and the other an everyday working class world. The dramatic nature of this poem appealed to me, with its interesting, distinctive characters and effective use of dialogue vividly highlighting the desolation that inevitably follows the fracturing of a relationship. The opening scene in this poem takes place in the bedroom of a wealthy woman. This lady's luxurious bedroom is described in vivid detail: the marble floor, the ornamented mirror and her 'rich profusion' of jewels that spill out from her satin jewellery cases. Clearly, this woman is very materialistic. However, her wealth (as is so often the case in the modern world) brings her no happiness. In fact she seems to be close to a complete mental and emotional collapse. When a man (probably her husband) enters the room where the woman has been sitting at her dressing table, brushing her hair, the 'dialogue' that follows reveals much about this woman's state of mind and a great deal about the quality of their relationship. There is serious doubt as to whether a dialogue actually takes place since the man's responses are not placed in inverted commas. The woman's mental distress is reflected in her desperate pleas not to be left on her own: 'Stay with me. Speak to me.' There is a serious communication problem between the two: 'Why do you never speak to me?' The man's grim and disturbing response (seemingly kept within his head) would seem to indicate that he too is mentally distressed: 'I think we are in rats' alley / Where the dead men lost their bones.' His responses are completely unrelated to the woman's questions. Their disconnection seems total, their relationship non-existent. This poem opened my eyes to the destructive effect of a disintegrating relationship on the mental and emotional balance of the people involved.

The second section of the poem presents us with a very different setting, as the poem moves from the ornate bedroom of a wealthy woman to a working-class pub in the East End of London. Sharing the dramatic quality of the first part of the poem, the urgent dialogue graphically portrays both the breakdown of a marriage and the harshness of a society devoid of compassion for the emotionally wounded. A woman is gossiping with her friends about a couple named Lil and Albert, a soldier who has recently been 'demobbed' at the end of the World War I. The conversation, while dispiriting, is entirely realistic. The relationship between Lil and Albert seems to be strained, with the woman telling of how she advised Lil to make herself 'a bit smart'. It seems that Albert is no longer attracted to his wife, having told her to get 'a nice set' of teeth, before adding, 'I swear, I can't bear to look at you'. The woman reminds Lil that after four years of army service, Albert 'wants a good time', warning that if she doesn't 'give it to him, there's others will'. Lil's explanation for no longer being physically attractive shocked me as she explains that it was the pills she took to induce an abortion that aged her so dramatically: 'It's them pills I took, to bring it off.' The harsh, depressing nature of Lil's life becomes clear when the gossiping woman refers to her five children ('and nearly died of young George.'). I was struck by the harshness of a relationship where a husband attaches greater importance to his sexual pleasure than his wife's physical health, and by the harshness of a society where there is little sympathy for Lil's plight: 'Well if Albert won't leave you alone, there it is, I said.' The barman's repeated announcement ('Hurry up please it's time') may have another level of meaning beyond his anxiety to close the premises, perhaps suggesting the inexorable passage of time and life's unending pressures. While this poem is utterly pessimistic, it is commonly believed that, as part of *The Waste Land*, it reflects the despondency that followed the horrific devastation of World War I.

Once again, this poem provides us with further evidence of the difficulty that Eliot's wide-ranging allusions can present for the reader. There are, for example, references to Shakespeare's *Antony and Cleopatra* and to a play by Thomas Middleton entitled *Women beware Women*. Yet, in another way, this poem has all of the accessibility and appeal of a television soap, such as (appropriately enough) *Eastenders* – we have a returning husband, a wife whom he no longer finds attractive, mention of an abortion and the possibility of an affair (perhaps with the female narrator, who seems to have every sympathy for him!) if the wife fails to 'smarten up'.

The only poem by Eliot that I found to be less than entirely pessimistic is *Journey of the Magi*. The aspect of this poem that I particularly like is its dramatic quality. Similar to *Prufrock* this poem is written in the form of a dramatic monologue. Also, the theme of searching for something meaningful in life cannot but appeal to modern day readers, so many of whom find their own lives devoid of meaning. One of Eliot's great achievements in this poem is transforming remote biblical figures into engaging human beings. He achieves this by highlighting the regrets ('There were times we regretted . . .'), doubts and uncertainties (inner voices 'saying / That this was all folly') that the Magi feel after leaving a world of luxury and ease ('summer palaces', 'silken girls') and facing into 'hostile' cities, 'unfriendly' towns and 'dirty' villages as they journey to witness the birth of the saviour. I think anyone who has ever attempted to follow his/her personal star could relate to the feelings of doubt experienced by the Magi. After travelling through harsh and arid terrain for so long, they find themselves in a very different world, a world of abundance. Images of life and fertility ('a temperate valley' that is 'smelling of vegetation', 'a running stream and a water-mill') suggest how the birth of Jesus will impact on the world. However, this sense of optimism is short-lived, with the imagery that follows more suggestive of Jesus' death on the cross than of his birth in a stable.

In conclusion, while Eliot's poetry can be challenging, it is always interesting and thought-provoking, offering a range of insights into various aspects of modern-day life such as human uncertainty, problematic relationships, the artificiality of a great deal of everyday social discourse, and the sordidness of the urban world.

Elizabeth Bishop

Biographical Note

Bishop (1911–1979) was born in Worcester, Massachusetts, USA. An only child, she never knew her father, who died when she was eight months old. Bishop's mother was deeply affected by her husband's death and spent much of her life thereafter in and out of mental institutions, before being declared incurably insane. She was permanently institutionalised in 1916, when Bishop was only five years old. Bishop was raised by various relatives in different locations. Her happiest times were spent in Great Village, Nova Scotia, where she was looked after by her maternal grandparents. She was later raised by relatives in Massachusetts, although she returned every summer to Nova Scotia for a number of years. The traumatic nature of Bishop's early years inevitably had a major impact on the rest of her life. As a child Bishop developed asthma, and was troubled by lung-related problems throughout adulthood. She also struggled to cope with the acute depression caused by the lack of a stable home environment and feelings of deep isolation.

Bishop's literary talent was apparent from an early age and she had several of her poems published in her High School magazine. From 1930 to 1934, Bishop attended the prestigious Vassar College where she was introduced to the writer Marianne Moore, who would become an important influence on her poetic career. By the time she left Vassar in 1935, Bishop was suffering from deep depression. She was ashamed of her sexuality (she was a lesbian) and had alcoholic tendencies.

After leaving college, a restless Bishop travelled widely for a number of years. Much of her travelling may have been prompted by her sense of being rootless and by her search for a 'home'. Bishop eventually settled in Brazil in 1951. She achieved a degree of personal happiness during this time, living contentedly with her partner, Lota de Macedo Soares. Bishop won the Pulitzer Prize for Poetry in 1956, the most prestigious of a host of major literary awards that she won for her poetic work. After Soares committed suicide in 1967, Bishop's life again began to fall apart and in 1971 she returned to the USA. She taught at Harvard for a number of years and later at New York University. Bishop spent the final difficult years of her life in Boston. She suffered from physical ill health in these years, while struggling to cope with her depression, loneliness and alcoholism. In 1979 Bishop died suddenly of a cerebral aneurysm.

The Fish

Much of Bishop's poetry follows a similar pattern, with close observation and detailed description of her poetic subject culminating in a moment of insight. In this poem we see how her scrutiny and graphic portrayal of the fish ultimately leads her to a greater understanding of the fish, and indeed of human life.

The poet's use of precise adjectives, well-chosen verbs, unusual similes and striking metaphors result in her vivid and realistic portrayal of the fish. Sound effects (particularly the use of alliteration and assonance) add to the poem's descriptive and musical qualities.

The fact that the poem is narrated in the first person ('I caught', 'I thought', 'I looked', etc) gives it a sense of immediacy, drawing the reader into the drama. In this poem the poet is a central character in the drama that she describes in such vivid detail.

The language used is simple, direct and conversational: 'I caught a tremendous fish'. The adjective 'tremendous' reflects her sense of excitement at having caught this large and impressive fish, while the adjectives 'battered and venerable and homely' suggest her sympathy and admiration for the fish.

The poet's remarkable eye for detail and effective use of imagery enable her to produce a vivid verbal painting of the fish. The simile that compares the fish's skin to 'ancient wallpaper' gives it a sense of comfortable familiarity, while an unusual simile helps us to visualise the patterns on its skin. The use of assonance: 'shapes like full-blown roses', suggests her sense of awe. The poet's observant eye also lingers on the less pleasant aspects of the fish: 'infested with tiny white sea-lice', 'the frightening gills'.

Having described the exterior of the fish, the poet now imagines its insides. An interesting simile describes how the 'coarse white fish' is 'packed in like feathers'. The poet's use of colour enhances the poem's descriptive qualities: 'the dramatic reds and blacks of its shiny entrails'. Another imaginative simile compares the fish's bladder to a flower: 'the pink swim-bladder like a big peony'.

As the poet looks into the fish's eyes, we sense a development in the relationship between poet and fish. Vivid imagery helps us to picture the fish's irises: 'backed and packed with tarnished tinfoil'. Once again alliteration and assonance are used to good effect, adding to the poem's descriptive and musical qualities. When the poet notes how the fish does not 'return my stare' when she looks into his eyes, we sense its strong, independent spirit.

The poet's respect for the fish is directly stated:

'I admired his sullen jaw'. The personification of the fish reminds us that, like the poet, he too is a character in this drama. At this point the poet observes the 'five old pieces of fish-line' hanging from the fish's jaw, each one symbolising its struggle against adversity. Well-chosen adjectives and verbs evoke the fish's determined struggle for survival: 'frayed . . . broke . . . crimped . . . broke . . . got away'. Bishop now sees the fish as a war veteran, comparing the hooks embedded in its jaw and the attached threads to 'medals with their ribbons frayed and wavering'. Her respect for this ancient survivor is reflected in the metaphor that describes these threads as 'a five-haired beard of wisdom'. The poet also comes to see the fish as a symbol of man's resilience and powers of endurance – like man, the fish has displayed the capacity to survive life's trials and tribulations. In assuming this symbolic significance, the fish is transformed into something more significant than itself. This moment of insight flows naturally from the poet's close observation and precise description of the fish.

As the poet stares at the fish she is filled with a sense of triumph, delighting in the victories of fish and man alike. This sense of triumph transforms everything, just as the oil in the pool of bilge at the bottom of the boat seems to spread a rainbow of colour throughout the boat: 'until everything / was rainbow, rainbow, rainbow!' The use of repetition underscores the celebratory tone. In letting the fish go, the poet expresses her admiration for the fish and for what it represents.

KEY POINTS

- Key theme is the ability of both the fish and man to endure and ultimately triumph over adversity.
- Precise, detailed description.
- Vivid imagery, unusual similes and metaphors.
- Poem is narrated in the first person. The conversational style gives the poem an immediacy that causes the reader to feel more closely involved in the drama.
- Sound effects (alliteration and assonance in the main) add to poem's musical qualities.

- The tone is one of awe and respect towards the aged fish, becoming joyful and celebratory towards the end.
- Repetition underscores the sense of triumph at the close of the poem ('rainbow, rainbow, rainbow').

The Bight

In this poem we again see Bishop combine detailed description, personal reflection and a moment of insight. The title of the poem refers to Garrison Bight, a bay in Florida, USA. The subtitle 'On my birthday' suggests the personal dimension to what, at first glance, appears to be a largely descriptive poem. A birthday is a significant milestone in one's life that often prompts reflection and self-evaluation. On a metaphorical level, the poet may be exploring her state of mind through her depiction of this natural scene. There is a strongly sensuous quality to her description of the disorder of the bay at low tide. We can visualise the 'sheer' (smooth, transparent) water, feel the 'crumbling' marl (clay deposits), smell the gas flame, which, when 'turned as low as possible', suggests the colour of the sea in the bight, and hear the marimba music into which the sound of the sea is transformed in the poet's imagination. The reference to Baudelaire is interesting because this poet has suggested that the external world may be reflective of one's state of mind. While the bight appears to be a tranquil natural scene, there is an underlying sense of danger suggested by the poet's description: 'the boats are dry, the pilings high as matches'. Even the personified marl seems sinister with its protruding ribs and 'glare', while there is a surreal sense to water that 'doesn't wet anything'. A second musical reference compares the sound of the dredges to 'perfectly off-beat claves' (wooden percussion instruments), underscoring the idea of the bight as a world lacking in order and harmony.

The depiction of the birds is utterly unromantic as they are described in terms of mechanical imagery. Indeed, at times this coastal scene is described as if it were an industrial landscape.

The pelicans crash into the gas-like water 'like pickaxes', while the man-of-war birds 'open their tails like scissors'. It seems that many aspects of this world are unproductive and ineffectual. The pelicans' efforts generally go unrewarded; they 'crash' into the sea, rarely coming up with anything to show for it'. The repeated hard 'c' sound effectively evokes the harshness of this world: 'Pelicans crash / into this peculiar gas . . . / . . . like pickaxes'. While the image of the sponge boats 'coming in with the obliging air of retrievers' is comforting and reassuring, the foul-smelling ('frowsy') boats convey a sense of neglect that reinforces the sense of disorder pervading this coastal scene. Another mechanical simile describes the drying shark tails 'glinting like little plowshares'. Storm-damaged small white boats 'lie on their sides, stove in, / and not yet salvaged, if they ever will be', further accentuating the feeling of disarray and general untidiness. The simile that compares the damaged boats to 'torn-open, unanswered letters' and the description of the bight 'littered with old correspondences' conjures up an image of a disordered desk. In overall terms this is a bleak scene lacking in beauty, order and coherence. Perhaps this rather chaotic natural scene is symbolic of the disorder in the poet's mind as she takes stock of her own life on her birthday. The final sound is that of the dredge: 'Click. Click. Goes the dredge, / and brings up a dripping jawful of marl'. On a symbolic level this image may be suggestive of the poetic process of digging deep for themes and appropriate images, just as the disordered bight may be representative of life itself in all its untidiness and incoherence. While the overall tone of the poem is rather dark, the insight the poet achieves at the close of the poem is uplifting: 'All the untidy activity continues, / awful but cheerful'. The poet now perceives that while life may be 'awful', we must approach it with optimism and good humour if we are to endure its disorder and disappointments.

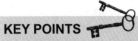

KEY POINTS

- The most obvious theme is the disorder of the bight.
- The poem may be read on a metaphorical level as a depiction of the disorder in the poet's mind.
- There is a familiar pattern to this poem, with close observation and graphic description leading on to personal reflection and a moment of insight.
- The birds are portrayed in a very unromantic manner, as is this entire natural scene.
- Unusual (mainly mechanical) imagery.
- The tone is generally dark, but the closing lines are more optimistic.

At the Fishhouses

This poem is similar in pattern to many of Bishop's poems, with close observation and detailed description leading on to a moment of insight. The fishhouses to which the poem refers were located at Cuttybank Island, Massachusetts, although the poem was probably inspired by the poet's visit to her childhood home in Nova Scotia in 1946. The poem opens with an image of a solitary fisherman awaiting the arrival of a herring boat. The opening lines have a strong sensuous quality. We can visualise the fisherman's 'dark purple-brown' nets in the fading light of dusk ('the gloaming'), smell the pungent codfish and almost feel the poet's reaction to it: 'The air smells so strong of codfish / it makes one's nose run and one's eyes water'. The assonant long 'o' sound evokes a serious, reflective mood: 'Although . . . cold . . . old . . . gloaming'

There follows a detailed description of the fishhouses in the everyday conversational language that we find in so many of Bishop's poems: 'The five fishhouses have steeply peaked roofs / and narrow, cleated gangplanks slant up / to storerooms in the gables'. The alliterative 'f' ('five fishhouses') and 's' ('slant . . . storerooms') sounds are typical of the musical qualities that proliferate in Bishop's verse. Fish scales are everywhere, painting the world of the fishhouses an attractive silver colour: 'All is silver'. Alliterative and sibilant 's' sounds evoke the musical quality of the sea: 'the heavy surface of the sea / swelling slowly as if considering spilling over'. The idea of the sea 'considering' suggests that it has a human capacity for reflection. In contrast to the 'opaque' (unclear) surface of the sea (suggestive of its dark, mysterious depths), every other aspect of this scene is apparently translucent (allowing light to pass through) because everything is covered in silver fish scales: 'the silver of the benches, / the lobster pots, and masts'. The strong sense of colour in this poem is reinforced by the reference to 'an emerald moss' growing on the small old buildings that are the fishhouses. It seems that the omnipresent fish scales beautify a world that most would find unappealing (it is, after all, a pungent smelling place of death). In a vivid word painting, the poet describes how 'layers of beautiful herring scales' completely line the big fish tubs, while 'the wheelbarrows are similarly plastered / with creamy iridescent coats of mail' (a memorable metaphor for the silver fish scales). Even the flies that crawl on

215

the scales are similarly 'iridescent' (rainbow-coloured). Throughout this passage we see the poet's remarkable eye for detail and her imaginative capacity to transform the everyday, and even the ugly, into something beautiful. We again see the poet's observant eye in her reference to 'an ancient wooden capstan' (a type of crane) 'with two long bleached handles / and some melancholy stains, like dried blood / where ironwork has rusted'.

It is towards the end of the first section of the poem that the first human interaction occurs, with the old fisherman ('a friend of my grandfather') accepting the poet's offer of a 'Lucky Strike' (a popular brand of American cigarettes). They talk of everyday matters such as the falling population and of the declining numbers of 'codfish and herring' as the old man awaits the arrival of a herring boat. The poet's keen eye for detail is again evident in her description of the 'sequins on his vest' and 'that black old knife, / the blade of which is almost worn away'. The 'sequins' are of course the scales that he scraped off the fish – even the old man's vest becomes transformed in the poet's imagination. The poet regards these scales as the fishes' 'principal beauty', once again reminding the reader of her ability to see beauty in the most unlikely of places and things.

In the second section of the poem we get a factual description of the ramp where the fishermen haul up their boats. Like every other aspect of this scene, the tree trunks that make up the ramp have been beautified by the fish scales ('thin silver / tree trunks'). The phrase 'down and down' does not just refer to the seaward direction of the tree trunks, but also to the movement of the poem, which is about to enter the depths of the poet's psyche.

The third section of the poem is the most challenging. Similar to *In the Waiting Room*, this poem moves from a description of the external world to an exploration of the interior world of the poet. This section opens with a paradoxical description of the icy waters of the North Atlantic: 'Cold dark deep and absolutely clear'. The paradox (dark – clear) may suggest the poet's difficulty in accurately describing and understanding the massive natural force that is the sea. No human being could survive in these freezing waters: 'element bearable to no mortal'. It is not uncommon for poets to employ the sea as a metaphor for the human psyche, and as this part of the poem develops, the poet explores the depths of her own consciousness through sea imagery. Similar to *The Fish*, the poet has an encounter with an animal – a seal that she has seen at this spot 'evening after evening'. The description of the seal is humorous because he is given human qualities: 'He was interested in music: / like me a believer in total immersion'. While the seal naturally enjoys being totally immersed in water, the phrase 'total immersion' when related to the poet may refer to Bishop's complete absorption in her poetic work or to the Baptist baptismal ritual that involves the adult believer being totally immersed in water. There is a surreal quality to the idea of the poet singing Baptist hymns such as 'A Mighty Fortress Is Our God' to the seal. The repetition of the earlier paradoxical description of the sea ('Cold dark deep and absolutely clear') may suggest the poet's difficulty in understanding the depths of her own psyche. The image of 'a million Christmas trees' behind the poet is obvious hyperbole (deliberate exaggeration), evoking the richness and abundance of nature. However, the fact that they 'stand / waiting for Christmas' points to the idea of death and decay that awaits all living things. Here there is an implied contrast between human mortality and the timelessness of the sea.

At this point the poet returns to her contemplation of the powerful, mysterious sea. She endeavours to understand the sea through her senses. Interestingly, she speaks directly to the reader: 'If you should dip your hand in, / your wrist would ache immediately, / . . . and your hand would burn / . . . If you tasted it, it would first taste bitter / then briny, then surely burn your tongue'. The freezing sea is here equated with fire as it too has a burning effect. In the closing six lines of the poem Bishop achieves a moment of insight. She draws an interesting analogy between the sea and knowledge: 'It is like what we imagine knowledge to be: / dark, salt, clear moving, utterly free'. Harsh natural images suggest that knowledge can be painful: 'drawn from the cold hard mouth / of the world, derived from the rocky breasts'. The closing lines suggest that knowledge is not fixed and static but, like the sea, is forever moving and changing as the repetition of 'flowing' indicates: 'flowing and drawn, and since / our knowledge is historical, flowing and flown'. The sea image is particularly apt, suggesting the vastness, power and endlessly changing nature of knowledge.

KEY POINTS

- In this poem, as in so many other of Bishop's poems, close observation and precise, detailed description lead on to a moment of insight (vision or understanding).
- Outer description is followed by intense inner reflection.
- Parts of poem have a surreal (dreamlike) quality – the final section presents us with the poet's stream of consciousness.
- Memorable imagery.
- Much of the language has a conversational quality. It becomes more complex in the third section of the poem as the poet struggles to comprehend the vastness and power of the sea and, ultimately, the nature of knowledge.
- Effective use of sound – alliteration, assonance, sibilance.

The Prodigal

As the title suggests, this poem is based on the biblical story of the Prodigal Son. The poet recreates this familiar tale in order to convey the debasement and ultimate redemption of the alcoholic. This is obviously a deeply personal poem because the poet was herself an alcoholic. The Prodigal Son is a metaphor for the alcoholic. In the poet's detailed description of The Prodigal's miserable, meaningless existence, we see the degradation and isolation of the alcoholic. Yet, this is essentially a positive poem that suggests that even the most debased human beings can rise above the dark depths of addiction and despair and achieve redemption by returning home to the family and society from which they have exiled themselves.

The structure of this poem consists of two sonnets. The poet focuses on the lowest and most repulsive part of the Prodigal's life – his time spent tending to and living with pigs. Her graphic descriptions effectively evoke a scene of depressing squalor and self-abasement (i.e.

self-degradation). The sensuous imagery of the opening lines immediately brings us into the foul-smelling, filthy sty: 'The brown enormous odour he lived by / was too close . . . for him to judge'. There is a suggestion here that having lived for so long in this squalor, the Prodigal has lost his sense of judgement – he seems to find it difficult to reflect on and assess his life. The image of 'the glass-smooth dung' is depressingly realistic, highlighting the poet's talent for precise description. The poet's alliterative description of the pigs looking up with their light eyelashes ('light-lashed') is also memorable. The reference to 'the sow that always ate her young' heightens our sense of revulsion. Despite being sickened by this, the Prodigal still manages to scratch the sow's head in a gesture of affection. Here we see that despite his dehumanising surroundings, he retains his humanity.

The lying, self-deceiving nature of the alcoholic is thrown into sharp relief (brought into clear focus) by his efforts to hide his alcohol: 'he

217

hid the pints behind a two-by-four'. However, the Prodigal is aware that there is a brighter world beyond the ugly pigsty. The sunrise transforms and beautifies this world of filth, briefly lifting his spirits: 'the sunrise glazed the barnyard mud with red; / the burning puddles seemed to reassure./ And then he thought he might almost endure / his exile yet another year or more'. Notwithstanding the harshness of his surroundings and his prolonged suffering and loneliness, the Prodigal is still moved by the beauty of nature. Here, as in *The Fish* and *Filling Station*, the poet presents the reader with an insight into the endurance and resilience of the human spirit.

The 'but' at the beginning of the second section of the poem signals a change in the Prodigal's life: 'But evenings the first star came to warn'. It is as if the Prodigal is being reminded of the need to take action to change the course of his life. We again see the poet's interesting use of imagery in her vivid description of the barn in the farmer's lantern light: 'overhanging clouds of hay, / with pitchforks, faint forked lightnings, catching light'. While the animals are 'safe and companionable as in the ark', it is clear that no human being should be reduced to living at the level of an animal.

Just as the early morning sun transformed the mud and puddles, the farmer's lantern 'laid on the mud a pacing aureole'. The lantern becomes a type of halo, which, like the sun in the first section of the poem, reassures and comforts the Prodigal. Towards the close of the poem we are again reminded of the disgusting filth in which he works: 'Carrying a bucket along a slimy board'. The reference to 'the bats' uncertain staggering flight' suggests the Prodigal's gradual, stumbling acquisition of self-awareness. The 'shuddering insights' that he acquires prompt him to return to the home and family he had abandoned, although he did not easily reach this decision: 'But it took him a long time / finally to make his mind up to go home'. On a symbolic level, this suggests the idea of the alcoholic once more becoming part of human society.

This poem then concludes on a positive note, with the lonely exile finally returning to the love, warmth and support of his family. It is also uplifting in its portrayal of the resilience of the human spirit – even in the harshest of conditions, the Prodigal retains his sensitivity of spirit.

KEY POINTS

- Key theme is the endurance / resilience of the human spirit.
- The isolation and self-abasement of the alcoholic is, clearly, a related theme.
- The poem suggests that beauty may be found in the most unlikely situations.
- Precise, detailed description.
- Startling metaphors: 'clouds of hay', 'pitchforks, faint forked lightnings'.
- Personification: 'the first star came to warn'.

Questions of Travel

This poem is located in Brazil, where Bishop lived for fifteen years. Travel was an important part of the poet's life and in this poem precise description of the exotic Brazilian landscape leads on to reflection on our need to travel, on its drawbacks and benefits. Put simply, in this poem the poet reflects on the pros and cons of travel.

While the first section of the poem conveys the richness and abundance of nature, there is a sense of travel-weariness on the part of the poet, as if she has experienced too much: 'There are too many waterfalls here; the crowded streams / hurry too rapidly down to the sea'. Visual and aural imagery combine to enable us to both visualise and hear the water pouring down the mountains, with the sibilant and alliterative 's' sound combined with the assonant long 'o' sound being particularly effective in conveying the noise of the water: 'and the pressure of so many clouds on the mountaintops / makes them spill over the sides in soft slow-motion, / turning to waterfalls before our very eyes'. The nascent (in their early stages) waterfalls are described as 'mile-long, shiny tearstains', a metaphor for the sadness that was, it seems, an inescapable feature of the poet's emotional make-up. The poet conveys the energy and non-stop movement of the natural world: 'the streams and clouds keep traveling, traveling'. The simile comparing the mountains to 'the hulls of capsized ships, / slime-hung and barnacled' helps us to visualise this scene, although it is not a very appealing image.

The second section of this poem is more philosophical in nature, with the poet posing a series of questions as she ponders our need to travel. She wonders whether or not we would travel if we thought 'of the long trip home', and if we should stay at home and simply imagine our destination: 'Should we have stayed at home and thought of here?' She suggests that, as tourists, we are like intruders into a world that is not ours: 'Is it right to be watching strangers in a play / in this strangest of theatres?' Interestingly, the poet views the impulse to travel as a form of impulsive childish behaviour: 'What childishness is it that while there's a breath of life / in our bodies, we are determined to rush / to see the sun the other way around?' She captures the often uncomprehending response of tourists to the historical remains of other cultures: 'stare at some inexplicable old stonework, / inexplicable and impenetrable'. Our response to such examples of historical heritage is uniformed and cliched: 'always, always delightful'. The poet views tourists in a very negative light in this section of the poem, suggesting that we would travel to the ends of the earth to see the smallest thing, such as 'the tiniest green hummingbird in the world'. This section of the poem concludes with the implication that tourists respond to new worlds in an entirely superficial manner. There is no meaningful engagement with a new, possibly rich, culture; instead we take our snaps in an instant and move on: 'And have we room / for one more folded sunset, still quite warm?'

While the second section of the poem presents us with the poet's arguments against travel, the third section focuses on its benefits. At this point the poet presents us with a series of detailed images that reflect her keenly observant eye and her wonderful descriptive powers. We are presented with some of the poet's striking memories of Brazil, those aspects of her Brazilian experience that it would have been 'a pity' to have missed out on. She mentions the trees along the road, which are described as having a 'noble' quality and as being 'robed in pink' (covered in flowers). She then speaks of a memorable aural experience: 'the sad, two-noted, wooden tune / of disparate wooden clogs / carelessly clacking over a grease-stained filling-station floor'. Here, alliteration and onomatopoeia combine to convey the distinctive sound of the clogs. The poet refers to clogs produced in other countries as being tested to ensure each pair 'would have identical pitch' in order to highlight the laid-back nature of Brazilian life. Another lingering visual and aural memory is of 'the fat brown bird / who sings above the broken gasoline pump / in a bamboo church of Jesuit baroque: / three towers, five silver crosses'. While the Brazilian people are not particularly concerned about clogs being perfectly matching, a great deal of time and care is involved in producing the intricate and highly stylised bird cage, which constitutes a most impressive artifact. The sharply contrasting attitudes of the Brazilian people towards the production of 'the crudest wooden footwear' and 'the whittled fantasies of wooden cages' speak volumes for their values and priorities. This section of the poem ends on a humorous note with Bishop comparing the monotonous sound of incessant rain to 'politicians' speeches', which thankfully also eventually end in 'a sudden golden silence'.

Having presented the cases for and against travelling, the poet, in the final section of this poem, tries to resolve her own inner debate as to whether it is better to travel or not to travel: 'Is it lack of imagination that makes us come / to imagined places, not just stay at home?' It seems that the need to travel is seen as the result of some sort of failure of the artistic imagination that should enable the poet to imagine different worlds without having to travel to them. The closing lines suggest that our choices are not as free as we might suppose: 'Continent, city, country, society: / the choice is never wide and never free'. The final line returns to a common theme for the poet, the lack of a stable home: 'Should we have stayed at home, / wherever that may be?' Ultimately, the question of where the poet belongs, the lack of a place that she can call home is a more fundamental issue than the value of travel. Where that issue is concerned, the litany of questions with which the poem concludes suggests that she has reached no definitive answer.

KEY POINTS

- Main theme is the value of travel.
- The vivid description of the first section of the poem leads on to a philosophical reflection on the merits and demerits of travel.
- Detailed description.
- Striking similes and metaphors.
- Imagery is varied and typically vivid.
- Effective use of sound: alliteration, assonance, sibilance.
- Series of questions at close of poem suggests that Bishop has reached no conclusive answer as to the value of travel.

The Armadillo

This poem suggests how both the human and animal worlds are vulnerable to man's unthinking destructiveness. In Rio de Janeiro, where the poet lived for many years, the local people sent up fire balloons (helium-filled balloons carrying paper boxes that self-ignite) as part of a religious festival honouring St. John. The reference to 'a saint still honoured in these parts' suggests a contrast between the importance of religion in Brazil and in the developed world. Bishop describes acts of violence without comment, allowing her vivid descriptions to speak for themselves. Once again, the poet's observant eye and descriptive ability are evident in her rich visual imagery and striking metaphors.

The poet describes how the fire balloons are released into the night sky. These balloons are frail and beautiful, but also dangerous. Their delicacy and beauty is suggested by the simile that compares the 'paper chambers' to 'hearts'. The repeated 'f' and 'l' sounds give us a sense of the balloons floating: 'flush and fill', 'flare and falter'. Their association with the stars and planets of the night sky accentuates their romantic dimension: 'it's hard to tell them from the stars'.

However, if these fascinating balloons are caught in a 'downdraft' of air, they can 'suddenly' turn 'dangerous', threatening both the human and natural worlds: 'Last night another big one fell. / It splattered like an egg of fire / against the cliff behind the house'. The egg metaphor effectively conveys the idea of the exploding fire balloons – what were once objects of beauty have now become a source of menacing violence. The house and its inhabitants, as well as the owls, the rabbit and the armadillo that live nearby are all endangered by this 'falling fire'. The verbs 'whirling' and 'shrieked' convey the owls' panic as they flee their burning nest. Birds and animals alike suffer as a result of man's carelessness: the owls are 'bright pink underneath', the armadillo is 'rose-flecked', while a striking metaphor ('a handful of intangible ash') suggests that the rabbit has already fallen victim to the fire. Even in the midst of this panic, the poet's observant eye misses nothing – the baby rabbit is 'short-eared, to our surprise'. The description of the armadillo is detailed but concise: 'a glistening armadillo left the scene, / rose-flecked, head down, tail down'. Despite its armour, the armadillo has no protection against fire.

The poet feels that her descriptions fail to fully capture the horror of this scene: 'Too pretty, dreamlike mimicry!'. While the poet's style is detached and she seems to be at a distance from her subject, it is clear that she is both moved and outraged by the animals' suffering (the baby rabbit is 'So Soft!'). The series of exclamation marks in the final stanza underscore the dramatic nature of this scene: 'O falling fire and piercing cry / and panic, and a weak mailed fist / clenched ignorant against the sky!' The 'mailed fist' metaphor signifies both the armadillo's defiance and vulnerability – it cannot understand or protect itself from this menacing fire. The armadillo symbolises all of those people and animals who fall victim to violence that they cannot comprehend, and over which they have no control. The fire balloons remind us that, despite mankind's finer spiritual and romantic instincts, we remain innately and unthinkingly destructive.

KEY POINTS

- Key theme is the vulnerability of both the human and animal worlds to man's unthinking destructiveness.
- Precise, detailed description.
- Description without comment, no overt moralising – allows readers to draw their own conclusions.
- Tone is generally detached. The poet observes without comment, however it is clear where her sympathies lie.
- Conversational quality to the language – one planet is described as 'the pale green one', the baby rabbit is 'So Soft!'.
- Use of striking metaphors.
- Use of alliteration and end rhyme give the poem a musical quality.

Sestina

This is a highly personal poem inspired by a childhood memory, more specifically, Bishop's recollection of the period following her mother's permanent institutionalisation in a mental hospital, which resulted in the child Bishop going to live with her grandmother. The opening stanza refers to September (suggestive of a dying year),

evening (suggestive of a dying day) and rain, immediately evoking a sense of gloom. While the references to the stove, jokes and laughing evoke a sense of warmth and cosy domesticity, the closing line in the first stanza reinforces the sense of sadness with which the poem opens. The old grandmother is 'laughing and talking to hide the tears'. The image of the old woman trying to hide her anguish from the child is quite poignant. The sense of despondency we feel in the opening stanza pervades the entire poem.

The second stanza presents us with the thoughts of the grandmother, who seems to be a superstitious woman. She believes that her own tears and the rain beating on the roof 'were both foretold by the almanac' (an annual publication that included a calendar, astronomical information, jokes and folk wisdom). Towards the end of this stanza we return to the familiar domestic world as the grandmother prepares tea: 'The iron kettle sings on the stove. / She cuts some bread.'

In the third stanza we see the child's perspective on the situation. As in *First Death in Nova Scotia* the young Bishop tries to comprehend her feelings by exploring them through the concrete objects around her. The child senses her grandmother's pain and repressed tears, transferring them onto the kettle. The drops of water spilling from the personified kettle are transformed into 'small hard tears' that 'dance like mad on the hot black stove, / the way the rain must dance on the house'. This second reference to the rain underscores the melancholy mood. However, on a positive note, the sense of life going on is conveyed by the image of the busy grandmother 'tidying up'.

Stanza four depicts the almanac in an ominous light as a bird of prey that 'hovers half above the child, / hovers above the old grandmother'. The child's consciousness of the sorrow that envelops the house is reflected in the manner in which she sees so much around her in terms of tears: the kettle sheds 'small hard tears', while her grandmother's teacup is 'full of dark brown tears'. The image of the old woman shivering conveys the chilling effect of grief or loss, but again we see domestic activity continuing with the grandmother putting 'more wood on the stove'.

There is a surreal quality to stanza five, with the child imagining the objects around her coming to life and engaging in a conversation: 'It was to be, says the Marvel Stove, / I know what I know, says the almanac'. The stove's remark suggests that there was a certain inevitability about what has happened to leave the child in the situation in which she now finds herself – without either of her parents (Bishop never knew her father because he died when she was a baby) and being raised by her grandmother. The almanac appears proud of its all-knowing nature: 'I know what I know, says the almanac'. The child now expresses her feelings visually, drawing a picture with her crayons. The 'rigid house' she draws may suggest her desire for a stable home life, while the man who features in this picture may represent the child's longing for the father she never knew. The deep sadness of the child's life is again conveyed by an image of tears: 'the child / puts in a man with buttons like tears.'

In stanza six, the grandmother is busy about the house when the child looks into the almanac. Again, we see the child's vivid imagination as she pictures how 'the little moons fall down like tears / from between the pages of the almanac'. While there are tears everywhere in this poem, the child herself never cries – she is sharply aware of the sorrow that enshrouds the house, but is not yet mature enough to fully understand it. She imagines the tears from the almanac falling 'into the flower-bed the child / has carefully placed at the front of the house'. Here we see the child's efforts to create an ideal home within the realms of her imagination.

The final three lines suggest that sorrow will be a growing feature of the child's future life, with an ominous declaration from the almanac: 'Time to plant tears, says the almanac'. The sense of life going on amidst sorrow and loss is conveyed by the grandmother continuing to hide her grief by singing as 'the child draws another inscrutable house'. The 'inscrutable' nature of the drawing points to the child's ongoing difficulties in coming to terms with the strange nature of her home life – a life without a father or a mother.

KEY POINTS

- Key theme is the child's difficulty in coming to terms with her life without her father and mother.
- Another theme is the idea that life continues to go on amidst sorrow and loss.
- A deeply personal poem reflective of the poet's troubled childhood.
- The child attempts to comprehend her feelings by exploring them through the concrete objects around her.
- Highly imaginative metaphors and similes.
- There is a surreal quality to the idea of the stove and almanac talking.
- Repeated use of tear imagery conveys a sense of pervasive sorrow.
- Simple, everyday language.
- The 'sestina' of the title refers to an old, formal poetic form with six six-line stanzas and a concluding three-line envoy addressed to the reader or to the subject of the poem.

First Death in Nova Scotia

In this poem Bishop recalls her first encounter with death. The poem is written from a child's point of view as she attempts to come to terms with the grim reality of death. The poet conveys the child's feelings of confusion; death is at once chilling, mysterious, attractive and frightening. The poet uses simple language and surreal imagery to convey the child's perspective on reality.

The deathly coldness of the parlour in which Arthur is laid out is suggested by the poet's use of repetition ('the cold, cold parlor') and imagery ('on his white, frozen lake'). The solemn mood is underscored by the assonant long 'o' sound in 'cold, cold . . . chromographs'. Death transforms the familiar parlour into a strange, cold world. Even as a child, the poet was observant, taking in every aspect of her surroundings. Everything her eye alights on is lifeless: the chromograph with the royal family, the stuffed loon and, of course, Arthur, her dead little cousin.

In stanza two the child is preoccupied with the loon. The fact that the personified loon 'hadn't said a word' since it was shot suggests the mystery of death. The metaphor of the loon's 'white, frozen lake' helps to convey the

cold atmosphere. The bewildered child finds something attractive about death; the loon's breast is 'cold and caressable', while its red glass eyes are 'much to be desired'. However, the references to marble and glass underline the idea of coldness and lifelessness.

The young child literally comes face-to-face with the reality of death when her mother lifts her up, and asks her to place a lily in Arthur's hand. The image of the coffin as 'a little frosted cake' is childlike and indicative of the young child's attempts to make sense of a strangely unfamiliar world. Death now becomes more frightening as the loon seems to come to life in the child's imagination, eyeing the coffin in a menacing manner: 'and the red-eyed loon eyed it / from his white, frozen lake'.

The child's perspective is again clearly evident in the description of Arthur as 'a doll that hadn't been painted yet'. The child believes that Jack Frost paints the leaves red in autumn, and imagines that he had just started to paint Arthur's hair red when he 'dropped his brush / and left him white forever', the final word signifying the finality of death. Thinking of the maple leaf, the child is reminded of the Canadian national anthem: 'the Maple Leaf (Forever)'. The associations made in this stanza clearly point to the workings of a child's mind, to the young Bishop's stream of consciousness.

The fairytale element in the closing stanza is anther example of the confused child's attempts to grapple with the grim reality of death. The child imagines that the royal couples invite little Arthur 'to be the smallest page in court'. Their warmth ('warm in red and ermine') contrasts with and highlights the cold (suggested by the adjectives 'white', 'cold', 'frozen', 'frosted') that is felt throughout the poem. However, there

is no happy fairytale ending to this sad drama. The child is struck by the fear that Arthur will be unable to escape from his coffin and reach the distant royal court. The final, poignant image is of a vulnerable, frightened little child alone in a cold world. The child pictures Arthur 'clutching his tiny lily', unable to travel 'roads deep in snow' and reach a place of warmth and security. The question in the closing lines highlights the child's confusion: 'But how could Arthur go . . .?' It is interesting to note that the imagined afterlife belongs to the realms of fairytale rather than religion.

KEY POINTS

- Key theme is the child's attempts to make sense of her first encounter with death.
- A related theme is the mysterious, unknowable nature of death.
- This poem presents us with a child's perspective (point of view) on death.
- Simple language and childlike imagery gives the impression of a child's voice.
- Metaphors (coffin was 'a little frosted cake'), similes ('He was all white, like a doll') suggest a child's attempts to comprehend death.
- Visual imagery, use of colour.
- Repetition of images ('his white, frozen lake'), adjectives ('white', 'frozen', 'cold') to underline the cold atmosphere.
- Use of assonance ('Cold, cold . . . chromographs'), alliteration ('cold and caressable').
- Fairytale element.

Filling Station

In this poem we once again see Bishop's photographic eye for detail. We again see how close observation and reflection lead on to a moment of insight. The theme of this poem is the unique beauty of everyday life. As the curious poet probes beneath the surface of the greasy, grimy filling station, she discovers that love can be found even in the midst of filth and ugliness. An unseen loving presence has attempted to give this oil-soaked filling station some of the features of a home.

The colloquial exclamation with which the poem opens gives it a sense of immediacy:

'Oh, but it is dirty!' The first three sections of the poem describe a place of filth and squalor. Every aspect of the filling station is 'oil-soaked, oil-permeated'. The phrase 'black translucency' serves as a good example of Bishop's talent for exact description. The conversational language is perfectly suited to the description of a very ordinary, everyday place: 'Be careful with that match!'

The extent of the dirt fascinates the poet: 'oil-soaked monkey suit', 'greasy sons', 'grease-impregnated wickerwork', 'a dirty dog'. Everything is 'quite thoroughly dirty' ('dirty' is repeated three times). However, the reference to a father and sons gives the dirty filling station an unexpected domestic dimension. The colloquial language employed to describe the dog ('quite comfy') reinforces the sense of a home in a world of grime.

The poet's sharp eye takes in every detail, including some surprising decorative touches that sharply contrast with the overall filth of the filling station – she observes the comic books, the begonia, even the 'daisy stitch' in the doily. Her curious mind probes beneath the surface of the scene, prompting her to ask a series of questions: 'Do they live in the station? . . . Why the extraneous plant? Why the taboret?' Most of all, she is fascinated by the doily: 'Why, oh why, the doily?' An unseen hand has attempted to create some degree of domestic order and beauty in this world of filth.

The 'somebody' who 'embroidered the doily' and 'waters the plant' is never named (we again see the poet's wit when she suggests that the plant is possibly oiled instead of watered). However, the suggestion is that it is a woman who has done her best to fashion a home in a world of overwhelming ugliness. Through a process of close observation and detailed description, Bishop acquires a further insight into human nature. It seems that people always have the desire and capacity to transcend (rise above) the ugliness of life. The world of squalor that is the filling station is given a certain beauty and harmony by a nameless woman's homemaking efforts – efforts prompted by her love for her family.

The arrangement of the cans of oil also reflects a desire to bring order to a depressingly filthy world. The cans of oil are arranged in such a way as to have a soothing effect on tense drivers: 'they softly say ESSO–SO–SO–SO to high-strung automobiles'. The personification of the cars is another example of the poet's memorable use of imagery. The very positive concluding line encapsulates the insight that the poet has gained: 'Somebody loves us all'. Put simply, the poet concludes that there is always someone quietly doing their best to improve the quality of our lives through generally unnoticed acts of love.

KEY POINTS
- Key theme is that love and beauty can be found even in the midst of filth and ugliness.
- A related theme is the indomitable nature of the human spirit.
- Precise, detailed description – a strongly visual poem.
- Conversational language – exclamations and questions give the poem a sense of immediacy, involving the reader in the scene being described.
- Colloquial expressions, e.g. 'a dirty dog, quite comfy'.
- Touches of humour.

In the Waiting Room

This poem describes the stream of consciousness (stream of thought) of the six-year-old Elizabeth Bishop as she waits in a dentist's waiting room while her aunt receives treatment. More particularly, it depicts a dramatic moment of self-awareness in the child's development. We see how she becomes aware of her own identity and separateness, while also achieving an insight into the extent to which her future life will be shaped by her gender. She comes to perceive the world beyond childhood as perplexing and terrifying. She senses that her future as a woman will inevitably involve a great deal of pain.

The language of this poem has a conversational quality which is typical of much of Bishop's verse: 'I went with Aunt Consuelo / to keep her dentist's appointment', 'I could read', 'I didn't know any word for it', 'an *oh* of pain'. The poem is spoken in the innocent, naïve voice of a young child. The delivery is simple and direct: 'It was winter. It got dark / early. The waiting room / was full of grown-up people'.

The child feels out-of-place in a room full of adults, and seeks refuge in the pages of the *National Geographic*. The pictures of distant lands and strange peoples introduce her to a world that is frighteningly different from the familiar world of the waiting-room with its 'overcoats, lamps and magazines'. The child is fascinated but terrified by every image she sees in the magazine: volcanoes, cannibals and black women who have mutilatated themselves in order to be sexually attractive. A familiar domestic image suggests the child's attempts to come to terms with a very disturbing sight: 'black, naked women with necks / wound round and round with wire / like the necks of light bulbs.' The child is so shocked by these women's elongated necks and so repulsed by their 'horrifying' breasts that she tries to distance herself from this terrifying introduction to the broader, outside world by focusing on the cover and date of the magazine.

Her absorption in the magazine is interrupted by her aunt's cry of pain. Sensing that her destiny as a woman will inevitably involve suffering,

the child suddenly empathises (identifies) with her aunt's pain. It is as if her aunt's cry of pain is strangely her own: 'What took me / completely by surprise / was that it was *me*; / my voice, in my mouth'. What follows has a surreal (dreamlike) quality to it as the child feels that both she and her aunt are 'falling, falling' into some unknown territory. She maintains her grip on reality by focusing on a concrete fact – her imminent birthday: 'I was saying it to stop / the sensation of falling off / the round, turning world / into cold, black-blue space'.

In a dramatic moment of self-awareness, the poet asserts her own individuality, while also insightfully acknowledging the female identity that she shares with all women: 'But I felt: you are an *I*, / you are an *Elizabeth*, / you are one of *them*'. While she is a unique individual, she is also a woman and, as such, destined to share in the suffering that seems to be the lot of all females, including her 'foolish' aunt and the mutilated black women. Startled by this realisation, the child returns from her trance-like state to the comforting familiarity of the waiting room, a world of 'shadowy grey knees, trousers and skirts and boots'. However, the significance of this dramatic moment of insight is not lost on her: 'I knew that nothing stranger / had ever happened, that nothing / stranger could ever happen'. The young child struggles to come to terms with the fact of being undeniably connected by her gender to a strange wider world: 'Why should I be my aunt, / or me, or anyone?' She has difficulty accepting the fact that her gender unites her with all other women: 'What similarities . . . held us all together / or made us all just one?' She senses that what makes her one with women everywhere is the pain involved in being a woman – at this point she again refers to the African women's 'awful hanging breasts'. This display of female sexuality continues to fill her with revulsion. Once again we see how, through observation and reflection, the child achieves a moment of insight.

The image of the bright, hot waiting room sliding

under 'a big black wave' suggests the idea of the poet drifting into unconsciousness. At the close of the poem, she is back in the waiting room, conscious of time ('February 1918') and place (Worcester, Massachusetts'). However, the reference to the war indicates that Bishop still perceives the outside world to be a hostile place.

The young Elizabeth Bishop waiting in the waiting room may be symbolic of the child waiting for adulthood.

KEY POINTS

- Key theme is the young Bishop becoming simultaneously aware both of her own individuality and the female identity that unites her with all other women.
- The onset of adult awareness and the resultant confusion is a related theme.
- Poem has a surreal (dreamlike) quality, moving from a detailed description of the external world to the surreal world of the speaker's stream of consciousness.
- A deeply personal poem.
- Precise description, e.g. 'rivulets of fire'.
- Striking imagery, e.g. 'necks / wound round and round with wire / like the necks of light bulbs'.
- Conversational language.
- Tone is one of shock, horror and revulsion.
- Use of questions suggest child's struggle to understand the frighteningly strange wider world.

Key Points on Style: poetry of Elizabeth Bishop

(Word Choice & Language / Imagery / Contrast / Variety of Verse forms)

Word Choice / Language

- The language of Bishop's poetry is, essentially, simple and straightforward. She tends to avoid obscurity. She felt that the physical world was real and language, carefully used, could communicate the essence of reality. It would be a mistake, however, to think that the simplicity of diction and accessibility of language make the poems superficial. Their apparent simplicity is deceptive. Each poem on the course offers a profound insight into life, nature and human experience. Take for example the language used to describe the fish's eye in the poem *The Fish*. The word 'sullen' suggests that the fish has human emotions and thus draws a connection between the speaker and the fish, creating a parallel and an intimacy between them. The fact that she uses words of comparison such as 'larger' and 'shallower' to describe the differences between their eyes, only emphasises further the similarities they share and which have already been mentioned earlier in the poem – 'blood', 'flesh', ' big bones ... little bones', 'entrails' etc.

- Bishop chooses and combines her words in a very artful, suggestive manner which enriches the meaning for the reader. Take, for example, her word choice in *Filling Station*. She mentions the 'dirty, oil-soaked monkey suit', the 'cement porch', the 'grease-impregnated wickerwork' and the 'dirty dog'. However, these are placed alongside a 'doily' which is 'embroidered in daisy stitch' and 'a big hirsute begonia'. The impact of these simple, descriptive words points the reader in the direction of the poem's deeper meaning – the fact that life is a mixture of ugliness and beauty and both can exist simultaneously.

- Word choice also functions to describe that which is obviously ordinary and familiar in order to bring out its quality of strangeness or its uniqueness. *Filling Station* and *In the Waiting Room* are just two examples of this technique which she uses throughout many of the other poems also. Look for other examples in the poems studied.

- The language of the poems is subtle and carefully crafted to achieve maximum impact on the reader, without overpowering obscurity or any attempt at ambiguity or complexity.

Imagery

- Bishop's images, like her word choices, are precise and realistic, reflecting her own sharp, keen intelligence and her moral sense. She was an artist as well as a poet and reveals an extraordinary capacity to capture significant scenes. We have already seen this in *Filling Station* but this feature is apparent in every poem. In *First Death in Nova Scotia*, the imagery powerfully recreates an early childhood memory. In a series of images, the poet reveals the impact of her first experience of death. Starting in a 'cold parlor', the poem moves effortlessly to the image of the chromographs, the 'stuffed loon' on the marble table, the coffin like 'a little frosted cake' and the image of the dead child clutching a 'tiny lily'. The colours red and white are repeated throughout the poem. The red eye of the loon, the red Canadian maple leaf, the red of the royal robes in the chromograph are all symbols of warmth and comfort which serve to highlight the whiteness of the dead child's face, the whiteness of the lily and the deep snow. The innocence and sense of wonder of the child speaker adds a profound poignancy to the occasion but also poses the profound question of the meaning of death and how one passes from one state of being to another: 'But how could Arthur go' ... and the roads deep in snow?'

- The majority of the images in Bishop's poems come from the incredible details of everyday life. It is this great gift of seeing the world through the eyes of a keenly aware observer that gives depth and richness to her verse. One example of this is the poem *In the Waiting Room* where the young poet has an intense moment of epiphany as she becomes aware of her identity. The imagery dramatises this moment of awareness. The simple description of the waiting room filled with 'gray knees, trousers and skirts', opens to a wider vista as the young girl leafs through the different cultures and wider world presented in a magazine. Details of the photographs build up to a growing sense of unease. Panic rises as the child realises that she has her own personal identity, but is also a part of something greater than herself and that demands will be placed upon her which will compromise her identity.

- Many of Bishop's images depict an intense concentration or contemplation of individual objects. *The Fish* exemplifies this characteristic. In this poem, Bishop describes the experience of catching and examining a fish. She begins by stating 'I caught a tremendous fish / and held him beside the boat / half out of water, with my hook / fast in a corner of his mouth'. She then describes the fish in detail and expresses her personal responses to it. By continuing to provide facts about the fish, she builds to the inevitable conclusion of releasing it back into the sea. Every minute detail in the imagery describes the process by which she arrives at the conclusion or her final action. This feature of style, where the poem builds to a conclusion or a question, is evident in many of her poems.

Contrast

- Many of Bishop's poems reveal their depths of insight by means of carefully chosen contrasts. In *In the Waiting Room*, there is a tension of opposites between that which is ordinary and that which is strange and unsettling. The dentist's waiting room, the people waiting, the clothing being worn, the child's approaching birthday are dramatically contrasted with the 'babies with pointed heads' and 'black, naked women with necks / wound round and round with wire'. There is a further contrast in the child's boredom and innocence when she entered the waiting room and the turmoil with which she leaves it. This is wonderfully symbolised in the image of the 'inside of a volcano' and the 'rivulets of fire'. Again, the poem builds image upon image to drive to her conclusion or to the questions which can only be half-answered or not answered at all.

- Contrast is also used to emphasise that which is known and that which is hidden. We see this in the poem *Sestina*. A warm, domestic scene of a child and her grandmother is powerfully contrasted with the underlying, unspoken sadness which permeates the entire scene. 'Tears' recur in almost every image in the poem – the grandmother 'hides her tears'; the child is watching the 'teakettle's small, hard tears'; the teacup is 'full of dark brown tears'; even the child's drawing shows a man in a coat with 'buttons like tears'. This hidden sorrow is contrasted with the act which the grandmother engages in to protect the child. She is 'laughing and talking' and telling the child 'It's time for tea'. Such use of contrast is both dramatically powerful and profoundly poignant.

Variety of Verse forms

- Although Bishop was not particularly attracted to formal verse patterns, her work displays a variety of structural forms. *The Fish*, *At the Fishhouses*, *Questions of Travel* etc. are all examples of free verse while *Sestina* is an example of an intricate form, of the same name, consisting of six stanzas of six lines and a concluding tercet (three-line stanza). The six final words of the first stanza are repeated in a different order in each of the remaining five stanzas and also in the final tercet. This very tight, structured form reflects superbly the strict control of emotion which exists in that poem, despite the enormity of suffering which underlies the surface.

• Lines with three stresses, or trimester patterns are often employed by Bishop. This gives rise to what look like long, skinny poems on the page. An example of this is *The Armadillo* and a similar metrical pattern is apparent in *The Fish*.

Sample Answer

The poetry of Elizabeth Bishop: A Personal Response

What I most admire about the poetry of Elizabeth Bishop is its combination of precise, imaginative description and thought-provoking insight. The poet closely observes and vividly describes the world around her. Her famous eye for detail and original imagery give her poetry a strong visual quality, drawing the reader into the world she describes. However, what makes her poetry particularly appealing is her desire to probe beneath the surface of things. We see how close observation leads the poet to inner reflection and moments of insight. These moments of insight, often dramatic and always interesting, help us all to better understand the world in which we live. Her poetry is rooted in personal experience, but has a genuine universal appeal.

I enjoyed *The Fish* for its unusual imagery, detailed description and uplifting epiphany (moment of insight). We are drawn into the poem by the first person narrative: 'I caught a tremendous fish'. The poet's respect for the fish is immediately conveyed – he is 'battered and venerable and homely'. A domestic simile helps us to visualise this huge, ancient fish, while evoking a sense of comfortable familiarity: 'his brown skin hung in strips / like ancient wallpaper'. Imaginative similes conjure up an image of the inside of the fish – his flesh is 'packed in like feathers', while his swim-bladder is 'like a big peony' (a large flower). An interesting shift in the poem occurs when the poet looks into the fish's eyes and begins to engage with him. Observation leads to reflection. The poet empathises (identifies) with the fish when she observes the five hooks that had 'grown firmly in his mouth'. Like the poet, I admired this fish for surviving the trials and tribulations of life. It is at this point that the poet achieves a moment of insight. The hooks are 'like medals with their ribbons / frayed and wavering', suggesting that the poet now sees this ancient survivor as a war veteran. This is a wonderful comparison. This ancient fish is an apt (suitable) symbol for the resilience (strength) of the human spirit and for our capacity to survive the vicissitudes (varying fortunes) of life. This insight has an uplifting effect on the poet and indeed on the reader. I particularly like the optimistic image with which the poem ends: 'until everything / was rainbow, rainbow, rainbow!' Having achieved victory through endurance, the fish deserves to be released.

The poet's powers of observation and description, as well as her remarkable ability to achieve insight through reflecting on ordinary, everyday experiences are again evident in *Filling Station*. The conversational tone draws us into the poem: 'Oh, but it is dirty!' The image of an 'overall black translucency' perfectly conveys the sense of overwhelming filth. The poet closely observes every aspect of the 'oil-soaked' station, even noticing how the father's monkey suit 'cuts him under the arms'. Her close observation of the unlikely domestic world that she encounters here sets her thinking: 'Why the extraneous plant? / Why the taboret? / Why, oh why the doily?' (her eye for detail is such that she even notices that the doily is 'embroidered in daisy stitch'). These questions reflect the poet's admirable curiosity to understand the reality that lies behind external appearances. Again we see how reflection leads to insight. The poet realises that some unseen person (probably a woman) has done her best to create some semblance of domestic order in a world of grime: 'Somebody waters the plant, /or oils it, maybe' (one of several lovely touches of humour in the poem). Even the oil cans are neatly arranged so as to soothe the fraught nerves of stressed drivers. I enjoyed the poet's clever use of personification as well as the repetition of the soothing 'so' sound: 'they softly say: / ESSO–SO–SO–SO / to high-strung automobiles'. The poet concludes that there is always someone doing their best to quietly improve the quality of our lives: 'Somebody loves us all'. As in *The Fish*, poet and reader are uplifted by a very positive, reassuring insight into human life. The human ability to rise above the ugliness of life means that beauty and love are to be found in the most unlikely places. I like the way Bishop reflects on a personal experience to discover an uplifting universal truth.

The Armadillo is also remarkable for its vivid descriptions, original images and moment of insight. Bishop is struck by the delicate beauty of the fire balloons which the Brazilian people released in honour of Saint John: 'the paper chambers flush and fill with light'. A well-chosen metaphor helps us to picture a constellation of stars: 'they steer between / the kite-sticks of the Southern Cross'. However, for all their beauty and romance, the fire balloons' possess a terrifying destructive capacity, which the poet vividly conveys with the image of an exploding 'egg of fire'. The armadillo is described with typical precision: 'a glistening armadillo left the scene, / rose-flecked, head-down, tail-down'. The poet's observant eye takes in every aspect of the scene, even noticing that a baby rabbit is 'short-eared, to our surprise'. The moment of insight occurs in the concluding stanza as the poet becomes aware of man's unthinking destructiveness. The fire balloons remind her of falling bombs, while the helpless animals come to symbolise all of the innocent victims of war and oppression. The seemingly tough and independent armadillo is pathetically vulnerable. I was struck by the closing image of 'a weak mailed fist / clenched ignorant against the sky' because it powerfully underscores humanity's vulnerability to forces of destruction. Here the poet offers us another thought-provoking, if grim, insight into the reality of life.

First Death in Nova Scotia describes a child's attempts to come to terms with her first experience of death. It is particularly poignant because we see the world through the eyes of an innocent, confused child. Even as a child Bishop was sharply observant, taking in every aspect of the cold parlour, including the old chromographs and the stuffed loon. The description of the lifeless loon as 'cold and caressable' effectively conveys the child's confusion when confronted by death. Bishop's images are typically imaginative: the marble-topped table becomes the loon's 'white, frozen lake', while Arthur's coffin is 'a little frosted cake'. The simile comparing little Arthur to 'a doll that hadn't been painted yet' is very moving, highlighting, as it does, the tragedy of a child's death. Through closely observing and reflecting on the situation in which she finds herself, the young Bishop gets a sense of the terrible finality of death. The child tries to come up with a happy, fairytale ending to this tragic happening by imagining that the royal figures 'invited Arthur to be / the smallest page at court'. However, she sadly concludes that her lifeless cousin, trapped in the embrace of death and 'clutching his tiny lilly' will be unable to travel 'roads deep in snow'. It is the child's perspective on death which makes this poem both interesting and poignant.

In the Waiting Room is another poem rooted in a childhood experience. What makes this poem particularly interesting is the manner in which it portrays the dawning of adult awareness in the young Elizabeth Bishop. Once again, the use of the first person and the conversational tone draw us into the poem: 'I went with Aunt Consuelo / to keep her dentist's appointment'. Again we see that, even as a child, the poet was very alert to the world around her: 'The waiting room / was full of grown-up people, / arctics and overcoats, / lamps and magazines.' The images in *National Geographic* introduce the child to a wider, frightening world, with the poet using a memorable simile to convey the appalling self-mutilation of African women: 'necks / wound round and round with wire / like the necks of light bulbs.' The image of their 'horrifying' breasts suggests the suffering involved in bearing and raising children. It is interesting to again observe how outer description leads to inner reflection. The poet's identification with the suffering of other women is suggested by the strange sense she has of her aunt's cry of pain coming from her own mouth: 'Without thinking at all / I was my foolish aunt.' Bishop comes to sense that all women are united in suffering. It is the inevitability of this female suffering that 'held us all together / or made us all just one.' This poem is again both wonderfully descriptive and strikingly insightful. While the poet is aware of her own individuality, it is as if all women fuse into one because of their shared suffering: 'But I felt: you are an *I*, / you are an *Elizabeth*, / you are one of *them*'. Poet and reader alike are challenged by a dramatic insight which suggests that individual identity is less important than gender in the shaping of a woman's destiny.

The Prodigal also combines detailed, imaginative description with memorable insight. The detailed description of the sty plastered 'with glass-smooth dung' effectively conveys the degradation of the prodigal or alcoholic who now lives at the level of an animal. However, the prodigal's enduring humanity (he feels a degree of affection for the cannibalistic sow) as well as his appreciation of beauty ('the sunrise glazed the barnyard mud with red') suggests that we all have the capacity to rise above the ugliness of life and grow as people. We are reassured by the poem's positive message that no one is beyond redemption: 'But it took him a long time / finally to make up his mind to go home.'

To conclude, I enjoyed Bishop's poetry particularly because of its moments of insight – her ability to probe beneath outer appearances and discover universal truths is very impressive. In terms of her style, I was struck by her remarkably vivid descriptions, and unusual similes and metaphors.

Sylvia Plath

Biographical Note

Sylvia Plath (1932–1963) was born in Boston Massachusetts. Her father, Otto, was a professor of entomology and her mother, Aurelia, also had an academic background. From the beginning it was apparent that Sylvia was a very intelligent, gifted child. She had her first poem published when she was eight years old. Her early childhood was happy, but the death of her father when she was eight had a profound effect on her. She was an outstanding student in secondary school and enjoyed some success as a writer before she had completed this phase of her formal education. In 1950 she won a scholarship to the prestigious Smith College. Her writing talent was widely recognised and she continued to have her work published. In the summer of 1952 Plath worked in New York as a guest editor for the popular *Mademoiselle* magazine. Self-obsessed and ambitious, Plath was prone to violent mood swings and depression. When she returned from New York she was exhausted and depressed. Her failure to win a place on a Harvard summer course run by Frank O'Connor saw her plunge into a black depression. The electric shock treatment that followed only served to exacerbate Plath's mental problems and she subsequently attempted suicide.

After recovering her health, Plath finished her degree at Smith College and went on to win a scholarship to study at Cambridge. It was here that she met Ted Hughes, a handsome, emerging young poet. They fell in love and married in 1956. After completing her studies at Cambridge, Plath taught for a period at her old university, Smith College, before the couple returned to London. Shortly afterwards, her first child, Frieda, was born. The following year they moved to Devon, where Plath went on to write some of her best known poems. In 1962 Plath gave birth to a second child, Nicholas.

Through all of this time Plath continued to wrestle with her inner demons. Her relationship with Hughes was a volatile one and their marriage grew more fraught, with the two eventually separating that autumn. This was a very difficult period for Plath (her letters to her mother reflect her growing desperation during this period), but she continued to write prolifically, producing intensely personal poems. It is ironic that she produced some of her greatest work when she was at such a spiritual and psychological low. At the end of 1962 Plath returned to London where one of the coldest winters on record combined with the problems associated with moving house exacerbated the depression which was a recurring feature of her life. Eventually, overwhelmed by her personal problems, Plath took her own life in February 1963. Her life, poetry and controversial death continue to be the subject of heated debate. While it is inevitable that her suicide should overshadow Plath's poetry, the tendency to view her work primarily in relation to her tragic death is simplistic. Her unique poetic voice is among the most distinctive of modern times.

When reading the poetry of Plath watch out for the following:

- The landscape of Plath's poetry is that of her own mind. She **looks inward** to explore her own emotions and thoughts.
- Her poetry can be life **affirming and positive** but is more **often dark and despairing**.
- **Symbolism** is fundamental to her work and this can create poems which are **obscure** and capable of **different interpretations**.
- Plath deals with issues of **identity**. Her poem *Mirror* is particularly relevant to this theme.
- The desire for **escape** and the conflict between a sense of **imprisonment** and **fear of freedom** are also major themes in her poems.
- An interest in the **role of women** in society, particularly as artists, is central to some of the poems.

Black Rook in Rainy Weather

This poem has to do with the business of writing poetry and with the often lengthy wait for poetic inspiration. The poet is out walking in a rain-drenched landscape struggling to find the inventive spark that is fundamental to the creative process. The gloomy-sounding title suggests the poet's personal gloom. The poem opens with a clear description of a rook perched in a tree, 'On the stiff twig up there / Hunches a wet black rook / Arranging and rearranging its feathers in the rain'. Resigned to her unproductive state, Plath does 'not expect a miracle' to set this commonplace sight 'on fire / In my eye'. In other words, she does not anticipate a flash of inspiration igniting her poetic imagination, enabling her to transform the everyday natural scene before her. Plath does not expect to discover a plan ('some design') in the unstable weather or some sign ('portent') in the falling leaves.

Expecting is one thing, desiring quite another. Plath sometimes yearns to establish a connection and achieve some communication with the world of nature, 'I admit, I desire / Occasionally, some backtalk / From the mute sky'. While Plath's expectations may be low, she remains hopeful of being struck with inspiration by some aspect of the everyday world, 'A certain minor light may still / Lean incandescent / Out of kitchen table or chair'. Inspiration is associated with light and fire because it illuminates and transfigures aspects of the everyday world. Inspiration is seen as a type of heavenly force ('a celestial burning') that can make the dullest things ('the most obtuse objects') special, and an insignificant moment sacred, 'Thus hallowing an interval / Otherwise inconsequent'. The mood of the poem is much more positive at this point.

Walking on in the rainy weather, Plath waits warily for the magical bolt of inspiration to strike her. She does not want to miss it if it should occur – 'for it could happen / Even in this dull, ruinous landscape'. The magic and beauty of the moment of inspiration is captured in the metaphor of an angel flaring suddenly at her elbow. Plath acknowledges that nature may yet inspire her, 'I only know that a rook / Ordering its black feathers can so shine / As to seize my senses, haul / My eyelids up …'. The dramatic nature of the moment of inspiration is suggested when the poet speaks of the bird seizing her senses, while the struggle for inspiration is evoked by the phrase 'haul'.

Plath longs for 'A brief respite from fear / Of total neutrality'. Put simply, she yearns for some relief from her fear of artistic barrenness. All artists dread a lack of inspiration and it is a common poetic theme. The 'season / Of fatigue' is a phrase suggestive of the poet's creative exhaustion, yet she remains stubbornly hopeful, 'Miracles occur'. Plath knows that inspiration is inherently 'spasmodic' and she waits patiently for the angel of inspiration to descend on her, 'The wait's begun again / The long wait for the angel / For that rare, random descent'.

KEY POINTS

- Key theme is the struggle for inspiration.
- Plath's dark view of life is suggested by a series of negative adjectives ('wet', 'black', 'desultory', 'mute', 'obtuse', 'wary', 'dull', 'ruinous' 'sceptical', 'ignorant') as well as verbs ('hunches', 'fall', 'trekking', 'haul', 'wait').
- The bleak physical world (suggested by such images as 'the desultory weather', 'this dull, ruinous landscape', etc.) is contrasted with the bright, optimistic world of inspiration (evoked by images of fire and light such as a flaring angel and the rook's shining feathers).
- Religious terminology ('miracle', 'hallowing', 'celestial', 'angel') suggests the spiritual

nature of inspiration.

- The language combines the everyday ('Although, I admit ...', 'I can't honestly complain', 'If you care to ...') and the archaic ('portent', 'hallowing', 'largesse'). The effect is to take the ordinary moment and to transform it into something extraordinary and powerful – even something holy!

- Notice the effective use of repetition. The repetition of 'fall' suggests inevitability – things have gone beyond their prime and she cannot do anything about that. The effect is a sense of powerlessness Plath is renowned for her skilful use of imagery which conveys the theme and tone of the poem vividly to the reader. *Black Rook in Rainy Weather* provides a perfect example of this feature of style. Her use of richly sensuous images engages the reader and involves them in the experience. We see the black rook as he 'Hunches' on a stiff twig and the 'spotted leaves'; we feel the wetness and discomfort as the rook is 'Arranging and rearranging its feathers in the rain'; we can almost feel the impact of 'haul' and 'seize' as the 'incandescent' light shines.

The Times Are Tidy

In this poem Plath passes comment on contemporary American society. She does this by juxtaposing the excitement, adventure and mystery of the fairy-tale world with the monotony, dullness and smugness of the consumerist world in which she lives. Plath is reflecting on American culture in the 1950s, an era of increasing materialism and political uniformity (the paranoia engendered by Senator McCarthy meant that few were prepared to challenge the political status quo). The title suggests the idea of an ordered, conformist society where nothing 'untidy' or out of the ordinary occurs.

The opening stanza implies that contemporary society is no place for heroism: 'Unlucky the hero born / In this province of the stuck record'. This image evokes a world that is unimaginative and boring. This is a world where the 'most watchful cooks go jobless'. The precise meaning of this image is unclear. Perhaps 'watchful cooks' refers to those who would dare to dissent from or criticise the values of the ruling regime. Such critics would have been 'jobless' after being blacklisted as communists or communist sympathisers. The image of the mayor's roasting spit ('rôtisserie') turning 'of its own accord' suggests the idea of a political regime that grinds on in its own interest. An alternative reading

suggests that unemployment is the result of increasing mechanisation. More generally, the cooking/eating image evokes a society that is self-absorbed and smug.

Unlike the world of fairy-tale and legend where heroic knights battle dragons, no adventurer could make a career for himself in the modern world: 'There's no career in the venture / Of riding against the lizard'. Modern-day cynicism leaves no room for mystery or romance – the dragon is 'Himself withered these latter-days / To leaf-size from lack of action'. When Plath declares that 'History's beaten the hazard', she implies that the modern world is safer, but unexciting.

This idea is underlined in the third stanza which refers to the burning of the last witch, 'The last crone got burnt up / More than eight decades back'. With her went all sense of mystery and magic ('the love-hot herb, the talking cat'). The closing lines are ironic in tone, 'But the children are better for it / The cow milks cream an inch thick'. Plath clearly does not believe that riches and luxury compensate for the loss of a sense of mystery and the disappearance of a spirit of adventure. Material wealth is no compensation for spiritual poverty.

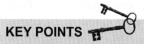

Morning Song

This deeply personal poem describes Plath's feelings following the birth of Frieda, her first child. The opening line points out that the child was conceived in love, 'Love set you going like a fat gold watch'. This unusual simile suggests that the new baby is precious and the moment of her birth golden. It also reminds us that the child has entered the world of time, a world where transience and mortality are unalterable realities. The image of the midwife slapping the baby's footsoles evokes the harshness of this world. The baby's 'bald cry' declares that she has now assumed her place in the wider world, 'Took its place among the elements'.

The atmosphere in stanza two is cold and the tone strangely detached. The naked child is a 'New statue. / In a drafty museum'. This striking metaphor suggests that the child is unique and precious, while also conveying her vulnerability in a cold ('drafty') world. Plath feels helpless to protect her child, 'We stand round blankly as walls'. She seems to feel separated from her child after she leaves the world of the womb and takes her place in the universe.

The detached tone is sustained in stanza three. The reader is startled by the astonishingly cold-sounding words with which this stanza opens, 'I'm no more your mother ...'. However, the rest of this sentence indicates that Plath is simply acknowledging the reality that the passage of time will inevitably alter her relationship with her child, 'Than the cloud that distills a mirror to reflect its own slow / Effacement at the wind's hand'. Just as the pool created by the cloud witnesses ('reflects') the disintegration of the cloud, so too will the child witness the demise of the mother. Again, this stanza is dominated by a sense of estrangement and powerlessness.

There is a change of tone in stanza four. The image of the baby's 'moth-breath' flickering 'among the flat pink roses' underlines the fragility of the baby, while also suggesting her delicate beauty. The metaphor of 'a far sea' suggests how the baby's breathing sounds to her mother.

The closing stanzas portray the mother-child relationship as we might expect it to be depicted. The mood is one of happiness and contentment and the tone is affectionate. We see Plath as an attentive mother instantly responding to the child's cry, 'One cry, and I stumble from bed ...'. She describes herself in a self-deprecating (self-mocking) manner, 'cow-heavy and floral /

237

In my Victorian nightgown'. An unusual simile suggests how she marvels at, and delights in, the baby's every movement, 'Your mouth opens clean as a cat's'. The metaphor of the whitening window square suggests that it is dawn – the spreading light 'swallows' the 'dull stars'. The closing image is appropriately joyful as the baby experiments with her voice and her 'handful of notes …/ rise like balloons'.

What makes this poem interesting is Plath's portrayal of the different emotions experienced by a new mother. She vividly depicts the complexity of these emotions. The feelings of joy and affection expressed in stanzas one, four, five and six are juxtaposed with the sense of separation, powerlessness and gloom that dominates stanzas two and three. Plath's portrayal of the mother-child relationship is realistic and never sentimental.

KEY POINTS

- Key theme is the complex mother-child relationship. Despite her delight at the birth of her child, Plath feels a sense of insecurity in her role as a mother.
- Unusual, sometimes startling, imagery. The descriptions of the child as a 'fat gold watch' and as a 'New statue. / In a drafty museum' are unusual and thought-provoking.
- Tone varies from the detached to the affectionate. This corresponds to the poet's conflict of emotion on becoming a mother. The poem ends on a note of delight and hope as Plath experiences the natural bond between herself and her child.
- Contrast is effectively used. The infant's vulnerability and fragility contrast with the mother's clumsy heaviness: the baby's 'moth-breath / Flickers' , her 'clear vowels rise like balloons'. The mother, on the other hand, is portrayed as awkward and heavy: she stumbles 'cow-heavy', covered in a 'floral …Victorian nightgown'.
- Notice how the poet uses inanimate objects: 'watch...statue... walls... mirror... cloud' at the start of the poem, but gradually moves to living creatures: 'moth... cat... cow' while the last images are those of a mother and child.

Finisterre

In 1960 Plath and Hughes travelled through Brittany, spending some time on the coast. As the title indicates, this poem is based on the coastal landscape of Finisterre (which literally means 'the land's end'). As with all of Plath's landscape poems, it can be read literally or on a symbolic level. The sea is a central image in Plath's work – it is often associated with fear and death. The poem is highly descriptive. Plath's description of the outer, physical landscape tells us much about the inner landscape of the poet's mind. This is a dark, sinister poem, with the idea of death implicit throughout. At this time Plath was keenly aware and fearful of the

death and destruction caused by war. She was horrified to see the maimed veterans of the Algerian war who were convalescing at a nearby resort. In addition to this harrowing personal experience, tensions were running very high on the international front, with a very real danger that America and Russia would plunge the world into a catastrophic nuclear war. It is therefore unsurprising that feelings of fear and despair pervade this poem.

Stanza one vividly describes the rocky shoreline, the turbulent seas and the cliffs surrounding the bay known as the Bay of Death. The poem opens with a statement, 'This was the land's end'. Beyond this lies the world of the sea. The opening image is striking. The rugged rocks are compared to 'fingers, knuckled and rheumatic, / Cramped on nothing'. The cliffs are also personified, with Plath suggesting that they give warning ('Admonitory cliffs'). The sea – powerful, menacing and destructive – is portrayed as 'exploding' around the rocks. There is a sense of awe at the enormity of the sea – it has 'no bottom, or anything on the other side of it'. Here Plath uses hyperbole (exaggeration) to underscore the terrifying vastness of the sea. Drawing on the folklore surrounding this bay, the poet suggests that the sea spray is 'Whitened by the faces of the drowned'. Imagery of death dominates this stanza – the rocks are depicted as 'Leftover soldiers from old, messy wars'. The sea seems to be at war with the rocks as it 'cannons' into them. However, the personified rocks 'don't budge', while some 'hide their grudges under the water'. The atmosphere in the opening stanza is gloomy and threatening. The language has overwhelmingly negative connotations: 'Cramped', 'Admonitory', 'exploding', 'drowned', 'gloomy', 'dump', 'Leftover', 'messy wars', 'grudges'.

The dark, despondent mood continues into stanza two, with more images of death. The flowers (normally a symbol of beauty) on the cliff edge are described as having been embroidered by 'fingers … close to death'. The mists become a metaphor for the souls of the dead. The description of the sound of the sea as 'doom-noise' suggests that the souls of the dead (the many people who drowned in this area) are in a type of hell, doomed to forever remain in the sea. The idea of death and resurrection is introduced. In a surreal image, Plath suggests that the mists that cover the rocks give them new life: 'They bruise the rocks out of existence, then resurrect them'. The souls of the dead rise towards heaven, but are 'without hope'. Their sorrow is suggested by the simile that compares them to 'sighs'. The poet imagines herself walking among these souls.

The surreal imagery continues as she imagines them stuffing her mouth with cotton. The image of being stifled may be suggestive of Plath's fear of being stifled in a creative sense through lack of inspiration. This strange experience is distressing for the poet who is 'beaded with tears' after the lost souls free her.

Stanza three sees a change of focus as the poet turns her attention to the marble statue of the Virgin Mary. This is the statue of Our Lady of the Shipwrecked, but the marble figure offers no consolation to those who need comforting. She is portrayed as cold, remote and uncaring. She is described as 'striding toward the horizon', oblivious of those who pray to her – a marble sailor and a peasant woman in black. The closing line in this stanza is heavily ironic, the patron of sailors and of all lost at sea 'is in love with the beautiful formlessness of the sea'. She is drawn to the destructive force behind the shipwrecks she was erected to protect against.

There is another change of focus in stanza four, which presents us with a typical Breton seaside scene. This stanza is devoid of the darkness and gloom that dominated the poem up to this point. The peasants sell laces and postcards, as well as 'pretty trinkets' such as 'necklaces and toy ladies' made from shells. Significantly, these shells 'do not come from the Bay of the Dead down there, / But from another place, tropical and blue'. This image reminds us that while the sea can be massively destructive, it can also be beautiful and tranquil. Even the Bay of Death has its own jewellery box of delicate shells. The poem ends with the comforting image of the locals offering the poet crepes, 'Eat them before they blow cold'. There is a striking contrast in mood between stanzas one and four. In place of exploding waves and rocks with grudges, we have good-humoured, generous peasants. However, while the mood in the closing stanza is relaxed and cheerful, this remains an essentially dark poem dominated by feelings of fear and hopelessness.

KEY POINTS

- A dark poem dominated by the theme of death.
- Highly descriptive – striking imagery.
- A poem rich in symbolism and suggestion.
- Personification gives a human quality to the various aspects of the seascape that inspired the poem.
- Dark, despondent mood is conveyed by language that is predominantly negative: 'Cramped', 'exploding', 'dump', 'Leftover', 'cannons', 'doom', etc.
- Repeated long vowel sounds ('exploding', 'faces', 'drowned' 'gloomy', 'rolled', 'doom', etc.) also evoke the gloomy mood.
- Notice the irony in the description of Our Lady of the Shipwrecked. The statue is meant to care for the living who pray to her for support. However, she is 'in love with the beautiful formlessness of the sea'.
- Sound is used effectively to convey atmosphere. Harsh 'd', 'ck', 'k' and 'g' sounds create a mood of foreboding: 'admonitory', 'knuckled', 'gloomy', 'dump of rocks', 'budge', 'grudge'. Long vowel sounds: 'exploding', 'faces', 'drowned', 'gloomy', 'old' etc. slow down the rhythm and combined with the harsh consonants reflect the harsh and resonating sound of the sea.

Mirror

This is a dark poem which reflects on a number of inter-related themes: the inevitability of old age and death, our preoccupation with image and the search for identity. Looking at her work in general, Plath regularly endows inanimate objects with human qualities. In this poem the mirror is personified and speaks for itself, describing its relationship with a particular woman. Giving the mirror a voice gives the poem a sense of immediacy.

The mirror expresses itself in a clear, direct manner, 'I am silver and exact'. It reflects things exactly as they are. It does not pre-judge – it has 'no preconceptions'. It is without bias, ensuring that the image it reflects is 'unmisted' by any feelings, positive or negative. The mirror is cold and emotionless. While a person may be dissatisfied or even upset by their mirror image, the mirror insists, 'I am not cruel, only truthful'. When the mirror states that it immediately swallows whatever it sees, we are reminded of the inexorable passage of time. The image

captured by the mirror at a particular point in time will never be exactly the same again. When the mirror describes itself as 'the eye of a little god' it sounds arrogant, but what is being implied here is our obsession with ourselves – we worship at the mirror that reflects our image.

The mirror describes how it spends its days meditating on the opposite wall. The mirror has been reflecting this wall ('pink, with speckles') for so long that it feels the wall is now part of itself, 'I think it is a part of my heart'. Only darkness and people 'separate' the mirror from the wall. The phrase 'over and over' suggests the passing of time.

The second section of the poem is concerned with the mirror's relationship with the woman on whose bedroom wall it hangs. The mirror declares, 'Now I am a lake'. This metaphor is easily understood – the flat surface of a lake is reflective like a mirror. However, a lake has hidden depths, so this metaphor also has connotations of danger. The woman searches the depths of the mirror/lake 'for what she really is'. The woman seems to be struggling to discover her identity and find her way in life. There is a suggestion here that the mirror reflects more than outer physical appearance, that it reveals deeper realities. The woman 'turns to those liars, the candles or the moon' because their light has a softening effect on her reflection. However, the mirror 'faithfully' reflects the woman's image. The reference to 'tears and an agitation of hands' points to the woman's inner torment. The fact that the mirror is 'important to her' indicates her insecurity. It would seem that she is deeply troubled by the ageing process. The line 'She comes and goes' again reminds us of the passing of time, with one day inexorably rolling into the next. The mirror seems glad to see the woman at the start of every day, 'Each morning it is her face that replaces the darkness'. The phrase 'each morning' is another reminder of the passage of time and of the importance of the mirror to the woman.

The closing lines are particularly dramatic. The lake metaphor is developed, with the mirror/lake describing how the woman has 'drowned a young girl' in its depths, while watching old age daily rise towards her 'like a terrible fish'. Day by day the mirror has recorded the ageing of the woman, witnessing her anguish. The closing image is startling and a little disturbing in its depiction of old age as an ugly, monstrous creature waiting in the depths for us all.

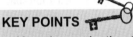

KEY POINTS

- Key theme is the transitory (passing/impermanent) nature of youth and the fears associated with growing old.

- Use of startling imagery can be seen in the poem. Some images are surprising in their imaginative quality and symbolism: the image of the mirror as 'the eye of a little god' which then becomes 'a lake', 'In me she has drowned a young girl, and in me an old woman / Rises toward her day after day, like a terrible fish'.

- Apart from the major image of the mirror in the poem of the same name, there are several symbols in the poem. The image of the woman who 'bends over' the lake, symbolises the human search for truth despite the horror of the reality. The 'candles' and the 'moon' symbolise dishonesty and self-deception. The 'terrible fish' symbolises the inevitable arrival of old age and death.

- Contrast is also evident. The mirror is honest – 'I am not cruel, only truthful'. This is contrasted with 'those liars, the candles or the moon'. Light is contrasted with darkness – 'it flickers. / Faces and darkness separate us over and over'; 'Each morning it is her face that replaces the darkness'. The 'young girl' is contrasted with 'an old woman'. The 'exact', 'four-cornered' two-dimensional mirror is contrasted with the 'lake', which has depth and hidden horror.

- The personification of the mirror gives the poem a sense of immediacy, enabling this inanimate object to speak directly to the reader.

- A very dark poem – the woman's world is dismal, cold and loveless.

Pheasant

This poem evokes and celebrates the special beauty of the pheasant. Upbeat in mood, it reflects Plath's appreciation of the natural world. The poem opens in a dramatic manner with the poet urgently pleading with another person not to kill the pheasant as he said he would, 'Do not kill it'. Plath goes on to give a variety of reasons why the pheasant should be allowed to live. She is still taken aback by the bird's presence, 'The jut of that odd, dark head, pacing / Through the uncut grass on the elm's hill'. Watching the bird fills her with pleasure. She is proud that the pheasant is on her land; indeed, she feels privileged to be graced with a visit from this special bird, 'It is something to own a pheasant / Or just to be visited at all'.

Plath insists that she does not view the bird in any kind of 'mystical' way. She is not pleading for it to be spared because she believes that it has a spirit. Instead, the pheasant has 'a right' to live because it fits so naturally and harmoniously into its present environment, 'It is simply in its element'. She believes that the bird possesses 'a kingliness'. She recalls how, the previous winter, it left its signature on their garden, 'The print of its big foot .../ The trail-track, on the snow in our court'. The word 'court' suggests that the bird has a legitimate right to be where it is.

The poet recollects how she marvelled at the beauty of the bird's bright colours set against the whiteness of the snow, 'The wonder of it, in that pallor'. She remembers the contrast between the pheasant's distinctive trail-track and the footprints of the other birds ('crosshatch of sparrow and starling'). She values the bird in 'its rareness', telling the person who had intended killing it, 'It is rare'. Despite its rareness, she declares that 'a dozen would be worth having' and imagines that 'A hundred ...– green and red / Crossing and recrossing' the hill would be 'a fine thing!'. Green and red are colours symbolic of life and vitality.

Plath delights in the pheasant's fine shape and richly coloured plumage, 'It is such a good shape, so vivid'. Abundant with beauty, the bird is a source of inspiration, 'It's a little cornucopia'. The pheasant 'unclaps' its wings, whose colour is captured in the simile 'brown as a leaf'. The idea of the bird fitting naturally into this environment is underlined in the closing lines, 'Settles in the elm, and is easy./ It was sunning in the narcissi'. Far from the bird being out-of-place, it is Plath who feels like an intruder, 'I trespass stupidly'. The final words echo the urgency of the opening lines, 'Let be, let be'. This repeated plea is directed at the person whom the poet addressed in the opening lines.

KEY POINTS

- Clear, direct statements reflect the poet's sense of conviction, 'It startles me still...It is rare...It is such a good shape...It's a little cornucopia'.
- The opening is dramatic in its intensity, particularly in the repeated use of the word 'kill'.
- Vivid, detailed description. Plath captures an image of the pheasant in a few words – 'green and red', which evoke the pheasant's vitality, 'a good shape', 'so vivid', 'a little cornucopia', 'brown as a leaf'.
- The personal voice of the narrator is a dominant presence. She invites us to share the experience with her.
- Short dramatic injunctions (commands) convey a sense of urgency, 'Do not kill it . . . Let be, let be'.

Elm

This is an intensely personal poem concerned with the theme of psychological suffering. There are two voices in the poem: that of the personified elm and of the woman she addresses. At times it is very difficult to distinguish between these two voices because they seem to merge, with the suffering of the elm and that of the female persona reflective of each other. The elm and the woman seem to share a common psychological identity and both can be identified with the poet herself.

As in many of Plath's poems, an inanimate object – in this instance an elm tree – is personified. It is the voice of the elm that we hear in the opening lines of the poem, 'I know the bottom … I know it with my great tap root'. Typical of much of Plath's poetry, the poetic voice is clearly troubled. The image of the tap root journeying deep into the earth may symbolise the individual journeying deep into his/her psyche. The elm knows what it is like to hit a type of mental and emotional rock bottom, to plumb the depths of depression and despair. The elm knowledgeably declares that it is this extreme state that the woman fears.

The elm asks if the sound of the wind blowing through its branches reminds the woman of the sound of the sea (in Plath's poetry the sea is an image commonly suggestive of threat and destruction), or of 'the voice of nothing', which was the cause of previous periods of insanity. It seems that the woman's despair was caused by disappointment in love. Love is described as 'a shadow' that you 'cry after'. The shadow image suggests that love is unreal. It may also imply that love has a darkening effect on the woman's life. Love has seemingly abandoned this woman, 'Listen, these are its hooves: it has gone off, like a horse'. The taunting voice of the elm is coldly insensitive to the woman's anguish. The world of this poem, similar to that of *Mirror* and *Finisterre* is bleak and harsh. At this point the elm becomes the galloping horse, telling the woman that it will continue to gallop away until her head is numb, 'Till your head is a stone, your

pillow a little turf'. This is a world that offers no comfort or consolation to the sorrowful woman. The repeated long 'o' sound in 'echoing, echoing' underscores the sense of loneliness and gloom that pervades the poem. This phrase suggests that the woman's anguish will not be short-lived because the sound of loneliness will continue echoing through her mind.

In stanzas 5-9 the elm describes the various forms of suffering it has endured. It has been tormented by the rain, the sun, the wind and the moon. The tree continues to taunt the woman, 'Or shall I bring you the sound of poisons?' This is possibly a reference to the sound of falling acid rain. The idea of a polluted environment is developed when the elm speaks of 'fruit … like arsenic'. The imagery in these stanzas evokes a post nuclear war landscape. With the Cold War intensifying, the threat of such a conflict was very real and preyed on Plath's mind. The elm describes how it has been 'Scorched' by sunsets, 'My red filaments burn and stand'. The metaphor of 'a hand of wires' perfectly captures the idea of the elm's parched, withered branches. Once again, this image has connotations of a nuclear disaster. It can also be related to Plath's personal experience of the electric shock treatment she received for her depression. The elm next describes the destruction done to it by the violence of the wind, 'Now I break up in pieces that fly about like clubs'. Again, a violent wind is associated with the immediate aftermath of a nuclear explosion. The tree finds the suffering unbearable, 'I must shriek'. The elm is also tormented by the moon, which is portrayed as 'merciless'. The moon, like the sun, scorches the tree with its light, 'Her radiance scathes me'. The elm wonders if, instead of being dragged involuntarily, it has captured the cruel moon in its branches. Repetition conveys a sense of urgency, 'I let her go. I let her go'. The barren moon is compared to a barren woman, 'Diminished and flat as after radical surgery'. The elm now declares that its sufferings are attributable to the woman, 'How your bad dreams possess and endow me'. Since the elm's fears have been transferred onto it by the woman, then clearly the fears expressed by the elm are also those of the woman.

From this point on, the elm and the woman are speaking in one voice. The speaker feels 'inhabited' by some dark presence symbolised by a bird of prey. The fact that 'Nightly it flaps out, / Looking with its hooks, for something to love' underlines the speaker's loneliness. Like an owl, this threatening presence is most active at night, conjuring up images of troubled, sleepless nights. The speaker is 'terrified by this dark thing' that sleeps within her. The image of an evil, predatory bird is developed, 'All day I feel its soft, feathery turnings, its malignity'. This 'dark thing' within the speaker refers to the dark, destructive side of her nature, which she fears she cannot control. The idea that the woman's pain is caused by lost love is again suggested by the description of passing clouds as 'the faces of love, those pale irretrievables'. The cloud image suggests that love is frail and transitory.

The poem concludes with a nightmarish image of a 'murderous' face in the elm's branches. This terrifying face is the dark side of the speaker's personality. The reference to 'snaky acids' indicates that the speaker is aware of the highly dangerous nature of her own dark, despairing thoughts. Such imaginings paralyse with fear ('It petrifies the will') and are, potentially, deadly. The closing line is particularly grim, 'These are the isolate, slow faults / That kill, that kill, that kill'. The poet is terrified that her inherent weaknesses could literally kill her.

KEY POINTS

- Key theme is the speaker's inner torment which makes this a deeply personal poem.
- The poem is a very good example of a more open, free style. It moves away from the very controlled form of her earlier poems thus adding to the sense of honesty and sincerity.
- Rhythm and rhyme are important. The poem is written in tercets (three-line stanzas) with no attempt at a rhyming scheme. The lines are free-flowing and varied in length which brings them closer to the natural rhythms of speech.
- Although rhyme is not used there is extraordinary sound quality in the poem. The poet uses internal rhyme: 'lie and cry', 'burn and stand, a hand of wires'; assonance: 'sleeps in me', 'inhabited by a cry / Nightly it flaps out'; alliteration: 'hooves...like a horse', 'moon is ...merciless'; repetition: 'Echoing, echoing', 'That kill, that kill, that kill'.
- Again, an inanimate object is given human qualities – at times it is hard to distinguish between the voice of the personified elm and that of the female persona it addresses.
- A complex poem rich in imagery and symbolism.
- Much of the language is simple and direct ('Love is a shadow', 'I am terrified by this dark thing', etc).
- A dark poem that conveys a nightmare world ('poisons', 'suffered', 'burn', 'violence', 'shriek', 'scathes', 'terrified', 'malignity', 'murderous', 'strangle', 'snaky', 'kill').
- Much of the language is simple and direct ('Love is a shadow', 'I am terrified by this dark thing', etc).
- A dark poem that conveys a nightmare world ('poisons', 'suffered', 'burn', 'violence', 'shriek', 'scathes', 'terrified', 'malignity', 'murderous', 'strangle'. 'snaky', 'kill').

Poppies in July

While the title suggests a joyful poem about the beauty of nature in summer, it proves to be misleading in its positive connotations. This poem is concerned with the speaker's inner turmoil. The voice of the poetic persona is clearly troubled. The opening metaphor sets the tone for the dark poem that follows, 'Little poppies, little hell flames'. The flowers are immediately associated with evil. The question the speaker addresses to the poppies implies that they can be dangerous, 'Do you do no harm?'. The fire image is developed with the observation that they 'flicker'. This suggests that the movement of the dancing red flowers resembles that of a flickering fire. The image of the speaker putting her hands 'among the flames' is disturbing because it seems to point to a self-destructive tendency. While flowers often inspire, watching the dancing poppies 'exhausts' the speaker. For her the poppies only have negative connotations – as the next image which compares them to 'A mouth just bloodied' and 'Little bloody skirts!' underlines. The image of the bloodied mouth startles the reader in its linking of the poppies with physical violence. It is certainly unsettling to see beautiful flowers being associated with violence and bloodshed.

Having reflected on the physical appearance of the flowers, the speaker now focuses on the drug (opium) produced by them. She wishes for the tranquillising effect of the drug, 'Where are your opiates, your nauseous capsules?'. It is a measure of the speaker's desperation for some avenue of escape from her world that she longs for the drug even though she knows it is sickening. It seems that violence or sleep are preferable to her present state, 'If I could bleed, or sleep'. Having described the poppy as 'A mouth just bloodied', the speaker's wish to experience pain is expressed in an extraordinary manner, 'If my mouth could marry a hurt like that!'. The glass capsule image ('Or your liquors seep to me, in this glass capsule') suggests her isolation from the world. It is also suggestive of a sense of stifling confinement. In the closing lines the speaker expresses her longing for the 'dulling and stilling' properties of opium. Exhausted from watching the energetic red poppies, she yearns for oblivion, for an inert world devoid of colour ('colourless. Colourless'). The contrast between the lively, brightly coloured flowers and the drowsy, colourless world for which the speaker longs is marked. Given that sleep is closely associated with death, the closing lines of the poem could be interpreted as a death wish.

KEY POINTS

- Key theme is the speaker's longing to escape from her world. It reflects a struggle. The vividness and movement of the flowers make the speaker feel as though she lacks energy and vitality.
- An intensely personal poem. The imagery reveals a sense of deep pain: 'hell flames', 'mouth just bloodied', 'bloody skirts'. This is so intense that the speaker longs for annihilation. There is a dark, despairing mood.
- Sharp contrast between the vividness and vitality of the flowers and the dull, lethargic world for which the speaker longs.

The Arrival of the Bee Box

Plath's father was a bee-keeping expert, writing two highly regarded books on the subject. In 1962, Plath and her husband decided to take up bee-keeping. This poem describes the speaker's unusual response to the arrival of a box of bees. It is a poem that can also be read on a symbolic level.

The poem opens in a straightforward, narrative-like manner, 'I ordered this, this clean wood box'. While the simile describing the box as being 'square as a chair' is comfortably domestic, the metaphor that follows is strange and unsettling, 'I would say it was the coffin of a midget / Or a square baby'. This image is suggestive of death and deformity, giving the box a sinister quality. The speaker is immediately struck by the noise emanating from the box, 'Were there not such a din in it'.

The speaker has an ambivalent attitude towards the box, being both fascinated and frightened by it, 'The box is locked, it is dangerous . . . / And I can't keep away from it'. Her inability to see into the box heightens her curiosity. The description of the box evokes a sense of claustrophobia, 'There are no windows . . . / . . . no exit'.

This sense of claustrophobia is reinforced by the startling, surreal imagery that follows. Peering in the little grid, the speaker senses the oppressive atmosphere within the box. Repetition emphasises the darkness of the box, underlining the sinister, threatening atmosphere, 'It is dark, dark ... / Black on black'. A grotesque image portrays the bees as African slaves, '... the swarmy feeling of African hands / Minute and shrunk for export'. The 'angrily clambering' bees are viewed as aggressive and menacing.

It is the noise generated by the bees that most horrifies the speaker, 'It is the noise that appalls me most of all'. The simile that compares the bees to a Roman mob suggests that she is in awe but terrified of their collective power, 'It is like a Roman mob / Small, taken one by one, but my

god, together!' The description of their buzzing as 'furious Latin' suggests their incomprehensible anger. The speaker feels that she cannot control them, 'I am not a Caesar'. The image of 'a box of maniacs' underscores the idea of something uncontrollable. The speaker comforts herself with the thought that, since she is the owner, they 'can be sent back' or 'They can die' if she chooses to 'feed them nothing'.

The speaker shows her more compassionate side when she wonders how hungry the bees are. Becoming more confident, she wonders what would happen if she simply released them, 'I wonder if they would forget me / If I just undid the locks and stood back and turned into a tree'. (This image relates to the Greek myth of Daphne being turned into a tree after pleading with the gods to help her escape from Apollo.) The reference to the laburnum and cherry trees (whose beauty is captured in a memorable image, 'There is the laburnum, its blond colonnades, / And the petticoats of the cherry') suggests the bees' natural environment. There is a sharp contrast between the confinement of the box and the freedom of the natural world.

By the close of the poem the speaker no longer feels so threatened, 'They might ignore me immediately . . . /I am no source of honey / So why should they turn on me?' Feeling newly empowered, the speaker decides to exercise her power in a positive way, 'Tomorrow I will be sweet God, I will set them free / The box is only temporary'.

This poem can also be read on a symbolic level. The bee box may be regarded as a symbol of the poet's unconscious mind, and the angry threatening bees as symbols of the dark, destructive aspects of her own personality. This symbolic reading suggests that Plath was afraid of exploring the depths of her psyche because this would involve unleashing the terrifying demons lurking there.

KEY POINTS

- Effective use of simile/metaphor. The bee box itself is concrete, solid, plain: a 'clean wood box', 'Square as a chair' and heavy. However, it has sinister connotations: it could be the 'coffin of a midget / Or a square baby' suggesting death and distortion. It is 'dangerous' and she cannot escape from it but must live with it overnight.

- The bee box can also be seen as a metaphor for imprisonment or repression. The poet feels that she is in some way a captive. Perhaps she feels that she is 'boxed-in' by the expectations of those around her.

- The bees may be seen as the interior life of the speaker, her true identity. Notice the deeply personal, repeated use of 'I'.

- Images are often startling in quality. The poet compares the bees to African slaves, a Roman mob and a crowd of maniacs. These images surprise the reader and provoke a series of associations which clarifes the themes.

- The mood of the poem fluctuates between a sense of being in control: 'I ordered this...', 'They can be sent back. / They can die. I need feed them nothing. I am the owner' and a sense of being controlled: 'I have to live with it overnight...', ' I can't keep away from it...', '...why should they turn on me?'.

- Rich sound effects are used throughout. Notice the variety of techniques: internal rhymes such as 'din in it', 'the box is locked'; alliteration; assonance. These, combined with repetition, create a poem rich in verbal music.

Child

In this poem Plath expresses her love for her child, while also revealing her inner torment. This poem starkly portrays the dark depression that regularly engulfed the poet.

The poem opens with the poet addressing her child, 'Your clear eye is the one absolutely beautiful thing'. This statement implies that everything else in the speaker's world is in some way tarnished, hinting at the poet's troubled mind. Plath longs to give her child beautiful experiences. She wants to fill his eye with 'colour and ducks, / The zoo of the new'. This imagery evokes a child's innocence and sense of wonder. Flower imagery ('April snowdrop, Indian pipe') suggests the fresh, fragile beauty of the child. The April snowdrop metaphor also reminds us that, like spring, the child is representative of hope and new beginnings. 'Little / Stalk without wrinkle' is a metaphor that suggests the child's

potential to grow and blossom. Plath longs for her child's innocent eye to take in only that which is beautiful and magical. The metaphor she employs is memorable, 'Pool in which images / Should be grand and classical'.

While the tone of the first three stanzas is largely joyful, the closing stanza is contrastingly gloomy. The poet doubts her ability to provide the beautiful, magical experiences that she wishes for her child. She worries about her child witnessing her emotional turmoil and being affected by her anxiety, 'Not this troublous / Wringing of hands'. The closing image is utterly bleak, 'this dark / Ceiling without a star'. The total darkness of the poet's depression conveys a sense of oppression and confinement. The fact that Plath committed suicide two weeks after writing this poem adds to its poignancy.

KEY POINTS

- Key themes are the poet's love for her child and her own depression.
- Use of clear, simple language. The language is almost simple enough for a young child to understand. There are references to childish things: 'colour and ducks', 'The zoo of the new', 'April snowdrop', 'Indian pipe'. This simplicity adds a tone of poignancy to the poem.
- Stark contrast between the joy and colour of the child's world and the despair and darkness that engulfs the poet.
- Notice the use of the superlative adjective – 'the one absolutely beautiful thing'. This captures the admiration she has for the child – admiration for its innocence, purity and beauty.
- Images of light and darkness are cleverly used in the poem. The light / darkness imagery is bleak and oppressive. Plath would like to provide her child with vast horizons of opportunity – a starlit sky – but for her there is only darkness without any guiding star or hope. In the same poem imagery is very powerfully used for maximum dramatic effect. The phrase 'wringing of hands' conveys powerlessness, anger and frustration. The image of a 'dark ceiling' suggests limitation and lack of focus, a type of imprisonment. Claustrophobia is apparent in the phrase 'without a star'.
- Stark, dramatic contrast between joy of the child's world and the despair and darkness that engulfs the poet is central to the meaning of the poem. The 'zoo of the new' is a perfect phrase to describe the variety and adventure of new experiences and things she intends for her child. This is contrasted with the 'troublous / Wringing of hands, this dark / Ceiling without a star'.

Sample Answer

'Why I enjoy reading the poetry of Sylvia Plath.'

I enjoy reading Plath's poetry for a variety of reasons. In exploring her own emotional, psychological and spiritual states, she helps us to better understand the fears, confusion and turmoil that we all experience at some point. Those poems concerned with the destructive power of depression have an obvious relevance in a modern world where this illness is becoming increasingly prevalent. While Plath's poetry tends to be more pessimistic than optimistic, it is not relentlessly dark. She writes about life's 'two electric currents, 'joyous positive and despairing negative'. Among the more positive aspects of her poetry are her love for her children and her love of nature. What I find most appealing about Plath's style are the remarkable precision of her language and her unusual and striking imagery.

Morning Song interests me because of the honest way Plath describes her complex response to the birth of her child. I admire Plath's lack of sentimentality – she is a loving, but intensely realistic mother – and her use of surprising imagery. The opening image is unusual, but witty, 'Love set you going like a fat gold watch'. This image suggests how the plump new baby is something very precious. While the equally surprising image of the new baby as a 'New statue. In a drafty museum' highlights the baby's unique and special qualities, it also suggests the harshness of the world into which she has been born, and her vulnerability. The image of the parents standing round 'blankly as walls' suggests their uncertainty and confusion. I was particularly taken aback by the following cold-sounding lines, 'I'm no more your mother / Than the cloud that distills a mirror to reflect its own slow / Effacement at the wind's hand'. However, I now realise that Plath is just being typically realistic – in the same way that a pool of water witnesses the disintegration of the cloud that created it, so will the child witness the parent growing old and dying. The final half of this poem offers us the beautiful, reassuring image of a loving mother tending to her child's needs. Plath's self-image ('cow-heavy and floral / In my Victorian nightgown') is self-deprecating, but vividly realistic. Reflecting on the image of the baby's mouth opening 'clean as a cat's', I could visualise the proud mother marvelling at and delighting in her baby's every move. I love the appropriately happy final image, 'And now you try / Your handful of notes; / The clear vowels rise like balloons'.

Few poems moved me as much as *Child*, a poem as beautiful as it is sad. Similar to *Morning Song*, this poem is a delightful expression of parental love. However, this poem also portrays the dark depression that regularly enshrouded the poet. The opening line clearly expresses Plath's love for her child, while hinting at her troubled mind, 'Your clear eye is the one absolutely beautiful thing'. The poet longs to give her child beautiful experiences. She wants to fill his eye 'with colour and ducks / The zoo of the new'. The 'zoo of the new' is a memorable image that conveys a child's sense of wonder and innocent delight. The images of the 'April snowdrop' and the 'Stalk without wrinkle' suggest the child's fragile beauty. The child's innocence and purity are evoked by the metaphor that compares his eyes to a pool. The poet reflects that this pool should only reflect images that are 'grand and classical'. Sadly, Plath doubts her ability to provide the beautiful, magical experiences that she wishes for her child. She worries about him witnessing and being affected by her inner turmoil, 'Not this troublous / Wringing of hands, this dark / Ceiling without a star'. I have never encountered a darker image than this in any poem. The darkness of the poet's depression is total – she is entirely without the light of hope.

Mirror is a darker poem that set me thinking about the inevitability of old age and death as well as humankind's preoccupation with image. While it may seem to be a very pessimistic poem, Plath is again being typically realistic in confronting the transitory nature of youth. Again, Plath's images are unusual and sometimes startling. The personification of the mirror enables the mirror to speak for itself, giving the poem a sense of immediacy. The mirror expresses itself in a direct, precise manner, 'I am not cruel, only truthful'. The description of the mirror as 'The eye of a little god' is very effective because it suggests how people almost worship their own reflections, such is the modern world's preoccupation with image. Interestingly, the poem suggests that the mirror reflects a reality deeper than physical appearance. The lake metaphor suggests how the woman looks into the mirror in an attempt to discover her identity, 'Now I am a lake. A woman bends over me / Searching my reaches for what she really is'. The woman who owns the mirror is a troubled individual, 'She rewards me with tears and an agitation of hands'. The mirror's declaration that 'I am important to her' emphasises our obsession with our own appearance. Again, a key idea is expressed in a wonderfully crisp manner. The poem ends with a shocking image. The mirror is a lake from whose depths the 'terrible fish' of old age daily rises up to meet the woman. While I dislike Plath's portrayal of old age as something negative and ugly, it is good that she encourages us to face up to some cold realities.

Elm is one of the most strikingly original poems that I have read. While this is a grim poem, it offers interesting insights into how a person feels when he/she hits a type of psychological 'rock-bottom'. Once again, Plath gives a voice to an inanimate object, the elm. It is interesting that the tree and the woman she addresses seem to share a common psychological identity, with their two voices ultimately merging into one. The opening line sets the tone for the dark poem that follows, with the elm declaring, 'I know the bottom ...'. It seems that lost love is the cause of the woman's torment. The transient nature of love is expressed in a clear, direct manner, 'Love is a shadow'. Love has galloped away like a horse. The repeated long 'o' sound in 'Echoing, echoing' underscores the lonely mood. The suffering of the elm reflects the anguish of the woman. When the tree speaks of how it has been scorched by sunsets, I was reminded of Plath's own experience of electric shock therapy, 'Scorched to the root. / My red filaments burn and stand, a hand of wires'. The idea of the elm and the woman becoming one and sharing the same dreams is strange, 'your bad dreams possess and endow me'. The speaker's fear of the dark side of her own nature is described in unusually concrete terms, 'I am terrified by this dark thing / That sleeps in me / All day I feel its soft feathery turnings, its malignity'. The nightmarish image with which the poem closes – that of a 'murderous' face in the elm tree – reminded me that no place is as frightening as the dark depths of our own psyche.

The Arrival of the Bee Box also deals – on a symbolic level – with the poet's fear of the dark aspects of her psyche. The bee box can be regarded as a symbol of the poet's unconscious mind. Again, Plath uses imagery that is truly startling – the bee box is described as 'the coffin of a midget / Or a square baby'. Plath is drawn to feel fearful of the bee box. Her fear of the bees suggests her fear of the demons deep within her own mind. The image of the rampaging Roman mob effectively suggests the destructive nature of her darkest fears. The poet's dilemma intrigued me – should she risk unleashing her inner demons by exploring them in her poetry? I admired Plath's courage in ultimately deciding to set the bees free.

Reading *Poppies in July*, I was immediately struck by the contrast between the joyful sounding title and the darkness of the poem itself. While the title suggests a poem about the beauty and richness of nature, this is in fact one of Plath's bleakest poems. I was surprised to discover that the poppies are actually symbols of violence and suffering, 'A mouth just bloodied. / Little bloody skirts!'. The metaphor comparing the flowers to 'little hell flames' is strange and sinister in its suggestion of evil. There are many disturbing aspects to this poem. The idea of the poet putting her hands 'among the flames' suggests a tendency towards self-destruction. I was struck by the poet's desperation to find an avenue of escape from her own world, 'If I could bleed, or sleep!'. The poet longs for escape or oblivion through the 'Dulling and stilling' effects of opium. This poem provided me with more insights into the private hell that was the poet's mind. She longs to reach a type of numb, inert state where everything would be 'colourless. Colourless'. Reading this poem we are reminded of how different kinds of pressure can drive people to search for some means of escape from their torment. Sadly, Plath ultimately opted for the most drastic means of escape. Her intensely personal poetry helps us to understand the mindset that prompted her to reach this grim decision.

Although I found Plath's poetry challenging and, at times depressing, there was much to appreciate and admire in her work. She made me think, and by admitting me to her innermost thoughts and feelings, she enabled me to feel a sense of compassion for a fellow human being who was profoundly disturbed but extraordinarily gifted.

Eavan Boland

Biographical Note

Eavan Boland was born in Dublin in 1944. Her father's career as a diplomat saw the family living in both London and New York before she returned to Dublin, aged 15, and completed her secondary education. Boland went on to attend Trinity College, graduating with a first class degree. Her peers at Trinity included other gifted poets such as Michael Longley, Brendan Kennelly and Derek Mahon. Boland lectured for some years at Trinity before devoting herself fulltime to her writing. She got married in her mid-twenties and her subsequent move to the suburbs had a major impact on her poetic development.

Though removed from Dublin's vibrant literary scene, Boland found inspiration in her experience of the suburban world. After much travelling, she appreciated the stability that married life in the suburbs brought. Realising that a predominantly male poetic tradition did not regard motherhood and the life of a housewife as 'fit material for poetry', Boland drew on her own experience as mother and housewife to give a voice to the thousands of women living in housing estates in the suburbs. Love, marriage, motherhood and the suburban experience now became her central poetic preoccupations. On the international stage, such poets as Sylvia Plath and Adrienne Rich were also using their experience of marriage and motherhood as subject matter for their poetry. Boland also explores such themes as Irish identity, the nature of the Irish historical experience and the role of the female poet in society.

The War Horse

This poem was inspired by a commonplace incident that occurred in the suburban estate in which the poet lived. Image and sound combine to draw the reader into the poem. It is a 'dry night' and a horse is wandering around the estate in which Boland lives. The horse has escaped from 'the tinker camp on the Enniskerry Road'. Onomatopoeia enables the reader to hear the 'clip, clop / Casual iron of his shoes', 'his breath hissing, his snuffling head'. The horse is regarded as a threatening, destructive presence 'as he stamps death / Like a mint on the innocent coinage of earth'. When Boland surveys the damage done after the horse has passed her home, she is relieved to see that 'no great harm is done'.

The poem becomes more interesting when Boland uses the language and imagery of war to describe the damage done by the wandering horse. A torn leaf is described as 'a maimed limb'. A destroyed rose is depicted as a 'mere line of

defence', and as a 'volunteer' that is 'expendable'. The connection between the damaged plants and the human victims of violence is very clear in the following image: 'a crocus, its bulbous head / Blown from growth'. The long 'o' sound helps to evoke a solemn mood. The crocus is depicted as 'one of the screamless dead'.

Boland's use of the terminology of war to portray the destruction wrought by the horse suggests that this suburban incident has prompted her to reflect on broader issues relating to our attitudes towards the threat and violence of war. When this poem was written in the mid 1970s, the violence in Northern Ireland was threatening to spill over into the Republic. When the threat of destruction has passed, the poet's feeling is one of relief, 'But we, we are safe'. The repetition of 'we' suggests the insular (inward-looking), self-absorbed mentality that prevails in this suburban estate. As the 'huge, threatening horse' ambles on, neighbours hide behind curtains. The destruction done by the horse may be seen as a symbol of the violence in Northern Ireland, while the refusal of Boland and her neighbours to confront the threat of the horse suggests the unwillingness of people in the south of Ireland to confront the violence that was blighting life in the North at this time. A rhetorical question sets readers thinking about our attitudes towards violence, especially the violence on our own doorstep: 'why should we care / If a rose, a hedge, a crocus are uprooted / Like corpses, remote, crushed, mutilated?' The adjectives 'distant' and 'remote' imply that we in the Republic of Ireland regard the Northern problem as being very far removed from us. Selfishly indifferent, we lack the 'fierce commitment' necessary to involve ourselves in a potentially dangerous situation.

The poem ends with Boland feeling a connection with her ancestors, who faced threatening, violent situations in earlier times, 'And for a second only my blood is still / With atavism . . . /recalling days of burned countryside'.

KEY POINTS

- Key theme is outsiders' detached, insular attitude towards the violence in Northern Ireland.
- An unremarkable incident that occurs in Boland's suburban estate prompts her to reflect on our attitude towards violence and war.
- The poem is written in a series of rhyming couplets.
- The language and imagery of war indicates that the poem is not just about the minor damage done by a wandering horse.
- Repeated use of 'our' and 'we' underscore our insular attitudes ('our laurel hedge', 'our house', 'our short street', 'we, we are safe').
- Other sound effects include internal rhyme and assonance ('hock and fetlock', 'blown from growth').
- Use of onomatopoeia enables us to hear the horse ('clip clop casual iron of his shoes . . . hissing breath . . . snuffling head).
- Rhetorical question prompts the reader to reflect on our attitude towards violence and war, particularly the violence on our own island ('why should we care if . . . ?').

Child of Our Time

This poem was inspired by the harrowing image of a dead child being carried from the rubble following a bomb explosion in Dublin in 1974. The title of the poem suggests that this innocent child was a victim of the times in which we live. This poem is both elegy (lament) and lullaby. A series of antitheses (contrasting ideas) in the opening stanza suggests how the tone of the poem alternates between tenderness and outrage. The antithetical style contributes towards the creation of a balanced tone. The opening stanza reflects Boland's desire to create some sort of order and harmony from the terrible chaos and 'discord' of the child's death, 'This song, which takes from your final cry / Its tune, from your unreasoned end its reason / Its rhythm from the discord of your murder'. Boland underlines the tragedy and terrible finality of the child's death, 'your final cry . . . your murder . . . the fact you cannot listen'.

In the second stanza the poet reflects on the failings of the adult world that contributed to the death of the child. The collective 'we' suggests a sense of collective responsibility, 'We who should have known'. The world of childhood is evoked by references to rhymes, soft toys and legends. Our duty was to create a safe environment in which this child could grow and learn. Ironically, the adult world must now learn from the dead child, 'We . . . must learn from you dead'.

The final stanza holds out the hope that we might learn from the child's death and rebuild around the child's 'broken image'. Boland attributes the child's death to our inability to communicate with each other ('our idle talk') and exhorts (encourages) us to find 'a new language'. Images and language ('idiom') relate to our culture, values and attitudes. The adult world stands accused, 'Child / Of our time, our times have robbed your cradle'. The final line has a prayer-like tone, expressing the hope that the death of the child – who may be taken to represent all innocent victims of violence – will awaken the world to the need for change, 'Sleep in a world your final sleep has woken'.

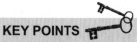

KEY POINTS

- Key theme of the poem is the unspeakable tragedy of a child's violent death and Boland's desire to put some sort of meaning on this senseless tragedy.
- The poem's long lines reflect the sad, solemn mood.
- The poet involves the reader in the poem in stanzas 2–3 ('We . . . our').
- Although the tragedy had its origins in the Northern conflict, politics do not enter into this poem, and names and places are not mentioned. In this way Boland highlights the universality of this tragedy.

The Famine Road

In this poem Boland reflects on the famine, the darkest and most traumatic period in Irish history and on the theme of colonial injustice. What is particularly unusual about this poem is the analogy that Boland draws between the suffering of the famine victims and the anguish of a barren woman. This is a dramatic poem with specific settings, 'characters', different voices and an element of conflict and tension.

The poem opens with Colonel Jones, an English official in Ireland, reading a letter from Lord Trevelyan. In a classic example of racist stereotyping, Trevelyan arrogantly dismisses the entire Irish nation as being 'as idle as trout in light'. He rejects the idea of giving the starving people any kind of charity, suggesting that both their bodies and weak characters would benefit from hard work. The 'toil' he has in mind is road building. These public works schemes were the government's response to the desperate plight of a famine-stricken nation. The infamous 'famine roads' rarely served any purpose other than sapping the little energy the starving people had, 'roads to force / from nowhere, going nowhere of course'. The image of the blood red seal on the letter suggests the callous indifference of the English administration.

The repeated harsh 'k' sound ('fork, stick . . . rock, suck') also suggests the harshness of these officials, who are happy that starving people 'suck April hailstones for water and for food'. An image suggestive of cannibalism underlines the desperation of the starving people, 'each eyed – / as if at a corner butcher – the other's buttock'.

Disease was as great a killer as starvation.

Boland highlights the misery of a typhoid victim who becomes an outcast ('a typhoid pariah') because of others' fear of contracting the highly contagious, deadly disease. The extent to which people are dehumanised by starvation is powerfully conveyed when Boland describes how the unfortunate man is left to die alone, with no one to say even a prayer, 'No more than snow / attends its own flakes where they settle / and melt, will they pray by his death rattle'.

Jones' letter to Trevelyan is smug in tone. The public works programme went better than they expected because the famine victims were too exhausted to even contemplate any kind of rebellion, 'sedition, idleness, cured / In one . . . / the wretches work till they are quite worn'. The image of corn being marched to the ships when people were starving to death dramatically highlights the theme of colonial injustice. The image of Jones coldly viewing the bones of famine victims from the comfort of his carriage underscores the heartless detachment of these officials.

Intertwined with the dramatic portrayal of the suffering of the famine victims is the depiction of the suffering of a barren woman. In the italicised verses the woman is addressed by a doctor who unfeelingly quotes statistics when discussing her infertile state, 'one out of every ten and then / another third of those again'. The voice becomes even more insensitive and upsetting, 'You never will, never you know'. The repetition of 'never' is particularly hurtful and the advice he offers ('grow / your garden, keep house') hollow and meaningless to the devastated woman. The unfeeling voice of the doctor reminds us of the callous tones of the English officials. The famine road is a symbol of the futility of the lives of both the famine victims and the barren woman. The poem reminds us that those in positions of authority are often lacking in humanity and compassion.

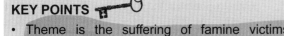

KEY POINTS

- Theme is the suffering of famine victims and the callousness of the English administration.
- Boland draws an analogy between the suffering of the famine victims and the anguish of a barren woman.
- The famine road symbolises the futility of the lives of both the famine victims and the infertile woman.
- A dramatic poem with specific settings, 'characters', different voices and an element of conflict and tension.
- The adjectives 'sick, directionless' aptly describe the plight of the starving people.
- The image of the blood-red seal suggests the cruelty of the English administration.
- Repetition of harsh 'k' sound evokes the harshness of the ruling regime ('fork, stick . . . rock, suck').

The Shadow Doll

In this poem Boland reflects on the nature and meaning of marriage. The poem was inspired by a Victorian porcelain doll that the poet viewed in a museum. The doll, a miniature bride, would have been sent by a dressmaker to a bride to help her decide on the design of her dress. As in *The Black Lace Fan My Mother Gave Me*, a concrete object prompts Boland to reflect on a range of issues associated with the particular object. The view of marriage expressed in this poem is very dark. Basically, marriage is perceived to be a form of imprisonment that confines, constrains and silences women.

In lines 1–9 the doll is described in a series of concrete images. The detailed description suggests the special, delicate beauty of the dress, 'They stitched blooms from the ivory tulle / to hem the oyster gleam of the veil'. However, the language used in relation to the doll evokes a sense of repression and containment, 'stitched', 'neatly sown', 'airless glamour', 'under glass, under wraps'. The doll would have been kept by the married woman and would have witnessed her unfolding life, complete with its 'visits, fevers, quickenings and lusts' (suggestive of sex, pregnancy and childbirth). Boland personifies the inanimate doll when she describes it as 'discreet'. Here she may be suggesting that women remain silent about their personal lives.

Lines 10–15 focus on the Victorian bride herself. As the bride-to-be views the doll in all its artificial perfection ('the shell-tone spray of seed pearls, / the bisque features'), she has a vision of herself in the place of the porcelain doll, 'she could see herself / inside it all'. Here she seems to gain a frightening insight into the restrictive nature of marriage.

The poem's final section (lines 16–21) switches focus from the Victorian bride-to-be contemplating her shadow doll to Boland on the night before her own marriage. Her endless repetition of her vows suggests her feelings of apprehension. A list of various items ('cards and wedding gifts – / the coffee pots and the clocks') suggests the typical pre-wedding clutter. Significantly, the closing image is one of confinement, 'the battered tan case full of cotton / lace and tissue paper, pressing down, then / pressing down again'. The repetition of 'pressing down' suggests a growing sense of claustrophobia at the prospect of the confinement of marriage. All of the suggestions of oppression and imprisonment culminate in the poem's final three words, which are set apart for emphasis, 'And then locks'. The clear implication of these words is that, where women and marriage are concerned, little has changed since Victorian times.

KEY POINTS

- Key theme is the way in which marriage represses and confines women.
- It is in examining a concrete object (the porcelain doll) that Boland is prompted to meditate on the nature of marriage from Victorian times to the present.
- Various images of imprisonment: the 'airless' glass dome that houses the doll, the locked suitcase, etc.
- Much of the poem's language has connotations of confinement: 'stitched', 'under wraps', etc.
- Repetition is used for emphasis ('pressing down, then / Pressing down again').

White Hawthorn in the West of Ireland

This poem describes a journey that Boland makes from her suburban Dublin home to the West of Ireland. This personal experience leads to the poet reflecting on the contrast between the confinement and boredom of the suburban world and the vastness and magic of the natural world. While Boland is a poet who regards life in the suburbs as suitable material for her poetry, her portrayal of the suburban world in this poem is distinctively negative.

The conversational tone of the opening lines draws the reader into the poem, 'I drove west / in the season between seasons. / I left behind suburban gardens./ Lawnmowers. Small talk'. This imagery evokes a dull, restricted, monotonous world. The regular full stops underscore the confinement and rigid order of the suburbs.

The contrast between Boland's normal humdrum environment and the wild landscape of the West is sharply drawn. The image of 'splashes of coltsfoot' with its sibilant 's' sounds suggests the beauty and tranquillity of nature. The oxymoron 'the hard shyness of Atlantic light' suggests the mysterious, indefinable nature of the light in the West of Ireland. (An oxymoron is a figure of speech which involves contradictory terms being used in conjunction with each other). The phrase 'the superstitious aura of hawthorn'

suggests that there is something mysterious about hawthorn. Boland has a longing to fill her arms with the hawthorn's 'sharp flowers'. She yearns to embrace the hawthorn and become one with the natural world, 'be part of that ivory downhill rush'. This image sharply contrasts with the images of confinement in the first stanza.

However, the poet's knowledge of the folklore relating to hawthorn causes her to pause and hold back from embracing the plant. In Irish folklore many superstitions surround hawthorn. Linked with the world of the fairies, hawthorn is associated with death and bad luck, 'the custom was / not to touch the hawthorn / . . . a child might die, perhaps'.

So the poet leaves the hawthorn 'stirring on those hills / with a fluency / only water has'. Here the hawthorn is seen as a mysterious, living entity. An energetic life force, it has the ability 'to re-define land'. Visitors are struck by the abundance of hawthorn in the western landscape. Boland states that 'for anglers and for travellers', it is 'the only language spoken in these parts'. The hawthorn now assumes a symbolic significance, representing the unique culture of the West of Ireland. Just like the other visitors, Boland cannot become part of this world, no matter how much she is drawn to the idea.

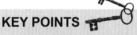

KEY POINTS

- This poem celebrates the unique beauty of the West of Ireland.
- Repetition of 'I' underscores the deeply personal nature of the experience at the heart of the poem.
- Poem contrasts the confinement of the suburbs with the freedom of nature.
- While regular full stops suggest the enclosed world of the suburbs, run-on lines evoke the unrestricted western landscape.
- Use of memorable visual imagery ('splashes of coltsfoot', 'that ivory downhill rush').
- Sound effects: – the sibilant 's' sound suggests the peacefulness of the West ('Under low skies, past splashes of coltsfoot').

Outside History

The theme of this poem is history's exclusion of the voiceless. In writing this poem, Boland remembers and honours those forgotten people who have remained 'outside history'. The poem opens with a factual statement, 'There are outsiders, always'. The natural image that follows depicts the stars ('those iron inklings of an Irish January') as being far removed from the reality of human life. They 'have always been / outside history'. The stars may be seen as symbols of myth – the idealised versions of Irish history. Under the stars real human history in all its pain and darkness unfolds, 'Under them remains / a place where you found / you were human, and / a landscape in which you knew you were mortal'. Boland sees history in a very negative light, describing it as an 'ordeal'.

Faced with the choice of myth or the real, painful world of history, Boland chooses the latter. It seems that she is 'only now' becoming aware of the 'darkness' of history. The image of 'roads clotted as / firmaments with the dead' suggests the devastation of the Great Famine. The image of people slowly dying underlines the terrible suffering that people endured throughout our history. The poet's compassionate nature is highlighted when she imagines us kneeling beside these dying people and whispering in their ear. The closing line reminds us that while we may remember and honour the forgotten victims of history, we cannot change or undo the wrong that was done to them. The closing line points to our collective responsibility for their suffering, 'And we are too late. We are always too late'. The repetition of 'too late' underscores the regretful tone. It seems that we are always too late in learning the lessons of history.

KEY POINTS

- Key theme is the forgotten lives of the voiceless.
- Effective use of imagery ('roads clotted as firmaments with the dead')
- Repetition of 'too late' conveys regretful tone
- Key words express the poet's deeply negative view of history, 'pain', 'ordeal', 'darkness'.

The Black Lace Fan My Mother Gave Me

Similar to most poets, Boland writes regularly on the themes of love and relationships. This poem was inspired by a black fan given to Boland by her mother. This fan had originally been given as a gift to her mother by the man who later became her husband. It was in fact the first gift that Boland's father gave her mother and is seen as a symbol of their love. Typical of Boland, she does not attempt to idealise or sentimentalise her parents' relationship. She describes their love in an honest, realistic manner. The fan represents the joy and stability of their love, but also its imperfection.

The opening line gives a sense of personal history being recollected, 'It was the first gift he ever gave her'. Its importance is underlined by the fact that its exact cost ('five francs') and the place where it was purchased ('the Galeries') are clearly remembered. Sensuous imagery evokes the atmosphere of pre-war Paris, 'It was stifling. A starless drought made the nights stormy'. A few crisp sentences give us a glimpse of their individual personalities, 'They met in cafés. She was always early. / He was late'. This particular evening, his purchase of the fan meant that he was even later than normal. Detailed description helps us to picture Boland's impatient mother looking down Boulevard des Capucines, before ordering more coffee and standing up as if to leave. Boland imaginatively recreates the scene, using sensuous imagery, 'The streets were emptying. The heat was killing. / She thought the distance smelled of rain and lightning'. The reference to the threatening weather may suggest that the relationship was problematical in some way or that the woman had doubts or worries in relation to the future of the relationship.

Stanza three gives us a vivid image of the fan. It is appropriately decorated with roses, the traditional flowers of love. The skilled craftsmanship that went into its creation is suggested by verbs and adverbs, 'darkly picked, stitched boldly, quickly'. While Boland appreciates the delicate beauty and elegance of the tortoise-shell, she is aware of the 'violation' of the tortoise that facilitated the creation of this love token. The description of the tortoise-shell as 'a worn-out gold bullion' suggests the rich, enduring nature of her parents' love. However, the following lines recall the dark hints of the opening stanza, 'The lace is overcast as if the weather / it opened for and offset had entered it'. The fan represents the beauty, longevity and imperfection of her parents' love. Put simply, it is a symbol not just of the romance of their early romantic days together, but of the real lifelong relationship – complete with all its ups and downs – that they have shared.

Stanza five returns to the scene of that stifling Parisian night. Thunder is in the 'airless dusk' – again, perhaps hinting at a stormy relationship. There is a sense of drama and anticipation, 'A man running. / And no way now to know what happened then – / none at all – unless, of course, you improvise'. Boland knows the history of the fan, but the story of her parents' love is incomplete, known only to her parents themselves. All we can do is 'improvise' or imagine how her parents got on through their years of marriage.

The final stanza is dominated by the image of a blackbird – the bird is another traditional symbol of love. The image of the blackbird is highly evocative. While the fan is beautiful, it has been affected by the ravages of time ('worn out'). It is, of course, also an inanimate object. In contrast, the blackbird is, like her parents' love, vibrant and alive. This closing image means that the poem ends on a triumphant, celebratory note, 'Suddenly she puts out her wing – / the whole, full, flirtatious span of it'. Her parents' love has weathered various emotional storms and survived. The adjectives 'whole, full' suggest a love that is balanced and complete, while the adjective 'flirtatious' suggests that the romance in their relationship remains intact. Sound effects (the alliterative 'full, flirtatious' and the sibilant 'flirtatious span') contribute to the upbeat mood at the close of the poem.

KEY POINTS

- Key theme is the nature of Boland's parents' relationship and love.
- The fan is a symbol of their love, as is the blackbird later in the poem.
- Sensuous images evoke the atmosphere in pre-war Paris.
- The story of her parents' early love is told in a clear, crisp manner (stanzas 1–2).

This Moment

This poem celebrates a special moment in everyday life. While *White Hawthorn in the West of Ireland* presents suburban life in a negative light, this poem suggests that everyday life in the suburbs has its moments of beauty. The opening lines set the scene, 'A neighbourhood

/At dusk'. The mood is peaceful. There is a sense of anticipation, 'Things are getting ready / to happen / out of sight'. The natural world seems to wait in expectation, 'Stars and moths./ And rinds slanting around fruit'. The stars will shortly rise, the moths flutter and the apples sweeten. However, for the moment, everything in the natural world seems to pause 'But not yet'. The sense of anticipation intensifies. The next image is beautifully simple and vivid, 'One tree is black. One window is yellow as butter'. This domestic simile is very apt.

The moment at the heart of the poem occurs when a child runs into the arms of his mother, 'A woman leans down to catch a child / who has run into her arms / this moment'. By referring to 'a neighbourhood', 'a mother' and 'a child', Boland suggests the universality of this special moment. The natural world seems to respond to and celebrate the moment when mother and child are re-united, 'Stars rise. / Moths flutter./ Apples sweeten in the dark'. The sibilant 's' sound that dominates the poem conveys a sense of perfect peace. The natural imagery evokes a sense of universal harmony. The short lines and regular full stops encourage the reader to read through the poem slowly, and to reflect on the special beauty of a commonplace event.

KEY POINTS

- Key theme is the beauty of the mother-child relationship.
- Vivid images.
- Economic style.
- Use of simple, everyday language.
- Effective use of sound.
- Mood is quiet and reflective.

The Pomegranate

The theme of this poem is the mother-daughter relationship and the manner in which it inevitably changes over time. Boland draws on the myth of Ceres and Persephone to underline the universal relevance of her own personal experience. The poem is written in blank verse which is similar to a natural speaking voice. This is appropriate for a poem in which Boland is clearly speaking from the heart.

The legend of Ceres and her Persephone tells of the abduction of young Persephone by Pluto, god of the underworld, who wanted her to be his wife. Devastated by the loss of her daughter, Ceres searched everywhere for her. As goddess of vegetation, Ceres threatened to interrupt all growth in the world until Celeus, the King of Eleusis, identified Persephone's abductor.

Ceres went to reclaim her daughter from the underworld, only to discover that, having eaten some pomegranate seeds, Persephone would be forced to spend half of each year in the underworld. When Persephone is with Ceres, everything grows, but as soon as she returns to the underworld everything starts to wither and die.

As a child, Boland was drawn to this legend ('The only legend I ever loved') because, as a child in exile in London ('a city of fogs and strange consonants'), she could relate to Persephone's exile in the underworld. Later, as an adult and mother, she could relate to the feelings of Ceres when she had to go out on a summer's evening searching for her own daughter at bed-time, 'When she came running I was ready / to make any bargain to keep her'. However, Boland realises that the special relationship between mother and daughter inevitably changes over time, 'But I was Ceres then and I knew / winter was in store for every leaf / on every tree on that road'. Boland is keenly aware of the universal, inexorable nature of the ageing process. Time would inevitably change the nature of her relationship with her daughter – this was an 'inescapable' reality.

Line 24 marks a turning point in the poem, with the movement from the past to the present. This section of the poem has a dramatic quality. The scene is set: it is winter, a starless night and Boland climbs the stairs. As she watches her teenage daughter sleeping, she is filled with conflicting emotions. The teen magazine and can of coke are typical of a teenage bedroom. It is symbolically significant that her daughter also has a plate of uncut fruit because this represents the pomegranate. In the context of this poem, eating the fruit symbolises leaving the world of childhood behind and entering the world of adulthood. The idea of eating the fruit also has obvious biblical connotations involving the loss of innocence. Boland now considers how things might have turned out if Persephone had not eaten the pomegranate, 'She could have come home and been safe / and ended the story and all / our heart-broken searching'. The use of 'our'

indicates that Boland is speaking for Ceres, for herself, and for all mothers. However, she knows that the relationship between mother and daughter must inevitably change. Just as Persephone 'reached out a hand and plucked a pomegranate', so will Boland's own daughter inevitably enter the world of adulthood and so change their relationship forever.

Aware of the kind of experiences awaiting her daughter in adulthood, Boland wonders what she should do, 'I could warn her'. While the poet recognises that the suburban world in which they live is far removed from the world of Greek legend ('It is another world'), she knows that even this world can be harsh, 'The rain is cold. The road is flint-coloured'. However, if she postpones the grief, she 'will diminish the gift' – perhaps a reference to the freedom to live her own life that she will grant her daughter. Every world has its share of pain and sorrow and, while Boland would like to insulate her daughter from the harsher aspects of life, she accepts that she too must live her life and learn through personal experience the things that Boland herself now knows, 'The legend will be hers as well as mine. / She will enter it. As I have'. These lines suggest an unending, universal, natural process. When her daughter wakes in the morning, she will put the pomegranate to her lips. The poet resolves to 'say nothing'.

KEY POINTS

- Key theme is the changing nature of the mother-daughter relationship.
- A personal poem to which every parent and child can relate.
- Mythical allusions suggest the universality of the poet's experience and feelings.
- The harshness of the modern world is evoked in vivid, dark images ('The rain is cold. The road is flint-coloured').

Love

This is a deeply personal poem, the theme of which is the changing nature of love. It was prompted by a visit to a 'mid-western town' in

Iowa in the United States where Boland and her husband lived in the early years of their marriage. The reference to myths suggests the extraordinary, magical nature of their love at this time. The reference to the bridge 'the hero crossed on his way to hell' derives from a tale in Virgil's *Aeneid* that describes Aeneas crossing the bridge into hell to see his dead comrades. In this instance Aeneas may be seen as a symbol for Boland's husband who often crossed this bridge over the River Iowa to visit their seriously ill infant daughter in hospital. That period in the family's life might certainly be described as hellish – Boland states that her infant daughter was 'touched by death'.

The family's old apartment is described in detail, 'We had a kitchen and an Amish table./ We had a view'. The language here is simple and crisp. A memorable metaphor suggests the strength and gentleness of the love that Boland and her husband shared at this time, 'And we discovered there / love had the feather and muscle of wings'. The wings image further suggests the power of love to elevate and inspire. The poet suggests the powerful, elemental force of their love when she personifies it as 'a brother of fire and air'.

Boland remembers how her ill daughter was 'spared'. When the poet again refers to the myth of Aeneas, she describes how, when his comrades hailed him, 'their mouths opened and their voices failed' – an image suggesting the impossibility of expressing intense emotion. This mythical allusion implies that Boland was unable to articulate the depth of love that she felt at this special time in her life. Just as nostalgia for his previous life spurred Aeneas on to visit his former comrades in hell, Boland is filled with longing to return to the earlier life that she and her husband shared.

Boland now reflects on the present state of their love, 'I am your wife./ It was years ago. / . . . We love each other still'. The latter line clearly implies that their love is not the same as it was during that traumatic period in their lives, although it continues to survive, 'Across our day-to-day and ordinary distances / we speak plainly'. Boland longs to return to that earlier time to once again experience that uniquely intense love, 'And yet I want to return to you / on the bridge of the Iowa river as you were with snow on the shoulders of your coat and a car passing with its headlights on'. This romantic image has a cinematic quality. At that time the poet saw her husband 'as a hero in a text'. Now she longs to 'cry out the epic question' and ask him if they will 'ever live so intensely again'. Boland uses an apt adjective to sum up the strength of this special love, describing it as 'formidable'. Drawing again on Greek mythology the poet depicts love as a male god, 'it offered us ascension / even to look at him'. The use of the religious term 'ascension' suggests the spiritual quality of their powerful love – this image connects with the earlier 'wings' metaphor, underlining the idea that love has the power to elevate and inspire, enabling Boland and her husband to transcend the problems of everyday life.

The closing lines underline the impossibility of the poet returning to that earlier time in her life or articulating the uniquely intense love that she and her husband once shared, 'But the words are shadows and you cannot hear me. / You walk away and I cannot follow'.

KEY POINTS
- Key theme is the changing nature of love.
- The language combines the conversational and the metaphorical, with mythical allusions suggesting the depth and complexity of their love.
- Use of memorable imagery.
- Tone is nostalgic.

Sample Answer

Write out the text of a talk that you would deliver to your class, outlining your response to the poetry of Eavan Boland.

Good afternoon classmates,

I found Eavan Boland's poetry to be original and thought-provoking. While female readers in particular appreciate Boland's poems on marriage, motherhood and the place of women in society, her work also has a wide appeal. She writes about history, violence, love and suburban life in a way that is fresh and interesting. I like the way she often uses a personal experience to reflect on an issue of universal importance. I admire her obvious compassion for all victims of violence and oppression and her anger at those who visit suffering and misery on innocent people. She has great powers of description and her verse has an appealing visual quality. Her use of sound effects to evoke particular moods is also very effective. I especially like her use of everyday, conversational language – Boland deals with issues that matter in language that we can understand.

I would first like to talk about *This Moment*, a poem of wonderful simplicity which conveys the magic of an everyday event. We could all relate to the heartwarming image at the heart of the poem: 'A woman leans down to catch a child / who has run into her arms / this moment'. Boland cleverly underlines the universality of this moment by writing of 'A neighbourhood . . . a woman . . . a child'. The poem's short lines and regular full stops create a sense of anticipation, while encouraging us to pause and reflect on the power and beauty of this moment. This poem contains one of my favourite images: 'One tree is black./ One window is yellow as butter'. This is a wonderfully simple, vivid image. I liked Boland's repeated use of the sibilant 's' sound to convey a sense of perfect peace. The way nature seems to respond to and celebrate the meeting of mother and child ('Stars rise. / Moths flutter. / Apples sweeten in the dark') underscores the naturalness of this special moment. There is a lovely sense of universal harmony in this poem.

I enjoyed reading the poem *Love* because it set me thinking about the way love changes over time. Again, the theme of this poem is both personal and universal. I admire the honest way Boland writes about her relationship with her husband. She seems to confide in the reader. She describes how her love for her husband was intensified by the traumatic experience of nearly losing her sick child. Simple details of her life in Iowa draw us into her domestic world: 'We had a kitchen and an Amish table./ We had a view'. I really like the image that she employs to suggest the beauty and strength of their shared love, 'And we discovered there / love had the feather and muscle of wings'. Her description of their mutual love as elemental ('a brother of fire and air') was memorable. I think you will agree that, as a class, we found the reference to an episode from Virgil's *Aeneid* quite challenging. However, when we teased it out, we discovered that by employing this mythical allusion, Boland was suggesting how it can sometimes be impossible to express intense emotion. Like Aeneas' comrades in hell, her feelings were too intense to be expressed: 'their mouths opened and their voices failed.' While the mythical allusions mean that this poem has its share of metaphorical language, more of the language has a lovely simplicity and conversational flow: 'I am your wife./ It was years ago. / . . . We love each other still.' Here Boland reminds us that love can grow and change over time. This poem contains another memorable visual image – that of her husband crossing the bridge with snow on the shoulders of his coat 'and a car passing with its headlights on'. I could almost picture this image on a big cinema screen. Many of us can relate to the idea of idealising a person you love: 'I see you as a hero in a text – / the image blazing and the edges gilded.' I think 'formidable' is an apt adjective to describe a really powerful type of love. Boland offers us some words of wisdom at the close of the poem when she suggests the impossibility of returning to the past: 'You walk away and I cannot follow.'

One of the reasons Boland appeals to so many readers is that she writes about life in the increasingly populated suburbs. In *White Hawthorn in the West of Ireland*, she highlights the contrast between the suburban and rural worlds. A few well-chosen words suggest how the suburbs are both physically confined and spiritually stifling: 'I left behind suburban gardens./ Lawnmowers. Small talk.' I love the way Boland combines visual imagery and the sibilant 's' sound to suggest the freedom, wildness and tranquillity of the western landscape, 'Under low skies, past splashes of coltsfoot'. I can see why she longs to become one with nature, 'be part of / that ivory downhill rush'. Boland's use of punctuation in this poem is very effective. Regular full stops underscore the confinement of the suburbs, while run-on lines suggest the unconfined freedom of nature. I like the way she portrays the West as a special, magical place where one cannot but be aware of 'the superstitious aura of hawthorn'. I noticed how she draws a sharp contrast between the fixed, orderly suburban gardens and the seemingly fluid, shifting landscape of the West where the hawthorn is 'stirring' on the hills and has 'a fluency only water has'. I was struck by the way she presented the hawthorn as a symbol both of the West's wild beauty and unique culture, 'the only language spoken in these parts'. I like the way she celebrates all that is special about the West, while at the same time, setting us thinking about the quality of modern day suburban life.

Boland is again critical of the suburban mentality in *The War Horse*. Again, I admire her ability to use a personal experience to reflect on an issue of wider importance. I like the visual and aural imagery that draws us into the scene: 'the clip, clop casual / iron of his shoes / . . . his breath hissing, his snuffling head.' An original simile captures the damage that the wandering horse does to a manicured suburban garden: 'he stamps death / like a mint on the innocent coinage of earth.' This poem becomes more interesting as Boland uses the language and imagery of war to describe the destruction done by this frightening invader – a damaged leaf is compared to 'a maimed limb', while an uprooted crocus is 'one of the screamless dead'. The destruction done by the horse becomes a symbol of the violence in the North, while the image of Boland's neighbours hiding behind curtains suggests our insular, uncaring attitude towards the violence in our own country. The use of repetition effectively underscores our selfish indifference: 'But we, we are safe'.

Classmates, most of us share Boland's interest in our past. I admire the compassionate way she writes about the famine, the worst catastrophe in Irish history in *The Famine Road*. Her use of dialogue really brings home the indifference and harshness of the English regime. We can almost hear the arrogant Lord Trevelyan casually dismissing an entire nation as worthless, 'Idle as trout in light'. Boland makes effective use of sound, with the repeated harsh 'k' sound ('fork, stick . . . rock, suck') accentuating the harshness of the officials responsible for 'managing' the famine. Boland's use of a familiar image to suggest the horror of cannibalism is particularly disturbing: 'cunning as housewives, each eyed – as if at a corner butcher – the other's buttock.' The image of the typhoid victim dying alone is also very shocking, suggesting how the famine dehumanised its victims, draining them of any sympathy for others. Our entire class was outraged at Jones' callously pragmatic view of the famine as a cure for Irish rebelliousness. One of the most interesting features of this poem is the way Boland compares the suffering and oppression of the famine victims with the pain and humiliation of an infertile woman. The doctor who coldly quotes statistics and glibly suggests that this unfortunate woman look after her house and garden is as arrogant and as unfeeling as Jones and Trevelyan. Boland reminds us that those in positions of power and authority are often lacking in humanity and compassion. The famine road metaphor effectively suggests how the lives of the famine victims and the infertile woman are similarly futile, 'what is your body now if not a famine road?'

Child of our Time is similarly powerful and thought-provoking. This is a poem that really sets us thinking about the violence in our own country and about our responsibility for that violence. Boland was inspired to write this poem by the harrowing image of a dead child being carried from the scene of a bomb explosion in Dublin. I admire Boland's desire to create some sense of order and harmony from the chaos and 'discord' of the child's death. I was struck by the irony of the adult world learning from a child: 'We who should have known how to instruct . . . / . . . must learn from you dead.' Boland rightly encourages us to 'learn' from and 'rebuild' around the child's 'broken image'. She points to our collective guilt for this tragedy when she refers to our inability to communicate ('our idle talk'). Classmates, we should respond to Boland's exhortation to develop 'a new language' of reconciliation. We all share the hope expressed in the poem's poignant closing line that tragedies such as this will wake us up to the need for change: 'Sleep in a world your final sleep has woken'.

In conclusion, my overall response to Boland's poetry is very positive. She addresses issues that are relevant and important to the modern reader, giving us much food for thought. Memorable images, conversational language and effective use of sound add to the appeal of her verse. Thank you for your attention.

Paul Durcan

Paul Durcan was born in Dartmouth Square, Dublin on 16th October 1944, the eldest of three children. His father, John, was a teacher who later became a barrister and then a circuit court judge in the west of Ireland. Durcan's youth was spent mostly between Dublin and Turlough, Co. Mayo. He claims that relations with John became strained when his father changed from being a humorous man to being a stern, demanding and distant father. Durcan blames this in part on the loneliness of the judicial career.

His relationship with his mother was warmer. Sheila MacBride Durcan came from a family famous for its literary and political heritage. Major John MacBride, a leader and martyr of the 1916 Rising, was Paul's granduncle. John MacBride was married to Maud Gonne (a woman who was loved by WB Yeats and who inspired much of his finest poetry). Sean MacBride, the son of the marriage, was Durcan's godfather. Sheila Durcan was in the legal profession too and performed extremely well in her law exams. She was obliged, however, by the customs of the day to stop working when she married.

Durcan began to study Law and Economics at UCD, but at 19 years old he was committed by his family to St. John of God psychiatric hospital. Durcan believes the fact that he didn't conform with his privileged middle-class family led them to take this step. He later attended a Harley Street Clinic, where he was treated with electroshock and barbiturates, and claims he narrowly escaped being lobotomised. He was incorrectly diagnosed as suffering from schizophrenia. He believes he was not suffering from any mental illness prior to this experience but his treatment left him with recurring depression and a permanent sense of isolation and loneliness.

Durcan spent three years in and out of various mental institutions until he ran away and began to associate with the poet Patrick Kavanagh, who served as a mentor to him.

Durcan's poetry owes a great debt to Kavanagh, fusing as it does the mythic and the commonplace, direct (even blunt) language, and the linking of loneliness with revelation. In 1967, attending a wedding at the Shangri-La Hotel in Dalkey with Kavanagh, Durcan met Nessa O'Neill, his future wife. They lived in London and raised two daughters, Sarah and Siabhra. In 1970 they moved to Cork, where Nessa taught in a prison. Their marriage ended in 1984.

It has been said of Durcan that:

'Poetry can often seem remote and removed from the real world but the beauty about Durcan's poetry is that it is of this world and, in particular, very much of Ireland.'

Nessa

Nessa is a love poem about the poet's wife, Nessa O'Neill. It opens with two facts: the date he met her and the place in which he met her. But the factual world of dates and places blurs into the mythic by the second line. The hotel (Shangri-La) is an allusion to a mythical place (it's from a novel by James Hillman), loosely based on the Buddhist paradise Shambala, where people are enlightened and live incredibly long blissful lives. The term roughly correlates to 'cosmic peace', a notion mentioned in another Durcan love poem, *The Girl with the Keys to Pearse's Cottage*. The Himalayas as a site of enlightenment is also alluded to in *Windfall*, a poem that charts the collapse of Durcan's marriage.

In the opening stanza of *Nessa*, the woman is presented as taking the lead: 'She took me by the index finger/And dropped me in her well'. The index finger may be sexually suggestive and being dropped in her 'well' may mean an initiation into sex. The young man seems overwhelmed and even spellbound by her power; the comparison to a well is striking. Wells are dangerous structures and have drowned many people in rural Ireland. They are also often associated with myths and fairytales, and they boast wish-fulfilling properties. The deep 'well' of Nessa's love is not calm or still; it is a 'whirlpool', a place of incredible energy and chaos, and the poet claims in a repeating refrain that 'I was very nearly drowned'.

Durcan often slips deftly from mythical visions to ordinary or even blunt dialogue. The second stanza opens with a direct order from his lover: 'Take off your pants, she said to me'. His awe is such that 'I very nearly didn't'. What follows may be a comic change of direction – she's offering to go for a swim – or it may be another sexual metaphor. Though there are some significant exceptions, water imagery is often used in Durcan's poetry as a token of the most sublime happiness and reassurance. The invitation to swim in the Irish Sea here could be an invitation to 'hop' into the sea of love itself. But again the refrain tells us that the sea is not calm but in chaos, a whirlpool that nearly drowns him.

The third stanza advances the dramatic verbs of the first two stanzas (took, dropped, hopped) by claiming he 'fell' in a field. She falls (in love) beside him, and he wishes to remain 'in the grass with her all my life'. The refrain returns, but now 'that was a whirlpool' has subtly changed to 'she was a whirlpool'.

The final stanza changes the tone as the poet addresses Nessa directly. Possibly in a sly allusion to the ancient Greek myths about mermaids and sirens, the poet's address comes complete with antique diction: 'O Nessa my dear'. Here it is unclear who is playing the role of siren singer, threatening the death of the unsuspecting sailor who hears it. The poet seems to be calling her into the sea now, to live with him 'on the rocks'. He asks her to let her 'red hair down'. Red hair is associated with mythic Irish ideals of feminine beauty, and letting one's hair down is a relaxing of all restraint and defence. It is to luxuriate in sensual play.

The closing four lines are especially charged, as they suggest that the couple will actually 'drown' each other in love, and then their ghosts will 'ride into Dublin City/In a taxi cab wrapped up in dust'. The fatalist tone is borne out by the closing refrain, which has shifted from the past tense of reminiscence, to the present tense: 'you are a whirlpool', and the almost-gleeful anticipation of the final line: 'And I am very nearly drowned'.

KEY POINTS

- The factual world of places and dates blurs into the mythical world in this poem.
- Note the deep significance of the image of the well.
- Water imagery is often used in Durcan's poetry as a token of the most sublime happiness and reassurance.
- Notice the change in the use of verbs and the change of wording in the refrain to mark the development of the relationship.
- Poet addresses Nessa directly in stanza four. This marks a change in the direction of the relationship.
- Note the variation of tense in the refrain in the final stanza.

The Girl with the Keys to Pearse's Cottage

Pádraig Pearse was a poet, barrister, and one of the leaders of the 1916 Rising, a role for which he was executed along with Durcan's uncle, John MacBride. (Durcan writes about this famous branch of his family in *The MacBride Dynasty*.) During the Rising, Pearse read aloud the Proclamation of the Irish Republic on the steps of the GPO, a document Durcan ironically alludes to in *Windfall*. Pearse also gave a speech/eulogy at the funeral of the fenian Jeremiah O'Donovan Rossa, an event referenced in Durcan's *Six Nuns Die In Convent Inferno*.

In his role as a member of the Gaelic League – an organisation that promoted the Irish language – Pearse built a modest cottage in Rosmuc, Connemara, where this poem is set.

On the surface, *The Girl with the Keys to Pearse's Cottage* is about unrequited teenage love. The poet (typically male in this genre) loves a girl from afar, but for unstated reasons does not – or cannot – bridge the divide between them. This fits with a larger pattern in Durcan's work, that of a man trying and failing to communicate across great gulfs of time (personal or national history), space (the Atlantic Ocean) or emotional distance (the anxiety that otherworldly beauty can evoke in a young man).

Thinking of the cottage, he visualises 'two windows and cosmic peace'. The home is presented here as a place to gaze out from, and in doing so, receive a kind of grace, not unlike the window of the poet's own home in *Windfall*. The cottage is humble: 'bare brown rooms and… whitewashed walls'. It is adorned with some heroic remnants: 'Photographs of the passionate and pale Pearse'.

However, as with hero-worship in general, the cottage looks better from a distance: 'I recall wet thatch and peeling jambs/And how all was best seen from below in the field'.

Fields are often used as symbols of a rural and romantic Ireland, and it is in such a romantic setting that the young trainee poet can be found practising his alliteration: 'Compiling poems of passion for Cáit Killann'.

It's never explained why Ms. Killann has the keys to the cottage, but she seems an appropriate keeper for the spiritual home of such an intense figure as Pearse. The girl herself cuts a striking figure, composed as she is entirely of contrasts: 'Her dark hair was darker because her smile was so bright', and dressed 'In sun-red skirt and moon-black blazer'. If there is symbolism attached to the clothing, it is unclear what it might be, but the red of the skirt may allude to the blood shed for Irish freedom, and the black to death. Or it may be a contrast between the 'cosmic' rotations of day and night (sun and moon).

Cáit is a virtual alien in her own land. She looks 'toward our strange world wide-eyed./Our world was strange because it had no future'. The 'our' is also unclear here. It could refer to the futureless romance between her and the poet, or it could mean 'our' in the sense of people living in the West of Ireland, or Ireland in general. This poem was written in the 1970s when Ireland was on the brink of a significant economic recession. Many people would soon have 'no choice' but to emigrate to countries like England or, in Cáit's case, America.

The final stanza aches with the pang of dashed teenage love, but also with the heartache of losing so many fellow countrymen and women to other shores. The notion that she has 'gone with your keys from your own native place' suggests that the emigrants have taken something with them, and left both the emigrants and those who remain somehow locked out of the home that should be the source of cosmic peace to all.

Durcan's taste for mingling painters into his own poetry emerges again – as in *Windfall* – when he references El Greco, the nickname of a genius artist who left his native Crete in Greece to live in what were then the centres of power (Venice and Rome) and who died in Spain far from his native land. His figures were known for their extreme elongated features and other-worldly appearance. Durcan blends the otherworldly character of Cáit's eyes with the 'Connemara postman's daughter's proudly mortal face'. Even though the young poet is tempted to celebrate her as a mythic being – or an ideal frozen in time like Pearse – it is her humanness, her grounded working-class roots, that ultimately speak to him. Her face is 'mortal', meaning that unlike a symbol, it will suffer and die. Perhaps here there is more than a celebration of the living over the legend.

KEY POINTS

- A recurring idea in Durcan's work is that of a man trying and failing to communicate across great gulfs of time (personal or national history), space (the Atlantic Ocean), or emotional distance (the anxiety that otherworldly beauty can evoke in a young man).
- Note the small details in the description of Pearse's cottage.
- There is a suggestion that the reality of the cottage is not quite as perfect as the image of cosmic peace which the poet remembers.
- Excellent use of alliteration and symbolism.
- The use of bright, dramatic colour makes the figure of the girl, Cáit Killann, stand out and may have symbolic connotations.
- The necessity of emigration in order to survive is alluded to in the poem – this was not the dream of Pádraig Pearse!
- The fact that the girl still holds the keys of the cottage suggests loss.
  Those left in Ireland are somehow locked out of their rightful heritage.
- Although Cáit is presented as an almost mythic character and associated with the work of great artists, the final picture is one of a real woman who was forced to emigrate. This can be read symbolically as a representation of the ideals of Pearse and the reality of modern Ireland.

The Difficulty that is Marriage

The opening line of this poem hits us with hard alliterative 'd' sounds: 'We disagree to disagree, we divide, we differ…'. The reader is thrust into the scene: a married couple in discord. Even the familiar phrase of reconciliation ('agree to disagree') is rejected and mangled into a deliberately confusing double negative – people disagreeing to disagree could be read as always choosing to agree, but this is not the case here. From the outset, the claim strains our sense of logic: do they fail even to 'disagree' in the sense that they don't fight openly, and instead 'divide' or 'differ' into the protective realm of their own silent, private opinions? It's hard to answer because Durcan doesn't show us the couple in action. Instead, we are transported from the opening line to what seems to be a nightly ritual: the poet regarding his wife as she lies 'curled up in sleep'. He describes her as 'faraway', and this is an important motif in Durcan's poetry: much of his work seems to struggle with conveying a message from across a vast gulf: a sea; sleep; death; memory; a foreign land; the tightlippedness of a remote loved one or family member.

The restless speaker arranges 'a mosaic of question marks' across the bedroom ceiling. He does this most nights so we assume he is disturbed, but then the tone of his inquiry seems joyous: 'How was it I was so lucky to have ever met you?' Again, we are thrown back on ourselves as readers – here is a man who is troubled, who can't sleep, can't find any middle ground with his wife, and cannot figure out how he is so lucky to find himself in this bind.

The difficulty of this paradox makes us notice the form of the poem. It's a sonnet, in that it has 14 lines and a natural break after the 8th line. Traditionally, sonnets can be intellectual exercises that introduce a problem or riddle and then try to solve it.

In the second line, Durcan claims to 'lie in bed' each night. The word 'lie' here could have a double meaning. He literally lies in bed beside his wife but may also be involved in a 'lie' about their relationship. Is this line an admission that he is struggling to make his own double claim: I love you and feel lucky to be with you, but I feel lonely and removed from you at the same time? Certainly, by the end of the poem he is making paradoxical statements: 'You must have your faults but I do not see them'. It's a contradiction: I know you're not perfect, but I think you're perfect. It is as if by day he differs and divides from his wife, but by night his mind is differing and dividing within itself. He claims he doesn't place her on 'a pedestal or throne' but in the same breath says he would 'rather live with you for ever/Than exchange my troubles for a changeless kingdom'. To give up a kingdom (presumably the eternal paradise promised in Christianity) in favour of the company of one's wife here on a 'changeling earth' (a corrupt substitute for heaven) is placing her on something of a pedestal, surely.

There is another difficult paradox here. The issue of mortality is a recurring theme in Durcan's work. Let us look at it more closely:

'I am no brave pagan, proud of my mortality'. The meaning of 'pagan' is unclear here. It's a word typically used to describe tribes of people who don't belong to Christianity (or the other religions of Judaism or Islam), and who believe in a spiritual existence where gods live in various elements of the natural world—like water, air, fire, or plants and animals. Some pagans believe in a personal afterlife (as the Greeks and Romans believed in hells and heavens) but others don't, believing instead in reincarnation or oblivion. Durcan here describes his ideal pagan as 'brave', which might suggest he considers wishing for effortless eternal life next to a Christian God as, in some way, less than brave. Does he see a truly rewarding life as one of struggle and maybe even discord?

Besides paradoxes, sonnets often concern themselves with romantic love. But this 'sonnet' is caught between romantic love and modern rejection of such a quaint notion. Metrical rhymes are discarded in favour of unrhymed blank verse, suggesting a kind of chaos or randomness even in this traditional poetic form.

Given the density of paradoxical claims being made in the poem, the title needs to be read very carefully. Note that Durcan doesn't call it The Difficulties of Marriage which would be banal and simply mean that marriage has difficulties in it. No, he implies here that marriage is difficulty. The difficulty is not simply that tension can emerge between two people who live together, but rather the sweet and subtle trap, or riddle, that is intense love. Perhaps the speaker doesn't love his wife in spite of their demanding relationship, but because of such demands. It is interesting to compare Durcan's poem Nessa here, where he explicitly pairs intense love with 'drowning'. He suggests that if they stay together they will 'ride into Dublin City/In a taxi-cab wrapped up in dust' possibly implying that they will become ghosts ('dust') and haunt the human world. He presents her as a whirlpool drawing him into her depths. This is not the language of a man who loves in spite of the whirlpool of fear or anger or difficulty, but because of it.

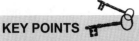

Wife Who Smashed Television Gets Jail

The tabloid-headline-style title launches us into a first-person voice. Lines 1-21 are the husband speaking directly to the judge who is evaluating the case of the smashed TV. The opening lines present the wife as being aggressive and threatening without any context for why she might be frustrated. The speaker is careful to use deferential phrases like 'my Lord' and clumsy, legal-sounding phrases like 'peaceably watching' to curry favour with the magistrate.

He claims they were simply enjoying the 1970s detective show *Kojak,* and that at the same moment that Kojak shoots a character with the same name as the defendant ('Goodnight, Queen Maeve'), the wife flies into a rage and smashes in the box.

The reference to Queen Maeve is particularly loaded. Maeve (or Medb) was a powerful and ambitious 'Warrior Queen' of ancient Connacht. She features in a cycle of myths, and is depicted as a complex character: forceful, sexual and uncompromising. She murders her rivals and takes many husbands and lovers – some of whom she kills or abandons. Her name may be associated with the English word mead, which is a sweet wine. As such, Maeve takes on the role of a goddess of sexuality, violence and intoxication. The violence is humorously echoed in the modern context by her way of taking on her 'rival' for affection and attention: the TV. Her mythical connection with intoxication is re-visited, again in a humorously petty way, when she suggests that 'We'd be much better off all down in the pub talking…'. This 'queen' has fallen a long way from her origins in Irish myth. But the presence of a powerful and uncompromising woman is still threatening to the judge. He is paraphrased (possibly by a reporter) in lines 22-26, and his argument is far more bizarre and illogical than anything Maeve has said or done. Justice O'Brádaigh trots out the well-worn claim that families are the 'basic unit of society' but then mangles that by arguing the

TV may be a 'basic unit of the family.' Following his twisted logic, any wife who prefers playing games in a pub over watching the family TV is a threat to the fabric of society! He orders her to be locked up and refuses any legal appeal, seemingly oblivious to the fact that in doing so he has broken up the actual human family by removing the wife and mother.

Looked at one way, this could be a darkly comical tale about how a cruel and disloyal mythical queen gets reincarnated in the 20th century and frightens some petty men into locking her up. But on a more serious level it depicts the power of unbalanced and self-important judges to split up families and incarcerate people for petty crimes. The poet seems worried about the Establishment's tendency to side with property concerns over human concerns, such as Durcan's on-going hunger for deep communication. He seems to be presenting the TV as something that can interfere with real family communication and corrode the deep ties that form when people play and talk together.

Given the mythical name of the wife and the Gaelic spelling of the judge's surname, there may also be a tension being set up between the Irish background of the speakers in this poem and the American culture of the TV shows they are watching. Perhaps the poet is implying that traditional Irish culture is being sold out in favour of foreign – and particularly American – passive pleasures.

KEY POINTS

- Note the tabloid-style title and the use of first-person narration. This creates immediacy and a sense of drama.
- In Irish myth, Queen Maeve is depicted as a complex character: forceful, sexual and uncompromising. The use of the name for the wife is powerfully symbolic. The violence is humorously echoed in the modern context by her way of taking on her 'rival' for affection and attention: the TV.
- Note the irony of the fact that the judge breaks up the family unit himself by removing the wife and mother.
- Durcan presents the TV as something that can interfere with real family communication and corrodes the deep ties that form when people play and talk together.
- The explicit references to the Irish names of Maeve and O'Brádaigh form an ironic contrast to the imported American TV series *Kojak* which was interrupted by the wife's actions.

Parents

Durcan's poems often display unusual titles, like *Madman* or *Six Nuns Die in Convent Inferno,* but *Parents* has a deceptively simple title, so our guard is down when we read the stunning opening line: 'A child's face is a drowned face'.

On a purely literal level, this probably means that a newborn's features, recently freed from the aquatic environment of the mother's womb, can look scrunched up and alien, like a watery corpse. But the deeper import of the line is that first-time parents, who are still overwhelmed by the enormity of their new role, tend to investigate their unnervingly calm sleeping baby at night-time and wonder if it is dead. The use of the verb 'stare' rather than 'gaze' or 'admire' takes us to an animal place of amazement and primal concern with keeping their vulnerable infant safe.

Like the sleeping wife and fretful-yet-loving husband in *The Difficulty that is Marriage,* this poem relates a scene of people trying – and failing – to communicate across a mysterious gulf or distance. The parents here are 'Estranged from her [the baby] by a sea'. The sea could represent sleep, but also the sheer difference between the consciousness of an infant and an adult.

Initially, the baby is presented as an exotic sea creature, something alien, being observed by the creatures that live on solid land: the grown-ups. But in the uneasy world of the poem, even this relation is not fixed. Everything reverses whenever the baby wakes: 'If she looked up she would see them…mouths open/Their foreheads furrowed –/Pursed-up orifices of fearful fish –/Their big ears are fins behind glass'. The baby's weak eyesight renders the image of her guardians as warped and muted, but even she could make out that these are worried fish watching her.

In another unexpected reversal, even though the baby is asleep, she is active, 'calling out to them', but despite their 'big ears' they 'cannot hear her'.

The theme of isolation, or the unbridgeable gap that can exist between family members even when they love and need each other, mingles with another related Durcan anxiety: the fear of homelessness. The new parents find themselves 'locked out of their own home', and that is what the arrival of a new baby can do: displace old comforts with new roles and scary new concerns. This mysterious sea creature has pushed the couple out of their familiar world and onto a strange isolated island. They are 'stranded' in the night, staring with awe at the marvel of their alien visitor. Note the repetition of key words: 'sea' ends the third, fourth, fifth, sixteenth and seventeenth lines; 'Father, Father/ Mother, Mother' echo in a ghostly manner, as if the child is calling out to them not from sleep but from the death the parents fear so deeply. In this manner, the poem conveys the intensity of the parents' love for their child without ever succumbing to sentimentality.

KEY POINTS

- The title of this poem is deceptively simple.
- The overwhelming responsibility of new parents when faced with a newly born child is explored in this poem.
- Like the sleeping wife and fretful husband in *The Difficulty that is Marriage*, this poem relates a scene of people trying – and failing – to communicate across a mysterious gulf or distance.
- Note the use of unexpected reversals in the viewpoints expressed in the poem (parents vs child).
- Themes of isolation, anxiety and homelessness are explored in this poem as they are in several other poems by Durcan.
- The poem conveys the intensity of the parents' love for their child without ever succumbing to sentimentality.

'Windfall', 8 Parnell Hill, Cork

Section 1 (Lines 1-37):

On the surface, the title is simply the poet's old address where he lived with his wife and daughters, but the house name (Windfall) can be understood to have two meanings at least. The first is that of a lucky win, something like a lottery, or the grace of God: a gift that lands in your lap regardless of whether you deserve it or not. The second meaning of windfall refers to fruit that has dropped from a tree without being chosen or picked, and in that sense may imply randomness, chaos or even an expelled quality. The first meaning – that of a jubilant lottery win – informs the first 112 lines of the poem (i.e. the vast bulk of it).

Durcan repeats 'home' six times in seven lines, as if turning the familiar word around and around until it becomes alien, exotic – like repeating your own name until it becomes strange. This de-familiarising of the basic stuff of life is something poetry has great power to do, and certainly Durcan is interested in helping us see how the profound and sublime can be found in even the most ordinary scenes and phrases. He claims that the throwaway statement 'Well, now, I'm going home' makes him feel 'sovereign' (like a king). In lines 8-14 he converts the view from his window – the seeming ordinariness of industrial Cork – into something worthy of great painters like Cezanne. Another painter, Goya, is referenced also, but this is more foreboding; Goya was famous for painting dark images of cruelty, madness and abandonment in places like war zones and lunatic asylums. There is a note of hyper-self-reflectiveness here, as Durcan shows us himself 'Dreaming that life is a dream which is real/The river a reflection of itself in its own waters/Goya sketching Goya among the smoky mirrors . . .'.

His tone lightens as he sketches a scene of domestic bliss: TV watching with the kids, wife knitting on the couch. The other houses have picturesque or sentimental names (meaning 'with love', 'without cares', 'little peace', 'little mountain', etc.) but their house means Pure Luck.

'It is ecstasy to breathe if you are at home in the world' (Line 19). This line connects to the reference to '. . . Buddhist Monks/In lotus monasteries' (Lines 24-25), because Buddhism teaches that letting go of egotistical struggle and self-regard is the key to happiness. Monasteries are seen as places for refugees from that worldly struggle for power or fame. The poet seems to be saying that as long as he has his home and family, he wants for nothing and so enjoys a profound calm. The lotus is a sacred flower that grows out of the muck of a lake, and Durcan presents his freedom of mind as blossoming out of the muck of 'homicidal' Cork City. In Buddhism, being born human (as opposed to animal) is considered a 'windfall' because you have a chance to 'wake up' from the whirlpool dream of life and death and achieve Nirvana, as Durcan puts it: 'A chance in a lifetime to transcend death'. Transcending death, in a Buddhist context, doesn't mean literally living forever; it means seeing through the illusion of the grasping ego that makes you feel separate from the world, and which holds onto anger, lust, envy, loneliness, fear etc. But even in his 'lotus monasteries' there are still dark thoughts, as Durcan sneers at the gap between the dreamy language of Ireland's Proclamation of Independence (our own country's claim to sovereignty), which promises to cherish each child equally, and the reality 'where the best go homeless'.

Section 2 (Lines 38-75):

This section opens with another scene from his 'high window' and again we see notions of connection to all of reality: 'shipping from all over the world'. The river Lee, like the poet-turned-family-man, is 'busy, yet contemplative'. The house is covered in prints of fine art, but mixed with the famous paintings is the even finer art of personal photos, the life and times of family members played out in holiday snaps doing 'ordinary' things like building sandcastles or camping. There are a few references to religious ceremonies (First Holy Communion, Confirmation Day) but there's no indication these holy rites are any more or less sacred than the other memories. The poet tells us he 'pored' over these images with his children often, suggesting that recollection is important to both him and them. This 'ritual' of remembering is presided over by the mother 'from a distance –/ The far side of the hearthrug'. Although she is watching 'proudly', there may be a hint of a gradual drifting apart taking place.

Section 3 (Lines 76-101):

Water imagery changes from river to sea. The children's home is 'Their own unique, symbiotic fluid'. Durcan's use of symbiotic is itself unique, because the term 'symbiotic' refers to the relation between species who mutually support each other. Because he's applying it to a medium here (water) and in the context of something being unique to each child, the mind naturally thinks 'amniotic', the womb sea we all float into the world through. If we allow this reading, the house is a great womb indeed, because even the parents partake in this 'private sea'.

Repetition is used ('a sea of your own' appears twice) to reinforce this notion of sovereignty. The family house is a place of playful inversions. You can 'hang upside down from the ceiling… hands dangling their prayers to the floorboards'. Here, prayers are grounded, and go down to the solid base of the home instead of up to a cloudy pie-in-the-sky heaven. All this playing is done with equanimity – a meditative trait of being able to find balance in even the most chaotic environments – in front of postcards from Thailand, a Buddhist country.

The sea world of the house breaks down into the minutiae (tiny details) of 'sands underneath the surfaces of conversations, / The marine insect life of the family psyche'. The family's life is being depicted as a rich and complex ecosystem enjoying a very fine but delicate balance.

This ecosystem seems complete into itself, like a meditating monk. The parents ignore the phone, disconnecting from superficial conversation so as to connect more thoroughly with each other. This is a kind of asylum, 'In which climbing the walls is as natural/As making love on the stairs'. 'Natural' is a strange word here, and may mean 'instinctive' or 'impulsive', implied by the act of having sex on uncomfortable stairs. 'Climbing the walls' sounds fun, but contains hints of going mad. Perhaps there are echoes here back to Goya's paintings of asylums, or Durcan's own psychiatric incarceration in his youth, but here the asylum lives up to its name: a shelter for refugees from the world.

The section ends with a curious claim: 'The most subversive unit in society is the human family'. This is an inversion of the usual 'family values' claim that the family is the basic unit of society. How and what does Durcan's happy family subvert? Perhaps there is something about love, fun, relaxation and instinctive life that is a threat to some other imposing project he sees at large in the world, like the global industrial activity he can see from his window.

Section 4 (Lines 102-113):

This section is composed of echoes of statements he or the children have made over the years regarding home. What's notable is how ordinary they sound; there's nothing here you haven't said a million times yourself. But by seeing the word 'home' appear on the page again and again, you begin to realise how inextricably linked the language of home and reassurance prove to be.

Section 5 (Lines 114-126):

The tone drastically shifts – suddenly Durcan enters into a confessional mode. He never states what he did, other than he was 'put out of my home' with 'good reason'. The third line inverts 'windfall' from happy win to becoming 'fallen' or 'felled'. Without the protective refuge of his family's home, he seems to cease being a human. He is relegated to 'creeping, crawling' about the 'alien' city of Dublin. He becomes restless as a bird 'beyond all ornithological analysis'. His chance to meditate in his monastery, to escape the endless cycle of rebirth, has been lost. He tumbles from 'Bed-and-breakfast to bed-and-breakfast', a creature of the wind.

Section 6 (Lines 127-137):

After imagery of water and wind, the final image is that of fire. He peers into 'other people's homes' and sees the family hearth as a primal need, something gathered around by every tribe known to man, from the ancient Native Americans to the modern middle class nuclear family. Even the TV functions as a fire of sorts, a light to gather around. His final lines are cold and technological, a radio operator trying and failing to speak from one side of the word Windfall to the other, from the sad to the happy, from the present to the past, from the isolated father to the unified family: 'Windfall to Windfall—can you hear me?' No answer.

His last line is a recycled one. The 'pet' suggests it was originally aimed at one of his children. Now he uses it to reassure himself, not a domestic 'pet' but a lonely animal lost in the street.

KEY POINTS

- Durcan is interested in helping us see how the profound and sublime can be found in even the most ordinary scenes and phrases
- Note the repetition of the word 'home' in the opening section of the poem.
- He converts the view from his window – the seeming ordinariness of industrial Cork – into something worthy of great painters.
- The poet suggests that as long as he has his home and family, he wants for nothing and so enjoys a profound calm – like that enjoyed by Buddhists.
- The poet emphasises the importance of recollections to himself and to his family as he pores over old photographs of major family occasions.
- Note the repetition of sea and water imagery and its connection to life. The family's life is being depicted as a rich and complex ecosystem enjoying a very fine but delicate balance.
- Note the dramatic shift in tone as Durcan is put out of his home and becomes homeless.
- Durcan uses the image of fire symbolically. It represents warmth, energy and togetherness.
- The final image of the poet as a lost 'pet' animal is deeply moving.

Six Nuns Die in Convent Inferno

The title of this poem reads like a dramatic newspaper headline, but the dedication beneath it contains the confounding pairing of the phrase 'happy memory' with a reference to nuns burning to death sometime after midnight on a specific date. This fusing of factual detail with dramatic flourish and sombre image with joyous language sets the complex tone for what follows.

Part 1, Section 1 (Lines 1-62):

The poem is narrated by one of the six deceased, though we never learn which one. Her opening lines are factual and simply locate where the nuns lived in Dublin city centre. However we quickly see a playful spirit emerge as she turns the grandiose description of Grafton Street as a paseo into a verb 'where everyone paseo'd'. A paseo can mean an elegant boulevard to stroll through, but originally it meant an entrance into a bullfighting arena – a place of combat and struggle and danger. The notion of struggle is touched on deftly in the very next line, as she remembers often passing the 'great patriotic pebble of O'Donovan Rossa'. Rossa was a member of the Fenians. He fled to New York in the 1870s to work as a journalist and to raise great sums of money to set up a 'dynamiters' school' to organise the bombing of British cities. Referring to his large stone monument as a 'patriotic pebble' seems to deflate that kind of martyr in the nun's eyes. Perhaps she is implying that we all seek freedom, but violence is a spiritually petty route to take.

She remembers passing 'tableaus' (a striking image of a group of people; often they are showing a scene from history, such as Jesus surrounded by his apostles at the Last Supper) of punks. The punks are rebels and freedom-seekers too, idealistic young people who find themselves self-exiled from the middle-class world of shopping and commerce that Grafton Street represents. They are like nuns or monks with 'half-shaven heads' or soldiers in 'martial garb', but the nun sees how 'vulnerable' they are, 'Clinging to warpaint and to uniforms and to one another' in much the same way as militants of all kinds and in all times have done. Although nuns are typically viewed as humble and meek, the punks' reactionary pose is nothing compared to how rebellious the nun sees herself: 'The wild woman, the subversive, the original punk'. One of Durcan's favourite words, 'subversive', is here, so we know he has warm feelings for her.

The nun seems surprised at her ability 'To opt out of the world and to/Choose such exotic loneliness/Such terrestrial abandonment'. This homelessness is the flipside of Durcan's lonely character who tumbles lost through the Dublin streets by the end of *Windfall*. Here the nun

celebrates her 'exotic' choice to turn her back on the instinctive life of sex and childbirth. Even so, she notes how banal her 'weird bird' life is, using 'A lifetime' three times to describe her humble bike, galoshes stored away, umbrella drying out – evidently a lot of time spent outdoors in miserable weather.

The nuns' dormitory high up in the convent is as 'eerie an aviary as you'd find/In all the blown-off rooftops of the city'. Her freedom is complex and not without conditions, because she returns every evening to an aviary (a large cage for birds) – one from which they cannot escape on the night of the fire.

As well as the bird image, she likens herself and her sisters to the crew of a nineteenth-century schooner. The image is of brave, tough voyagers – people without roots. The specific nature of the vehicle also echoes back to exiles like O'Donovan Rossa who set sail for cities like New York en masse in the nineteenth century, hunting for freedom of one sort or another. The nun and her sisters use their 'schooner' to follow an ancient 'young man' who 'lived two thousand years ago in Palestine'. She notes that he was a 'subversive' too, and 'died a common criminal' in the eyes of his prosecutors.

Section 2 (Lines 63-84):

Suddenly the narrator takes us into the terrifying heart of the fire, but the language is not that of fear. Even the flames are 'the arms of Christ'; the fire is likened to its opposite – the cooling waves of the sea (a common Durcan motif for comfort). The burning nun's mind is chaotic as she hops from the 'disintegrating dormitory' to a beach excursion 'the year Cardinal Mindszenty went into hiding'. Mindszenty was a Hungarian who opposed fascism and communism and believed in religious freedom. He was labelled 'subversive' first by Nazis, who imprisoned him, and then by communists, who locked him up for even longer. He was finally stripped of his titles by the Pope and took refuge in the US embassy in Budapest. He died in exile in Vienna. Through his various trials he clung to his title of 'Prince Primate', much as the punks do to their safety pins and warpaint. There is thus a marked twinning of courage and vulnerability throughout this poem.

As she burns, the narrator's mind darts between her happy beach memory, the allusion to the trials of Mindszenty, and the nuns' banal fantasies of darning that fugitive-martyr's socks. It's difficult to know if the effect is meant to be comical or disturbing. Is this a clever wit, or the rambling of a mind scared out of its wits?

Section 3 (Lines 85-131):

Durcan's fascination with water and joyous drowning is revisited as he manages to turn a fire victim into someone reflecting on how 'Christ is the ocean . . . We are doomed but delighted to drown' (compare the poet relishing his being swallowed into the whirlpool of love in *Nessa*.)

Looking back on her terrestrial life, the narrator concludes that she and her celibate sisters are 'furtive' rebels, 'mothering forth illegitimate Christs/In the street life of Dublin city'. She is careful to use the word 'illegitimate' here, making a point that the law of the land rarely if ever overlaps with the law of Love, and that the spiritual life is often rebellious or subversive. The narrator is profoundly unselfish, not even grasping onto her own life. She reflects on what a 'refreshing experience' it is to lose things: 'How lucky I was to lose…my life'. This stands in stark contrast to the married man in *Windfall*, whose 'luck' falls away once he loses his place in the world, even though he lives on.

The nun's mind makes a characteristic dart from profundity to the small detail as she remembers the book she was reading that fateful night: Conor Cruise O'Brien's *The Siege*. O'Brien was a diplomat and scholar of sectarian unrest. His own relationship with Ireland's struggle with English colonialism was uneasy, and he switched from Nationalism to Unionism later in life. *The Siege* is about sectarian conflict in the Middle East, Jesus' birthplace, between Palestinian Arabs and Zionist Jews seeking refuge in their own state after the horrors of the Holocaust. Oddly, the nun mentions only the price tag of the book. Perhaps this is a sly allusion to the materialism that Durcan's subversives are always fighting against in some way.

Section 4 (Lines 132-147):

This short surreal section shows us the nun drawing the fire dragon to her breast, ecstatic in death. The imagery focuses pointedly on her fulfilling the biological function of giving birth that she has foregone in her celibate life, but here all the nuns are 'frantically in labour' to their deaths. Before the fire she describes them as 'sleeping molecules', implying they are part of a larger fabric. The crisis of death serves to wake them up to a higher reality. A blur of figures attend to them: phantom doctors and nurses help them 'giving birth', while Christ alternates as an 'Orthodox patriarch' and a fireman 'splashing water on [their] souls'.

The six names of the deceased are presented as a memorial in text. The closing image is of joyous innocence: frisky kittens in the sun.

Part II, Section 5 (Lines 148-154):

The second part shifts to an omniscient narrator. It tells of Jesus listening to the Grafton Street punks, and then addressing them in astonishment: 'I tell you, not even in New York City/Have I found a faith like this'. Whether he is referring to the faith of the nuns or the punks is not clear. The reference to NYC seems arbitrary, but could be an ironic allusion to O'Donovan Rossa, who managed to drum up huge sums of money in New York to fund a bombing campaign in England.

Section 6 (Lines 155-165):

The final section shows us the nuns' ghosts after the park is locked and the whole world has receded. They kneel by the Fountain of the Three

Fates, an ironic spot as it refers to pre-Christian (Norse) characters called Norns, who control the fates of gods and men. The monument has a deeper significance, as it was a gift from the German people to Ireland for giving shelter to their war refugee children during World War II. Moving back further in time, St. Stephen's Green was a site for public executions – often in the form of burnings. Reciting the Agnus Dei (Lamb of God) conveys its own irony, not only because it refers to letting Christ in 'under my roof' (as the nuns burned under their own roof), but also because the words are attributed in the Gospel of Luke to a Roman centurion – a representative of power and war. Durcan refers to the recitation as a 'torch song'– the allusion to fire is obvious, but a torch song is often a song about unrequited love. Were the devoted nuns truly loved by a god who let them burn? Perhaps we all feel unworthy of love to some extent, but the closing lines (from an ancient soldier to an ancient punk) suggest that we are all refugees in some way, and behind all the uniforms and poses of power, the only thing we have to cling to at last is the 'aid' of love itself.

KEY POINTS

- The title of this poem reads like a dramatic newspaper headline. Note how tragedy and happiness are mixed in the language of the opening.
- Complex, symbolic images are used throughout.
- Note the unusual linking of the speaker with punks. Although nuns are typically viewed as humble and meek, the punks' reactionary pose is nothing compared to how rebellious the nun sees herself: 'the wild woman, the subversive, the original punk'. Christ is also seen as a subversive in this poem.
- Repetition is used effectively. 'A lifetime' is repeated three times to describe her humble bike, galoshes, umbrellas drying out – evidently a lot of time spent outdoors in miserable weather.
- The description of the fire uses language associated with comfort rather than fear.
- The reference to Cardinal Mindszenty, a subversive, helps to link the notions of courage and vulnerability throughout this poem.
- Surreal, multi-layered imagery is effectively used to describe the nuns' deaths.
- The closing lines (from an ancient soldier to an ancient punk) suggest that we are all refugees in some way. Behind all the uniforms and poses of power, the only thing we have to cling to at last is the 'aid' of love itself.

Sport

Like many of Durcan's poems, *Sport* is autobiographical but differs from his typical approach in its directness. There are no flights of fancy, no surprising combinations of metaphors, images or scenes. Instead it recounts a single memory: the day the poet played in goal for his hospital's Gaelic Football team. As a young man, Durcan had been committed to St. John of God psychiatric hospital against his will. His internment is ironically 'celebrated' in this poem again and again as he uses the now-defunct phrase 'Mental Hospital' six times while describing his impressive performance on the day of the match.

He uses the second person ('you') to speak to his father, a stern circuit court judge whom Durcan believed was profoundly disappointed in him. The opening lines are achingly sad: 'There were not many fields/In which you had hopes for me'. The term 'fields' can mean 'areas of expertise' but here we see the poet setting the scene on a literal field – a playing pitch. He notes that his father took the effort to drive him fifty miles to the game, and this detail can be read as thanking his father for the opportunity, or illustrating how driven and demanding his father was to see his son excel at something. He says his father stands on the sidelines to 'observe me'. Unlike the verbs 'cheer' or 'support', 'observe' is a detached, clinical word. 'Sidelines' sound removed, distant, far from the action. The poet seems to be grouping his father with the psychiatrists and other authority figures who feel responsible for his well-being, but don't love him.

Durcan describes the huge, almost animal-like men he is defending the goal against: 'gapped teeth, red faces/Oily, frizzy hair, bushy eyebrows … over six foot tall/Fifteen stone in weight… All three of them, I was informed,/Cases of schizophrenia'. He is presenting these men as monstrous, and this is often how society regards the spectre of mental illness itself – something looming, threatening, dangerous. These men are the faces of chaos.

The poet notes that no one knows the truth of anyone else on the field: 'There was a rumour/That their centre-forward… Had castrated his best friend'. This extreme action (which may or may not have happened) is attributed to a 'misunderstanding'. The poet makes use of extremely vague language, such as 'rumours' and 'misunderstandings'. Perhaps Durcan is implying that everyone committed to a psychiatric ward – or at least in his case – is there due to a breakdown in communication. Certainly there is no real or effective communication between himself and his father, who only manages a terse 'Well played, son' at the end of the match. Even though the poem is directed to 'you' there is a tired sadness in the tone that suggests this message is too late to reach its real audience. It feels like a letter he has written but knows he'll never send.

But there is euphoria here too, and moments of pride. The speaker surprises himself at his courage and skill in the heat of the game: 'I made three or four spectacular saves'. He attributes his father's presence as giving him 'That will to die/That is as essential to sportsmen as to artists', but this is a very loaded compliment. The phrase 'will to die' could mean a burst of courage and selflessness – of self-sacrifice – but it could also mean a self-destructive drive that draws you into acts of masochism or self-damage. He says he wanted to 'mesmerise' and be 'mesmeric'; both verb and adjective are derived from an infamous eighteenth-century hypnotist called Franz Mesmer. Mesmer was a 'quack' doctor who used a variety of bizarre techniques to 'heal' his patients, many of whom were hysterics. One method involved the patients swallowing a fluid containing metal while Mesmer ran magnets over them to create a healing 'magnetic tide'. His theories of animal magnetism were discredited as 'imagination', and he spent the last twenty years of his life in self-imposed exile, a recurring theme in Durcan's work. The poet might be taking a dig at the psychiatric professionals here, although it's possible he is simply using a word we hear often in the context of great performances in art and sport: the audience feels lifted up by an other-worldly spectacle of grace under pressure.

Despite the elements of wry humour and fleeting pride, the underlying tone in *Sport* is one of sadness, not only the personal sadness of being seen as a disappointment, but also the general poignant 'spectacle' of mental illness, and the gaping hole that is left when communication breaks down. All we have left to separate the 'winners' from the 'losers' are numbers on a scoreboard.

KEY POINTS

- Note the unusually direct approach in this poem which focuses on a single memory.
- The repetition of the words 'Mental Hospital' emphasises the sense of stigma Durcan felt at that stage of his life.
- The poet's uneasy, detached relationship with his father adds a poignant tone to the poem.
- Durcan presents his fellow inmates as being monstrous. This is often how society regards the spectre of mental illness itself – something looming, threatening, dangerous.
- The underlying tone in *Sport* is one of sadness, not only the personal sadness of being seen as a disappointment, but also the general poignant 'spectacle' of mental illness.

Father's Day, 21 June 1992

This poem shows Durcan as an emotionally complex writer. It fuses comedy and wit (and shades of farce) with genuine poignancy. It opens on a naturalistic scene: a man frazzled as he rushes to pack and run out the door to his waiting taxi. It is at this most frantic and inconvenient moment that his wife chooses to spring a request on him: bring a huge threatening-looking axe with him down on the train to Cork to loan to her sister. He protests, suggesting his sister-in-law settle for a 'simple saw'. How does an axe differ from a saw? Is one more 'simple' than another? One difference that jumps to mind is that the action of an axe seems more violent. One hits the tree repeatedly until it falls.

The speaker seems paranoid about his neighbours, claiming that 'the whole world' is 'inspecting' the waiting taxi. This may imply that he's already worried about how his marriage (and his character) might come across to others. His anxiety seems unfounded until we learn later that his relationship with his wife is indeed in trouble and doesn't hold up under scrutiny.

His wife, for her part, seems cool to the point of being cold. Despite his show of fluster and hurry, she keeps her request firm, and her language simple: 'Yes, if you wouldn't mind, that is'. The pronounced politeness – her show of reasonableness – could be interpreted as a technique called 'passive-aggression'. This is when a person puts pressure on someone to do something, but acts as if they are being perfectly calm and polite, making the put-upon person feel like they themselves are being unreasonable. It works on her husband; he folds under her request like a sofa bed: 'I decided not to argue the toss. I kissed her goodbye'.

The axe in question is set up 'behind the settee'. This is significant: not only is the axe (an implement of violence) hidden from plain view until the last second, but the location is also noteworthy. For Durcan, the couch (or settee) is a stand-in for the heart of the home.

It is where the family gathers to lounge and live their comfortable, instinctual life. The tool of destruction lurks right behind where he tends to relax the most.

She presents the axe to him, 'neat as a newborn babe'. It is naked, as painful truth is always naked. The comparison to the baby is comical, but there's a sadness under this wit too. As we saw in *Parents*, having a child can be traumatic in a way. It alters the nature of the couple's relationship forever. Durcan may be suggesting through this linking of images (axe=baby) that having children changed them from a 'couple' to a 'family' (it is Father's Day, after all), but once those children grow up and leave the house, the father and mother must rediscover who they are, and if they do not like who they find themselves to be, the tree of family life may suddenly transform into an axe ready to split the man and woman apart.

The second part of the poem is set on the train to Cork. He claims the whole way down he is beset by 'Guilt feelings', but we don't know why he should feel guilty until he confesses to his fellow traveller, a stranger in the seat near him: 'I am feeling guilty because she does not love me'. This is the irrational language of love. In his mind, the speaker believes it his own fault that he is not loveable, and lists off some feeble attempts to explain it to himself: he takes up too much of the bed; he is 'coarse' in his attempts to have sex with his wife; he eats pasta the wrong way. This is a man struggling and failing to communicate with the passenger on the train, with his wife, even with himself. He doesn't even choose to speak, instead he 'overheard' himself talking to the passenger, as if he is purely passive and has no control over what he does or how he does it. When the passenger eyes the axe and departs the seat without leaving the train, we see a comic scene (He's mistaking the author for a crazy man!) but really there is the spectre of depression looming in the final stanza. The speaker feels isolated: 'we sat alone/The axe and I'. Outside, the 'green fields' – symbols of youth and fertility – flee from him. He is not young, he will have no more children, and the daughters he does have are 'gone away' too. Unlike the frenzy of the opening lines, there is a quietness to this end, but it is a desperate one.

KEY POINTS

- *Father's Day, 21 June 1992* shows Durcan as an emotionally complex writer. The poem fuses comedy and wit (and shades of farce) with genuine poignancy.
- 'The axe behind the settee' is a significant image, not only for its connection to violence but because it is hidden behind a piece of furniture usually associated with relaxation and calm.
- An excellent simile occurs when the poet describes his wife presenting the axe to him, 'neat as a newborn babe'. It is naked, as painful truth is always naked.
- The final image in this poem is that of the poet struggling to come to terms with the breakdown in his marriage and feeling unable to communicate.
- Despite moments of brilliant wit, the poem is profoundly sad and disturbing.

The Arnolfini Marriage

Ekphrastic art is art that describes the beauty of a detailed object, often a painting or sculpture. The word 'ekphrastic' comes from the Greek 'ex' + 'phrazein' = to point out or explain. It has a rich history, going all the way back to the epic poet Homer, for instance, who could describe the beauty of an ornate shield. In modern English, ekphrastic poetry is typically poetry about visual art. It aims to interpret a painting or sculpture, and sometimes speaks as if it were the voice of the original work talking to us as a character; it was a popular genre of poetry in the nineteenth and twentieth century among scholar-poets.

Durcan's *The Arnolfini Marriage* is from his collection of ekphrastic poems *Give Me Your Hand* (1994), loosely based on paintings in London's National Gallery. Considering most people feel lost when looking at 'official' art, Durcan's book title suggests reassurance: perhaps he is offering his hand as a guide. Or perhaps the paintings are reaching out to the poet, asking him to have faith and follow them into their mysteries.

The Van Eyck painting which this poem describes is a tangle of uncertainties. We know it was painted by Dutch artist Jan Van Eyck in 1434, but almost every other detail is disputed. For instance, scholars disagree on what the title should be: 'The Arnolfini Portrait/Marriage/ Wedding/Bethrothal/etc.' are just some suggested names. Experts differ on whom it depicts (which Arnolfinis? There are a few candidates), their relationship (are they married, engaged?) and even whether the woman is pregnant or not (the bulging of her dress may suggest wealth or fertility rather than an actual pregnancy).

Durcan's interpretation starts with the title; obviously he has decided this is a portrait of a married couple. The poem speaks to us in the cool measured tones of the wealthy subjects on the canvas. Everything about them is measured, even their speech, which unpacks in neat three-line stanzas.

Whether due to historical uncertainty about their exact identity, or from a detached aristocratic attitude, they keep their introduction simple: 'We are the Arnolfinis'. They follow this greeting with a terse cautioning: 'Do not think you may invade/Our privacy because you may not'. Already the poet has pulled the rug out from under us; the couple send mixed messages, inviting us into their home (into their marriage), but immediately telling us not to get too comfortable. The purpose of this painting, Durcan suggests, is not to invite outsiders in, but to show them what they are missing out on. It's all an elaborate boast. Theirs is 'The most erotic portrait ever made'. They appeal to the artist not to portray them with sentimentality, but for that cooler intellectual virtue: to do justice to their 'plurality,/Fertility, domesticity, barefootedness'. The plurality may refer to the prospect of offspring – thereby increasing the number of Arnolfinis – or it may be the more abstract boast of how they enjoy a distinctness from each other (note the physical distance between the man and woman) while still being able to claim the sovereign sense of 'we' that is celebrated in *Windfall*. Boasts of 'domesticity' may be in contrast to the robust farm labourers of the day – who would be red-faced and large like the huge schizophrenic country men we see attacking the goal in *Sport* – and not pale and slender-fingered like this couple.

They present their bed 'As being our most necessary furniture'. Again, this could be a sexual boast, but it may also allude to a convention of the time where guests were received onto the bed as if it were a couch. Couches feature in Durcan's poetry as a kind of 'heart' or centre of a living room.

'Our brains spill out upon the floor'. This confounding line in stanza 5 throws us back on ourselves. Since the terrier is sniffing the 'minutiae of our magnitude', it may mean that the couple's greatness is manifest in small details. These people must have substantial resources. Perhaps the 'brains' here mean that their intellect is expressed in the profusion of rich materials (dress fabric, curtains, bedsheets) that 'spill' out before us. Like most wealthy people, they think they have come by their good fortune through their own brilliance.

Stanza 6 could have come from *Windfall* – it is the closest to warm and intimate that the speakers attempt. But there is a smugness underlying it, as if they were rare creatures to enjoy intimacy: 'Most people are in no position to say "we"'. Again, this is the language of implied exclusion. And by stanza 7 the exclusion turns explicit and personal. They are virtually pointing a finger at the divorced poet, and accusing him of being a failure: 'Are you? Who eat alone? Sleep alone?'

The final stanza seems to be a different speaker, or at least a radical break in the tone of the poem. TV programmes on RTÉ are still interrupted to make way for the Angelus, a call to prayer and reflection. This poem plays on the notion of reflection, hinting at the literal reflection of the self-aware painter who worked himself into the mirror on the wall between the figures of man and woman. Durcan is hinting at how he has worked his own concerns into this poem about one of the most famous self-referential paintings in art history. The term 'reflection' could also be used in the sense of a meditation: 'To do justice to our life as a reflection'. The reader might find an echo here back to *Windfall* when the poet reflects, yet again, on famous painters, and considers how life is a dream that is also real.

The final two lines are enigmatic: 'Here you have it:/The two halves of the coconut'. A coconut is another exotic food, like the oranges in the painting. It is a sphere, and sometimes spheres and circles are symbols of the perfection of God – consider the domed (half-sphere) mirror on the wall surrounded by a circular frame made up of tiny religious scenes.

Coconuts, like the mysteries of religions and marriages, are hard to crack open and get inside. But if you are smart or strong enough to get within that rough, resilient exterior, there is rich food indeed, and a sea of warm nourishing milk awaiting you.

KEY POINTS

- The poem speaks to us in the cool measured tones of the wealthy subjects on the canvas. Everything about them is measured, even their speech, which unpacks in neat three-line stanzas.
- The poem is an elaborate boast as the couple in the painting appear to be taunting the viewers. They introduce themselves but also insist on maintaining a distance.
- Like most wealthy people, the Arnolfinis think they have come by their good fortune through their own brilliance. Unusual images are used to indicate their brains.
- The language used by the Arnolfinis is that of exclusion which has a rather smug tone.
- The final stanza seems to be a different speaker, or at least a radical break in the tone.
- Durcan hints at how he has worked his own personal concerns into this poem about one of the most famous paintings in art history.
- Coconuts become symbolic of the mysteries of religion and marriage – tough exteriors but warm, nourishing centres.

Rosie Joyce

On the surface, this poem is a joyous three-part ode to the birth of the poet's granddaughter. But there are layers here that delve beneath the birth of the child, touching on ancient history and reach up into the possible shoots of future political growth.

Part I

The opening image is one of birthing labour, as the 'hot sun pushed through the clouds,' and the child is born. The second stanza paints a world where everyone seems to be celebrating, setting out bright china on picnic rugs.

The first explicit religious allusion is when Durcan notes Rosie was born on the Christian holy day: Sunday. Durcan is in the middle of a mock-epic journey through Ireland when he learns of her 'incarnation' (a metaphysical term for when a god takes human form on earth). The intensity of this mystical language is offset by the perfunctory notice he gets from his son-in-law (whose name – Mark – is coincidentally that of one of the apostles) announcing the great event. It simply conveys the child's gender, weight and birth time, and affirms that all is well.

Part II

The first four stanzas of Part II are an extended representation of the world breaking into bloom in celebration of their god Rosie's arrival. This is followed by the poet making his way to Dublin, a city that has been presented by him in other poems as the site of his 'homelessness' since his divorce. Now the city is a source of fortune to him, and he refers to 'Each canal bridge' as 'an old pewter brooch'. The reference to pewter may be significant given that it immediately precedes his sudden flashback to his father making such an epic journey himself, the judge/ father 'relishing his role as Moses'. Pewter was an alloy technique used in the making of metal, weapons, ornaments etc. It was devised in ancient Egypt, and Moses was the leader who led the oppressed slaves out of Egypt under the guidance of a benevolent god. The theme of escape from oppression (via a god's assistance) may be implied here. However, where the poet's father asserts a 'Great Divide' between the people, be they Egyptians and Jews, or East Coasters and West Coasters in Ireland, Durcan counters this with an alternative vision of reality:

'There are higher powers than politics/And these we call wildflowers or, geologically, people.'

The poet seems to be claiming that political divisions – those that have woven our history – are imaginary or at least petty, whereas nature (our mountains, rivers, flora etc.) is real. He uses the term 'geologically' to make us think of timescales. People are geological (in the sense of occupying a huge stretch of time) relative to the lifespan of flowers. And of course our greater environment (rivers and mountains) dwarfs the lifespan of humans, likening us, and even the incarnation Rosie, to ephemeral wildflowers.

Durcan alludes to the journalist Jonathan Philbin Bowman's show *Daymaker,* which focused on events that made people's day. But Durcan is exclaiming this phrase in a new way, as if the child's birth is a celestial event, like the god of Genesis who makes/creates the day. For Durcan, Rosie makes – or renews – life. With her birth, the poet's three-year long depression breaks and lifts: 'But you saved my life'.

Part III

This short final section is laden with allusions. Two of the main ones are considered here. On his return from Dublin to Mayo, Durcan meets John Normanly, a man he is obviously friendly enough with to stop and talk to and mention by full name in his poem. He points out that John (another apostle but also a possible allusion to John the Baptist) is an 'organic farmer' and that he is connected with the 'Western Development Commission'. That organisation is an ecologically conscious attempt to create sustainable farming and energy practices in the West of Ireland, and plays into Durcan's belief that it is the land itself, the living things on it, that matter. This idea of the hopeful eco-politics of Rosie's (rosy?) future is presented in contrast to the old corrupt cronyism of Irish party politics. Durcan uses Pádraig Flynn, an Irish politician whom Durcan considers corrupt, as an example of political cronyism.

Normanly and Durcan 'wet our foreheads' (baptise themselves/get drunk) in a discussion of John Moriarty's autobiography. Moriarty was a mystic and philosopher who travelled widely and practiced a variety of jobs, including teaching English literature and being a live-in gardener for a monastery in Oxford.

The autobiography Durcan and his friend are discussing is called *Nostos,* which is Greek for 'homecoming'. Durcan references the book here because he feels himself returning to full human life (coming home), redeemed by the 'incarnation' of new life that is his grandchild. But there may be more implied by the literary allusion. Moriarty is something of a nature poet himself, and mentions in the book that he would prefer to celebrate the mountain itself rather than cheer a Moses on top of it. This may be a subtle rejection of Durcan's own judge father as Moses, holding up the tablets of the Old Testament. Rosie is presented instead as an avatar of a New Testament, which may be love of the true things of life: wildflowers, people, clean water and fertile soil, and the ancient dark mountains that stand firm before the dawn.

KEY POINTS

- This poem is a joyous three-part ode to the birth of the poet's granddaughter.
- Christian images, heavy with allusion, are interspersed with prosaic details about the child's weight, height and time of birth.
- In the second part of the poem the poet seems to be claiming that political divisions – those that have woven our history – are imaginary or at least petty, whereas nature (our mountains, rivers, flora etc.) is real.
- For Durcan, Rosie makes – or renews – life. With her birth, the poet's three-year-long depression breaks and lifts: 'you saved my life'.
- The short final section is laden with allusions.
- Rosie is presented as being a symbol of love and of life.

The MacBride Dynasty

Durcan's poetry verges on prose in this piece. Durcan was related to both the MacBride and Gonne families on his mother's side. *The MacBride Dynasty* is more telling than showing, as the speaker remembers a visit to his grand-aunt (and one-woman national institution) Maud Gonne when he was a young boy and she was an elderly woman. Taking a mythical cue from Yeats, Durcan likens his own mother to a 'vengeful goddess/Spitting dynastic as well as motherly pride'. A dynasty is a line of rulers or

other prominent and powerful people, and it is clear in the poem that the MacBrides consider themselves to be an 'alpha' family in Ireland. His mother is going to 'show off' her 'walking, talking little boy' to Maud Gonne, referred to as 'the servant of the Queen'. This title works in two ways, as Gonne claimed to have received a vision of the mythical 'Queen' of Ireland, Cathleen Ní Houlihan, as if to imply she had been chosen to follow the path that best served the creation of an Irish sovereign state. The title of 'servant' also works ironically, because Gonne – born in England – chose to reject rule by the British monarchy, and is hardly servile in her manner at all. If anything, Gonne is depicted as enamoured with her role as a cultural treasure, 'keen as ever to receive admirers'.

Durcan mocks her as a vain and even ludicrous old dame of the theatre, noting that 'Only the previous week the actor MacLiammóir/Had been kneeling at her bedside reciting Yeats to her/His hand on his heart, clutching a red rose'. The scene is overwrought with forced artfulness and reverence. W.B. Yeats was a poet, playwright, and statesman, an obsessive admirer of Maud Gonne, and one of the founding 'myth-makers' of the emerging Irish republic. He stands as a giant in the history of Irish mythic poetry, and one imagines that the subversive Durcan would have an uneasy relationship with such a figure, given Durcan's own love of mythic imagination, but distaste for official state propaganda.

The young boy views the aged Gonne through a nightmarish lens: 'sticking out her claws/To embrace me, her lizards of eyes darting about/In the rubble of the ruins of her beautiful face'. This could be read as a cruel rendering of an old woman, or simply an honest recreation of the emotional outbursts very young children are given to. He flees, and is found and 'quieted' by his cousin Séan.

From line 26 on there is a vague but sustained attack from Durcan's mother on Maud Gonne. She is accused of being 'disloyal' to her husband (Durcan's mother's uncle, John MacBride) but it is never explained what she did. In point of fact, Maud Gonne separated from John MacBride and accused him publicly of drunkenness, domestic abuse and molesting Iseult, her 11-year-old daughter from a previous marriage. This airing of 'dirty laundry' in public may be the greatest offence to insular family consciousness, especially dynastic consciousness. The grandmother's voice chimes in here like a ghost, singing John's praises, and the poet describes him as the 'pride of our family'.

Instead, the ire is focused on Gonne, who is described as 'not worthy of Mummy's love'. The idea of being 'worthy' (or not) of love is something that haunts much of Durcan's poems. He struggles to be worthy of his father's love in *Sport* and struggles to be worthy of love from his wife in *Windfall* and *Father's Day*. *Rosie Joyce* is about being redeemed by a love that forgives and accepts unconditionally. But none of that is made explicit here. Instead, the closing lines are hard and cold. The collective pronoun 'we' is used to envelop and warm members of a family, but also to exclude others. Here, 'We', the dynastic family, will 'tolerate' Maud. She may remain as a central prop in the propaganda of the early Irish state, but 'we would always see through her'. This dismissive tone may be an ironic attack on insular family politics, or it may be a sincere and direct attack on the use of self-aggrandising myths in political art. Given that the poem is being recounted from the perspective of a young child, it's hard to know exactly how much we should take its claims at face value. One thing is certain: the vagueness of the accusations and the cold judgemental quality of the tone – so out of place in a Durcan poem – suggest we should tread carefully in how we read what is being said.

KEY POINTS

- Notice the prose-like quality of the style in this poem.
- Maud Gonne is depicted as enamoured with her role as a cultural treasure, 'keen as ever to receive admirers'.
- Note the poet's use of irony throughout the poem.
- There is a mocking tone as Durcan describes Maud receiving the attentions of the actor MacLiammóir.
- The physical description of Maud Gonne has a nightmarish quality.
- The idea of being 'worthy' (or not) of love is something that haunts many of Durcan's poems. Here, Maud is seen as being unworthy of love because of her separation from and allegations against John MacBride.
- Note the use of the collective pronoun 'we' to include the members of the family, but to exclude Maud Gonne.
- The poem has a cold, judgemental quality which is not very typical of Durcan and may be more of a reflection of the views of others towards Maud. It is almost as though Durcan remembers being a child and absorbing the attitudes of his mother and grandmother.

Sample Answer

What I like and/or dislike about the poetry of Paul Durcan.

Write a personal response to this statement supporting the points you make with reference to the poems of Durcan on your course.

(Intro: Personal initial reaction to poems)

On first reading, I confess I found Paul Durcan's poetry confusing, and even a little slapdash. The conversational, colloquial tone felt like it clashed with the weird imagery, which hopped from idea to seemingly-unrelated idea. The images and metaphors were certainly striking, but I struggled to make sense of it all. Now, having read the poems several times and considered motifs that occur consistently, what emerges isn't confusing, but is instead a complex portrait of a complex man: The Difficulty That Is Paul Durcan.

(2nd para: consideration of titles, introduction to mix of tones/modes: factual, subversive, mystic, comic)

The first thing that might throw the average unsuspecting reader is how Durcan mixes up a few registers, or voices, that you don't usually find together. For instance, his titles often read like tabloid headlines: *Six Nuns Die in Convent Inferno, Wife Who Smashed Television Gets Jail, Sport, Madman*. Others are banal, like addresses (*Windfall, 8 Parnell Hill, Cork*) or dates (*Father's Day, 21 June 1992, Ireland 2002*) or simply names (*Nessa, Rosie Joyce*). But then we read the poems, and the bland – or tabloid – titles don't prepare us for what comes next. Far from factual or journalistic detail, we encounter a mix of political subversion and mystical comedy.

(3rd para: Durcan as 'subversive')

Let us consider the subversive aspect first. Durcan, as far as I can tell, isn't a satirist and never seems to attack any particular political party or social movement. Instead, his upset is a more general grudge against suffering from – or himself being – a vague historical disappointment. In *Sport*, he addresses his father directly and says outright that 'I was fearful I would let you down'. He manages to do a good job in goal, but keeps underlining that he was playing for a 'mental hospital', and that, even considering how lowly he felt by being committed against his will, 'Seldom if ever again in your eyes/Was I to rise to these heights'. I think this poem is subversive because mental health – even today – is stigmatised. Most individuals and their families keep any hint of depression, anxiety etc. hidden from public view. But Durcan lays it all out for us. It's extremely confessional. This level of honesty, of admitting not only to having been committed, but wanting approval from Daddy so badly (and failing to get it) is unsettling. And it's moving, because any time an adult man takes off the mask of strength or certainty it is a kind of political act. Anyone who says: let's stop pretending everything in our personal life or in our nation is fine is being subversive.

(4th para: Developing 'subversive' reading and adding 'mystic')

Durcan keeps returning to the twin themes of privacy and family throughout his writing. In *The*

MacBride Dynasty he pulls out more dirty laundry when he reveals the way his mother's family closed ranks on Maud Gonne, his grand-aunt. They are punishing her for 'disloyalty' to John MacBride when she publicly humiliated him by accusing him of drunkenness and abuse of her daughter. The MacBrides allow the living legend, Gonne, to remain part of their 'dynasty', but they secretly reject her: 'For dynastic reasons we would tolerate Maud' but she will always be 'not worthy of Mummy's love'. Again, I think there's something subversive and even angry about the notion of being 'worthy' of love. This is a strikingly candid portrait of how ugly family politics can get behind closed doors. Because of the family ties to the Easter Rising and the birth of the Republic, *The Girl with the Keys to Pearse's Cottage* still feels personally subversive. Durcan describes Pearse's tourist-attraction cottage as having 'wet thatch' and 'peeling jambs', and points out how it's better viewed from a distance than up close. Symbolically through the cottage, Durcan is presenting the national martyr-hero as a stand-in for all official propaganda: glorious from afar, but not holding up well upon close inspection. The girl he fancies from a distance has to leave the country and move to America because Ireland cannot support its young. More disappointment, more imagined failure in the eyes of elders.

This fusing of personal and national and/or historical disappointment bleeds into *Windfall* too. Durcan paints a cosy portrait of enjoying a loving family (stealing 'a subversive kiss' with his wife while ignoring the ringing phone) only to lose that love and find himself 'homeless'. In a moment of foreshadowing this exile, he takes another dig at the language of the Proclamation, claiming he lives 'In a country where all the children of the nation/Are not cherished equally'.

(5th para: painterly quality of mystic writing—motif of water)

But countering this epic disappointment is the cool, painterly, even mystic element of the poet's work. For all the restless movement of Durcan's poems, he seems to find brotherhood with painters: people who show us a still scene. *Windfall* likens the view of Cork from Parnell Hill to something Cezanne or Goya would produce. *The Arnolfini Marriage* lets the painting of the austere couple speak back to us from across the centuries. *Nessa* paints idyllic scenes of a young couple falling in love in a field, and *Rosie Joyce*, about the birth of his granddaughter, shows us a joyous portrait of 'sky blue-and-white china in the fields/In impromptu picnics of tartan rugs'. Present in most of these poems is the motif of water. It takes many forms and can be a chaotic whirlpool of love in *Nessa* or a private sea of intimacy in *Windfall*. Durcan's use of water imagery is as complex as the man himself. In *Windfall* he hits us with this cosmic head-scratcher describing the Lee: 'The river a reflection of itself in its own waters'. Even the fire in *Six Nuns* becomes water, which becomes Christ Himself: 'Christ is the ocean...Christ is the fire in whose waves/We are doomed but delighted to drown'.

(6th para: resilient [humour] and self-pity)

Shades of self-pity can creep into Durcan's work at times. Even though he attributes the phrase 'Exotic loneliness' to a dead nun, we get the impression he sees himself as being a romantic exile. First his parents cast him out (as in *Sport*) and even in maturity he presents himself as 'creeping, crawling' and 'homeless in Dublin' in *Windfall*. In *Father's Day* he acts as if deserted by daughters: 'all the green fields running away from us/All our daughters grown up and gone away'. But even so, I can't reduce the man to being merely a martyr. I can't imagine what it's like to be committed to a mental hospital as a teenager or to get electroshock therapy either. Perhaps the most likeable element of Durcan's work is how he weaves humour into so much of his poetry. We get absurd scenes of accompanying an axe on a train, and a weird 'aviary' of the nuns. There's the crazy and yet impressive Queen Maeve of *Wife Who Smashed Television Gets Jail,* and the smug enigma that is the couple in *The Arnolfini Marriage.*

What I like and respect most about Durcan's poetry is that it isn't used to hide from reality or soften it. His absurdities and playful images come across instead as a way to explore the awesome mysteries and crippling disappointments of life a bit more safely, like the way divers use their tanks to go deeper into dark waters.

Guidelines for answering exam questions: Poetry

Type of Questions

Leaving Certificate Higher Level Poetry questions tend to be general in nature. Questions essentially look for a candidate's personal response to a poet's work. Personal engagement with the text must be supported by detailed textual knowledge.

Examples:

(a) Write a personal response to the poetry of Sylvia Plath.

(b) Write an introduction to the poetry of Eavan Boland.

(c) Account for the popularity of T.S. Eliot.

(d) Explain what you liked and / or disliked about the poetry of John Donne etc.

If a question is slightly more specific, the terms of the question must be addressed and kept in focus. However, at the heart of all poetry questions is the idea of personal engagement with the text.

The following are examples of slightly more specific poetry questions:

1. Write an article for a school magazine introducing the poetry of Sylvia Plath, to Leaving Certificate students. Tell them what she wrote about and explain what you liked in her writing, suggesting some poems that you think they would enjoy reading.

2. What impact did the poetry of Paul Durcan make on you as a reader? Your answer should deal with the following: (a) Your overall sense of the personality of the poet, (b) The poet's use of language/imagery.

What does personal engagement with the text involve?

*   Comment on themes, subject matter.
*   Comment on the relevance of a poet's themes.
*   Explain why a particular poem is worth reading.
*   Say why you can relate to or 'connect' with certain themes.
*   Discuss how particular poems had a particular impact on you.
*   Explain why a personal poem has a universal appeal.
*   Say which poems you most enjoyed.
*   Comment on aspects of a poet's style:
*   Language: accessible? simple/complex? etc.
*   Imagery: vivid? precise? unusual? etc.
*   Sound effects: alliteration, assonance, onomatopoeia, rhyme, etc.

    Note: Your personal response must be grounded in the text – support your points by appropriate reference to and/or quotation from the poems on your course.

EXAMPLES OF THE LANGUAGE OF PERSONAL ENGAGEMENT

- *I can relate to this poem because . . .*
- *This poem remains relevant because . . .*
- *I enjoyed this poem because . . .*
- *What I liked / disliked about this poem was . . .*
- *This is my favourite poem because . . .*
- *This poem opened my eyes to . . .*
- *This poem helped me to understand . . .*
- *This poem had a profound impact on me because . . .*
- *This poem offers interesting insights into . . .*
- *This poem set me thinking about / made me aware of . . .*
- *I particularly like the image of . . .*
- *The image of . . . effectively conveys the idea of . . .*
- *The image of . . . is particularly striking.*
- *The vivid imagery fires my imagination . . .*
- *I like the way the poet compares . . .*
- *The poet employs a powerful metaphor to . . .*
- *This unusual simile is effective because . . .*
- *The poet's use of sound is particularly effective here because . . .*
- *The use of everyday, conversational language made the poem very accessible . . .*
- *I love the poet's wonderful use of detail . . .*
- *The poet's eye for detail brings the character / scene to life . . . etc. etc.*

- It is also important to write in the appropriate form and to employ the appropriate register (type of language).
- For example, you may be asked to write your response to a poet's work in the form of a letter in which you speak directly to the poet.
- If your response takes the form of a speech/talk, use conversational language / employ a chatty tone, etc, etc.

STRUCTURE YOUR ANSWER
- Brief introduction, addressing the question and outlining your response to it.
- One point (for example, a poet's use of imagery) or one poem per paragraph. Brief conclusion, referring back to the question.

Remember:
- Avoid summarising poems – remain focused on your key points. Aim to be analytical / discursive in responding to a poet's work.
- The emphasis throughout your response should be on personal engagement grounded in the text. Regularly quote from and refer to text to support points made.
- You do not have to discuss a fixed number of poems, but it is difficult to produce an impressive response discussing fewer than three poems.

RESPONDING TO THE UNSEEN POEM

In responding to this question, you must display an ability to personally 'connect' with the poem and the poet. You are expected to make intelligent use of the text to support your interpretation.

Look at the shape of the poem. Is it organised in stanzas? Is it written in sonnet form? Are any lines set apart from the rest of the poem? For example, the final line in Heaney's *Mid-Term Break* stands alone to emphasise the tragic nature of his young brother's death ('A four foot box, a foot for every year')

Note the title of the poem – it has not been chosen at random. What does the title suggest? Does the poem fulfil the expectations suggested by the title? For example, the title of Rosita Boland's poem *Butterflies* suggests that what follows will be a beautiful nature poem, whereas this poem is in fact concerned with the terrible destruction caused by landmines – the title is therefore ironic. In contrast, when we read *The Daffodils* by William Wordsworth, we expect – and get – a poem about the beauty of nature.

It is important to remember that a poet chooses his/her words very carefully to express his/her feelings. Words may be used literally or metaphorically

('I turned to ice', etc). They may be selected for their connotations / associations ('The waters of the canal pouring redemption for me' suggests the idea of an experience that is almost religious, etc.). Words may also be selected for their sounds.

Make a note of your first impression which will, naturally, be general in nature. What did you think of the poem's opening and closing? Did anything in particular strike you? A word? A phrase? An image? Were certain words suggestive of a particular mood or idea? Did the poet make use of repetition? Was the imagery primarily visual or did it appeal to a range of different senses? Are there any colours in the poem? If so, what feelings do you associate with these colours? Does the poem make use of contrast?

Your second reading of the poem will need to be more focused. Try to identify the dominant feeling in the poem and make a note of the key words and images that convey this feeling.

How would you describe the language? Is it formal or colloquial / chatty? Modern poets use the language of the modern age, ensuring that their poems are readily accessible. Is there any unusual use of language? For example, in Longley's poem *The Badger*, the poet uses the language of birth ('delivery...tongs') to describe the death of the badger. In his poem *The Tollund Man*, Heaney uses the language of religion ('consecrate...pray') when writing about a long dead pagan. Does the poet invent any new words, and if so, how effective are they? For example, in *Lines Written on a Seat on the Grand Canal, Dublin*, Kavanagh describes the water pouring from the lock as roaring 'niagorously'.

Discuss the poet's use of imagery. Are certain images particularly effective? An image is basically a word-picture which may consist of a single word or a number of lines. Similes and metaphors are types of images. Does the poet make use of comparisons and, if so, are they effective in conveying a particular idea?

Consider the poet's use of punctuation. For example, regular full stops can serve different purposes. In her poem, *This Moment*, Eavan Boland makes regular use of full stops to create a sense of expectation. Regular full stops also help to create a reflective mood. A full stop at the end of a poem suggests a sense of closure, while its absence suggests the idea of something unresolved. Emily Dickinson often ends a poem with a dash or a question mark. Regular question marks suggest uncertainty.

What happens between the beginning and end of the poem? How do the poet's thoughts and feelings develop? Does he/she achieve some insight as the poem develops?

Consider the poet's use of sound (alliteration, assonance, onomatopoeia, rhyme, etc). Different sounds help to suggest different moods. For example, an alliterative 'b' sound can suggest a noisy atmosphere, a repeated 'd' sound a gloomy one and a repeated 's' sound a sense of peace. Are certain vowel sounds repeated and, if so, to what effect? For example, the repetition of broad vowel sounds helps to convey a serious, sad or lonely mood ('Alone, alone, all alone', 'staring face to face', etc.)

Key Points – Mention the following:

- Title of poem.
- Key theme.
- Shape.
- Opening.
- Key words / phrases / images.
- Way in which ideas develop.
- Use of sound.
- Conclusion.

Remember:
- Your response to the poem must be supported by intelligent use of the text.
- Show an awareness of literary terms in your response.

Key Literary Terms

ALLEGORY – A piece of writing that has both a surface meaning and another, deeper meaning. The purpose of an allegory is often to illustrate a moral or truth. *Example:* On the surface George Orwell's *Animal Farm* is a simple tale of animals taking over and running the farm on which they live. On a deeper level, this tale highlights the corrupting effects of total power. (Orwell had the old Soviet Union in mind when he wrote this novel.)

ALLITERATION – A run of words (usually consonants) starting with the same letter. *Examples:* 'Billy Brennan's barn' – Patrick Kavanagh. 'In the sun the slagheap slept' – Philip Larkin.

ALLUSION – This occurs when a writer refers to a well-known character, event, historical happening or work of literature. *Examples:* In *The Pomegranate* Boland alludes to the myth of Ceres and Peresphone. In *The Cage*, Montague refers to Homer's poem *The Iliad*, '…for when / weary Odysseus returns / Telemachus should leave'. In *September 1913* Yeats refers to Irish history, 'Was it for this the wild geese spread / The grey wing upon every tide?'

AMBIGUITY – This occurs when a word, phrase or sentence is open to more than one interpretation. *Example:* 'I am king of banks and stones and every blooming thing' – Patrick Kavanagh.

ANALOGY – A comparison made to show how two things are similar. Similes and metaphors are based on analogy. *Example:* 'Hope is the thing with feathers / That perches in the soul' – Emily Dickinson.

ANTITHESIS – This refers to the juxtaposition of contrasting phrases or ideas. *Example:* My words fly up, my thoughts remain below' –

ARCHAISM – This refers to a writer's use of old-fashioned (archaic) language.

ASSONANCE – This occurs when a vowel sound is repeated in words close to each other. *Example:* 'But ranged as infantry / and staring face to face' – Thomas Hardy.

BLANK VERSE – This is unrhymed iambic pentameter (each line consisting of ten syllables). *Example:* 'Your batman thought you were buried alive / Left you for dead and stole your pocket watch' – Michael Longley.

CLICHÉ – This refers to a well-worn, overused expression or phrase. *Examples:* 'Tomorrow is another day', 'raining cats and dogs', 'a crying shame'.

CLIMAX – This refers to a moment of great intensity in a play or dramatic poem. *Example:* Having reflected deeply on the plan to murder Duncan, Macbeth decides not to go ahead with it. However, Lady Macbeth intervenes and Macbeth succumbs to her powers of persuasion. At the close of a very tense scene, Macbeth declares: 'I am settled and bend up each corporal agent to this terrible feat.'

CONCEIT – This is an unusual metaphor or comparison used especially by metaphysical poets such as John Donne. *Example:* Donne compares his lover and himself to the two legs of a mathematical compass to suggest how they will never be separated, even when he embarks on his travels, 'As stiff twin compasses are two, / Thy soul the fixed foot, makes no show / To move, but doth, if th'other do'.

COUPLET – This refers to two successive lines of verse, usually rhymed and of the same metre. *Example:* 'I lift the window, watch the ambling feather / Of hock and fetlock, loosed from its daily tether' – Eavan Boland.

DIALECT – This refers to a form of language spoken in a particular geographical area, which contains words and expressions not found in the standard language.

DRAMATIC IRONY – This occurs in a play when the audience knows more than a particular character. It is very ironic that having been betrayed by the Thane of Cawdor, Duncan then bestows this title on Macbeth, little knowing that his apparently loyal and trustworthy kinsman plans to muder him.

ELEGY – This is a poem of lamentation, a poem mourning the dead.

EMOTIVE LANGUAGE – This is language that evokes an emotional response in the reader. *Example:* 'I touched his head, his thin head I touched' – Michael Longley.

EPIGRAM – This is a concise (short) and witty saying. *Example:* 'But wild ambition loves to slide, not stand / And fortune's ice prefers to vertue's land' – John Dryden.

EPIPHANY – This refers to a moment of insight / understanding, such as Elizabeth Bishop achieves in the closing lines of *The Fish.*

EUPHEMISM – This is a gentle or indirect way of expressing something drastic, offensive or unpleasant. *Example:* He passed away.

FIGURATIVE LANGUAGE – This refers to language which makes use of simile and metaphor to express an idea. To speak figuratively is to speak metaphorically.

FREE VERSE – This is verse that is unrhymed and unmetered. It is widely used by modern poets. *Example:* 'I caught a tremendous fish / and held him beside the boat / half out of the water, with my hook / fast in the corner of his mouth'. – Elizabeth Bishop.

HYPERBOLE – This refers to the deliberate use of exaggeration or overstatement to emphasise a point. *Example:* 'Ten thousand saw I at a glance / Tossing their heads in a sprightly dance' – Wordsworth.

IMAGERY – This is a general term which embraces similes, metaphors, symbols. Basically, it refers to any type of word-picture.

IRONY – Verbal irony occurs when one thing is said, while the opposite is meant. *Example:* 'For men were born to pray and save' – Yeats. Irony of situation occurs when a situation is very different from what the protagonist believes it to be.

LYRIC – This refers to any short poem which directly expresses personal feeling.

METAPHOR – This is a type of image that directly compares two things, without using 'like', 'as' or 'than'. *Examples:* 'I turned to ice' – Derek Mahon. 'a leaping tongue of bloom' – Robert Frost.

MOTIF – This refers to a recurring theme or feature in a writer's work.

ONOMATOPOEIA – This occurs when the sound of the word suggests the sound being described. *Examples:* hissing, sizzled, clanging.

PARADOX – This refers to a statement that appears to be, but is not, a contradiction. *Example:* The freezing ice burnt my hand.

PATHOS – This refers to a quality in literature that evokes a deep, sympathetic feeling in the reader.

PERSONA – This refers to the voice or speaker in a poem. The persona is usually – but not always – the poet.

PERSONIFICATION – This is a technique whereby a writer attributes human qualities to an animal, object or idea. *Example:* The happy sun smiled down on us.

PETRARCHAN SONNET – This refers to a sonnet which consists of an octave/octet (set of eight lines) and a sestet (set of six lines). The octave presents us with a situation or problem which is resolved in the sestet.

QUATRAIN – This is a four-line unit of verse.

RHYTHM – This refers to the movement or flow of words.

SHAKESPEARIAN SONNET – This consists of three quatrains and a rhyming couplet.

SIBILANCE – This is a whispering/hissing 's' sound. *Example:* 'Its surface seems tilted / To receive the sun perfectly' – Longley.

SIMILE – This is a type of image which compares two things using the words 'like', 'as' or 'than'. *Example:* 'One window is yellow as butter' – Eavan Boland.

STYLE – This refers to a writer's individual way of expressing his/her ideas.

SYMBOL – This is a word or phrase which represents something real and concrete, but also represents something other than itself. *Examples:* A dove is a symbol of peace, a flower a symbol of beauty.

THEME – This refers to a key idea in a piece of writing. (There may be more than one theme.)

TONE – This is the attitude of the writer towards his/her subject. A tone may be joyful, angry, bitter, self-pitying, etc. etc.

SAY NO TO BULLYING
NOBODY DESERVES TO BE BULLIED
TELL AN ADULT YOU CAN TRUST

This Anti-Bullying campaign is supported by the Department of Education and Skills with the
co-operation of the Irish Educational Publishers Association

//:DON'T REPLY/
KEEP THE MESSAGE/
BLOCK THE SENDER/
TELL SOMEONE YOU TRUST://

WWW.WATCHYOURSPACE.IE

Don't Accept Bullying

This Anti-Bullying campaign is supported by the Department of Education and Skills with the co-operation of the Irish Educational Publishers Association.